Ascending into Miracles

The Path of Spiritual Mastery

Jennifer Hoffman

An imprint of Feed Your Muse Press, LLC
www.feedyourmuse.com

Ascending into Miracles – The Path of Spiritual Mastery

Copyright © 2011 by Jennifer Hoffman

Printed in the USA and distributed by Feed Your Muse Press, LLC. For more information visit us at www.enlighteninglife.com

Feed Your Muse Press, LLC
A division of Enlightening Life OmniMedia, Inc.
P.O. Box 7076
Lee's Summit, MO 64064   USA

Cover design by Karen Taverner and Jane Behrends

ISBN10 0982194935

ISBN13 9780982194935

Acknowledgment

I would like to acknowledge the millions of loyal and faithful clients and
audiences of the Enlightening Life weekly newsletter and radio show
whose messages of love, gratitude and appreciation,
as well as their support and generous testimonials
have been my light on this journey, begun in 2004,
as I shared these insights and messages with you.

This book is dedicated to you and I hope that it is a
powerful light on your mastery journey.

You have my deepest gratitude and appreciation
for the light you have been for me in the many years
that we have walked this path together.
Jennifer Hoffman

Other titles by Jennifer Hoffman

Books:
30 Days to Everyday Miracles
The Difference Between a Victor and a Victim is I AM
Be Who You Are – And Fearlessly Live Your True Purpose
The E-Business Primer

CDs:
Cord Cutting and Healing Meditation
Chakra Clearing Meditation
Communicating With Your Angels and Spirit Guides
Maternal Energetic Emotional Imprint Clearing

Audio Programs:
Guilt and Shame Healing and Transformation
Aligning the Trinity
The Path of Spiritual Initiation
Manifesting Your Mastery

For additional titles please visit www.ascendingearthangels.com

Foreword

Dear Reader,

Have you wondered what's been happening in your life lately? Have you lost your job, been deserted by your friends, has your romantic life fallen apart or is nonexistent (and has been for quite a while), or do some of your family and friends treat you like you are invisible?

Are you restless, ill at ease, unable to focus, and do you feel off center and ungrounded?

Do you sometimes feel so disconnected that you wonder if you're on another planet or in another dimension?

What is happening to you is also happening to many others around the world. It is part of a shift in the global consciousness, the birth of a new paradigm, a movement that, after gathering power over eons of time, has finally reached critical mass. This shift is the culmination of lifetimes of spiritual growth and learning and its purpose is our ascension into the miracle vibration and spiritual mastery. This book is your guide to that process.

We, and by 'we' I mean all of humanity, are experiencing a paradigm shift, a change in the way we view ourselves, the world around us and our place in it. The changes that are occurring are so profound that many fear that these are the 'end times' that have been predicted and that we are witnessing the final stages of humanity's destruction. But that is not what is happening—the earth is not going to implode or explode and humanity will not be eradicated. However, everyone will be affected by the profound changes that will occur everywhere. This is an opportunity for us to re-think our lives, to rid ourselves of the beliefs and perceptions that have held us back from the life that we were meant to live, filled with peace, love, joy and abundance.

We are ascending from the fear and ego-based consciousness of the material human into becoming a spiritual human. With this movement we can step out of the karmic energies that have been the focus of our lifetimes and into higher vibrations of being. Now we can embrace our spiritual mastery and claim our power as co-creators with the Universe. This is our journey into mastery, where we remember our divinity and allow ourselves to become whole, which is the state of balance between body, mind, emotions and spirit, and to live life mindfully, with intention and awareness of our place in the Universe.

The transformation of the human consciousness paradigm is possible because we are releasing long held patterns of thinking and behavior and creating an opening into a new vibration of being.

Each of us has the chance to accept our spiritual mastery (or not) and here you can find information on what is happening, why it is happening now, and how you can best utilize the energy that is part of this process. The doubts, concerns and fears you have are similar to those that clients have been sharing with me for many years and some of their stories are included as examples in this book. Once you understand this process, embrace its lessons and allow transformation to occur in your life, you will have a much better understanding of your life purpose, and with an awareness of the availability of new and different choices, can learn how to create a reality that is more peaceful, prosperous, happier and fulfilled.

This book was written to help guide you through your process of healing, learning, growth and transformation that is your mastery journey, enabling you to step into your spiritual mastery and create the life of your dreams. It will explain the ascension journey -- what it's all about, the kinds of changes you can expect and how to work with them on all levels, individually, globally, planetary, universally, for humanity and for yourself. It is an amazing time and each one of us plays an important role. It is my hope that with what you learn in this book you will embrace your own awakening, identify the areas in your life that are shifting and learn to flow with the changes.

This book is for everyone who is on the path of spiritual mastery. You are each travelers on the path leading us to the new earth and the miracle vibration. This is the end of life through karma and destiny and the beginning of living through manifestation, intention and creation. You need information, support and guidance to understanding what is happening and why, so you can identify, embrace and integrate the unfolding opportunities for growth and healing that are now present. If you are afraid, confused or in doubt, know that you are not alone.

There is an underlying methodology to what you are experiencing and the information in this book is here to help you understand, accept and integrate the various changes that are occurring in your life and all around you. The challenges may be great but so are the rewards, which include renewal, rebirth and re-alignment with our collective spiritual Truth, replacing the old with new and different energetic vibrations. You can learn more about this process and find more tools for learning at www.ascendingearthangels.com and www.enlighteninglife.com.

We are supported through this process by powerful energies who patiently watch and wait as we move through our journey of consciousness into spiritual mastery. They are with you and with us all as we learn, heal, grow, transform and ascend into miracles.

Many blessings,
Jennifer Hoffman
March 2011

NOTE: There are many client stories referenced in this book and each one was chosen because it contained details and experiences that best highlighted the topic of discussion. While these are true stories of real people, names and details have been changed to protect their identities and ensure that they remain anonymous.

You will notice that I frequently interchange the words God, Creator, Source, Universe, All-That-Is to describe what I believe is the central power of the Universe. And this central power is sometimes referred to as He or She. Although I believe that God is gender neutral, I find it inappropriate to refer to God as 'It'. I do believe that there is a central, uniting power in the Universe that we are both an integral part of, is part of each of us, have come from and are returning to, that we are not and cannot be separate from God because we each embody a spark of God essence. Thus, when I speak of God I am also speaking of that aspect within each of us that glows with the divine essence and light that we are created from and have always been part of. The use of those words is an attempt to address the many names that describe this cosmic force and are not meant as an acknowledgement of any religious or spiritual belief or preference.

Table of Contents

A Paradigm Shift

The earth and humanity are undergoing a paradigm shift, the creation of a new earth that is the dawning of a different era. Some call it the end of days, a time when the earth as we know it will cease to exist. Others believe that it is the fulfillment of an ancient Mayan prophecy, marked by the end of its calendar on December 21, 2012. There are many theories and predictions about this time and we can join the doomsayers and believe that the earth and its inhabitants will be destroyed by a giant cataclysm. Or we can take a different perspective and view the changes as an internal shift, a move from the material to the spiritual, a re-joining of humanity's connection to its spiritual Source.

The potential destruction of the planet is the stuff of Hollywood dramas and while some earth changes may occur, the real drama and excitement will arise from the transformation that happens within every member of humanity as each of us is provided with the choice to either ground our path in the material world or acknowledge a more spiritual alternative. This is an invitation to choose the path of spiritual mastery, as part of our commitment as the architects of this new reality.

We do not have to wait for 2012 for the new reality to occur because it is happening now and has been building for more than twenty years and longer. Some say that it first began with the introduction of the Internet, a technology that has connected the family of humanity in an unprecedented way. Then, in 1995 the planet Uranus entered its own sign for the first time in 84 years. This event marked the first time that most of Earth's people experienced Uranus in Aquarius, a time of shifting energies, concepts, beliefs and lifestyles that has changed our lives irrevocably. Where we once would never have imagined a world with instantaneous computer and cell phone connection, it is now impossible to imagine the world without it. And we have Pluto in the sign of Capricorn for the first time since the mid 1700s. The American Revolution and the end of the British Empire resulted from its last visit to this sign. What kinds of changes will we experience with this transit? We will have to wait and see.

But we have more tangible, personal evidence that the world is changing. The rise and fall of the Internet bubble caused company failures, massive unemployment and a shift in the concept of work and the new, unpredictable nature of employment. We now live in a global economy, where nations cannot operate in political, social or economic isolation. No longer can something happen in one place while others go on about their daily lives in ignorant, self-centered bliss. We are inextricably connected to each other, all of the time. None of us lives in a vacuum although each of us is on our own path, learning the lessons that our soul requires for its return to wholeness. This new paradigm is the end of the "human human" and the beginning of the spiritual human.

In 2003 we experienced the Harmonic Concordance, in which an unusual planetary alignment created a Star of David symbol in the sky. This was another mass activation of the energy of transformation, resulting in additional levels of profound changes ranging from job losses to unexpected relocations, financial devastation and what has amounted to forced life reorganization. An aging population, Alzheimer's disease, and economic and employment uncertainty have also shifted the social dynamic as we are given opportunities to assess what we do with our time and energy and whether it is expanding or contracting our dreams.

These changes affect everyone, regardless of age, culture, income level and gender, and as they occur, those affected must reflect on their life, livelihood and lifestyle as the old is removed, compelling them to review the direction of their life path and make a choice to commit to follow one that is more balanced on all levels, spiritual, emotional, mental and physical.

With these changes we are also becoming less polarized and more accepting of each other as we acknowledge the fact that we are all connected through bonds that transcend time and space. With technology that links people and continents instantly, we have truly become a human family. On other levels, we are less tolerant of old rules and beliefs about divorce, single parenthood, same sex relationships, and other lifestyle choices and insistent on changing the rigid boundaries of judgment and condemnation that created the lifestyle standards we once lived by. As a global society, we are less tolerant of injustice, inhumanity and suffering and are more vocal in our demand for justice, dignity and fairness. Our commitment to enforcing change where we believe it is needed creates a global call for the transformation of our social systems as we are no longer willing to accept the status quo.

This level of transformation exacts a price from each of us, that we re-examine ourselves, our life choices, our relationships and to redefine who we are in context of the wholeness of our being and our connection to our goals and dreams and to consider ourselves as an important part of the human family. Through our stronger connections we are more aware of our individual and collective responsibility for the state of our planet. Yet while many of these changes are welcome, they are also frightening as they propel us into an unknown and potentially fearful future. Who or what do we count on, when everything has changed and the familiar structures we once organized our lives around are no longer dependable or available? We live from cell phone call to cell phone call, wanting that connection to someone, anyone, to help us deal with the feelings of alone-ness and separation that arise from the sudden knowledge that although we are connected, each of us is on our own path and responsible for our individual reality.

Those of us who have been part of the spiritual movement for many years find that we too need comfort, explanations, and support. Our lives are changing minute by minute and we can no longer define a strong foundation on which we can stand. We may often feel as lost and abandoned as those who have no experience in spiritual matters. In some ways, we may even feel let down by the spiritual system that we have so long believed supports us as we go through our own dark night of the soul. Although this illusion of separateness exists, activation of the new reality means that we will be connected to each other as never before, but in new and different ways.

Where does this take us and where does it end? There are many junctures and crossroads on this journey, which will continue to affect ever growing numbers of people. But it is not about the destination, this is a journey in consciousness, a time for humanity to choose a more loving, tolerant, accepting and compassionate path on individual and collective levels. Opportunities to make this choice will be plentiful, as we will find in the coming years. There is a purpose to the process and answers to many of its questions will be apparent once we have been through the experiences that will, at times, try our souls, make us question our mission and purpose and challenge us to uncover inner sources of strength and wisdom that we were unaware we possessed.

Those of us who have already embarked on this path, who understand what it is about and who have some idea of what to expect, will be called   to share this information with those who are just stepping onto this path -- and who have no idea what they are getting themselves into. There is a significant population that is unaware of the magnitude of this paradigm shift and who will need this information to make sense of what is happening. Everyone has some degree of awareness that the world is changing and the old world is quickly moving out of the way to prepare for something different. This   is a voluntary decision and while we have free will and can choose any path, it is a time to surrender and acknowledge that there is another dimension to life beyond what we have been willing to acknowledge for many lifetimes.

This new paradigm is not replacing the one we have always known, nor is it a new reality that will be forced on us by some cosmic, galactic or divine mandate. It is the new energy for the earth and a logical, planned path of spiritual growth that we will create as our commitment to the fulfillment of our mission of bringing heaven on earth. We have been setting its foundation with the learning of each lesson, the transformation of fear into love and our commitment to ascension. It has slowly been gathering strength and momentum as we turn away from the path of karma and destiny and move towards powerful, dynamic, fulfilled living and into co-creation with the Universe.

The new earth is a return to our divinity and an acknowledgement of our Source connection. This is why we are here and it is why we have returned, lifetime after lifetime. We are now at the crossroads of this path and each choice, decision, thought, word and action carries us farther into our divinity, closer to Source and into the realization of our mastery. We have, and have always been, spiritual beings having a human experience, travelers on the path of ascension and builders of the new earth.

How To Use This Book

This book is a guide for your mastery journey and the information it contains is focused on the ascension process and all of its components. You may feel sad, angry, excited about or confused, disillusioned and worried by some of the information you find here. Some of it may challenge your existing beliefs and at the same time, provide you with new insights into your life and potential. Be sure to answer the questions in each chapter as they will help you to personalize the information for your life journey.

You may read the chapters in any order but it is suggested that with your first reading you complete this book in chapter order, because as you progress through each chapter you are clearing energy, shifting your energetic vibration and learning principles that will guide you through a process of healing and transformation that is a prerequisite to mastery. After you have completed your initial reading of this book, you may select a chapter at random and the one you choose will be the one that answers your questions.

Within each chapter are questions that are designed to help you apply the principles to your own journey into spiritual mastery. You may want to keep a journal or notebook handy as you read each chapter and answer the questions that provide you with a deeper understanding of its principles and allow you to apply them to your life. This will help you apply the lessons of that chapter to your personal mastery experience.

Now, let's begin your mastery journey into the miracle vibration as we discuss what spiritual mastery is.

What is Spiritual Mastery?

For many years we have known that these times were coming, many prophecies have warned us that these times could be difficult and even disastrous for the planet. And some may think that the changes we are undergoing are disastrous—economic and political uncertainty, high unemployment, a banking and credit crisis, the exposure of corporate greed, political corruption and the general uncertainty we face today could be interpreted as signs that we have failed in our journey of reconnection to our Source and our divine heritage.

But this is part of the mastery journey, in which our fear-based beliefs are exposed so that we could make the choice for transformation, showing us where we have been focusing our energy and intention and allowing us to create new paradigms for our reality. The purpose of the drama and chaos is to awaken us from our self-induced slumber through which we have long been masters out of touch with our mastery and allow us to remember who we are, divine spiritual beings having a human experience. When we awaken and re-member that we are co-creators with the Universe, we realize that our humanity is merely a disguise that we adopt as part of our spiritual path. Mastery is a journey into wholeness, where we integrate all aspects of our self, physical, mental, emotional and spiritual, returning from our journey of disconnection into reconnection with our self, our Source and our power.

Spiritual mastery is the goal of each lifetime and we achieve it when we are able to accept our spiritual truth and understand that our true soul purpose is to learn, heal, transform and ascend into higher energetic vibrations. We achieve mastery each time we learn acceptance, forgiveness, compassion and love, for ourselves and for others. It is not a one-time process, nor is it something that marks the end of our journey. Each level of mastery we can achieve creates a new beginning that arises from the ashes of a previous set of beliefs and perspectives, and an opportunity to move to a new level of being.

Spiritual mastery takes us from our smaller view of our individual world and gives us a much broader perspective, where we can see how each of us affects and is part of the whole. It takes us out of our single-minded, ego-based humanity into a more balance spiritual and human perspective. Once we achieve spiritual mastery we continue with life lessons but in different ways. There are some who believe that in order to achieve mastery we must become like the enlightened ones who have preceded us, such as Jesus, Buddha or the ascended masters. This sets a standard that would put mastery out of the reach of all but a select few and is simply not true.

Mastery is available to each of us but since we are each on an individual journey, our path is unique to us and so is our mastery. We all share the same kinds of struggles as well as the potential for the reward of mastery. While we may look to others for clues to help us with our journey, what we can accomplish in our life depends on what we are able to learn and the level of mastery that we are able to achieve through our own efforts.

We achieve mastery with enlightenment, which represents a quantum leap in our understanding of ourselves, our path and purpose. This is both a completion and a connection into a new level of being, representing an individual accomplishment on a soul level that resonates throughout our energy field. With enlightenment we have learned a lesson that alters our life path because we have a deeper, broader and higher level of understanding about our purpose, a renewed commitment to our spiritual nature, a belief in our divinity and a desire to live through our spiritual truth. The material world is still an integral part of our journey but it is balanced with spirit.

For some enlightenment may mean overcoming a single fear or belief that they have held for lifetimes. Their mastery lies in finding their power and truth. For others it may be learning compassion and to give and receive love. Their mastery lies in allowing surrender and learning acceptance. For many, mastery lies in understanding forgiveness and extending unconditional love.

While we tend to look for a common denominator in all things, in the area of spiritual mastery that common denominator only exists in the purpose of the journey, to heal our separation and reconnect to our Source, the All-That-Is of our universal Home. We are connected to Source like the spokes on a bicycle wheel, each supporting and connecting with the others through their shared central connection. We may not even realize that we are on the path to mastery and simply believe that we have had some challenges and overcome them. But that is because our mastery depends on fulfilling the objectives of our soul contract and accepting the learning and healing purpose of our life path. And achieving mastery is not found at the destination, it is learned within the journey itself.

The journey to spiritual mastery is a movement from our self-centered, ego-driven perspective of the world, to reconnect to Spirit. Everything that happens to us is our own creation, a reminder of how powerful we are. Everyone is part of this process, whether or not they follow a spiritual movement. For some, it will arrive as a subtle reminder that there is a spiritual purpose to life, along with opportunities to choose that.

For others the reminder will not be so subtle and will come via situations and circumstances that will allow them to choose a different path or remain on the one they are following. Some may experience a sudden awakening to a realization of their purpose, unexpected or sudden clarity about their lives, a deeper understanding of their human and spiritual duality and a need to merge the two, a change in beliefs and perspective that will free them from fear.

This is a process that will be unique to every individual — no one will experience the path of spiritual mastery in same way. Each will transform and become enlightened, or not, according to their abilities and desires. These energies provide everyone with the same opportunities and each person will accept as much or as little as they believe is essential to the life experience that is their soul's journey in this lifetime.

Therefore, categorizing how one undertakes or accomplishes the path to spiritual mastery is a difficult process because there is no single way to describe what will happen and how we will respond to it. But if we look carefully, we can clearly see evidence of the opportunities all around us. The human family has a global connection via the Internet and email. We are increasingly interested in spiritual healing, communicating with the 'other side,' the development of psychic and clairvoyant abilities and other psychic phenomenon. The entertainment industry produces popular movies about spiritual matters. There is an increasing interest in natural healing and alternative medicine. All of these factors are indicative of a new interest in our spiritual aspect, the acknowledgement of another level of consciousness.

In the material world, we see evidence of this happening as well. An organic farmer in Oregon was once a New York banker. A business executive, healed of cancer, becomes a hospice worker. Today's spiritual healer was once an internist. Massive corporate layoffs force people to reassess their priorities and seek employment that feeds their soul, not just their bank accounts. Corporate dirty deals are uncovered and the perpetrators jailed. Politicians know that their constituents are watching them and can assemble grass roots protest movements with the click of a mouse.

These all represent aspects of the journey into spiritual mastery, and it begins as we disconnect from what we know and are no longer able to accept life "as is" or work within the status quo. We are forced to look deep within ourselves and discover what is important to us and whether our life is in or out of integrity with our hopes and dreams. If we don't like what we see many opportunities will be presented to help us to make changes. These changes may seem to occur randomly but nothing in the Universe is random. Their purpose is to allow us to take a more objective look at 'how we always do things' and choose to do the things that make us happy, enrich our lives and honor ourselves, our truth and our spiritual roots.

The invitation to accept spiritual mastery comes when we are ready for it and once we step into it, we will have to, one way or another, live with integrity, being true to ourselves. It will free us from the expectations, beliefs and perspectives that we have lived with, accepted as truth and suffered under for years. Some of these changes will feel like they are imposed on us and they may be difficult, others will be easy. Some of the changes will be confusing, others will arrive with crystal clarity. Once we have gone through this process though, no matter how dramatic or subtle our experience, we will emerge on the other side as one reborn, with a new perspective, ready for a new experience of life and living. These changes may involve leaving or losing personal relationships, changing jobs, moving to a new city, state or country. We may break ties with long-held friendships, family members or religious beliefs. We may decide to change our lifestyle, simplify our life or totally change our belief system.

Of course, we can also choose to not participate, to maintain our life exactly as it has always been. That option is available to everyone. But, on both an individual and a global level, its time has come and those who choose to not participate may find that the world is a much different place. It will no longer be possible to hide dark secrets, to keep the truth from people, including ourselves. It will no longer be possible to fake our way through life, pretending that we enjoy what we are doing, laughing on the outside while we're crying on the inside. We will be forced to examine every aspect of our lives and our values and make changes where our truth is not being honored.

When it is time for us to make life changes the Universe nudges us gently, offering subtle (or not so subtle) clues that we need to look in another direction. After a while, the nudges become more insistent, then they become sharper and finally, if we do not respond, all doors close until we are forced to look at the one which we, perhaps out of fear, refused to look at before. When it is time for our life to change, we must be willing to walk through the only door that is left open to us. If we ignore the longings of our soul long enough, the soul will put up a fight to force us to acknowledge its urgings.

Yet, despite every positive, life affirming reason to undertake this journey, we still have to consciously choose to embrace the path of spiritual mastery. We do have free will. And it is must be our choice, one that cannot be taken lightly. Once we have stepped onto the path of spiritual mastery, we are permanently changed. Our perspective will be altered and that may include starting over, being alone for the first time in our life, or embracing a lifestyle that we would never have considered before. All of these are choices that will be possible because barriers to our spiritual growth will dissolve and fears that may have once held us back will be released as we are faced with the opportunity to choose the life we want to live instead of the one we believe is our obligation.

Why is this possible now and why is it so important? Theses change are possible because we are completing the end of humanity's cycle and have completed the full range of experiences that were necessary to bring us full circle, from separation to reconnection to Source, from fear-based victim consciousness to a willingness to acknowledge our divinity and accept our spiritual mastery. Until the collective consciousness reached critical mass and agreed to raise their vibrations, this was not possible. But we now have the cooperation of enough of humanity's membership to enable mastery to occur.

Without this shift in our awareness of who we are and a willingness to change from our fear-based consciousness to embrace unconditional love, we would have continued to suffer and struggle, to remain separated and in danger of fulfilling the doom and gloom prophecies foretelling a disastrous end of the world.

The responsibility that our potential for mastery entails is enormous because we are the first of Earth's inhabitants to undertake a shift of this magnitude, to realize our ability to become one with the All That Is, our God Creator, to achieve multi-dimensional living and to become one with our Truth. While we have seen examples of paradigm shifts in history -- the Renaissance period in Europe was such a shift, as was the American Revolution, but never before in the history of humanity have so many people been willing and able to change their view of reality on such a large scale and had the information and resources with which to do it. It is an awakening of global proportions, a paradigm shift that has never before been experienced on this planet.

The nature of our spiritual understanding is an individual process and each one of us has to make our own choices on our spiritual path. We cannot rely on the choices or opinions of others and we have unlimited freedom in choosing what we will do. This individual aspect of our life path is one that we are uncomfortable with for we have learned to be part of the group instead of standing alone. As societies we have become homogenized and have learned to adopt an accepted way of being, living and interacting. This makes one aspect of spiritual mastery so difficult for us — we each have a unique and different experience of this process of transformation so there is no single way to experience it and no two people will experience it in the same way, although we may find ourselves around others whose experiences are somewhat similar to ours. But we cannot look at someone else's experience and use it as a model to predict what we may go through.

It is not possible to adapt our healing journey to mirror that of those whom we see as having successfully completed this process. We cannot use others' experiences to make our own easier. Part of our mastery journey lies in discovering what this means to us, to create our own connection to Source, to find our own inner guidance and learn and heal at our own rate, within our own capabilities and find our own way through the experiences our soul has selected to help us reach our own level of mastery.

Consider these questions for your personal mastery journey:

Are you aware of how your path to mastery has unfolded or is unfolding now?

Do you see how the events and experiences in your life contribute to your mastery journey?

Can you see how the people in your life have contributed to your mastery path?

Did you consciously adopt your spiritual path or were you nudged by the Universe? How did that happen?

What does your mastery journey look like and are you willing to be a conscious participant on this journey?

Are you aware of how you are participating in humanity's mastery journey?

Are you willing to consciously walk in your mastery every day, with every thought, word, action and belief?

Making the choice to embody mastery means making the choice to live in our truth, acknowledging ourselves as powerful beings with unlimited potential for joy, love and peace. Living in the Truth means that every second of every day, we never waver in our absolute belief and trust that we are one with our Creator. It means being absolutely honest with and true to ourselves, all of the time. It means being able to let go of every part of our life that is not serving our Highest Good and is out of integrity with our dreams and soul purpose to live a joy-filled life.

It is a new paradigm for us and we can do it – we have been preparing for this moment for many lifetimes. We will learn to make choices from our power and purpose rather than from our fear and understand that those choices may not always be obvious, easy, make sense or they may take us totally out of our comfort zone, including choices about our most cherished relationships. We move from the vibration of fear into higher potentials where we have access to the vibration of miracles.

The Miracle Vibration

We describe miracles as extraordinary events that defy natural law, logic and explanation. But they are simply the movement of energy from one place to another. We believe that miracles happen when we are blessed, rescued or saved at the time we need it most. We think that miracles are created by God but they actually originate within us. They are created when we tap into the flow of Universal energy, free of fear and doubt, with full faith that our prayers will be answered and our needs met. And they are always met, but not for the reasons we have come to believe, such as God having pity on us or having a stroke of luck. Our needs are met at these moments because we have absolute faith that our prayers will be answered and this puts us in the miracle vibration, a level of energy where are fully utilizing our creative abilities to manifest exactly what we want at the moment we want and need it.

Within the miracle vibration we are flowing with the Universal energy, which is the dynamic energy of creation. This energy creates everything around us. It is a ceaseless current that responds to our every thought and word. It never judges or criticizes our choices because it acknowledges our perfection and wisdom. We are always interacting with this energy, consciously and unconsciously, and create an endless flow of reality with it. When we are free of fear and doubt, fully present in each moment, we flow with this energy and create effortlessly with it. But in the presence of doubt and fear, our interactions are difficult, sporadic and the flow of creation is not smooth and effortless. When we are able to access our mastery and connect to the energy at the highest levels, we are at the miracle vibration. And this is when the extraordinary is accessible because nothing is impossible. We 'ascend into miracles' because their vibration is at a higher level than that place where we experience lack, life is difficult, challenging and there is drama and chaos. And we must be at the vibration of miracles in order to access them with effortless grace and ease.

Miracles are not the life saving, extraordinary events that save us from disaster, although that is generally our experience of them. They represent the highest potential for our reality, what is possible for us when we shift our perspective regarding our possibilities and accept a new level of consciousness for ourselves and our reality. They represent our ability to be free of the memory, fears and restrictions of the past and open to the prospect of a limitless, abundant future that unfolds one step at a time. The possibility of miracles lies in our ability to believe that they are possible. Do we believe we deserve miracles? That is another prerequisite, for we must believe that we deserve to have all that we want before miracles will manifest for us.

The miracle vibration is a new paradigm for humanity and represents a reality where everything is possible and what we want is immediately available to us. Within this vibration we are not worried or fearful, we do not have doubts and misgivings about whether we are doing is the right thing or whether we are in the right place at the right time. We know that everything has a purpose and meaning and when an experience has fulfilled its purpose in our life and we are complete with it another one will be presented to us.

In the miracle vibration we live with an understanding of the importance of the past and the lessons and experiences it has for us. But we do not live in the past or bring those experiences and their energy into the present. The past merely serves as a source of information that we use to guide us in the present moment. It is a reminder of the outcome of previous choices and decisions and how we have previously used our power.

With the past as a known reference point we can make more informed, powerful and conscious choices in the present. The lessons of the past allow us to be consciously mindful of each moment, fully aware that we are always presented with an infinite number of choices for the next step of our journey. Whatever we choose is the right thing for us at that moment. Other choices will appear as we are ready for them.

Within the miracle vibration we are aware that we live in a state of connection — each of us is connected to our spiritual Source and to each other. Our Source connection enables miracles to happen because it is our direct connection to the flow of the Universal energy. This energy is responsive, creative and non-judgmental. The miracle vibration does not flow from an energetic vacuum where blessings go to the deserving, most enlightened or to those who carry the highest vibration. By simply believing that miracles can happen, we create the energy that allows them to happen. We create miracles according to what we want but what we ask for or create for ourselves we do for everyone else and we must be willing to have our miracle available to everyone else in order for it to happen. Each person receives according to their needs and beliefs and each person contributes to the miracles of the whole of humanity.

Consider these questions for your personal mastery journey:

Are there any miracles you would like to create in your life?

Do you see patterns of the past in your current reality?

Are you willing to take responsibility for your reality by accepting the power you have to create every aspect of it?

Do you feel connected or disconnected from Source? Are you aware that when you are disconnected you are not in the flow of the energy that creates miracles? What are three things you can to do be more connected, powerful and in alignment with your heart's desire for your life?

Do you believe that you are a miracle machine? You must, if you are going to create miracles.

Are you willing to be open to your miracle ability and believe that miracles can happen for you?

Think of one miracle you wish to create in your life. Keep your focus on that miracle every day for one week and expand it to everyone in the world. Then watch for the signs that it is coming to you and have faith, for that is how miracles are created.

It is an exciting opportunity and a new challenge, as we are the first generation of humanity to access this level of connection, understanding and willingness to integrate our divinity within our humanity and to enter the miracle vibration. We are redefining humanity and creating a more caring, gentler and more conscious level of human being. The miracle vibration is voluntary and it is available to us as a choice but is not forced upon us. We have to choose it and we may be faced with different opportunities to do so.

Our choices reflect whether we are ready for this level of spiritual awareness and if not, we will have other opportunities at a later time. Whatever we choose is what is best for us, provides us with opportunities to learn, heal and transcend our life lessons and within the dynamic universe we live in, there are unlimited choices because reality is a potential state of being that responds to our energetic vibrations and our willingness to acknowledge our mastery.

The Potential of Reality

Within the miracle vibration we have access to unlimited potential realities and can choose any of them. What we are aware of and how we access these realities depends on our energetic vibrations and beliefs. The reality we live in, on an individual and collective level, is an illusion that reflects our beliefs, thoughts and energies, mirroring the potential reality that we have chosen. If our thoughts and beliefs are of lack and limitation, then our reality will reflect that. If they are of abundance and expansion, our reality will reflect that too. Changing our thoughts and beliefs changes our vibrations, which then creates a new illusion for our reality and expands its possibilities. Individually and collectively, the world we experience is a reality that we selected from a vast pool of potential realities whose available choices are determined by our energetic vibrations. At its most basic state, the world is an illusion that we can transform at any time by changing our vibrations, which allows us to choose from a new and different array of potential realities. We can, for example, create a world of chaos, drama and fear or one that exists in love, joy and abundance for everyone. The world is simply a reflection of the mass consciousness that created it.

What are the potential realities available to each of us? After all, we do not all want the same things and how do we choose what is right for us? Anything we could possibly want is contained within our field of potential but how do we know what is in it?

There are three questions to ask that will help you determine that:

What do you want and are passionate about?
What do you focus your intention on?
What is the first thing that comes to your mind when you say "I wish …"?

Our reality is limited to our field of potential, which is actually limitless because it exists as different levels of potential with different energetic vibrations. We can connect to the level that we resonate with energetically and this determines which level or elements within our field of potential we are aware of and can connect to. Anything outside our range of energetic vibration is a potential that is off limits to us. With each shift in our energetic vibration we expand our field of potential to include these different possibilities.

It is impossible to create a reality that is outside our level of energetic vibration, because this creates an energetic mismatch which we will feel as blocks, feeling stuck, and a lack of progress or flow. Once we raise our energy that new level of potential becomes available to us. That is why we can ask for something, wish for it, focus our intention and still not receive it at that moment but may receive it much later. The answer lies in whether our energetic vibrations will allow us to connect to that level of potential.

Our thoughts create our reality too. In fact they are the most powerful tools we have available to us. Some of my clients say "But I have been doing my inner work, changing my thoughts and beliefs and I am not manifesting what I have asked for." How can that happen, if they are focused on what they want and managing their thoughts and beliefs? Their focus was on what they wanted to create but the Universe is aware of all of our thoughts, and it is the lowest vibration we are expressing, consciously or unconsciously, that determines what manifests in our reality. So if we are being positive and confident on the outside but are inwardly fearful and doubt our abilities, guess which energy level we will be creating our reality from. Right, at the level of our doubt and fear. And nothing in our outer reality will change until we release the doubt and fear we feel on the inside.

Even though many other realities are available to us, our energetic vibrations must match them in order for us to be aware of and connect to them. No matter how much we may want or how many times we ask for a new job, relationship or wealth, our level of energetic vibration must match what we are asking for or we are violating the Law of Attraction, which states that attraction occurs between things with similar levels of energetic vibration. This does not mean that change is impossible, we can create a reality that differs from what we are currently experiencing, but we have to be in the vibration of the different reality for it to manifest.

For example, someone with an empty bank account has chosen a reality that reflects their level of vibration with respect to financial abundance. Whatever they believe about money and their ability to have it in their bank account has created this as their reality. They may want to create financial abundance and are speaking the right words but their thoughts may include fear of lack, not believing they deserve abundance, afraid that money will not manifest in the right amounts at the right time, or any other thoughts that focus on lack. The Law of Attraction is allowing them to attract abundance according to their level of energetic vibration.

Can they create another reality? Yes, if they shift their thinking so they can be consciously focused on creating abundance, having it appear in their life, believe that they deserve to have unlimited abundance and trust that money is available to them in an unlimited supply. Their belief in lack, that there is not enough, has something to teach them. When that lesson is learned and they no longer have to experience it, they can raise their energetic vibrations and attract an abundance of material resources.

Here is a client story that reflects this principle. Douglas is a graphic artist, who is intelligent, creative, talented and loved by his clients. He does wonderful work, has won awards and is recognized by his peers for his abilities. With all of this going for him, it would seem that his business would be thriving. But it is not. Douglas often has trouble paying his rent and other bills, has no savings and often has to ask family and friends for money to meet his financial obligations.

While Douglas is talented, he admits that he continually sabotages his business' success. He does not believe he is worthy of success and has a fear of being penniless. His childhood was marked by poverty as his alcoholic father spent all of the family's money and Douglas remembers that he often went to bed hungry. He was ridiculed by other children for his ill-fitting, ragged clothing and by his teachers for sleeping in class and not doing his homework. They did not know that the family had no money for food or clothing and Douglas' sleep was often interrupted by his father's drunken rages. While Douglas tried to create a successful business, his thinking was focused on fear, lack, and anger at his father. And his reality mirrored those thoughts. To create lasting success he had to change his thoughts so he stayed focused on being successful, instead of his fear of poverty and lack. And he   had to learn about forgiveness, release and acceptance.

With spiritual mastery we connect to our ability to create a reality that reflects our Highest Good, which is the best and most wonderful outcome possible for us. In fact, we create our reality every day, with every belief, thought and word. Whatever our reality is at the moment, whether we are happy or sad, rich or poor, at peace or in chaos, we have created it. For many generations we held the belief that we were victims, of nature, of our social, religious and political systems, victimized by our past and destiny, and that our reality was out of our control. This victimhood has been our state of being for so long that we believe it to be true. The energetic vibrations of the new earth are bringing our victimhood to the forefront, identifying each fear, limiting belief and perception as they are out of alignment with the higher energies we are trying and want to create. Our choice is to either succumb to our fears or to overcome and heal them. Will we continue to be victims of our fear-based reality or find the inner resources to change it? We can if we are willing to change our vibrations to create new potential realities for ourselves and for the world.

We have been tasked with creating a new paradigm for ourselves and for the world which will contain potential realities that are new to the earth and to humanity. This new paradigm is built on the foundation that we have created through our transformation and the healing work that we are now doing. With each healing experience we are refining the energies of the new paradigm and releasing the energies of fear, polarity, and limitation, to choose light over darkness, abundance over lack, joy over sadness and love over fear. Each time we heal an aspect of ourselves we remove that energy from the earth's vibrational field and its field of potential and release all realities that are associated with that energy.

Energized by our healing and release work, the new paradigm gathers force to allow all of humanity overcome its powerless victimhood and become empowered victors. We can change the world we live in by changing the potential realities humanity can connect to, raising the vibrations of the energies so that war, discord, hatred, and violence are simply not energetic possibilities. This reality is possible through the current transformation in global consciousness. The new realities available to us are grounded in self and spiritual empowerment, which includes the end of karma, respect for the Earth and all of its inhabitants, a re-awakening of our own 'godhood' and reconnection to the Source, becoming spiritual human beings. On an individual level, we can choose a life of unlimited abundance, peace, freedom, joy and love. On a collective level, we can choose peace, love and joy for the world. It is our collective intention that will allow us to choose the reality for the world beyond 2012 and we have the power to create a world as we wish it to be.

We are co-creators with the Universe and we create on two different levels, in our own life and for the world. Each shift in our vibration creates a corresponding change in all fields of potential, ours and that of the world. Every step we take away from fear and into its higher vibration, unconditional love, moves us and the world away from fear and into a higher vibration. The fear paradigm has been creating humanity's reality for eons of time has now outlived its usefulness and will no longer work on a massive scale, as it has in the past.

The growing interest in all things spiritual has been slow, but steady. And that will increase exponentially in coming years for several reasons: people are afraid of what is to come, they are afraid of what might happen if they do not acknowledge their spirituality, they receive fewer assurances from and have less confidence in the world's political, social and religious systems and they are tired of the status quo. But mostly, they are tired of being afraid, sad, angry, hurt, disappointed and feeling that their lives are out of control. They are ready for new choices that reflect their need for joy, their desire to experience their power and their willingness to know different ways of being.

Consider these questions for your personal mastery journey:

List three things you like about your current reality and three things you dislike about it.

Do you sabotage your success because you want to create a wonderful reality but your fear gets in the way?

Name two potential realities that you would like to create for yourself.

Writing as quickly as you can and without thinking about what you are writing, make a list of everything that you believe is contained in your field of potential. Do some of the things on the list surprise you? Remember that this represents your potential at this moment and it will change each time you shift your energy and raise your vibrations.

How are you experiencing life as a victim and what can you do to change that? What are some ways you can help change the earth's field of potential, raising its vibrations by changing your own?

These are not new concepts. With each generation spiritual teachers have come to teach this information, often to an unreceptive and unappreciative audience. In each lifetime we attempt to shift the fear paradigm with varying levels of success. And we feel powerless against the mass consciousness, thinking that our small efforts have little effect. Yet each of us has the power to shift fear-based realities when we understand our role as Lightworkers, those who carry specific energetic vibrations for the world, and remember that our mission for each lifetime is to introduce new potential realities and to remember ourselves as individual sparks of Divine Consciousness.

The new paradigm will usher in the opportunity to see miracles in action, to live a life free of drama and fear, the end of karma and the beginning of heaven on earth. All of these are aspects of our individual and collective fields of potential, but only for those who actually believe that this can happen and who refuse to accept the fear paradigm as the basis of their reality

We are here to create heaven on earth, where all of humanity is awakened and embraces their Source connection and will be fully aware that we are all one through our divine connection. This is the purpose of the new earth and the new paradigms, and the reason that we have been coming here, for millennia, to learn this lesson. This is our path of ascension, the journey we undertake with each lifetime. And to know what we must do we must understand ascension.

The Path of Ascension

What is the path of ascension, where does it lead us and what is the final destination? Is learning our lessons a prerequisite to ascension? What happens after that? Do the lessons ever end and then what do we do? Is Ascension a final day of reckoning, where we are judged by our Creator and those who are worthy will leave the earth for heavenly realms? Will we be visited by extra-terrestrials who will remove those who have reached ascension and then destroy everyone else and the planet?

Ascension is the culmination of our journey into spiritual evolution that started with the beginning of the human cycle, when we first separated from Source. It ends when we return to Source and complete the cycle. It has lasted for eons and is the central focus of each lifetime. While the ascension process involves all of humanity, it is not a standardized process of spiritual evolution. Each of us is on our own, individual ascension journey, which is defined as transcending the material, human experience and creating a balance between our human, ego-based consciousness and our spiritual, divine consciousness.

This is a process of transformation, accomplished by raising our vibrations to move out of the third dimension into higher dimensions of being. Each of us will connect with the dimension that matches our vibration and then we will cycle through another ascension process as we create the possibility of journeying into higher and higher vibrational potentials. The lessons continue but they are at different levels, as our core lessons are still active. We simply have a new perspective on them with each step forward we take on our journey.

How does this work? Think back to at least five years ago and a choice that you had to make at that time. Would you make the same choice today or for the same reasons? Your perspective on that choice is different because you have a different vibrational energy than you did then (maybe not, but that is a different matter). The point here is that we are always ascending, always growing, learning and transforming. Just as everything in nature renews itself with the change in the seasons, so do we.

This is not a sudden, permanent leap into a new dimension. Instead, we go back and forth, moving forward into a higher dimension and back into the third and the lessons it contains. Each time we access a higher level we are able to see the additional healing that we need to do, so we return to the previous energetic level to do the healing work. While we are ascending and moving out of our vibrational comfort zones we are processing vast amounts of information and energy until we have fully mastered the lessons of our lifetime at a variety of energetic levels. Then we can choose whether or not we will fully ascend into a higher vibration and move into the lessons it has for us. Taking time to rest when our bodies tell us they are tired, being quiet and still when we need time to regroup, and staying focused on our ascension goals will help us stay on the path. While we do not remember what has occurred in previous lifetimes we are all experiencing familiar lessons, in new and different ways, as part of our ascension path.

There is no final day of judgment when it will be decided whether we are worthy of entering Heaven, the reward for having been 'good enough' during our lifetime or whether we would go to the dire alternative. When we believe this, we accept that our lives here are relatively meaningless and that the work that we do has no redeeming, ongoing value until after we die. But the ascension journey does not happen in the spirit world, it happens here on Earth. And ascension is not a day or an event, it is not even a moment in time or a reward. Ascension is simply the path that we embark upon in each lifetime to reconnect to Source, embrace our power and remember our divine selves. Ascension is our life purpose and objective, and the path that we are on every day.

Every time we embrace a spiritual concept such as forgiveness, gratitude, abundance, compassion or unconditional love, we move farther along the path of ascension. This does not mean that we have accumulated enough points so that we can ensure our place on the spaceship (in case it does come); it means that within our personal spiritual journey, we have raised our vibrations and have accomplished an aspect of our purpose here. When we are able to forgive someone who has wronged us, make a powerful choice for ourselves, stand in acceptance of others or ourselves, or even choose to create peace, joy and unconditional love in our own life, we have ascended. In effect, we have transformed the energy in our lives so that we no longer live with judgment, fear, hate and chaos. And that is what ascension is, moving beyond fear into unconditional love, balancing the spiritual and material and creating heaven on earth.

The key to understanding ascension is in remembering that we are each on our own spiritual journey, one that cannot be shared or even understood by anyone else. Our personal spiritual journey encompasses the lessons that our soul has chosen for this lifetime. They may be experienced within the soul group that we have worked with for many lifetimes, but they are part of our own, unique path. Since our path is unique, so is our ascension experience. This is also true of the ascension path of every other person on the planet. We can look at humanity as a group of souls, all of whom are ascending individually and together. When one person awakens to a conscious awareness of their ascension path, they create an opportunity for many others to awaken along with them.

Every decision that we make, every choice that we consider, every word that we say or thought that we think are all part of our ascension journey. Will we make decisions that move us into powerful opportunities? Can we make choices that open us to our unlimited potential? Do our words reflect our spiritual understanding? Are our thoughts creating the reality that we desire? Ascension is not about being 'good enough' to lead a powerful, joyful and abundant life; it is about raising our vibrations to create the Heaven on earth that is our birthright. Ascension is not about being 'good enough' to deserve what we desire; it is remembering that we are limitless beings and deserve to receive limitless blessings. This is not new information for us, it is what we have always known but have forgotten through our human experience. It is a reconnection to the memory of our divine heritage, the knowledge that we are already everything that we want and hope to be, do and have.

As we turn our intention to changing our reality, gaining greater spiritual knowledge and living our lives within the context of our spiritual understanding, we are on our ascension path. We can also choose to not ascend — the Universe will not judge us either way. But fulfilling our spiritual contract involves walking the path of ascension, where we choose to step outside of what our mind knows is possible and open ourselves to the limitless possibilities afforded by our collective Source, where we choose to forgive rather than continue our karmic experiences with others, and where we choose peace and unconditional love as a way of life for ourselves and for all of humanity.

To know where you are on your ascension path, look at your own life and consider these questions:

Are you happy with yourself and your life?

Do you have fear, anger or unresolved issues in any area of your life?

Do you live in chaos and lack or with peace, joy and abundance?

Are you doing exactly what you want and enjoying every minute of your day?

Is your life filled with people who love, honor and respect you?

Have you had moments of bliss followed by deep sadness? These are opportunities to choose which dimension you want to be in and your moments of bliss give you a glimpse into another dimension of being.

Can you change the thinking that creates the sadness so you can be in a state of constant bliss in each moment?

Ascension does not happen when we decide that we are finished with our journey on earth and create a way to leave the planet, it is our life journey and we live with the evidence of our ascension progress in our everyday lives. Every aspect of our reality reflects where we are in our ascension journey, which level of vibration we are expressing and which dimension we are in. Whether we are consciously aware of our life purpose as a journey of ascension or not has no bearing on the process because as our divine purpose it is inter-woven within the threads of our life. Sometimes lifetimes are spent in complete ignorance of our ascension purpose so that we can know what it is to be completely disconnected from our spiritual side. In another lifetime we will have the opportunity to know ourselves in a different way and to embrace ascension and reconnection.

When we consciously choose the ascension path and are focused on its learning and transformation we are saying "YES" to our soul's longing for healing and reconnection to Source. When we are unaware of this purpose our life is a series of events, some good and others challenging, that we struggle through without understanding their purpose or relevance. We miss the opportunities to choose with our heart instead of from the ego, or from love instead of fear. Each time we choose to ignore the lessons and our ascension we are given other opportunities to make that choice. With introspection we can find the patterns in what happens to us and who they happen with. Relationship lessons are delivered by successive partners, each one similar to the previous one. Lessons in abundance arrive in cycles, where prosperity is followed by lack. Periods of peace are followed by periods of drama. When we arrive at the point where we will consider transformation as an alternative to what we have previously chosen, we connect with our ascension path. It is not an obligation but it is an aspect of the life purpose that we choose with each lifetime.

Ascension is a faith-based path, whose rewards are subtle and sometimes hidden, meaning that we do not know what turning our consciousness towards becoming more spiritually aware, raising our vibrations and choosing higher energetic vibrations will bring us and often our lives seem to get worse before they improve. Healing requires faith in the process, in ourselves and in the rewards that come with spiritual understanding. Faith requires trust in a benevolent Universe, knowing that the rewards of ascension lie within the journey, not the destination.

Ascension requires all of these things and more, knowing that by moving our consciousness in other directions, we are choosing the path of integration, inviting Spirit to partner with us within our human experiences. This is not a choice of being spiritual over being human, it is a blending of these two energies, where we release the densest energies we have embodied over countless lifetimes of believing we were disconnected, to accepting the truth of our divinity, become one with the highest expressions of our aspects and energies.

What happens if we choose to not ascend? By that, I mean choosing to live unconsciously, unaware of the meaning and purpose of lessons, to forego releasing karma, to renounce forgiveness, gratitude and unconditional love. Are we punished if we do not make the choice? The short answer is "No" because the Universe never punishes or judges us for anything, as it views all of our actions as being perfect. But over the longer term, we have a soul contract for ascension to fulfill and we will continue to receive lessons until we are willing to learn and transcend them. That will take as long as it takes, including this entire lifetime and others. When we resist our lessons they do not go away.

They just come around again, inviting us to make different choices until we make those that allow transformation and ascension to occur.

Choosing the path of ascension moves us forward on our spiritual journey and has both tangible and intangible rewards. The tangible rewards will manifest in the form of greater peace, abundance, joy and discovering that life flows more easily. The intangible rewards include the fulfillment of our spiritual contracts and the freedom from fear which opens us up to the energy of unconditional love and access to higher dimensions of being.

But to do this we must be willing to be led by spirit instead of solely by the ego. With a conscious choice for ascension we agree to allow our spiritual self to become the leading force in our lives and gently guide the ego towards working in partnership with it. This is an acknowledgement of our divinity that leads to a search for balance between our human and spiritual selves.

Here our two selves merge to manifest our purpose of becoming a spiritual human with limitless possibilities. Our choice for ascension does not guarantee a peaceful life and our lives can become more chaotic, difficult, and confusing as we shed our emotional and psychic baggage. We have not chosen the wrong path, we are simply in between where we were and where we are going, a void we must cross to create the next step on our spiritual journey. We are in the gap between fear and understanding, light and dark, a pause between steps on our journey. This is something we go through, not around, as we are faced with every fear, every emotion and experience that has ever created pain in our lives, all at once.

Getting through these experiences is easier when we remember that we are being provided with an opportunity to review everything that has ever held us back and to agree to release it. Once we do that, we do not have to experience it again and even if a similar situation appears, we will not respond to it in the same way. But that is little consolation for us when our life is turned upside down and nothing seems to work. Our time in the void is temporary, as we process the energy that we are ready to release. Then we can experience the 'peace that passes all understanding' as we see life through the eyes of absolute clarity, know that peace and love are more than a possible choice, they are the only choice.

How do we ascend? We do it through a desire for change and transformation, which happens at the moment when we look at our life and are ready to move in a different direction as our current reality is unsatisfying and unfulfilling. An initial feeling of discomfort is followed by a period of self examination that can either be destructive if it is in the form of criticism and judgment, or constructive, if viewed from the realization that we are uncomfortable because our energy has shifted and we can no longer connect with our current reality.

We can choose between two responses, fear or power. If we choose fear then we are simply not ready to ascend into a higher vibration and we will have another opportunity at another time. If we choose to respond through our power, using our spiritual knowledge to accept our shifting energies, then we have chosen to ascend and we must take action by allowing change to occur.

Our desire for transformation invites change and whatever arises in response to that is something we are capable of and have been asking for. The Universe rushes in to help us when we are willing to put our spiritual truth into action through our desire to transform. We must know that when we are guided to act it is because it is time, whether or not we think we are ready. Ascension is our life purpose and all we have to do is say "YES".

Putting ascension into practice happens through our actions. We can believe, think and know all kinds of spiritual truths. Our call to action asks that we show ourselves and the world that we will live by what we know to be true. Putting our truth into action, in what we do, how we interact with others and how we apply our spiritual truth in our material reality shows us where we are on our ascension path. The action is in the form of what we are ready to become and what we do—to become the highest expression of our potential, forgive those who have hurt us, forgive ourselves for our limiting beliefs, accept ourselves and others within the limitless boundaries of unconditional love, willing to speak our truth in all things and to bless ourselves with joy, peace and abundance.

When do we achieve ascension? We achieve it every day, in many ways. Each new level of understanding, every desire for transformation, our willingness to forgive unconditionally, each truth we reveal to ourselves, moves us farther along this path. It is a journey has no end and if our focus is on getting to the end of our ascension journey as quickly as possible, we are missing the

31

point of the experience. There are no standards to measure whether or not we are fulfilling our ascension journey, how far we have come or how far we have yet to go, other than what we feel. Are we still afraid, confused and unsure? Or are we at peace, in acceptance and with an understanding of who we are in the grand scheme of the Universe?

Ascension is an unfolding process, where each new understanding puts us in a place where we can learn on a different level, where each layer of fear that we remove allows us to experience life from another perspective. We began our life at a certain level of ascension and we will end it at a new and different level. What happens in between is what is important for this is the learning that allows our vibrations to shift and new dimensions to open for us.

Instead of being one long, endless journey, our ascension path is a series of steps, some of which seem large and unattainable, others small and easy, each one requiring an energetic shift, a vibrational lightening and a willingness to realize new potentials. There is proof of our progress, which we can know as a feeling of peace and joy that comes with renewal of our Source connection, the gift of miracles, the fearlessness that is ours when we step into our power, acknowledging that we co-create our reality with the Source and that we have the ability to create the life of our dreams.

The ascension path has no destination. There is no reward or prize for being the best, the fastest or the most efficient at ascension. It is not a contest. It is an individual journey, one that is uniquely ours. It is the lessons and learning that we experience along the way that mark our success. Each victory, no matter how small or insignificant it may appear to be, is important to our soul's growth. And each time we transcend a lesson we have made progress on our continuing ascension path. Every day brings new opportunities to create a life of peace, joy, unconditional love and unlimited abundance that is the reward for choosing the path of ascension.

Consider these questions for your personal mastery journey:

What lessons are you experiencing now that mark your ascension journey?

Can you identify any people who are helping you with your ascension?

Are you experiencing cycles of release and healing at this time? Can you see their purpose in your ascension journey?

How can you put your spiritual truth into action in your life?

In what ways is your energy shifting and how can you use that transformation to create a different reality?

Do you see any results of your ascension journey in your daily life?

Are any aspects of your life unfulfilling or unsatisfying and can you see how your dissatisfaction is preparing you for the next step on your ascension journey?

Do you have any goals for your ascension – is there something you would like to do with your life that your ascension process is awakening you to?

Who is responsible for introducing the energies of ascension? The Lightworkers, those who carry specific energetic vibrations for transformation and the new earth paradigm. They are the pioneers, those who are preparing the final stages of the ascension path for humanity and they are everywhere, working in big and small ways, to ensure that ascension occurs.

The Role of the Lightworker

Lightworkers carry a special energetic vibration and have volunteered to be on the planet at this time because they are uniquely qualified to withstand the rigors of the energetic transformations of ascension and then use their learning to help others. They are called Lightworkers because they each hold a specific light vibration that they have agreed to maintain during this process of growth and transformation. Together they bring in a new vibratory collective to set the new energetic paradigms and vortexes that are necessary for our individual and collective transformation to occur. Many of them have agreed to be here because this time is important and even critical in humanity's evolution. They are the ascension pioneers, those who have experienced many ascension cycles, beginning with Lemuria and Atlantis, and are here again to ensure that there is energetic support for this ascension cycle.

Lightworkers have been present on the earth for eons and their time here has often been challenging. They have always been present to teach and heal and were tasked with introducing spiritual truths in different times as part of the effort of raising humanity's consciousness throughout the ages. Their efforts often led to various forms of persecution, including being chastised, tortured, killed, beaten and starved or worse. Many Lightworkers still carry the memory of their persecution in their cellular memory, which is why they tend to work quietly, in the background, and are sometimes reluctant to openly talk about their work and teachings.

Many Lightworkers carry strong memories of their participation in the last great healing cycle, which occurred with Atlantis. At that time there was an opportunity for ascension similar to the one we are experiencing today and Lightworkers were also gathered to bring their light and energy to the process. While they gladly participated in creating the energies that would help Atlantis complete the human cycle, those in power had a hidden agenda. The energy that was released on the earth, without the balance of spirit, destroyed the city and everyone in it. Many Lightworkers still bear emotional scars and guilt from having watched those they loved and were trusted by annihilated as the city slowly collapsed and fell into the ocean. The Lightworkers were also destroyed, but not before they were able to see what had been done with their energy in that ascension cycle.

This ascension cycle has similar energies as that of Atlantis except this time there is a focus on the balance between the spiritual and material, which will prevent a recurrence of the Atlantean disaster. The Atlantean experience is why many Lightworkers are reluctant to use their gifts and are afraid that they will participate in the ascension to once again have their power misused and the earth destroyed. But that will not happen because the lessons of Atlantis were learned and the focus today is creating heaven on earth, instead of the manipulation of energies to create an earth-like heaven, dominated by ego-based energies, as was attempted in Atlantis.

All Lightworkers have the memory of a strong connection to Source. This memory is what has sustained them through their own healing and growth journeys and it is the strength of their connection that allows them to hold that energy for others as part of their transformation work. But this has not made their life any easier. In fact, Lightworkers often experience the most intense of these energies long before they are felt by others. And they often suffer their effects in dramatic ways, through physical illness, emotional issues, financial problems and difficult relationships. By experiencing and overcoming these issues, they are able to create new paradigms for healing, establishing new vibrations by transforming fear-based energies into their higher aspects.

Many Lightworkers work alone, in isolation, away from people and distractions. They do not necessarily do this by choice; it is easier to process energy when they are not around others because they are often highly empathic, able to access others' energetic and emotional fields and vibrations. Since many people carry a lower fear vibration, being around these energies creates additional work for Lightworkers, as they unconsciously process all of the energies around them.

But this aspect of their journey is changing, as enough energy has been transformed and the collective energetic vibration is now higher. There is enough conscious participation in raising energetic vibrations that allows light to become the dominant energy. With the collective consciousness at a higher level, an important part of the Lightworker role has been completed and another can begin, integrating the material and spiritual worlds, making new connections in places where they did not exist before, creating a spiritual context that allows the two worlds, material and spiritual to co-exist in harmony. Soon Lightworkers, who have removed themselves from the material world and focused their energies in more spiritual endeavors will be integrated into professions that were formerly considered non-spiritual, bringing with them the energies of transformation and integration, as part of their mission to create heaven on earth.

Who are the Lightworkers? They are the spiritual teachers who present the world with new information, solutions and enlightenment. They are the energy workers who provide healing services that help balance energy, clear blocks and heal on a soul level. They are those who work tirelessly for change, who insist on disrupting the status quo, pointing out new alternatives. They are the people you work with, go to school and live with. Some do not even know they are Lightworkers and simply do what comes naturally to them. But through their efforts others learn, heal, are transformed and access higher energetic vibrations. Lightworkers are everywhere, are present in all walks of life, in all professions and do their work in a variety of ways. Some are very public and vocal, others are quiet and prefer to remain in the background. Each of them has a special task to do, an energetic vibration and light to carry and a mission to fulfill at this important time.

Are you a Lightworker? There are certain characteristics that most Lightworkers have, some or all of them may be familiar to you:

• You feel different from others and do not fit in. You have always felt this way, even as a child.

• You have always had strong spiritual experiences that can include seeing angels and other spirit beings, hearing and speaking to them and being aware of their presence.

• You often experience ringing in your ears and hear sounds others do not hear.

• You feel drawn to help humanity in some way and have great compassion for others.

• You have a strong interest in spirituality and enjoy learning about it.

• You are very sensitive to the emotions and feelings of others.

• You have always known that you are here to serve a higher purpose, even if you do not know what that is.

If you are curious about Lightworkers, then you probably carry this energy and have wondered why your life is such a challenge and you cannot seem to have a normal life like other people. You are here at this time because you are needed and your participation is important. Your life has been difficult because you came here to transform energy and while that was happening you were functioning within dense energetic vibrations that   were very uncomfortable for you. Now that much of this transformation has occurred, you can rest and work on a level that is much less intense and demanding. While your work is not finished, it can be much easier and you will find more people like you, who vibrate at your level, to be with, as you play your role in the ascension and complete your own mastery journey.

Our mastery journey is a road to enlightenment, where we shed the density of the third dimension and its emotional connections and move into higher, lighter dimensions. If you are wondering how all of this applies to you and to your life, it's very simple. Each of us is born with a story to experience, one that echoes with the pain and joy, fear and love, sorrow and laughter that we have experienced over lifetimes. Our mission is to heal and transform that story. But first we must understand what it is.

The Story of Your Life

Our agreement to move forward into spiritual mastery includes a promise that we are willing to do the healing work that we have agreed to undertake on our life journey. And this promise involves cleaning up the energies of the past. Each of us has a past that includes all of the energies we have accumulated in all of our previous lifetimes, consisting of the emotions, beliefs, perceptions and the stories that were our life journeys. With each lifetime we accumulate these energetic imprints that we then use to prepare us for the next one. The totality of these energetic imprints creates the energies of the world we live in. All of the suffering, pain, drama, chaos and fear that are present on the earth at any moment represent the energetic imprint that humanity has created over eons of time. And we now have the opportunity to change every aspect of these energetic imprints and enter high realms of being to change humanity's story from victim to victor, dark to light, chaos to peace and fear to love.

On an individual level, this process entails reviewing every aspect of our life to find any areas that conflict with our true nature as divine spiritual beings, which prevent us from achieving our highest potential. Central to this process is defining who we are, not in terms of what we know to be true about ourselves, based on our past experiences, but within the context of our divinity, instead of the ego. To learn who we are we must understand the story of our life, the set of beliefs and perceptions that we use to define, explain and create our reality because this is where our energy is grounded. Without our intention to change it, the story is an endless loop, repeating every emotion and belief we have adopted in every interaction and situation. Changing it changes the course of our life and of humanity's karmic destiny.

Our story is developed throughout the course of each lifetime. It creates our life theme and the patterns of action and reaction that repeat in everything that we do, everyone we meet and every situation we create. This story has several purposes: it encompasses the lessons we have come to learn as part of our spiritual healing and awakening, it guides our behavior, creates the foundation for our reality and it protects us by ensuring that we remember the experiences that caused us pain. We then unconsciously draw events, situations and people to us that serve to   prove that our story   is true. Sometimes our stories have a positive theme—"I am a wonderful person and everyone loves me." Often, though, the stories have a far different theme—"I am unlovable, I am unlucky, I am not worthy of success." Because we judge life through our emotions, it is the difficult and painful life events that have the greatest impact on us, through which we create the stories that we believe and then work hard to prove to be true.

But we do not begin life with a fresh page on which we can build our own life story. We are born with a story that includes our karmic history and that of our soul group, past lifetimes and the karma and history of our parents, family, culture, gender and even our country. We also unconsciously draw to us those people whose story reflects ours. Some of these stories are simple, others are much more complicated. Each individual has a story and each story is different. One person's story would not make sense to anyone else because a story can only be perceived as meaningful and logical through its owner's eyes.

As we experience the life events that help us build on our story, it begins to take on a life of its own and it can take over our lives until we become the story. Our painful and emotionally significant life events become part of our story and build on its theme, reinforcing its truth for us. Depending on the emotional impact of the events that we experience, our story has the potential to create a far different outcome for our lives than we may want because making our story true means that we surrender our freedom and free will to the story.

As we progress through the paradigm shift that is ascension we will be given opportunities to remember, examine and to change our stories so that we can understand how we have created our life story and what it will take to change it. Before we address how to change a story, though, we must first understand where it began and how it was created.

As an example, let's start with a simple story. We all know that a kitchen stove can be hot and burn us if we touch it because at some point in our life, usually during childhood, we touched a hot stove and burned our fingers. Someone probably told us to not touch the stove because it was hot but we had to try it for ourselves—what did we know about 'hot' without experiencing it for ourselves? Once we burned our fingers, we could define what 'hot' meant and were careful to not touch stoves again. But we probably avoided every stove, assuming that they were all hot and would burn us. Was every stove hot? Probably not, but we weren't going to take that chance, so we most likely avoided every stove that we saw, just in case. We did not have to touch a stove to know it could be hot. Based on our experience we believed that every stove was going to be hot.

That's a simple story but it also has profound implications because it caused us to assume that our one experience with a hot stove would be repeated with every stove. And it would prevent us from going near stoves because of our fear of getting burned. What else would we avoid because our first experience with it caused us pain?

This is an example of a projection that we make based on our story. And this is the key element of understanding our story. It is not the story that has significance, it is the projections and assumptions that we make based on our story that give it life, meaning and continuity. As our story becomes more complicated, the projections that we make based on our experiences also become more complicated. And they begin to have a greater effect on how we live our lives, the choices we make and the people that we attract and associate with. They can even have an impact on our choice of jobs, where we choose to live and what we do with our life, such as how much success and prosperity we will feel safe with.

Here's a more complicated story. We are in love with someone and have agreed to marry. As the wedding date approaches our partner betrays us by having an affair with someone else. Emotionally devastated, we choose to end the relationship. And we create a story based on this event -- we are unlovable, every relationship will end in betrayal, whoever we love will break our heart and we will never allow ourselves to fall in love and be hurt in that way again.

This becomes our story about relationships and it may manifest in different ways. We may avoid relationships altogether or we may unconsciously draw relationships to us that make our story true. Every relationship may indeed end in betrayal and we may be unable to meet someone with whom we can fall in love or we may experience a series of relationships that end with our heart being broken. While these events may further devastate us, they also reinforce our story. And as we continue to repeat those events, each one that works out the way we know it will and that further convinces us of the truth in the story.

And then the story takes on a life of its own. Not only do we see examples of the story in our romantic life, they also begin to manifest in our career, with our friends, where we live and within many of our life choices. People we once knew and trusted may turn against us, a brilliant career may end suddenly, we may be forced to move away from a place we once loved and our life may be filled with events that cause us to believe that the entire world is determined prove that we are unlovable, unlucky and unworthy.

But that is the purpose of this process, to reveal our life themes that are based on pain and fear and reflect our story, and to change the course of our life from one that repeats the story to one that creates new possibilities through transformation.

First we must realize that the story, especially the one that we are born with, originates in the past. Every iteration of that story, within each event that creates an opportunity for us to make our story true, also provides us with the tools to prove it false, to heal it and create a new and different story. So each time an event that reinforces our story is presented to us we have several options -- we can look at it through the lens of the story and add one more reason to believe that it's true. Or we can look at the event as an opportunity to understand what we need to heal, release it and practice forgiveness, which is essential to changing our story, and then create a new and different reality. Each time we forgive we remove a layer of the story and create a new opportunity to change it, bringing us closer to our power and allowing a different reality to become possible.

This information is an important aspect of your healing journey. So take a few moments to consider your life story and what it means to you in terms of the choices you make, experiences you create and the people you draw to you.

Ask yourself these questions:

What does your life story look like?

Whose story is it? Is it yours or was it passed on to you by your family or others close to you?

Do you know what its theme is?

What have you done in your life that makes this story true?

How many people in your life at this moment uphold and support your story?

When did your story begin? Can you remember the first time you told yourself this story?

Can you see the pattern of events that reinforce it in different situations?

Are you ready to make a change, to create a new story by viewing the situation differently, by applying forgiveness and allowing yourself to release your belief system?

Are you willing to undertake a shift in your consciousness knowing that it may open doorways to potential realities that you may never have considered before?

Our ascension journey is a new life path and our stories prevent us from being fully present within it. They are all about fear, pain and loss and while they may be true, they are from the past. Ascension occurs in the present moment, which is where we exist on our mastery journey. As we move farther into ascension we will release the need for the stories in our life, whose memories cause us pain, and allow ourselves to find joy in new stories of love, fulfillment, joy and abundance.

All it takes is a willingness to change and the faith to believe that with trust and intention miracles can happen. The doorways to the abundance of joy, prosperity and light that the Universe has for us are available when we are ready to release our story and forgive ourselves and others.

How do we know our story is being activated? When we begin to see the difference between the past and the present and when living through the past no longer serves us because we have changed our story. What we need to know is how to remember the past.

How To Remember The Past

Our life experience consists of two periods of time, the present moment and everything that happened before it. We call these periods the present and the past. (The future depends on each choice we make in every moment so it is not part of our energetic reality.) The present is this moment and it is constantly changing. The past is simply all of the events that occurred until this moment, and its energy is fixed. We cannot change what has happened in the past so those are the 'facts' that we have created based on our experiences in the past. It is, in fact, impossible to have lived without accumulating these past experiences. They are what gives our life its distinct look and flavor; makes us who we are today and forms the basis of our belief systems and perceptions of the world.

But the past is more than a collection of experiences — it is how also how we shape our future. Our past experiences remind us of what to do and not do in order to be happy, safe and secure. They also prevent us from repeating behaviors that once caused us pain. But to what extent do they play a role in creating our present and future and, if we live in the present moment or the 'now,' is there room in our lives for the past? How do we remember the past and apply it to our lives so that it adds to our journey instead of limiting it?

We need the past in order to help us navigate the present. Imagine a life without a past, where every day we had to repeat every experience, over and over again, never remembering anything that would help us navigate through our daily life or avoid life's pitfalls. Imagine getting into your car each day and not remembering how to drive because you could not remember what you did the day before. The ability to remember the past is a primitive brain function that is designed to help and protect us. But without conscious intention, the past can become, as Shakespeare said, "prologue to the future". Without the right perspective, the past replays as an endless loop in our present, that either re-creates the past or through fear, prevents us from ever experiencing anything because we are too afraid to take a step forward.

Our memories of the past can be a two-edged sword because while they help keep us safe, they can also prevent us from moving forward into a new and different future. And our memories of the past can become distorted, so that something inconsequential can, over time, become a major incident. This is especially true of events that happened long ago, such as during our childhood. This is something that I have personally experienced and shared with clients and listeners over the years. Here is how a past incident in my life profoundly affected my future.

When I was five years old, I fell while running to ride a friend's tricycle and injured my knee badly, requiring eight stitches and a brief stay in the hospital. A week later, I became very ill and had to be hospitalized. With a dangerously high fever, my condition was critical and I experienced physical death and had a near death experience, during which I was told that it was not my time and I had to return to earth. A week later I awakened from being in a coma, paralyzed from the neck down. After six years of painful physical therapy I could move and walk again.

Although I have few memories of my long hospital stay and of those years of limited mobility, I do remember how I felt as the one in the wheelchair who, later, had to walk with the aid of leg braces and crutches. My parents reminded me many times that "I nearly died" during my illness. While their intentions were good, what they and the experience taught me was that if I went after what I wanted (going after the tricycle), I would die. At the very least, I would suffer terrible consequences (my paralysis).

It took me many years to relate my overwhelming fear of following my dreams to this experience although I could see a pattern in the how my life would suddenly come to a halt at various times when I tried to make changes. Although I could not explain the fear I felt or the reason for it, I often watched helplessly as my dreams would come to an end and I was powerless to stop the process. And this occurred in five year cycles. Once I understood the link between the past and the present, understanding how my fear of the past and memories of its painful consequences prevented me from pursuing what I wanted in the present moment, I was able to release this memory of the past and alter the cycles so I could fearlessly and confidently pursue my dreams.

Our memories of the past can be represented in our present reality but the reasons behind them are oblivious to us because their long-forgotten details are planted deep within our subconscious. These memories become proof that we are not worthy, should not expect joy or success, and are limited in our ability to control the outcome of our reality. Every painful or challenging experience can become distorted and turn into a memory that paralyzes us and prevents us from living a full and happy life.

This was the case for John, a client who was once a successful business executive and now drifted from one low-paying job to the next. When the company he managed was taken over by a competitor, John had to fire hundreds of employees, many of whom were his friends and had been with the company for decades. Then he was fired without notice by the new company owners. John lost the job he loved, the career he had worked hard to build and many friends. He felt responsible for the takeover and the loss of his staff's jobs. In his mind, the entire incident was his fault so he was unwilling to step into another executive role with that level of responsibility.

He then turned down any attractive employment offers and instead, struggled financially because he would only accept entry level jobs with minimal responsibility that paid far less than he deserved. His memory of the past kept him stuck and unable to move forward. When would this be resolved? When he could make peace with the past and not allow the past to create his present. When he could control how he chose to remember the past and instead of focusing on the last few difficult months of his job, remember the many years of success and satisfaction he had enjoyed there.

Unfortunately, it is not the happy memories of the past that we recall, over and over again, it is the painful ones. They haunt us as we consider whether we could have done something differently, been a better person, tried harder or done something to avoid the experience altogether. This endless recycling of the past serves no other purpose than to make us feel bad, to remind us that we are unworthy. And it stops us in our tracks.

And this is what we remember of the past. The details of the actual incident may be unclear but the emotions are not. They serve as powerful reminders of our mistakes, failures, and how badly we can be treated by others. The incident itself is simply an event, it is the emotions that we have attached to it that have nearly unlimited power over us.

How does this work in the present? Here are some examples:

A mean-spirit, dominating and controlling parent will create a fear of authority figures.

An embarrassing childhood moment will create a permanent sense of inadequacy.

A traumatic event, whether it happened to us or to someone else, is the beginning of a lifetime of avoiding any attempt at taking a risk.

A disappointment will prevent us from ever attempting anything like that again, no matter how much we could benefit from it.

A betrayal will prevent us from trusting others in any situation.

It is only when we can separate the emotions from the past that we can understand the lessons they represent and gain the knowledge that we need to move in a different direction. They were never meant to create pain that would carry over into the rest of our lives. Their purpose was to teach us spiritual lessons from which we could gain knowledge that would help us create a new and different future.

The past has its own language, represented in the present by words like 'can't', 'don't', 'never', and 'always'. These refer to things that once happened which we are determined to avoid repeating. The negative context in which we use those words only enhances the powerlessness they create in us. For example, if we end a challenging relationship, we could fear that we will 'never' have another relationship or vow that we will 'never' have that happen to us again. And instead of keeping similar relationships out of our life, we avoid them altogether. This is how the past repeats in the present.

Consider phrases like 'I'll never do that again,' or 'I can't take that chance' or 'things never work out for me'.

Do you use them to speak about things in your life?

Can you remember the original event they represented in detail or do you remember the emotions, especially the painful ones?

How often do you use those phrases to describe your life situation right now?

Where does the past occur? In the past, of course, which was days, weeks or years ago. But does it really? From a time perspective that is true. But from the mind's perspective that is false because the mind remembers everything as though it is happening in the moment. So the painful breakup you had at age twenty still hurts when you remember it thirty years later. The memory of the prize you won at age ten can still make you smile at age forty. Do you see what the mind does with the past? It brings it into the present because it does not have a concept of time.

Consider these principles for your personal mastery journey:

Think of a painful event in your life that happened at least five years ago. As you remember it, can you feel the pain in the same way? Do you feel angry, hurt, upset or sad?

Now consider a very joyful event in your life that happened at least five years ago. As you remember it, can you feel your heart lifting, do you feel truly happy and are you smiling?

Look at your life today and consider one difficult event you are experiencing. Can you find any connection to what you are feeling from your past? Is a cycle repeating, have you re-created a story and is this an opportunity for you to change it?

Our ascension journey asks us to make peace with our past by learning to accept it as part of our life journey. Nothing can change it or make it different and there is no reason to. What we did in the past was simply part of our soul contract, whose experiences brought us to where we are in the present moment. At the time we created whatever was the right, best and most perfect thing for us. No matter how much we regret what we have done or what has happened to us in the past, there is nothing that we could have done differently then. We needed that experience and its energies so we could create something different in the future.

It is not possible for us to avoid our memories of the past because they are always with us. It is more fulfilling and helpful to see them for what they are, life events in the larger context of our soul's healing journey. And then to look at ourselves and those with whom we experienced these events with compassion and forgiveness. When we deal with the past we can learn to create a new future, one that is free of the past hurts and disappointments, one in which we learn to make different choices, to create new experiences that use the past as a tool for learning. The past then becomes our key to wholeness instead of a continuing reminder of our limitations and separation from Source.

The past is a template for the present moment because it contains the information about our karma and soul contracts, the soul group connections and our soul agreements that give us clarity about our life purpose. These spiritual lessons become especially important when we learn how to remember the past so that we can accept the past as what it is, valuable insight into what we need to overcome as we heal and transform ourselves into spiritual humans and ascend into mastery. One of the lessons of ascension is to accept and heal the past, which will then free us to move forward in the present. Until we heal the experiences of the past, they remain with us in the present and create the foundation for our future.

When we unravel the past and acknowledge its role in the present and then transform its many beliefs, we can quickly come to realize that we have based much of our lives on things that simply were not true, or were not as powerful as we once believed them to be. So what happens next? How do we define our next steps if the foundation of our lives has been erased? Even if the past is uncomfortable, it is a known quantity. Creating a new future, one step at a time, can be frightening when we have nothing on which to base it. The question that we are faced with is not "what am I going to do next," but "what is going to happen next". Because when we move away from the past, the future is no longer predictable.

Not knowing what to do next is often what stops many of us from making changes in any area of our lives. When we have done things the same way for a very long time and suddenly have the opportunity to do things differently, we are faced with the concepts of freedom and power. Arriving at the point where we realize that everything in our lives is under our own control is both empowering and frightening. Not having the past on which to base our actions or decisions always brings us to the same place -- what happens next? If the familiar is no longer an option, we are faced with the unknown. Can we create our life differently? As the saying goes, "the longest journey begins with the first step" and so it is when we make the decision to release ourselves from the grip of the past into a new and unencumbered future.

We do not have to drastically change our lives in a single day, nor do we have to dismantle everything that we have done in the blink of an eye. But we do have to take that first step. All the Universe ever asks of us is that we are present in the moment that we "show up" for new experiences with a willing and faithful heart. Showing up means that we are willing to walk through the doorways that open up for us, with faith that in that moment because it is the right thing for us to do. So as we move beyond the past we are faced with opportunities to make different choices. For some, it may mean saying "no" with conviction, or saying "yes" to living life with passion and confidence. For others, it may mean leaving old, destructive habits behind and yet others, creating new lifestyles or ways of being. Each and all of these things is a possibility for us once we learn to see life beyond the past, to give ourselves a chance to experience new blessings and to move through life fearlessly and with confidence, knowing that there are no mistakes in the Universe, only an unfolding array of choices that reflect that moment's mindset, and when we are willing to change, we can step into a new place of power and understanding.

The past will always be part of our lives, part of what we once did, who we once were and how we once felt or acted. When we move beyond it, we can focus on what we are doing now, today, in this moment, who we are and how we create a life of joy and abundance using the knowledge gained in the past as information for the present moment. All it takes to heal the past is the willingness to remember, to forgive, to heal and then step forward in another direction.

Consider these principles for your personal mastery journey:

How does your past mirror that of your family, soul group, partners or friends?

Can you see the patterns of action and reaction that you engage in?

Can you identify one or two situations from your past whose memory limits you in the present moment?

Are you aware of any language you use, such as 'can't', 'don't' or 'never' that limits your forward movement today?

Do you see the role that your past plays in your current reality?

What information have you gained from your past that is helpful to you in the present moment? Can you use the past as information and detach from the emotions that accompany these memories?

Are you willing to forgive yourself and everyone else for your past?

What is the key to mastery? There is one thing we must do to become masters and that is to practice forgiveness with everyone. Not with those who are easy to forgive but with those who have given us the most pain, been our most challenging teachers, who we feel least deserve our gift of forgiveness. The path of forgiveness is hard because we must be willing to quiet the ego which reminds us of how much someone does not deserve it and listen to the still, quiet voice of Spirit which reminds us of our journey, its lessons and healing purpose, and that if we are going to live through our divinity we must learn to forgive our humanity.

Forgiveness

With ascension we progress through an energetic continuum whose path leads from the third dimension into higher dimensions of being. When we are in this flow there is more synchronicity in our lives--we ask for what we want and it appears, we connect with people who fulfill our desire for love, joy, peace and abundance and we feel powerful in our life. But the manifestation process is not always smooth and a desire to change is not immediately followed by a new and better alternative. Sometimes there is a gap in the flow from desire to manifestation and we must survive being "in the gap" before what we want to create comes to us. While we are "in the gap" all activity and flow seems to stop and we feel stuck or unable to move. Or, it appears that more is being taken away from us than we are receiving.

The gap is a space between planes of consciousness. Since we live in a linear, third dimensional world, we view the process of moving through the dimensions on a linear level, going from the third to the fourth and fifth and so on. But they exist in a different perspective. The first three dimensions are on one plane and other dimensions exist on different planes. We need to create a bridge that takes us across this dimensional space and the bridge between the third dimension and higher planes is forgiveness, which is the release of emotional energies, in the form of the karma that we share with others. The only way we can move from one dimension to the next is via this bridge, which we create when we forgive.

Each journey from one plane of experience to the next is completed when we learn its lessons. Because we are in the dimension of karma and fear, the lesson of the third dimension is forgiveness, which enables the healing of the emotional and karmic issues that we share with others. These issues block us from manifesting what we desire and prevent us from crossing into other dimensions where karma does not exist. In order to fully shift from our current plane of consciousness we must clear all of the issues associated with our third dimensional experience because we cannot function in two different planes of existence. In simpler terms, we cannot shift from the third dimension into any other dimension and take our emotional and karmic baggage with us.

During the time that we are in the gap these karmic issues are brought to our attention in ways that are impossible to ignore. Every belief and emotion is tested while we are in the gap. Every fear and anxiety is highlighted to help us find a common denominator and create an opportunity to forgive ourselves and those in our soul group for that experience. The gap is also a test of faith. Do we really, truly believe that if we abandon all of our old patterns that the Universe will help us create better opportunities? The gap experience can be short or long, depending on how willing we are to apply total, unconditional forgiveness to everything and everyone in our lives.

What is the solution for those who are stuck in the gap? We may spend a lot of time looking for solutions, try many different avenues of experience and look to others for answers but every avenue takes us back to ourselves and to forgiveness. And our final answer is actually a question. Who do we need to forgive, including ourselves, and what are we holding on to because we cannot or will not forgive? Where does our desire for change and transformation clash with what has yet to be forgiven?

While being in the gap can be extremely frustrating and challenging, it is an opportunity to distill our karmic issues to their core. For many that involves discovering how they are allowing judgments, anger, fear and expectations to block their ability to manifest what they want. It also involves clearing many layers of emotional pain and karma through complete and unconditional forgiveness. We generally have a lot of time to do this because while we are in the gap, all distractions are removed and sometimes our lives are simply taken apart so we can put them back together.

Because we are shifting to another plane of consciousness crossing the gap may involve several stops and starts. These may appear to be blocks to our progress but each time we emerge from the gap we heal another layer of our consciousness. Each emotional issue or block we heal allows us to sever emotional and karmic bonds. Each time we forgive ourselves and others we move closer to shifting fully into the next plane and we release the people and things that have worked together, bound by our soul's commitment to healing, to prevent us from moving forward on our path.

Consider these principles for your personal mastery journey:
Is there an 'unforgivable' person, situation or event in your life?
Are there people that you know you should forgive but are having trouble completing that process?
Do you have feelings of sadness, pain or regret over things that have been done to you?
Do you wish that certain people in your life would have behaved differently?
Are you able to forgive them knowing that by doing so you also release yourself from them?
Can you begin the forgiveness process with them, even if it takes multiple times?
What would you do in your life if you did not have the sadness or regret that you carry over the 'unforgivable' things or people in your life?
What would your life be like if you were free of any guilt and shame that is associated with the people you may not feel you can forgive?

For many people forgiveness can be a very difficult choice because they believe that forgiving is the same as saying that whatever the other person did was all right and it did not matter. That is not the true essence of forgiveness, which is a release of karma and emotional attachment and a return to our original vibration of unconditional love. It is a release of the fear-based emotional bond that we have with others, which is often the glue that holds us to our shared karmic circles, cycles and soul group commitments. It does not mean that what they did was acceptable, allowable or fair and in many cases it probably wasn't. But those are judgments, which are part of the forgiveness work that will release them. The result of forgiveness is the end of a shared struggle, a removal of our emotional ties, energetic cords and karmic history that allows us to move from a life path designed by karma to one of unfolding creation. Forgiveness releases us from experiencing the same kinds of karmic dramas, over and over again, with people who have been part of our karmic circle for eons.

Consider this: every person that you cannot or will not forgive holds you back from living a happy, fulfilled life because you cannot fulfill your soul's

healing purpose until you can forgive them. Anyone that you cannot unconditionally forgive maintains a connection with you, as they are plugged into your
energy field at the level of what needs to be forgiven and that connection is a
permanent bond until you are willing to release it through forgiveness. How
many people do you have plugged into your emotional system right now? If
you do not forgive them, then you maintain a connection to them and you allow
them to maintain that connection with you. That connection does more than
sap your emotional energy. It robs you of your dreams, your goals and your
ambition because it keeps you entangled in your karmic relationships and at
their level of energetic vibration. All of these connections also prevent you
from being able to shift to a higher level of consciousness.

Before continuing with this section, consider this exercise:

Imagine, right now, that you are carrying everyone that you could   potentially forgive with on your back. This includes everyone that you have been
angry with, hurt by, abused by -- anyone who has ever caused you emotional
pain in your lifetime. Write down their names. How many people are on your
list? One, three, five, ten--or more? How hard do you think it is for you to
move forward if you are carrying all of those people on your back?

Are you ready to forgive them so you can release them and move forward to
create a new reality? Remember that forgiveness is applied to situations that
are based in the past and if you are feeling stuck in your life, it is because you
are stuck in the past. Use the forgiveness letter in the Appendix to complete
your forgiveness work, and forgive and release each person as you are ready to.

We cannot cross the gap into higher dimensions of being if we do not
forgive because the prevailing energy in higher dimensions is unconditional
love. No matter how much healing work we do, if it is not accompanied by
unconditional forgiveness we are holding on to energy that cannot exist in a
higher dimension. Let's talk about that for a moment. Are you now thinking,
"Does that mean that if I forgive everyone I have to love them too?" Yes, but
not in the way that you may be thinking about. You can have unconditional love
for someone that you do not want to be associated with. Forgiveness addresses
energetic connections and once those are released that level of connection does
not exist. Now you can create a new energetic level of connection that may
involve no physical contact or communication. You can love them   uncondi-

tionally and see them as being on their own path, without the cords of judgment, pain and fear connecting you. Then you can be free of this experience and create a different paradigm for your life.

Having unconditional love for someone means that we are detached from our beliefs and judgments about what they have done so we can understand that they are in their own space and we accept them exactly as they are (which does not mean that we have to continue to associate with them, we just have to stop judging them). Whatever they do or whoever they are is simply a reflection of their energetic vibration. With each judgment we put ourselves within their vibration; with forgiveness, we disconnect from it. Without judgments we are in complete acceptance of them as a divine being, with no thoughts or opinions, good or bad, about any aspect of their being.

Unconditional love removes the karmic connections that we have with them so any energetic connections at that level are severed. Where there is unconditional love, karma cannot exist. Our paths intersect through our karma, giving us an opportunity to repeat and continue the cycle or heal and resolve a karmic debt to end the karma. The person we must forgive in order to move on with our life journey is someone that has held this energetic place in our life for many lifetimes.

Each person in our life has a purpose, which is to mirror some part of our healing and they hold an energetic space to help us with our soul lessons. Think about that a moment. Every person in your life is here to help you learn and grow and this aspect of their life is offered as a sacrifice to help you. Their soul is willing to risk creating further karma with yours so that you can learn to forgive and then release them with unconditional love. And moreover, they trust that you will be able to forgive so that you can all move into higher dimensions of living. If you don't forgive them the karma continues. Whatever happened between you in this lifetime, can you consider that in another lifetime you did the same thing to them, or worse? It is possible, and very likely, that in this lifetime they may be seeking revenge for what you have done to them in another one, and providing you with an opportunity to forgive as well. Remember that karma works in both directions and in different lifetimes we are the abuser and the abused, the victim and the aggressor. It may be a challenge for you to see yourself as an aggressor or abuser in this lifetime, but that may not have been the case in other lifetimes.

With practice, forgiveness becomes a habit, as do detachment and being non-judgmental. Use the Forgiveness Exercise in the Appendix to begin the process. You may have to repeat the exercise several times before you are truly comfortable with forgiving everyone on your own list. If you can't forgive the most 'unforgivable' person on your list, try it first with those who you believe you can forgive more easily.

When we have learned to forgive and made it a life practice our life purpose begins to open up to us, as it is no longer blocked by the connections and karma that have prevented us from accessing our higher aspects of being. This is the key to masterful living, which is much more than the acquisition of material goods, career success, the right education or finding the right partner. It is a journey of spiritual initiation, from which we gather the tools for our mastery. This is a journey to enlightenment, the reward of ascension and the path that we take with each lifetime, which is an initiation into our divinity.

Life as a Spiritual Initiation

As we begin to understand that the purpose of our life transcends the accumulation of wealth or material goods and the true nature of our life path lies in the accomplishment of our healing and spiritual growth, we realize the importance of our presence and what is at stake. Then we are stuck, wondering what to do next, afraid of the consequences we may face and questioning our priorities to create balance between our material needs and spiritual   understanding. Can we accumulate wealth without becoming its slave? Is it possible to follow a spiritual path and be part of the material world? How do we balance our dreams with our life purpose? If we are spiritual beings, why is our life so challenging?

These are questions we need answers to as we contemplate our journey and wonder whether we will ever find peace of mind instead of the challenges that seem to follow us throughout our life. These issues serve a greater purpose as they are part of our spiritual initiation, the process that we undergo to expose our life story and find our power so that we can transform fear into love and experience life from a point of spiritual understanding.

This initiation process has a focus, to bring forward our life lessons, the soul wounds that we came to heal and to help us move into a new levels of vibration and consciousness. By following the initiate path we are encouraged to find and connect to our spiritual resources, and learn how to use spiritual tools to meet the challenges that confront us. This is an individual experience, and although we are faced with challenges that appear to be more than we can handle, we are really just facing ourselves. The purpose of the initiation journey is to allow us to face what we fear in a powerful, transformative way so it becomes the stepping stone to the next part of our life journey. And so we begin our spiritual initiation and step into our own darkness so we can find our light and become initiates of our mastery journey.

What is initiation? In ancient societies, they were special ceremonies which marked the passing from one phase of life to another. These ceremonies were a series of tests and challenges that became the physical embodiment of every doubt, fear, anxiety and worry that a person could experience as they moved from one life stage to another, generally from childhood into adulthood. The initiation ritual, which involved removing someone from the protection of the group or society and forcing them to experience a series of trials alone and unprotected, helped the participants develop their inner strength to create the powerful resources which would help them survive and surmount the challenges they would face in their lives.

Modern societies have replaced the individual initiation with ceremonies that mark collective rites of passage, such as high school or college graduation, marriage and retirement. The rituals that challenge an initiate to face and conquer their deepest fears so they are prepared to move confidently into the next life stage, allowing them to find and perfect their inner resources, are no longer utilized. What we are missing in today's world is the initiation process that prepares us internally — emotionally, mentally, physically and spiritually — to establish a strong connection with our inner guidance so we live life confidently, knowing that we are able to face, resolve and transform any challenge.

We enter the world with issues to review and release, lessons to learn, and karma to heal. Our soul creates opportunities to work on these issues through different life experiences. We can look at these situations as challenges that we must overcome, bad luck or a form of divine punishment. Or we can see them for what they are, steps on our journey of learning, healing and growth whose purpose is to move us forward along our spiritual path. The initiation is an important part of this journey of awakening and its four parts, birth, the trial, the lesson and enlightenment, each play a role that allows us to shift our energetic center from fear to love, in helping us establish a more powerful, balanced and conscious energetic presence.

In the birth phase, we are presented with a situation that is a choice point where we decide whether we have learned enough to choose another path. Our choice determines whether proceed into the trial, which is the experience we have created to bring our fears to the forefront. Eventually the lesson is revealed to us and once we understand the lesson we achieve enlightenment and have successfully completed the initiation. Then we move forward along our spiritual path, to the next initiation process.

The challenges we face are the representation of our fears, life story, pain and soul contracts. We must stand alone, which is representative of our separation from Source, without the benefit of anyone's assistance and are removed from our group — which could be family, friends, job, partnership or living situation. We must find ways to develop our inner resources, find our own inner compass and connect to our Source connection to successfully complete the initiation. Then we become one with our spiritual center and re-create our belief system so that it is based on spirit instead of the ego, to respond to life from a point of love instead of fear.

And each of the four aspects of spiritual initiation has a lesson for us. While each part is a journey unto itself, they work together to ensure that we learn what we must to arrive at the journey's end and satisfy the terms of the initiation — to grow spiritually and become Source-centered in preparation for the next step of our journey and its lessons. Like our multi-dimensional Universe, spiritual growth is a non-linear process that does not conform to the third dimension's perspective of time, space and movement. It is an evolutionary spiral whose core consists of our life lessons. Each time we are able to achieve enlightenment at a particular level, we move up the spiral, with a new vantage point of our lessons. Our success is measured by how we apply the enlightenment we have achieved as we go forward in our life. And each new level of enlightenment provides us with knowledge, information and tools to make different choices as future lessons arise, each one designed to move us farther along our evolutionary journey into our evolving mastery.

Phase 1 -- Birth

With the birth phase our spiritual initiation journey begins. Here we face a life challenge that is an opportunity to develop new perspectives. Like our physical birth when we enter the world, we re-create the birth process each time we move into a new life event. So, a new job is a kind of birth, as is a new relationship, a geographic move or even a difficult event such as the death of a loved one, a painful separation or an illness. With each birth process we have to learn new coping and living skills, understand how we have contributed to this challenge and then find the inner strength and spiritual resources to overcome it.

But hidden behind the apparent newness of the birth process is a core life lesson, created from lifetimes of karma and representing an aspect of healing our soul wants to complete. Each birth process faces us with our soul's healing purpose which, unless we have experienced some form of enlightenment from previous lessons, we are unable to see because of the strong reaction that we have to the emotions, particularly fear, that the birth process awakens in us. We are literally blinded by our emotional response in a birth situation so that we are incapable of seeing beyond what is happening to us. The temptation to redeem ourselves, recapture lost aspects of our power, vindicate past wrongs, be 'right' and prove ourselves worthy, limits our perspective on the birth process and we are drawn into the initiation journey and lose control.

There is another aspect to the birth process that we are unaware of until long after we are in the trial and lesson, and that is our ability to choose. With each new birth phase we are asked to apply our spiritual growth and knowledge to see beyond what appears to be happening and recognize the healing purpose behind this situation. Within each birth experience is a chance to either repeat challenging lessons or take a giant leap into enlightenment. Can we apply what we have already learned and bypass the upcoming trial? Doing so confirms that we have indeed achieved a milestone on our journey. If not, then we still have things to learn from that type of situation and our choice will be to move into it.

While our first few experiences with the birth process may take us by surprise, if we have learned our lessons we may be able to see when a birth process is forming and decide how we will move forward, from the emotions or with detachment, from the energy of fear or our inner power. How we feel about ourselves and others, the belief that we need to heal through pain, the role we take in others' healing, whether we feel we need to conquer a situation by force, willpower and sheer determination, all affect how we will choose to act during this part of our initiation. This is where we learn whether we respond to lessons from ego or from spirit, with detachment or judgment, from unconditional love or fear or whether we need confirmation of our power. But we may not be willing to apply this level of spiritual understanding and are completely unaware of our choices. So we prepare for battle and move into the trial.

Consider these principles for your personal mastery journey:
Have you experienced a birth process recently?
What kind of challenge are you facing?
Is this similar to something you have experienced in the past?
What kinds of emotions are awakened and are you aware of their karmic connections?
Who is part of the birth process and what is their connection to your karmic past?
What choices do you have and are you aware of them?
Can you identify a less challenging path and are you willing to take it?

Phase 2 -- The Trial

The choices that we make when we are faced with the details of the birth process will determine what happens in the next phase of our initiation, the trial. This is the challenge portion of the initiation, where we are presented with the task that we must accomplish in order to move ahead to the next stage. During the trial we will face our deepest fears, doubts, worries and anxieties and learn about the beliefs and perceptions that we have accepted to create our life and our reality. The trial challenges us to fight for our physical, emotional and spiritual survival. If we do not have the spiritual knowledge and understanding to end the process as we are entering the birth stage of our initiation journey, we step into this next phase fully expecting the worst and hoping that we will exit alive and unscathed.

What we encounter in the trial depends on what we wish to learn, more importantly, what our soul has agreed to help us learn as part of its commitment to our spiritual growth. The trial could involve the emotional energies that result from the loss of a job, the breakup of a relationship, an illness, having to deal with a difficult person or facing a life-changing decision. During a trial that involves the loss of a job we may have to cope with feelings of loss, worthiness and uncertainty while we decide what to do next. Do we find another job, create a new career, start the business we have always wanted or stay home, depressed and angry, and do nothing?

If we are dealing with an illness, our own or someone else's, we have to face our fear of death or of living through or beyond the illness. Perhaps we must learn to choose for ourselves, to fulfill what we want in life, rather than make choices on behalf of others, or limiting our life choices to what we believe others want or expect from us. Within relationships, trials can reveal many issues such as the fear of abandonment or betrayal, fear of being alone, our lack of self love, accepting others' choices or being willing to take a stand for what we want and reject anything that does not fit those parameters.

How we interpret the trial determines how quickly, easily and efficiently we are able to move through it. Will our response be one of hopelessness, grief or resignation? Do we act decisively and confidently or fall into depression and despair? Or will we be able to recognize its similarity to prior experiences, utilize the spiritual knowledge that we have already acquired and find the inner strength that will allow us to make different choices than we have in the past?

The key to understanding the purpose of the trial is to remember that we are here to heal karma and that process requires that we come face to face with our karmic wound. It is a wound that can and must be healed as we progress through this process of transformation. If we do not heal it this time, it will appear in our lives, again and again, until we do. We are able to recognize the trial for what it is if we look at it with detachment, resisting the temptation to react from our fear-based emotions and take a spiritual perspective. Will we respond to our deepest fears, anxieties, doubts and worries in the same ways or will we be able to look at them through the lens of our spiritual understanding?

Trials are not a form of spiritual punishment, although they can feel like they are. Instead, they are an opportunity to heal our karma, recapture aspects of our soul's light that we have lost through lifetimes of pain, and to use our spiritual knowledge and understanding to make different choices than we have in the past. That's sometimes difficult to do when we are in a situation that has turned our life upside down but that is the purpose of the trial, to allow us to face our fears and connect to our inner strength.

When we connect to our spiritual source and look for solutions and resolution from spirit, the trial's purpose and meaning will become clear. Then we can see it for what it is -- an event whose purpose is to empower our healing process -- instead of another block on our path. As we face the trial and decide how we will address it, we must also remember that we have a choice as to how it will affect us, how deeply we will become involved and whether or not the trial will become our life's focus. Will we resist the temptation to become emotionally involved in the trial and re-live the karmic experience? Or will we see the trial as a healing opportunity? That is always our choice. Keeping our focus on the healing aspects of this process and its role on our path to mastery will help us to quickly move through the trial and into the next stage of the initiation, the lesson.

Consider these principles for your personal mastery journey:
Are you going through a trial at this time?
How is situation like others you have experienced in the past?
What choices did you make then and what are you considering now?
Can you identify a karmic wound that this trial is revealing to you?
Who is involved and what role do they play for you in your initiation?
What are you being asked to release so you can move forward in your life?
What emotions, including fears, are being revealed to you?
What is the most powerful way for you to resolve this?

Phase 3 -- The Lesson

The third phase, the lesson, is the central theme of the initiation, representing what we must learn in order to arrive at the final stage of initiation, which is enlightenment. The lesson represents the learning that we must absorb in order to heal our karmic experiences, the spiritual knowledge our soul wishes to obtain through this experience. Every life experience has a lesson to teach us. In fact, our entire life is a lesson in spiritual growth and understanding. That is a concept that we can understand once we have moved beyond the one block to our spiritual growth, fear. Fear is our natural, human response to a challenge, whether it involves our career, finances, relationships, or personal growth. Some people live their entire lives in a state of constant fear, unable to move forward, accomplish their goals, and realize their ambitions, because they are afraid of what might happen in the future or of repeating what happened to them in the past. That is the purpose of the lesson -- to understand the source of the fear, to identify the learning that needs to occur, absorb it and then release the fear, soul wound and karma.

The lesson can take many forms and appear in many different ways. Perhaps the lesson is to value ourselves more, so we are faced with a situation where we must assert our self-worth.

Perhaps it is to forego a relationship that we know will be full of challenges and create one that is more self-affirming. If we have accepted this type of relationship in the past, believing that the other person will eventually change, then this becomes a lesson for us -- we must trust our judgment and learn when to walk away from situations that will cause us emotional pain.

Perhaps it is a lesson in integrity and we will be faced with a situation where we must stand within our integrity, even if it means walking away from a job, a person or other situation that challenges us at this level. The lesson can involve learning to choose what is best for us and saying "no" to someone who insists that we follow their plan for our life. Or making a choice to take action in spite of our fears.

Each of us will have different lessons because we are each here to heal our personal karmic issues. But the purpose of all lessons is the same, to help us acknowledge the aspects of ourselves that require healing, move them into the light of understanding, resolution and transformation. The lesson is apparent to us once we are able to move away from fear and see the experience for what it is, a healing opportunity. What did we need to understand, to realize about our life and what needs to change to make transformation possible?

When we can ask that question we have reached enlightenment and the lesson that is learned becomes part of our permanent memory because while the brain maintains a history of painful experiences it also keeps a record of what we have learned from them. Each time we learn a lesson we are able to retain the memory of our learning so that the next time a similar situation arises for us --and it will -- we can identify it for what it is and make a choice to respond from our spiritual center instead of through our emotions and fear. Then we are at the final stage of the initiation process, enlightenment.

Consider these principles for your personal mastery journey:

Have you identified the lesson you are learning from your experience?

Is it a familiar lesson that you have experienced before?

What is the purpose of this lesson in your life?

Can you see how your choices in the past contributed to different outcomes for this lesson?

How is this one different from other lessons you have experienced?
Do you feel you have learned this lesson and are ready to release it?

Phase 4 – Enlightenment

Enlightenment is the final stage of the initiation, where we have attained spiritual mastery at this level and are prepared to move on to the next stage of our spiritual path. This both an ending and a new beginning, with opportunities to view ourselves and our life from a transformed perspective and with a new level of understanding. It is important that we realize the true meaning of enlightenment, which is the attainment of knowledge and understanding. It does not mean that once we achieve enlightenment we are finished with all of our lessons and can spend the rest of our life never encountering another problem or difficulty. What it does mean is that we can approach each new lesson with a higher level of understanding that can help us move more quickly through the process and achieve enlightenment in each lesson with less pain and anguish, knowing our spiritual initiation for what it is, a process that allows us to heal, learn, grow and ascend into our mastery.

How do we know when we achieve enlightenment? We are enlightened when we acknowledge our greatness and perfection. When we look at ourselves with forgiveness and acceptance and we extend those sentiments to everyone in our life. When we look at a situation, recognize the lesson and allow ourselves to do something different, to make a choice that reflects our self love through our willingness to live powerfully, effortlessly and fearlessly. When we can choose peace over pain, love over fear and step into each experience with understanding instead of emotion, we have reached enlightenment. It is something that we achieve every day, in many different ways.

Like our spiritual evolution, enlightenment is also a process of growth and change. Enlightenment and the peace and understanding that accompany it is a gift from the Universe, an acknowledgement of a job well done, a glimpse into the unconditional love that is our birthright and the power that we have through our divinity. Each time that we are faced with a new challenge, if we look at it in as an initiation process we can look for and embrace the solutions that will lead to enlightenment and peace.

Consider these principles for your personal mastery journey:
Have you reached enlightenment in your initiation journey?
Do you understand the purpose of this experience with respect to your soul's healing journey?
Are you complete with this initiation and ready to release it?
Can you acknowledge yourself for what you have accomplished?
Do you feel more powerful, confident and enlightened?
Are you ready for the next phase of your spiritual journey and willing to take on new challenges?

Sometimes we resist the initiation process, are unwilling to participate in the lessons and instead of inviting their challenges, we feel threatened by them and close ourselves off from the learning process. The power of choice extends to choosing to walk the path of karma and there is value in resistance, as it points the way to our blocks, fears and where we need to heal.

What we resist is what we don't want to hear, listen to, acknowledge or pay attention to. It is where we have our blinders on, where we are afraid to look for fear that our worst fears will be realized. It is often the place where we feel most powerless and out of control. We often resist the truth, not because of the truth itself but because of what we are afraid the truth will show us about ourselves. Resistance shows us what we are afraid of and we learn a lot about ourselves by understanding what we resist, which is explained in Donna's story.

Donna's husband had been unfaithful to her for the duration of their twenty year marriage. His extra-marital activities were known to many people, except Donna, although she may have secretly suspected his infidelity. When he finally asked for a divorce so he could be with another woman, Donna was devastated and felt used and betrayed by the man she had stood by and supported for many years. As she processed her pain, Donna was forced to look at how long she had resisted acknowledging the truth about her marriage and her husband. She knew that she ignored the signs of his infidelity and refused to admit to herself that she was married to a man who did not honor his commitment to her. Donna also realized that her resistance to the truth   was based on her fear of abandonment and betrayal, lessons her husband had helped her learn.

Perhaps she could have ended the marriage on her terms if she had been willing to see the truth about her relationship, instead of finding comfort in her denial. Did resisting the truth of his infidelity make him faithful in her eyes?

Would acknowledging the truth have made her feel unworthy of being with a loving, faithful partner? The truth was painful but resisting it did not mean that it was not true. And she eventually had to acknowledge that her husband's actions were not a reflection of her worthiness or value. He was a lesson she had brought into her life so she could heal her own karma and resolve her fears.

Understanding that the lessons of betrayal and abandonment were hers to learn and transform, and that by choosing an unfaithful partner she had created the situation that would help her learn them, gave her clarity about this path of initiation that she had chosen. And with this came enlightenment, forgiveness of herself and of him, and peace. Through understanding her resistance and learning the purpose of this situation she found the power to accept the truth and heal her heart.

There is great value in knowing what we resist and we can use this information to understand what is blocking our joy. At the right time and when we are ready, we can face our resistance and find its blessings. Where we resist is where we are afraid, unsure, powerless, and feel out of control. There is much value in knowing this and understanding the truth behind our resistance often holds the key to our happiness and enlightenment.

Consider these principles for your personal mastery journey:
Is there a truth that you are resisting?
Do you secretly know this truth but feel that if you do not acknowledge it, then it is not true?
What fears are giving power to your resistance?
Can you find the blessing in your resistance and use it to empower you, instead of making you feel powerless?

There is no set time, format or guideline for the spiritual initiation process, each one can be short or long, depending on how much time it takes for us to learn the lessons and achieve enlightenment. We will complete many spiritual initiations during the course of our lifetime, each will present a unique set of challenges, with a different aspect of a lesson to learn. As we attain the state of enlightenment in each initiation we move farther along the evolutionary spiral that is the path of our spiritual growth and mastery. But once it is over we are not finished, as we will continue to move through various initiation processes, each of which acts to bring other areas of healing and forgiveness to our attention, moving us farther along our mastery path.

And as we each accomplish this on an individual level, it is being repeated on a global level on our planet. Everyone and everything is shifting, changing, moving along a spiritual path whose ultimate destination is the realization that we are One, connected and always within reach of our loving, benevolent, infinite Creator. And our goal of reconnection is not for our Creator's purpose but for ours, reminding us of the masters that we are and have always been.

After Enlightenment, What's Next?

There is a belief that the new paradigm for humanity will eventually mean the end of the human existence as we know it. And that is partially true for it will mean the end of the fear and the pain that have been the foundation of humanity's experience. While we hope that these changes will release us from having to experience life's trials and difficulties, we will still be humans living in a human environment and although we may achieve enlightenment, the learning is far from over. Enlightenment merely acknowledges that we have achieved a certain level of understanding that will allow us, when faced with a similar lesson, to be aware of an expanded field of choices at higher and higher levels of energetic vibration. Enlightenment will allow us to look at the human condition with detachment and compassion, knowing that the point and purpose of life is to know joy and that pain and drama are options that we can choose to participate in—or not.

What happens after enlightenment is described in the Taoist saying "Before enlightenment, carry water. After enlightenment, carry water." While enlightenment may give us a sense of peace and empowerment, all it means is that we have the internal tools to help us have a different perspective of our external environment. Nothing else really changes. We still have to make our way through the world, live our lives and navigate through the obstacles that appear on our path. But with enlightenment we are aware of the many different energies we are surrounded by and how they interact within each experience. Then we can consciously choose those we wish to incorporate into our reality and life path.

If only we could achieve enlightenment and then be done with the learning, healing and growing. Our journey would certainly be easier if this were the case. And in some ways it is, as each time we achieve another level of enlightenment we also achieve new levels of Source connection, self realization and the peace that accompanies them. But our work is not finished. It just expands into another level and moves us in other directions.

The gift of enlightenment is one of understanding, a realization of why we are here, what our journey is all about and how we can create the peace, joy and unconditional love on the earth plane that our soul longs for. Each level of enlightenment gives us the ability to continue our journey with new strength and resolve. We are empowered with the understanding of our mission and purpose, strengthened by our success and ready for the next step on our journey.

As our lives unfold from one experience to another we are provided with new opportunities to ascend to new levels of enlightenment. Will we ever be finished? The goal of our journey is not to finish, it is to bring the energies of heaven to earth, blending the spiritual and material worlds and create a new paradigm for ourselves and for humanity. That is the unfolding process of enlightenment and we will be finished when it is completed, ready for the next enlightenment and ascension cycle. All we have to do is play our part, participate in the process and know that the Light is always with us on every step of our journey of enlightenment.

Once we have achieved enlightenment our task becomes a challenge to 'be' enlightenment in our own lives, to practice what we have learned and share this knowledge with others. That may take many different forms but will probably not entail joining an ashram and sitting atop a mountain meditating all day. The Universe has far greater plans for those who have struggled through this process and come out on the other side, for it is their task to help others with their journey.

With enlightenment we may be thrust into the world, to help those that we would once have considered beyond help or who once rejected us for our spiritual beliefs and practices. These may be our old friends, family members and people who fell out of our lives during our journey of healing and transformation. Enlightenment is confirmation that we have succeeded in our individual process of transformation, but it is also a message that our work has just begun and a directive to live in a more focused, intentional, conscious and spirit-directed way.

So if we continue to experience lessons and have no assurance that successfully completing our journey will bring us relief, what's the point? Why work so hard to achieve enlightenment if it simply brings us to yet another lesson? Why do we put forth so much effort only to have to do it again?

The answer to these questions is the same, the purpose of our presence here is to grow spiritually, moving upwards along our evolutionary spiral into higher levels of energetic vibration. We do that by experiencing as many lessons as we can in order to gather enough spiritual tools to move us along our spiritual path. If we learn nothing from our lessons then we have not accomplished our objective because we are not here simply to experience lessons, but to learn from and eventually move beyond them. Each new lesson has its special gifts and blessings and one of our tasks is to find the gifts, learn from them and then transform them into a higher vibration, which is the blessing. The more challenging the lesson, the greater its blessings. We just have to learn how to sift through the pain to find them.

Consider these principles for your personal mastery journey:
Can you remember a challenging life experience you have had?

Do you remember the point at which you realized that there was a lesson to be learned from this experience?

Do you remember what the lesson was and has it been repeated in your life since then?

Are you aware of the blessing of this experience and have you used that blessing in other areas of your life?

If this lesson was to be repeated in your life, could you recognize it and choose to avoid it?

Enlightenment is an unfolding process of learning, healing, growth and transformation. The presence of every situation and experience, every teacher and lesson is an opportunity to gain enlightenment in some area of our life. When we are ready to accept ourselves as spiritual beings having a human experience, acknowledge our divinity and power, and be willing to learn and heal, we have completed the lessons that allow us to be enlightened. It is not something that happens in one event, it is a process that unfolds throughout our lifetime.

And as Lightworkers, we can share our enlightenment with others, spreading the light and helping each person to make conscious and informed choices. For sharing light is why we are here, re-establishing ourselves as centered, grounded and powerful is our goal and reconnecting humanity to its collective Source is the objective of our enlightenment. Once we are aware of our truth we are empowered and never have to be in fear again. Sharing our empowerment benefits all of humanity and creates support for new energetic vibrations.

This is a celebration of our accomplishments, spiritual growth and desire to reconnect with Source. It is at this time, as humanity embraces this paradigm shift and evolves into spiritual mastery with the completion of each spiritual initiation that the concept of "peace on earth and good will to humankind" can truly become a reality. And enlightenment is another step on the creation of the spiritual human.

Spiritual initiation brings us face to face with our karma, the path of atonement, pain and suffering that we have created as our own form of retribution for what we believe we have done wrong, to ourselves and others, in past lives. Enlightenment brings us peace and understanding, freedom from karma and in touch with our power. It is another step on our mastery journey and is available to everyone. Can we believe that we can achieve enlightenment just by learning our life lessons? We can, if we can embrace enlightenment and become the enlightened ones.

Who Are The Enlightened Ones?

Our spiritual journey is a path towards enlightenment, where everything is designed to assist us in achieving wholeness in body, mind, emotions and spirit. Throughout this journey we are provided with many opportunities to heal, grow and transform our fear-based ego centered life experience into one of spiritual mastery. As we move towards this goal we look for teachers and guides to help us along our path, seeking those who we believe have already achieved enlightenment or who are more enlightened than we are. We believe that they can provide us with lessons in enlightenment and speed the process. So when we are faced with people who teach us difficult lessons we believe that they are less enlightened then we are. How did we attract someone who was so unevolved? But we are looking at this the wrong way because everyone is enlightened, in their own way.

By defining enlightenment as the attainment of mastery and then defining mastery as some exalted state of being, we place enlightenment out of most of humanity's reach. That concept brings to mind spiritual perfection, at the level of an avatar or ascended master such as Jesus or Buddha, being more spiritual than human. Few of us can envision that level of being so does this mean we won't ever be enlightened? How can we, in our humanity, become spiritual masters? We can because enlightenment, like every part of our journey, is an aspect of our own levels of mastery.

Enlightenment is not reserved for those who are extraordinary, spiritually advanced, masters or students of a special teacher. It is part of the process of evolution, growth and transformation that is our life journey. The word 'enlightenment' means to embody light, to shed light on or to clarify. For some, enlightenment may mean finding the light to overcome a single fear or belief. For others it may be lighting the way to their power and learning to accept and assume control over their reality. For all of us this is a lesson in spiritual mastery that is designed to meet the requirements of our soul contracts. It may take an entire lifetime to move ahead one level or we can move through multiple levels of growth and enlightenment in a single leap in consciousness. Our ability to become enlightened depends on many things, including our willingness to heal and grow and our commitment to our spiritual journey.

Everyone is here to heal something, whether they realize it or not. This includes lessons to learn, soul wounds to resolve and the evolving options for transformation. Even those who appear to be stuck in the same healing cycles can achieve enlightenment and the difficulties they experience are part of their enlightenment journey. Whatever they manage to learn or achieve and how easy or hard they make their path does not make them any less enlightened than someone who chooses an easier path to learning.

Difficult lessons are no more or less enlightening than easy ones. Challenging lessons may point to a need to learn about resistance and fear. Maybe we need to be a persistent negative force in someone's life to help them with their soul learning. Or we need that element in our life for our own soul's growth. Maybe the lesson is learning to set boundaries. Maybe the lesson is about self love. Whatever lessons we experience with and through others, enlightenment occurs for everyone. It just isn't the same for everyone. Who can be the judge of another's enlightenment?

Judging who is enlightened assumes that we are all learning the same lessons, in the same way and at the same rate. What each of us needs to learn is only known to us, as defined in our soul contract. It is not possible for us to know what someone's lessons are, just as we cannot know how important certain experiences are to them. So we can never know someone's level of enlightenment. When we view enlightenment as a sort of spiritual hierarchy or contest we are forgetting that we are all perfect and connected, on the same path to reconnection. We are one, emanations from the same Source, divine sparks of light from the same Central Sun. Each person is always at the perfect level of enlightenment they can achieve at any moment in their lifetime. It is an individual process, so comparisons cannot be made. When we engage in comparison we are in judgment of others and often ourselves. We are not privy to the importance or value of someone's lessons, just as we are not able to see the full scope of what their soul came to experience in any lifetime.

Can we receive enlightenment from teachers or those who believe they have something to teach us about being enlightened? That depends on how we believe we can achieve enlightenment. Since every aspect of our life journey is a contract between the ego, soul and Source, who can tell us that we are enlightened, other than ourselves? One thing is sure, there are no shortcuts to the process. We are enlightened through our own learning and we should be wary of those who profess to be able to hand out enlightenment like merit badges or certificates of accomplishment.

A few years ago I attended an event that featured a well-known spiritual teacher who professed to be a master who could bestow enlightenment on others. The event was sold out and many people were anticipating becoming enlightened by listening to his message. The teacher's demands for his presentation included sitting in a special recliner, placed on a raised platform, with a particular brand of very expensive bottled water. Then he was more than thirty minutes late for the presentation.

As he began to speak I felt a wave of nausea wash over me and I knew that I needed to leave. The information was not right for me and I was very uncomfortable with the way this teacher presented himself as an enlightened being (and he stressed that everyone else was not) and the ego energy that dominated his teaching. When a friend, who also attended, asked me about my early departure I told her that I was uncomfortable with him and his messages, so I left. She said that was also uncomfortable but because he was so highly regarded she was not sure that her feelings were correct. It had not occurred to her to leave because she didn't feel right about his teachings.

There are many teachers who have information to assist us on our journey to enlightenment and each one has something to offer us. Our lesson with teachers can be to learn discernment as we must choose whether their information and energy are right for us. Or they can help us with a specific aspect of our learning and then when we have learned all we can from then, it is time to sever the relationship.

The value of any teacher's input to us is limited — they cannot give us what we cannot create for ourselves and cannot teach us what we are not yet ready to learn. And no one can give us the enlightenment that we are not prepared to receive. Asking whether something is right for us allows us to choose the path to enlightenment that is best for us. And to do so in a way that feels right and will attract the teachers who will best serve us on that part of our journey.

Enlightenment is a process of learning and clarification. So each time we learn a lesson, we become enlightened. Each time we face and overcome a fear, we become enlightened. Each time we are able to heal a soul wound, we become enlightened. The process can happen with anyone we connect with, from a spiritual teacher to a stranger on the street. Even people who we believe have no spiritual background can be our greatest sources of enlightenment. And we can choose our teachers by asking ourselves whether what they have to offer us is right for us. If not, we can find another teacher.

Consider these principles for your personal mastery journey:

Who do you believe helps you on your path to enlightenment? Remember that it is not just the people who are kind and loving who are your teachers, everyone is your teacher.

Do you have a teacher you look to for enlightenment and are you comfortable with the information they share with you?

Is there a difficult teacher in your life? Can you identify what this person is teaching you about and find the enlightenment in this experience?

Can you see all of your teachers as being enlightened?

In which areas of your life have your teachers been an enlightening resource?

The idea that everyone is enlightened and that everyone is our teacher can help us see the value in each relationship. If we view everyone as enlightened and honor their journey, no matter what type of life experience that entails, we move into the space of non-judgment, acceptance, detachment and unconditional love. And we can decide who we will allow to share our own journey. This is where we need to be if we are to embrace the opportunities of our mastery journey and to create a world where peace, joy and unconditional love are available to all. And it will bring us peace as we remember that when we shine our light and work on our own issues, we allow others to do the same in the perfection of their soul's journey of growth, healing, love and return to Source.

How do we know that we are enlightened? Enlightenment is the process through which our soul learns, grows and heals as we reconnect to the divinity that we all carry within us. Is there an issue we feel complete and at peace with? When we think of the situation and the people involved, can we feel joy, satisfaction and gratitude? Rather than anger and frustration, can we feel acceptance and a sense of knowing? That is enlightenment. We began our journey as enlightened and we will end it with greater levels of enlightenment. Can we accept enlightenment as our own, individual process of spiritual mastery?

When are we enlightened? Part of enlightenment is acceptance of who we are, our lessons, our journey, the healing that we have to do and the growth that we have come to achieve. For many of us, acknowledging our Source connection is an enlightening moment. We have experienced countless lifetimes in order to reach that stage in our spiritual evolution. Being aware of our divinity is another enlightening moment, as is realizing   a lesson and why we have had to learn it. Whatever we master in our lifetime is cause for celebration — only our soul and God know how long it has taken us to achieve it.

When know we are enlightened when we feel at peace with ourselves, we can accept ourselves for who we are and be proud of what we have achieved. If we view enlightenment from a soul level, what can seem to be the smallest, most insignificant lesson can be an enormous achievement in enlightenment, one that we have taken many lifetimes to learn. Confirmation of our enlightenment can arrive in many ways, from the manifestation of a cherished dream to recognition of a lesson's message. Enlightenment is not our final destination, it is simply a step on the cycle of learning, healing and transformation that is the purpose of our life journey. In fact, enlightenment marks the end of an initiation process and the beginning of another one.

We don't have to defend our beliefs or spiritual growth to anyone. And anyone who challenges that is another teacher for us. Are we aligned with our beliefs and can we support them through our words and actions? Do we need someone to validate or justify our enlightenment or can we be confident in our own knowing? We know we are enlightened when we feel the peace and understanding that comes with it. And as we complete one phase of that process we are prepared for the next one. Peace, joy and understanding are the gifts of enlightenment. Any time we are in those energies is an enlightened moment.

We have learned about spiritual initiation and its gift of enlightenment. To achieve this we must understand our karma and those who help us with our karmic journey, our soul group. In order to understand enlightenment and embrace our lessons, we have to understand what we came here to learn and its purpose on our healing journey. This is the foundation of our human experience, the most challenging aspect of humanity. Our karma holds the keys to our learning and is the source of all of our pain and fear. So we must explore our karma, soul contracts and soul groups to understand why enlightenment is such an important part of our journey. Karma is what we came to heal, the soul contract is our reminder of that commitment and our soul group is who we heal with.

Karma, Soul Contracts and Soul Groups

I once took a screenwriting class and was amazed to learn that the first rule of screenplay writing is that a screenplay cannot exceed one hundred twenty pages in length and most are between ninety and one hundred pages. Even the longest films are developed from a document that is at most one hundred twenty pages of content. Yet within those pages is all of the drama, intrigue, mayhem, romance and passion that can entrance, shock, thrill and move an audience.

We each enter life with our own screenplay, in the form of a soul contract that is imprinted in our minds, hearts and souls. It contains the details of our karma, the scenes, emotions and events that will govern the course of our life. The actors in our screenplay have been carefully selected to help us experience and resolve our karma, whose healing and transformation is the purpose of our lifetime. In essence, every lifetime presents us with a pre-written screenplay that describes every decision and action that we will take, defines the characters that will be featured and determines the flow of events. The ending has been written too, but it can be changed when we understand the concept and nature of our karma.

What is karma? It is the collective energy of the emotional experiences that we have had over the course of our lifetimes, the totality of everything we have ever done or said to every person we have ever interacted with or any situation we have ever been in. Any emotional energy we have left unresolved in a lifetime or trauma that we experience leaves an energetic imprint in the earth's matrix, which is the unfinished business we must resolve in another lifetime.

Our karma creates connections with the people we have experienced it with and these connections are very compelling, nearly impossible to resist and often set dramatic life changing events into motion. We have a soul contract with them, an agreement to experience our karma so one of us can end it.

One example of the irresistible nature of karmic connections and the damage they can do happened in a group I was part of, in which two of the participants had an obvious physical attraction to each other. Although they were each married to other people they were soon involved in an affair because the attraction was too strong to resist. Their spouses and families found out about their relationship in a dramatic series of events that resulted in hurt feelings, interrupted lives and difficult choices that had to be made. The activation of their karma had a ripple effect on everyone around them that caused much pain and changed lives.

Why were they willing to risk everything for this relationship? The emotional connection was too strong to resist and represented unfinished business from previous lifetimes that they knew they had to complete. Could they have acted differently? Yes, if they could have detached from the emotional energy of their karma. But the moment they met, their soul contract was   activated and within the awakened energy of their past life karmic connection they knew no other option than to be together. The ramifications, effect on their marriages, and the feelings of the other people in their lives, did not matter. What was their next step? They had   to decide whether they would leave their marriages and be together or separate and try to re-assemble their broken lives.

Not all karmic connections are this dramatic and end in such a painful   way. For example, two women introduced themselves and chatted while standing in line at a restaurant. They felt a strong connection and agreed to meet again. Within weeks they had become friends and felt they had known each all of their lives. They had a strong past life connection as friends and that was their karmic connection, to be supportive friends to each other.

Why do we make these kinds of connections? They are the people in the screenplay of our lives, with whom we have a karmic past. They are the members of our soul group, those with whom we share two things, karma and a mission to heal it. Our soul group is the cast of characters that will help us create the energies of our karma and ensure that we become the best embodiment of these energies so we can deliver the best performance of our karmic screenplay. We incarnate with these souls in each lifetime with the purpose of experiencing our karma. Our connection is through our soul wounds and we play multiple roles in different lifetimes so we can learn every aspect of our karmic experience. In one lifetime we are the teacher and they are the student. Then in the next lifetime we reverse these roles.

We continue in these cycles, switching the roles of teacher and student, aggressor and victim, abuser and abused, until one of us decides we are ready to forgive, which ends the karma and allows us to move out of the soul group and into another one, or which changes the soul group dynamics so we are no longer focused on healing karma and can experience our energetic connections in different ways. This occurs on many levels -- personal, within families, cultural groups, societies and nations. In fact, the family of humanity also has a soul contract and karma with the planet Earth.

The agreement for healing we have with our soul group is also part of our soul contract, which we create before each lifetime to determine how our healing journey will unfold. The details of these agreements are so deeply ingrained in our subconscious mind that we are not even aware of their existence. We can live our entire life not understanding why we make and even repeat certain life choices even though we know we will not be happy with the results. We can go from one abusive, painful relationship to another, not understanding why we attract that kind of person. We often repeat the lives of our parents, who repeated the lives of their parents, and so on. Even if we wish, try and hope for something different, we often feel powerless to change, so strong is our compulsion to act out the destiny that is defined by our karma and the contract we have created to ensure that we experience it.

Why is all of this important in our journey of spiritual mastery? Because we cannot raise our vibrations, move into higher levels of being and be fully in our power until we have resolved our karma and the density that is shaped by the energies that are associated with it. Why is this happening now? Because we, as the family of humanity, have decided that we are ready for karma to end and to transform the energetic imbalance that lifetimes of karma has created on earth. And it is required for ascension to occur because, as we mentioned earlier, we cannot move into higher dimensions of being and take our emotional and karmic baggage with us.

Karma is responsible for all of the fear, wars, hate, betrayal, disappoint-ments, sadness and anger that we experience on all levels of our human existence. Lifetime after lifetime, we return with the intention of transforming it, only to stop at the emotions that karma awakens within us and, unable to go any further, we come back to repeat the exercise.

But in this lifetime things are different. We have new sources of energy available to us and a deeper understanding of our spiritual nature. Our new vision of ourselves as spiritual beings allows us to go beyond the limitations of our humanity, finding and drawing on our inner resources to address karma from a different perspective. Through our willingness to become multi-dimensional beings and consider life beyond karma, we have given ourselves the opportunity to choose whether we will continue to experience life through our karma or move into a higher vibration, which allows us to create life as we want to live it. This moves us from karma into creation, where we are no longer bound by our karmic destiny and can create the life from a powerful, spirit-led and karma-free perspective and extend that to creating the kind of world we want to live in.

When we choose the path of spiritual mastery we are given a new perspective on karma and its role in our life, with the power to resolve it. Our new energetic paradigm shifts our viewpoint so we are aware of both the karma and the healing it requires. This is an entirely new concept for humanity, having a spiritual viewpoint of our emotional DNA and access to alternative potentials for its transformation. Karma is recognized through awareness and healed through forgiveness, which becomes possible with a shift in our energetic vibrations. This disrupts the connections to lower vibrating energy, which loosens the energy around the karma and reveals it as without its energetic support it can no longer be hidden from us.

When karmic energy is activated our fears are brought to the forefront and our karmic history comes to life in the present. As we read in an earlier chapter, this is our path of spiritual initiation, and the birth, trial and lesson are all focused on revealing and resolving the karmic ties that bind us to our soul groups and contracts. These karmic dramas can elicit very strong emotional reactions which are merely replays of how we have acted with that person or within that kind of situation in the past. Our commitment to mastery gives us the tools we need to view our karma from a new perspective so rather than becoming mired in the emotions we can pause and reflect before we choose to act. New questions can be asked, such as why we are feeling these particular emotions, what they mean to us, what lessons we must learn from this experience and then decide whether we are ready to release ourselves and those around us from it.

Then our challenge becomes how we will resolve the karma. Can we heal and release it or do we still need the karmic experience for a while longer? As you read this chapter, pay attention to the various people and situations that appear to you because they will be the people and situations you are going to work with as you continue on your own journey into your mastery by healing your karma and moving into the energy of creation. They are part of your soul contract, the agreement you have with Source to heal your karma. And everyone in your life is part of your soul group, souls you have known for eons and with whom you have contracts for healing. Whether they are the most difficult or the most wonderful people in your life, they play a very important role and hold the key to your karma and its healing.

The Soul Group

Our soul group consists of the souls we incarnate with again and again because we share unfinished business and unresolved emotional energy from previous lifetimes that has created an energetic imbalance between us and they join us in each lifetime to help us work through and complete our soul contract for healing and karmic resolution. And since we share the responsibility of creating the unbalanced energy, as teacher or student, victim or aggressor, abuser or the abused, we also share the responsibility of transforming it. Everyone we know in our lifetime is part of our soul group, which includes our family, children, partners, friends, co-workers, neighbors, acquaintances and even strangers. The person who stops to help in a moment of need is part of our soul group, as is the person who steals a purse or wallet. Our birth mother is part of our soul group as is a father-in-law or an adoptive parent. Within each soul group interaction is a purpose, a lesson, a blessing and a chance for forgiveness, healing, release and transformation.

Soul group relationships differ according to the shared soul level promises and karma. They can be among the most wonderful, fulfilling, cherished relationships, or they can be those that we dislike intensely, are the most challenging, that cause us our greatest sorrow and pain. Every person in our soul group, including us, knows their roles and lines well, as we have played them many times before and do our best to deliver them perfectly, creating the scenario that will help us perform our part in the karmic experience and lead us to the choice of continuing it into the next lifetime or ending it forever. This is our life purpose, to complete the unfinished business of our previous lifetimes and we do that with the help and participation of our soul group.

The members of our soul group are our 'soul mates', a term that is used to describe the ultimate romantic relationship, but that is a misinterpretation and an over-simplification of this term. Soul mates are energies that we have a soul level connection with, through our interactions in other lifetimes. These connections can include romance but they extend far beyond that. The co-worker who sabotages your work, the friend you love as a brother or sister, the neighbor you fight with, the beloved teacher who influenced you in grade school, are all soul mates. A soul mate relationship can be the most wonderful or the worst relationship you have ever had. A soulmate is anyone who mirrors your soul energy in some way, but especially, someone who brings forward the wounds that you have agreed to heal in a lifetime, and is often the person who have those wounds with.

How do you know you have met a soul mate? There is a strong sense of connection and knowing, an emotional response that you cannot ignore. You can have a 'love at first sight' encounter with a soulmate, as well as an instant dislike. You know that this is an important relationship, no matter how you initially feel about it, one that will change your life in some way. Soulmates show us where we need healing, which is why these encounters can be so wonderful and challenging, why they bring forward such strong emotions and why we cannot resist them, no matter how hard we try.

We connect with a soulmate when our soul knows that we are ready for the next phase of our healing. In that moment we make a connection that may seem like an accident or that fate is at work, but it is really another opportunity for us to go through this experience and apply everything we have learned up to that moment to help raise our vibrations and resolve our karma.

What happens in a soulmate encounter? We connect with a set of emotions that relate to our shared karmic experience. If this is a romantic relationship, we feel love, connection, a sense of destiny, a knowing that we are meant to be together. And we are, but perhaps not for the reasons we think because we have issues to resolve with this soulmate that require us to be completely emotionally committed to allow the healing to occur and that may involve betrayal, abandonment, unrequited love and separation. Our healing may also involve being able to love unconditionally, surrender, learn acceptance, detachment, receive love and allow an intimate, heart-level relationship to happen for us.

Whatever happens within the relationship will let us know what energies need to be healed through our interaction with this person. And we will go through those experiences until we get to the healing. Then we must choose whether we are willing to release the karma through forgiveness, of ourselves and of the other person and to heal or not. Sometimes the healing involves ending the relationship forever and that can be devastating. Other times, the healing takes the relationship to another level and allows us to experience our soul mate within a new and different energetic vibration.

The history of a soul mate connection can be helpful in understanding issues surrounding the current relationship. A client's karmic reading revealed that the man she was in love with had been with her in many lifetimes, some of them quite happy. But in most of those lifetimes their happiness was short-lived and they experienced separation, sometimes in violent ways that included death, betrayal or abandonment. In this lifetime she was heartbroken because what she thought was going to last forever had just ended when her soul mate suddenly left town with little notice. They had such a strong connection, were so close and everything felt so right. What had happened?

In the karmic reading I saw that in a previous lifetime they had been together as husband and wife with many children and had a very happy, peaceful life. The woman was an herbal healer and the man a farmer. Then at age forty the husband became quite sick and even though the wife was a gifted healer, nothing she did helped him and he died, leaving her alone with her children. Devastated by this loss, she threw her herbs into the river and vowed that she would never heal anyone again. She spent the rest of her life mourning her husband and died a sad, lonely and brokenhearted woman.

In this lifetime, their connection had been "love at first sight" and they spent every moment together. She knew she had found her soul mate. Who else could she have such a strong connection with? Then she noticed that he began to pull away and while she was confused, she thought it would pass. When he called and told her he was moving far away, she was distraught. What had she done? Why was he doing this to her? What about their relationship?

She had not done anything wrong and nothing was being done to her — this was the wound that he had come to help her heal, to experience the separation that had always occurred in their relationships and to make a choice to either be devastated by this loss or to accept it as his role in her life, to teach her to move on and to release him. He also had a wound to heal, to make choice to live his life and accept the love and blessings that he could have or to run from love and commitment, as he had always done in prior lifetimes. They had replayed this scenario countless times together, each meeting beginning with feelings of love and connection that they could not ignore, followed by a short relationship and then betrayal or abandonment. She had abandoned her own life in the past, out of grief and sorrow, and he had abandoned her out of fear of commitment, of not being able to meet her needs and his own lack of self love. What would they do this time?

In the present lifetime, he was given the choice to stay with her and build a fulfilling relationship. But he chose to not do that and left her behind once again. For her, the knowledge about their soulmate connection and past life history gave her the strength to forgive and release him and the relationship. Even though she spent some time mourning him and the loss of the relationship, she knew that this was for her benefit, that she could stay upset and grieve indefinitely or let herself heal this soul wound and move her relationship experiences into a different energetic vibration. He did not achieve that level of soul growth and would be able to have that opportunity again, in this lifetime or another, with someone else.

Forgiveness and release will allow her to find a partner with whom she does not have this karmic lesson. Her karma with this aspect of her soul group was over because she processed the information she received and used it to make a choice for her soul's growth and could now create a relationship that did not contain this lesson for her. While we cannot bypass our karmic lessons and the soul wound healing that we have agreed to do in this lifetime, once we have accomplished the healing, we do not have to repeat the experience.

In other types of relationships, a soul mate can be a difficult or abusive parent who has unresolved emotional issues with us. For example, a client was sad that her relationship with her mother had always been marked by jealousy and even as a young child she knew that her mother was very jealous of her.

A reading revealed that they had been rivals for the same man in a past life and the mother had been rejected by him, in favor of my client. The mother's anger and jealousy had carried over into the present life. The two had agreed to come together again so the mother could resolve her jealousy and my client her guilt.

Because she felt guilty about her happiness and had carried that guilt into this and other lifetimes, she never allowed herself to be as happy and successful as she could be in any aspect of her life. Although in this lifetime the former romantic rivals were mother and daughter, the mother was unable to control her feelings of jealousy and that is what defined their relationship. Through understanding and forgiveness my client was able to release her guilt and to realize that her mother's jealousy was her own lesson and that she no longer needed to be "less than" she was, hoping that her mother would finally accept her.

A soul mate relationship can exist between friends, as was the case with a client, Jane, who had experienced a series of painful losses in her life, beginning with the death of her mother at age seven. The shining light in Jane's life was her friend, Lisa, whom she loved as a sister. Lisa was someone she could lean on, depend on and who 'mothered' her when she needed it. During our karmic reading I saw that Lisa had been Jane's mother in a previous lifetime and she had also died when Jane was young. Through their soul mate relationship she had agreed to help Jane with her lessons when she became an adult and to become the supportive mother figure she needed to come to terms with her mother's death, as well as move out of the loss, sadness and pain that she felt, which attracted those kinds of relationships to her.

Everyone we cross paths with has a soul mate connection with us, representing a karmic connection that we can resolve. And remembering that we have unfinished business with this person, energy that needs closure and a past connection to release or benefit from in some way allows us to see everyone in a karmic context. Instead of asking why this is happening to us, we can focus on what we have to learn from this experience, what we have to teach each other and what needs closure. Knowing this makes it easier to resolve and heal our karma more quickly because we ask the questions at the beginning point of our connection instead of waiting until we have gone all of the way through it to understand what has happened.

Releasing karma means ending soul contracts that we have had with our soul group from the beginning of our existence. It means releasing emotional attachments to people and situations, which are the central element that defines our relationships with them. For example, we may dislike a family member, which is an indication of a strong karmic bond. They may have abused, betrayed, hurt or abandoned us in this lifetime, which we can view in one of two ways. We can see it as something they have done to us out of their selfishness, meanness, inconsiderate behavior or thoughtlessness. Or we can look a little deeper and see it as part of our karmic journey together. One question we can ask is, if this is how they   are treating us today, what did we do to them in another lifetime?

Here are some questions we can ask to help identify our karma with others:

Is this some kind of retribution that they think we deserve, as payment for something we did to them in a prior lifetime?

Or is this part of our healing journey together, to experience this kind of difficult connection and find the inner strength to change the dynamics of our shared energy?

Are we ready to forgive that person for whatever they have done to us, release them and move on?

Are we willing to forgive ourselves for the role we played in creating and extending the karmic connection?

Would this process be easier or more difficult if we knew that through the process of release and forgiveness we could either establish a different relationship with them or sever our ties to them altogether?

Can we accept that whatever they have done to us in this lifetime, we have also done to them, or worse, in a previous lifetime?

Consider these principles for your personal mastery journey:

What kind of relationship do you have with your father, mother or other family members?

Can you see the karmic bonds and lessons that you share?

Do you see that within karmic relationships there is a pattern of reciprocation and an exchange of roles?

Are you aware of the healing that you can do to release yourself from these patterns?

Are you ready to release them so that you can connect to them on a different level, or release them altogether?

Are you ready to forgive them for their role in the karma, and yourself too?

In order to accept the role of our soul group in our karma and to understand how we can end it, we must be aware that we can live powerfully and step into our power. So please take a few moments to consider who is in your soul group and what they are teaching you.

Take a few moments to answer these questions about your soul group:

Name one person you believe loves and supports you unconditionally.

Name one difficult or challenging person in your life and the lesson they are presenting you with, as well as the opportunity for growth and healing that you believe this is creating.

What is one lesson that you are going through at this moment?

Which members of your soul group are helping you with this lesson and how is each one contributing to your learning and healing?

What lesson did your parents teach you through the way they spoke to you, treated you and interacted with you?

Who in your soul group is blessing you with a lesson at this time, whether that lesson is challenging or easy and what is the lesson they are helping you with?

How can you interact with your soul group in a powerful way that allows you to experience the lessons they have come to help you with and finalize them, if necessary, so you can either move out of this soul group or end your contract and shift the dynamics of the relationship?

How you will interact with your soul group, and everyone else in your life, is defined in your soul contract, the agreement for healing you have committed to for this lifetime. It is the focus of your lifetime and until you understand and transform it, governs everything you do, everyone you meet, every situation you encounter and everything that happens.

The Soul Contract

A soul contract is the blueprint for our life path, an agreement that we make between ourselves and Creator to heal our soul wounds, which have resulted from the pain we have both caused and experienced in previous lifetimes. This pain creates a fear-based energetic imprint in the earth's energetic field, a reminder of our unfinished business in that lifetime that we must return to resolve. So each time we struggle, suffer, forget our divinity and blame others, God and our separation for our problems, we create an energetic imprint that we will have another lifetime to heal and transform. We call this energy karma and it is simply an energy whose vibration reflects a fear-based belief in our separation from our divinity and perfection. The same type of energetic imprint is created whenever we cause pain for others and the resulting imbalance of emotional energy must be resolved with them in another lifetime. Energy does not disappear; it must be transformed through healing and forgiveness, as part of our ascension process.

We created these energetic imprints in other lifetimes where we have been both the abuser and the abused, the victim and the aggressor and without knowledge of the alternatives, our lifetimes can become patterns of revenge and retaliation, or submission and powerlessness. Our soul is wounded during experiences of deep emotional trauma and marked with an emotional and energetic imprint that interrupts the energetic wholeness of our spirit. These wounds encompass many different kinds of experiences that can include betrayal, abandonment, fear, rejection, murder, suicide, poverty or wealth, success or failure, or the right use, abuse or misuse of power — the list is limitless.

We carry these wounds from lifetime to lifetime, hoping to find resolution through the lessons we create with selected partners from our soul group. In the absence of the spiritual understanding we gain through enlightenment, we use force, oppression, revenge, and power to resolve the lessons to our benefit, which means that we use any means to justify the end of our choice, so we can feel powerful once again. With spiritual understanding, we address the wounds with compassion, love and forgiveness.

The energetic imprints of these soul wounds is contained within our emotional DNA, the history of the emotions we have experienced in all of our lifetimes, whose energetic vibrations we share with our soul group. When our karma is triggered, through a situation, person, memory or experience, our emotional DNA is activated and the memory of all of the pain and emotion that has been previously associated with that kind of experience is available to us. With this activation, we are on a karmic path, where have a choice to heal and create a new future or repeat our karma.

Our soul contract sets the template for the wounds and pain that we are to work with and through this energy the past that we have an opportunity to heal becomes our present reality. By holding emotional energy, past life experiences and soul group dynamics, soul contracts define the details of our karma and map the path of our destiny for each lifetime. Note that we are given an *opportunity* to heal and that does not include hints on how to do that or the best way to proceed. We have choices available to us that we must select from.

One choice can be to resolve our karma by overpowering, outsmarting or out- maneuvering the one who previously caused us pain. Another choice is to take the path of healing and forgiveness. Another is to ignore the entire situation and pretend it does not exist, suffering in silence until it goes away. Whatever we choose, eventually we will arrive at the point where we can have the courage to face our contract, choose the path of forgiveness and raise our vibrations to another level, allowing us to practice compassion, detachment and forgiveness, which ends the karma and that aspect of the soul contract.

The activation of a soul contract occurs when we are triggered by a person or an event or experience a powerful emotion. This can be a time of great drama, confusion, chaos and change and each thought, decision and action is either a step forward out of the karma or a step back into it. Karma is like a dance between two people and when one person stops dancing the dance is over. We stop dancing when we intentionally apply forgiveness and compassion so our part of the karma is healed. Then we are no longer involved in the dance and our part of the soul contract is completed. We can move on and the other person has to choose what they will do next. The destination is our transformation, or the end of our contract, where we have chosen to end our story with them in a new and different way.

We have soul contracts with our family, friends, children, spouses, partners—everyone in our life is someone we have a contract with and every situation is an opportunity for the contract to be activated, brought to our attention and resolved or repeated. Knowing what these contracts are, recognizing when they appear in our life, who we have them with, when they have been activated and how to end them gives us a greater power over the unfoldment of our life purpose. While our journey would be more pleasant if we could remember our soul contracts, we do not and if we did we would probably do all we could to avoid them.

We may already be familiar with the terms of our soul contracts because they are present in the everyday challenges that we face in our life. Every trial, drama, problem, pain, disappointment, betrayal, and sorrow is merely a repetition of something we have already experienced, as well as our joys and blessings. The challenges have wounded us in such a deep and powerful way that we return to resolve them and find peace. Recall the earlier story of the client whose relationship ended when her partner moved away and left her. In a former lifetime, she had been devastated by the death of her husband. Their initial meeting in this lifetime began the karmic cycle and his leaving was the trigger that activated this soul wound and contract, putting the energies in place to allow her to experience them so she could choose to heal. Would she be devastated and fall into a depression that overtook her life, as she had in her past lifetimes? Or would she move beyond the grief and shift the energy to heal the karma, thus ending this soul contract?

To heal these wounds, the past life experience is re-created in a way that allows us to recapture their emotions through the people and situations involved and how they are presented to us. Our objective is to learn to make different choices. What we choose is entirely up to us—there is no right or wrong choice in this process. We have an option to complete our soul contracts or not, to start or stop at any point in the process as long as we understand that there is a choice and we are at a level of understanding that allows us to be aware of it. Without this level of understanding, we repeat the details of our soul contract over and over again, in lifetime after lifetime. We cannot skip or overlook soul contracts; we can only go through them to the best of our abilities. With understanding, we recognize the contract, become aware of its meaning, details and purpose and can make the choice to resolve it.

There are different kinds of soul contracts and the type we choose depends on the work that we have come to do within a lifetime. Not all soul contracts are painful and difficult. Some soul contracts, which could be defined as 'good' are the ones that are easy, providing us with lifetimes where we do not experience pain or emotional drama. Perhaps we have chosen a lifetime where we experience wealth, joy and love. We may have a contract with someone that involves being a friend, confidant and loving supporter. Maybe we chose to find peace and fulfillment in being of service to others and that brings us happiness. We can choose contracts that include fulfilling relationships, a loving family and friends, a peaceful and stable life.

Do you have a 'best friend', someone who is like a sister, brother or parent to you? Are you closer to that person than anyone else and you know that they will be there for you no matter what happens? You have a soul contract with that person that involves love and support. I often see these kinds of contracts between best friends, people who meet and have connection that lasts for many years. Within these relationships there is no judgment, only acceptance and a connection that is often stronger than that found within a birth family.

We may call our challenging contracts 'bad' but they are our most powerful lifetime experiences as they reveal many layers of healing. These occur in lifetimes where we have chosen to end a cycle with our soul group and are finalizing aspects of our healing work with them. They can involve karmic paybacks, where we may be persecuted by someone for what we did in a past life. Or we can be presented with an opportunity to persecute them for something they did to us. Or we need to learn to choose compassion over other emotional responses. With lessons in power, we may choose to experience powerlessness from people or situations and learn how to reconnect to our power.

We may think that because a soul contract's lessons are so important they would be presented to us in a way that would guarantee our success. And in a way they are, but they are usually presented in the form of strong challenges that we must overcome. Many of us have soul contracts to learn about power, compassion, fear, anger, and to fearlessly use our gifts. And although we may be brilliant, creative and talented, our lives are chaotic and filled with drama. And we become stuck in depression, addictions and despair, unable to move forward because we allow the lessons of our soul contract to overpower our life. Our reality, which could reflect the powerful use of our gifts, becomes a tangled mess of dysfunctional relationships and powerless choices.

Our soul contract can be presented in the form of family relationships that include physical, mental, verbal and emotional abuse, intimidation, aggression, neglect and anger. These carry over into our adult life and we have a choice with each lesson to find our power and heal our karma or allow it to consume us and our dreams. Until we surrender and become aware of our life purpose, to heal the karma, we will continue to receive lessons in power from family, friends and others around us, until we understand, heal and transform these energies.

How do we know when our soul contract is activated? That is the purpose of our spiritual initiation, letting us know that it is time for us to get to work, bringing our karma to our attention and setting us up for the choices we will make. Our soul knows that it is time, we are ready and it helps us to create the situation that is necessary for us to remember the karma and create transformation. The soul contract is activated with an event that awakens our emotional DNA, brings to our fears to the forefront, connects us with our past and any memories that are associated with this type of situation. Now we are fully in the energy of our karma and all of its associated feelings, emotions, beliefs and thoughts. The purpose of this process is to bring us to healing but when we are in the throes of our karma, healing is often the last thing on our mind because this can be a rough time. It can take all of our physical, emotional and mental resources to simply survive what is happening to us. Depending on the soul contract and karma, the people and situations involved, we can be re-living some of our most challenging life lessons.

What can we do when we are in this transformation, experiencing karma, struggling with life lessons and afraid? We can start by paying attention and be in the present moment. Look at what is happening around us, who is involved and the fears rising to the surface all offer information on what is happening, the opportunities for healing we are being presented with and the possible choices we can make. By detaching from the emotions and fear we become aware that we have options to end this without suffering by asking the right questions. Instead of asking questions like "Why is this happening to me" or "Why did this person do this to me", which reflect on the victim energies that we feel or our belief that we cannot overcome this challenge, more powerful questions are:

What is the lesson for me?
Where is the healing occurring?
Why did I create this?
What is the purpose of this experience?
What is my contract with these people and this situation?

What is the best step for me to take to end this now?

Healing and transformation are our life purpose and it is through our soul contracts that we create the possibility for that to happen in a lifetime. So as we are able to detach from the outcome, to consider options other than to be involved in the karma and going through the entire initiation process, from beginning to end, we can consider ending our soul contract. This is possible to do when we are willing to recognize the contract, karma and lessons, are open to transformation, and then do the healing and forgiveness work so the release can happen.

Once we decide to end contracts our lives can go in a different direction. The journey and everything we encounter on it is more important than the destination. And we are constantly making choices to heal or not, to obtain closure or to create additional experiences that allow us to heal and grow. What do we want to do next? Without a soul contract, our lifetime becomes a blank page. First, though, we have to look at the promises we have made across our lifetimes, promises that we will keep, no matter what it costs us to keep them.

The Soul Promise

At some point in one of our lifetimes, something happened to us that was so memorable that we made a promise which was imprinted on our soul. Within this promise we swore to do whatever it took to resolve, heal or change it. And each lifetime from that moment on has focused on completing this promise. A promise on this level has such a strong level of commitment that we will do whatever it takes, on all levels, physical, mental, emotional and spiritual, to fulfill it.

And because these promises occur on a soul level we are not even aware that we made them or what they are. What we are aware of is a sense of uncontrollable destiny, a feeling that we must do something and no matter how hard we try, we cannot avoid it. Although we are not aware of the details, there is a sense of urgency about them and an inner knowing that they must be completed. Even so, we feel helpless or powerless to avoid the situations we are presented with, even though we try because on a soul level we also know that each time we try to complete this, there is an impact on our life that involves some kind of commitment that we must keep.

These promises are revealed to us as we step into our mastery because they are part of the soul wounds that we have come to heal and resolving and completing them is important to our progress. Without resolving our soul level promises and forgiving ourselves and anyone else involved, we will stay in them forever, trying to fulfill them or until we have the insight and understanding to be able to let them go. As with karma, when we raise our vibrations we disrupt the energy flow to our soul promises with two results, first they are no longer hidden from us so we begin to understand the reason for our fears or actions and second, we disrupt the energetic connection with them so they begin to lose their power and the control they have in our life.

Souls level promises represent what we unconsciously care about, a silent driving force that compels us to act, even when we do not want to. I wrote about these promises in *Be Who You Are*, which describes how soul level promises affect how we unconsciously, and often with the best of intentions, make choices and decisions that have a profound effect on the flow of our life. We can have these promises with ourselves or with others. A soul level promise that we make to ourselves involves things that we will 'never or 'always' do or be.

We could make a soul level promise to never marry again, or to never have children.

We can make a promise to never leave home or to never hurt someone again, or to never allow ourselves to be forced to do something we do not want to do.

We can make a promise to always be faithful to a partner, no matter what, or to protect and never abandon someone.

These promises are based on judgments we make of our actions or those of another, where we hurt or betrayed someone or saw another hurt or betrayed and we cannot forgive ourselves or feel responsible for what has been done. In fact, we can feel so responsible for someone's choices or what happens to them that we vow to do everything in our power to prevent it from happening again.

A soul promise we make to others may involve re-creating a situation so they will make a different choice. For example, a mother who felt she abandoned her children in a previous lifetime will try to make it up to them by being constantly available to them and may even bring in a child who cannot live without her support and attention, such as a child with special needs or one who is hurt or disabled in an accident and cannot live alone. Or a man or woman who has been betrayed by a spouse may constantly seek partners who will betray them, hoping that by being long-suffering and patient, the person will change their ways. Or if they have been an unfaithful partner, they will attract unfaithful partners because in their guilt they believe that this is what they deserve. When unresolved, soul level promises become part of every lifetime and we re-create their details in many different ways.

Soul level promises are generally born from fear and involve experiences where we were once hurt, embarrassed, or shamed in some way or did this to someone else or watched helplessly as someone else suffered. And they are very powerful motivators. They can cause us to repeat experiences, over and over again, not understanding why things in our life don't change or why we seem to make the same choices or attract situations that bring us unhappiness. They are largely responsible for our self sabotage, those situations in life where we destroy our own creations, through motivations that are so unconscious we can be asking ourselves what we are doing as we are in the process of unraveling a cherished dream, a hoped for opportunity or the fulfillment of a long-held desire. With a soul level promise in place, we can feel unworthy, unable to move forward and undeserving of any blessings because we have unfinished business that compels us to delay our path until we can resolve this issue.

Within soul level promises are unconscious or unspoken commitments to others that may involve promises to be available to them, to not make certain changes until they are ready for us to do so, to consider their needs before our own or to complete obligations to them before we allow ourselves to move on. These unspoken commitments will interfere with any changes that we wish to make in our reality because until we have resolved them we will block any miracles or changes that can occur in our life, including our ascension and mastery.

How do these promises work? Here are a few examples to help you understand how they work and uncover any soul level promises you may be fulfilling in your life.

Ada was a gifted musician, who showed an interest in music at a very early age and told her parents that she wanted to play the violin. But her parents thought that girls should play the piano and boys played the violin. So they told her she could study music if she played the piano, which she did, while her brother, who wanted to play the piano, played the violin. Then, when she turned 18, after playing a concert she told her parents that she had always wanted to play the violin, was finished with the piano and would never play again. And she never did.

Her soul level promise was focused on not allowing others to force her to do things she did not want to do. In her anger and frustration she decided to end her musical career, although she could have been a successful musician. Instead, she married and had children. Many years later, Ada admitted that she regretted the decision to abandon her musical studies, which she had done to spite her parents and assert her authority over her own life, in fulfillment of a soul promise. 'What a waste of talent,' she said of herself.

In the fulfillment of her soul promise, Ada ignored her gifts and the life she could have led. Was her parents' insistence on her playing the piano possibly steering her in the right musical direction? Could she have learned to play the violin at a later point in her life? Yes, but her soul level promise, arising from a past life experience and her anger towards her parents, which was also part of her contract in the current lifetime, prevented her from doing so. And she regretted her decision her entire life but was too proud to admit it or to do anything to change it.

This soul level promise story is about a woman who did not allow herself to have children because of her experience in a previous lifetime:

Julie was in her forties and childless, although she desperately wanted children. Despite undergoing multiple costly fertility treatments and other types of medical intervention, she was never successful at conceiving a child. This subject came up for her during a reading because of the deep sadness I could feel in her energy field. When I asked her about children, her eyes filled with tears as she told me of her longing for a child and her many unsuccessful attempts at conceiving. I was surprised that she had never been pregnant because she had children's energy all around her.

As we continued with the reading I described a lifetime in which she had six children, whom she loved very much. Her children were the focus of her life and she was a kind and loving mother. One winter, disease went through their village and her children became very ill. They died, one after another. Each time one of her children died her heart broke a little more until, as her last child died in her arms, she promised herself that she would never have children again because she never wanted to experience that level of pain and heartbreak.

In her current lifetime, although Julie desperately wanted children, she admitted that she was afraid they would die, and it was something she thought about often when she was trying to become pregnant. With the knowledge about her prior lifetime and the soul promise she had made, Julie could understand why she had not been able to get pregnant and make a choice to resolve this promise and end it. She was also told that if she had become pregnant and given birth, the baby may not have lived, to allow her to resolve the issue of heartbreak and to experience the death of a child so she could resolve her pain in a more powerful way.

Do you have a 'best friend' in your life, someone who is closer to you than anyone else although you are not related? You have a soul level promise with this person, one that you may not be aware of:

Terry and Elaine had forged an instant friendship when they met in grade school. As children they were always together and later decided to attend the same college. They married at the same time and eventually lived in the same city and neighborhood. Their friendship had lasted more than thirty years and when they came to me for a reading, they came together.

Their deep connection was the first issue that appeared in their reading. They had been friends through many lifetimes and even shared a soul promise, which was to be a source of support and inspiration to each other. In other lifetimes, when one had been troubled or had challenges the other was always there for support. In this lifetime the same pattern was created. Terry had a difficult childhood, marked by divorce, separation, abuse and loneliness. Elaine was her only friend and the only person she could share her deepest feelings and thoughts with. She admitted that without Elaine she may not have been able to cope with her life. Elaine was fulfilling her part of their soul promise, as Terry had done with her in the past.

And a final one that addresses a relationship issue:

Dave knew that his wife cheated on him but did not want to admit it. Although her behavior deeply hurt him, he was not willing to confront her or make a decision to fix his marriage or end it. In fact, as he professed as his reading began, he actually felt guilty about his wife's behavior although he did not understand why.

During his reading I saw that both he and his wife had soul level promises that they were helping each other with. In a previous lifetime, Dave had been his wife's father and he had forced her to stay at home and take care of him, refusing to allow her to marry. By the time he died, she was too old to marry and spent the rest of her life alone, deeply resentful and bitter because of his treatment of her. Her soul level promise was that she would have the emotional freedom she wanted and his was that he would allow this kind of behavior because of his remorse over having denied her a chance to marry and fulfill her wishes for her life in their previous lifetime together. When Dave realized the dynamics of their relationship he could forgive himself, acknowledge his wife's behavior and decide what he would do about it, whether he would seek recon- ciliation or divorce.

There are many kinds of soul level promises and the ones you may have made will affect you in different ways.

Do you believe that you have made a soul level promise that blocks you from doing something you really want to do or that represents a commitment to someone in your life?

Are you ready to release it, forgive those involved and step into the opportunities that are available to you when you acknowledge and are ready to use your gifts and talents?

We are standing at the threshold of creating the life our dreams — we, along with our soul level promises, are the only thing that stands in our way. When we ask for our soul level contracts to be revealed, the soul level promises that may be connected to them, will also come forward so our release work allows us to transform all areas of this experience. Remember that the Universe always responds to our every request and if what we ask for does not manifest   it may be because we have unspoken or   unconscious commitments that need to be released before we can manifest the reality of our dreams.

Here are some questions to ask yourself about your soul level promises:
Can you identify a soul level promise that is present in your life?
Are you aware of the people involved, how they are presented in your life and what you have created to help you resolve them?
Are you ready to forgive yourself for what you did in a previous lifetime that created this contract so that you can move on?

Are you also willing to forgive anyone else involved so that they can move on as well, instead of remaining in your life to help you fulfill your contract?

There are other energies of the past that affect us in each lifetime in powerful ways. These are vows, curses, promises and decrees that carry strong energies of karma and destiny, forging permanent bonds between us and the people with whom they are made until we release ourselves from them. Our decision to step into our mastery requires our willingness to heal, to complete our unfinished business with ourselves and others so we can shift our energetic vibrations. Without our willingness to do this work, our mastery is within our reach but we will not be able to fully grasp it until we can choose to heal everything that is part of it, including our ancient promises that bind us to a long forgotten past.

Vows, Curses, Promises and Decrees

There are energies of the past that can affect us strongly in the present, in the form of promises that we have made to others, curses that have been issued against us or by us, or vows that we have taken for or against something. These are emotionally charged statements that we have made in a lifetime that affect us on many levels. They are imprinted in our emotional DNA, soul and cellular memory and have a very high fear-based emotional vibration. Their energies are replayed, again and again, until we remember them, forgive ourselves and anyone else involved and let them go. And they manifest in many ways, as you can see by some of the examples I have encountered with clients during sessions.

One client had made a vow of eternal poverty after having stolen money from her family in a previous lifetime. In this lifetime, she was never able to attain financial security.

After years of expensive and difficult fertility treatments which did not result in a pregnancy, a client discovered that she had died in childbirth in numerous lifetimes and had promised she would never become pregnant again. In this lifetime she unconsciously feared that becoming pregnant would result in her death. She had to release this promise and her fear to become pregnant.

Another client had been cursed by her sister in a previous lifetime because of an incident involving a man in which she had married her sister's suitor, and the sister, unable to find a husband, had lived a bitter, lonely and impoverished life. In this lifetime my client was unable to maintain a long term relationship and financially supported her sister.

A vow of protection made to a friend many lifetimes earlier, kept a client bound in a difficult, loveless marriage to the friend in this lifetime who was now her husband.

A curse made by a jealous rival many lifetimes before had kept a client sick and bedridden for more than thirty years, because she believed that she was unable to live a full and productive life.

This may seem like the stuff of horror novels or movies but these energies are very real, create discord and disharmony in our life and they play a significant role in our karmic history and healing. Vows, curses, decrees and promises contain very powerful energy that is based on fear and a strong emotional response. This energetic vibration is so strongly rooted in our subconscious and unconscious mind that it affects every aspect of our life. Until we are able to raise our vibrations enough to disconnect from this fear-based energy we will continue to feed it through our thoughts, words and actions.

Releasing these energies requires awareness and forgiveness. Our mastery journey will reveal these energies to us for transformation and their release will greatly assist in creating peace and harmony for ourselves and all of humanity.

Vows are promises that we make to perform certain acts or behave in a certain way. They are made on the level of the ego and are focused on what we will do or not do either in the course of our life or in a specific situation. We can take a vow of poverty or chastity, vow that we will protect or save someone or agree to a vow that dedicates our life to a specific purpose. In other lifetimes we take on vows out of guilt or service, regret or atonement. The vows we have taken can compel us to forego our life journey on behalf of someone else.

And they will follow us until we release them. Someone who has taken a vow of celibacy in one lifetime can find it difficult to have a romantic relationship until the vow is released. Those who have financial problems may have taken a vow of poverty in one lifetime that creates an inability to accumulate wealth. As mentioned earlier, a client was shown how her current financial problems were related to a vow of poverty she had taken in a lifetime where she had stolen money from her family, reducing them from financial abundance to destitution. In her remorse she took a vow of poverty not realizing that she was creating an emotional imprint that would follow her through her lifetimes until she released it.

Whenever we take a vow we will create lessons that challenge us to heal and release it because it contains fear-based energetic imprints that are part of a lifetime's healing purpose. Once we raise our energetic vibrations we can no longer sustain the vow's energy requirements and can then disconnect from it. Vows can involve emotions such as self judgment, unworthiness, remorse or regret and are based on an ego-based interpretation of ourselves and our life journey that is made through fear. They are released through forgiveness, acceptance, abandonment of judgment and reconnection to our divine sovereignty in our life.

Curses involve some kind of evil, misfortune or ill will that is wished towards another. Generally directed towards someone whom we believe has done us harm, a curse directs specific emotional energy towards its recipient and moreover, invokes the power of Creator to do so. When we deliver a curse we take on the role of a vengeful higher power, acting as judge, jury and executioner and stand in judgment of that person and their actions. Our primary focus is revenge and we want to ensure that someone pays for what has been done to us or someone we love. In this space we are disconnected from Source and standing in fear.

While it may be hard for us to believe that we could curse someone, in other lifetimes we have had many different kinds of experiences. In one lifetime, for example, a client was shown how she was cursed by a man's wife for breaking up their marriage. In this lifetime, she never married and the one man she loved was married and refused to leave his wife. She spent her entire lifetime alone, never marrying or having children.

Cursing someone reflects our desire that whatever we believe they did to us happens to them, and more of it. This is where we are taking the place of Creator because while we know that their actions will be returned to them, according to Universal law, we want to ensure that it does. Yet by connecting to that energy and speaking the curse, we are also placing ourselves in that energy and become part of it. So the curse that we wish on others becomes our own curse. We release curses through forgiveness; we continue them through our need to have revenge or our own lack of forgiveness.

Whether we give or receive a curse, its powerful emotional imprint becomes enmeshed in our emotional DNA. When we accept a curse and incorporate its energy into our own emotional body, we acknowledge our wrongdoing and give our power away to the person who curses us. When we are the one to delivers the curse we are trying to take energy from someone else in repayment for what we think has been done to us or lost to a person or situation.

What makes curses powerful is the fear and guilt attached to them. Our fear creates a strong energetic vortex that empowers the curse and makes it a permanent part of our emotional body. Its presence allows it to infiltrate our karma, attracts similar energies and manifests itself energetically into successive lifetimes. There are two components to curses. First, the recipient must believe that the person delivering the curse has the power, means or reason to do so and second, they have enough responsibility, guilt, fear or remorse about their actions to believe that they deserve the curse. These emotions build the curse's emotional foundation and allow it to be continuously present until there is a conscious intention for release.

We can also curse ourselves. Harsh words spoken in a moment of fear, anger or self judgment are very powerful and carry a strong energetic imprint. Take the example of a client who, in a previous lifetime, had a difficult life and was married to a brutal, violent man who killed her and her children. At the end of her life she cursed herself for being a woman and attributed her powerlessness to save herself or her children to her female gender. In other lifetimes she struggled with these same kinds of relationships because the curse created an energetic imprint that attracted brutal, violent people and situations. She also had serious health problems involving her reproductive organs, a symbol of her femininity.

Curses are another form of emotional energy that can be released once the presence of the curse is recognized and its energy disconnected through forgiveness.

Promises and decrees are a type of vow that we make as an assurance of our worthiness, value and responsibility. When we make a promise we make a personal commitment to ensuring that something is completed and take full responsibility for making it happen. If we could see promises on an energetic level we would see many cords that bind us to the person or situation that we made the promise about. In other lifetimes, promises are the energetic glue that binds us to people or situations until we release them. Like vows and curses, promises have deep emotional connections and strong energetic imprints because they are made in moments when we feel powerless, responsible, or want to prove ourselves in some way.

We can make a promise in one lifetime out of deep grief or sadness that follows us through many lifetimes.

A client came to me because he was having problems with his daughter, who had become very rebellious and would not listen to him. He had an overwhelming fear that something would happen to her, making him over protective and creating even more problems within their relationship. His karmic reading revealed a previous lifetime where his daughter had drowned before his eyes and he was unable to save her. Because he thought he was responsible for the drowning and that it happened because of his carelessness, he promised himself that he would never let harm come to her again. So in each lifetime he returned with her to honor his promise. It was also revealed in his reading that she had drowned because he had warned her to not go near the water and she had not listened to him so the drowning was her fault, not his. In order to release this promise he had to forgive himself for his belief that he was responsible for her drowning. This would then release his fear that something was going to happen to her in this lifetime and he could be less protective of her.

We release promises by forgiving ourselves and transforming our guilt, sadness and regret into acceptance of the divine order of the Universe.

As we release the soul level promises and other energetic commitments we have with others there is one thing we must remember. All of these situations exist because we have a need for healing in these areas. Anyone who connects with us at a karmic level mirrors our own healing needs. This is why we must forgive to release our karma because as we forgive, we heal our own soul wounds and can transform all of our pain and suffering into joy.

Ending Soul Contracts

We can end soul contracts, soul level promises, vows, curses, promises and any other agreements we have with our soul group. For that to become possible two things have to happen, one of us has to be willing to forgive the karma we share and we have to be in acceptance of everyone's free will to choose their path and make their decisions. We must be willing to honor each member of our soul group's free will, even if it is contrary to what we know is good or right for them, goes against everything we believe and rejects everything that we have been trying to teach or help them with.

This may mean that the soul contract ends in unpleasant and painful ways, without the kind of closure we need to know that we did the right thing, our work on their behalf was rewarded, the light we have been carrying for them has helped spark their transformation and that they appreciate our efforts. Ending the contract may feel like a door slamming in our face and we may think that we have failed but that is not the case. Despite our frustration and disappointment, we did all we could and what we now realize, that we have never been able to know before, is that each person has sovereignty over their soul contract and their life path, which means they can make the choice to heal, or not, and that is the right choice for them at that time.

Under these circumstances, we have two choices, to move on with our life or to wait for the person to make their transformation and join us. While the choice is governed by our free will and either choice is right, we must know that this situation has happened before, probably in the same way, and all of its aspects, including the frustration and disappointment, are part of the karmic journey we share with this person. If our choice is to wait for them to change, that has probably been the choice we made in the past. Will we do something different this time?

At this time everyone is being presented with choices as to which path they will take and one of those choices involves the ending of soul contracts. If the required level of learning and spiritual understanding has been achieved, the soul will allow the contract to end. But if not, the healing lessons continue and the one who has extended the healing must choose to move on while the other returns to their karmic lessons. That is why many relationships today are ending suddenly, without explanation or the kind of closure that provides some degree of comfort. We may feel that this person, who is so close to us emotionally and energetically, has no concern for our feelings, broken heart, anger or powerlessness. And they don't because that is not their perspective. They are viewing this journey from their own life path and their choice is the right one for them. We are not a consideration. In fact, we are powerless over this person's choices and must accept that no matter how much light we give them, no matter how evolved we have become, we cannot make choices for anyone, or influence their choices.

If you are nodding your head at this point because you can relate to this situation, you should know that it has happened to you before, with this particular soul. There have been lifetimes where you came together for healing and to move forward together, on a new path away from your karma. You chose to do the healing work and your partner was unable to honor that choice, so they decided to continue with their karmic lessons. You have the choice to stay or go, to get on with your life and your soul's growth or to wait for the person to transform and raise their vibrations to allow healing to occur. But you can't do it for them and although you have tried in many different ways in past lifetimes, the journey always comes to this moment, where one of you must decide whether to stay in the healing cycle or raise your vibrations and move forward. And if you decide to wait, you are doing what you may have done in a past lifetime, pausing your own spiritual growth in the hope that someone would complete theirs.

Mastery is not focused on healing others, it is focused on healing ourselves. The realization that everyone is on their healing journey while they are participating in ours and has something to teach us is an enlightening moment that can transform lifetimes of pain. This is a karmic experience for everyone and your choice to move on may represent a victory that you have been unable to achieve for many lifetimes. Know that you are not alone, that you are experiencing a transition that this paradigm shift has brought to the forefront for many. And make your choice knowing that what you have completed or outgrown will be replaced with something that matches your new vibration.

You will know when a contract is ending when someone begins to pull away or suddenly leaves. Or you are faced with a situation in which it is so obvious that someone does not want your help that you have to make the choice to let this person go because staying with them is the more painful option for you.

In these relationships one person has a greater awareness of the healing, providing the other person with an opportunity to raise their vibrations in a quantum leap of healing. And in many lifetimes the other person is not ready, so they end the relationship through betrayal, dying, physical or mental illness, or abandonment. And the karmic cycle comes around again in another lifetime, another cycle of healing or denial, of coming together or pulling away.

This was the case for Sue, a client who had had tried for years to transform her relationship with her brother and help him deal with the aftermath of their childhood. Their parents were emotionally and physically abusive and her brother, who was older, had taken the brunt of the abuse. As an adult he was angry, confused and bitter. Sue had tried to help him, giving him spiritual books, allowing him to stay with her when he was between jobs, which was usually the case, talking to him and even delaying a move to another area so she could stay close to him. When he began taking drugs and she caught him stealing money from her, she knew that she had to make a choice. As painful as it was for her, she decided to let him find his own path as she could no longer tolerate his behavior.

So she moved away to take a new job and kept contact to a minimum. It took several years for him to begin to call her again and he let her know that he had been seeking treatment and was putting his life back together. Now, instead of Sue forcing spiritual information on him, he asked for it and was willing to read the many books that she had provided him with. Over time, he did heal his anger and was able to forgive their parents but he had to make that decision for himself.

Making the decision to let someone go because staying in their energy is too painful or difficult is not an easy choice. Our commitment to them and their healing often represents a strong soul level promise that arose from one or more lifetimes of shared karma or even prior to that, from the moment of our original incarnation when we agreed to separate and come back together at this time. This is the cycle that occurs within karmic cycles, a soul promise for healing is made, a contract is created, an atonement is promised and then through many lifetimes we reunite to get closure and release the karma, hoping that the promise of healing will finally be fulfilled and the contract ended.

This karmic cycle is activated when it is time for the healer in this scenario to make a choice, to continue to martyr or sacrifice themselves on the other person's behalf or to make a decision to honor their path and let the other person find a different healer to work with. The other person also makes a choice, to stay on their current path or to accept the healing. This often happens in connections with partners, parents or children, where there is a strong soul level obligation to heal and a willingness to sacrifice on behalf of someone's healing. For Annie, a woman who had spent most of her life trying to accommodate her mother's healing, there was a difficult choice to be made.

Anne was nearly sixty and lived near her widowed mother in a town she disliked. Although she had traveled extensively in her life and would have preferred to live in many other places, she was always drawn back to her mother, with whom she had a distant and cold relationship. Every five to seven years something would happen to her mother, an illness, an accident or other situation in which she required assistance and Anne would receive a telephone call. And Anne would respond by stopping her life and either traveling back and forth for months at a time to help her mother or she would uproot herself and move closer to her. Determined to understand why this was happening, Anne called for a karmic reading. And she received the insight she needed to help end this contract.

The karmic reading revealed that in Anne's most recent lifetime her mother had been her husband, a controlling man who was emotionally and physically abusive, who wanted to know her every move and insisted that she stay at home, tending to his needs. After years of tolerating the abuse, Anne decided to leave him and began to make preparations for her new life, which included plans to move away, find a job and create the happiness that she had not been able to have in this marriage. On the day that she told him she was leaving, they had a terrible fight and her husband pushed her down a flight of stairs, killing her.

When Anne heard this she began to sob uncontrollably, remembering the pain she felt at having her life end just as she was preparing to create a new life for herself. But she saw the terms of their soul contract and understood why she felt such a strong obligation to help her mother. She had returned to allow her mother to let her go, something her mother had been unable to do in their previous lifetime together and was unable to do in this one. The mother was still emotionally abusive, controlling and afraid to be alone, insisting that Anne stay close to her. The only solution was for Anne to release herself from this promise and end the contract, forgive her mother/husband for killing her so she could finally live her life on her own terms and be happy.

It was a huge turning point in her life, through which she was able to release herself from this contract. She also realized that her mother had to find her own source of power and do her healing in her own time. Anne could not help her atone for what she had done and had to stop re-creating the situation in which she allowed her mother to have opportunities to allow her to leave, hoping that it would end differently. And she did feel partly responsible, believing that had she stayed in the relationship with her husband she would have avoided the situation. When she was able to release her sense of obligation and allow her mother to be responsible for her actions and her healing, she created the possibility for her mother to make her own choices with respect to the karma instead of sacrificing her own life, re-creating the karma to allow her mother to choose to let her go and have closure with the situation. Through forgiveness and release Anne finally found peace and was able to move on with her life.

Pause for a moment to review your soul contracts:

Can you name a soul contract you have with someone in your life?
Do you see how this contract has shaped, governed, or ruled your life?
Do you understand how this person participates in the contract you share?
What sacrifices have you made in your life to honor your part in this contract?
Are you ready to release yourself and them from your contract?

Are the people that we decide to release from our shared soul contracts going to find their power? That is up to them. Will they honor us for the role we play or have played in their life? That is also up to them and we cannot wait for their acknowledgement or gratitude. Soul contracts offer healing for all participants but whether that healing is embraced is up to each individual. Our path to mastery requires that we find and connect to our power and remember that each of us is powerful, each of us has the same Source of power and can connect to it in our own way and within the scope of our level of spiritual growth and understanding. Each person is in charge of their own healing.

When you believe that you must be part of someone else's healing you are relinquishing your power to them and limiting the amount of power that you allow yourself to express in your life. You are also seeing that person as powerless. One of our lessons in mastery is to be in our power. To do that we have to release ourselves from living in atonement for what we believe we have done.

When we live in atonement, we are constantly seeking God's forgiveness through others when what we really need to do is forgive them and ourselves.

Living In At-Onement

Everything that we do is perfect in every way. The Universe never judges, criticizes or condemns us. Every moment is lived to the fullest extent of our potential within that moment. When we are able to recognize greater potential within ourselves, we change our focus and direction and expand our possibilities. We do not make mistakes or errors in judgment. So there is nothing that we have to be sorry for or guilty about, there is nothing that we have to apologize or make amends for if we feel that we have not been or done all that we are capable of. We are asked to live in atonement but not in the way we have been led to believe.

When we live in a way that reflects our Source connection we are always "at one" with the highest expression of our Self. This allows us to live at our highest possible vibration and to raise our vibration with each experience. When we are at one with Source we are in alignment with Universal Law and with unconditional love. This is the place of instant manifestation, miraculous living and peace. Being "at one" is the highest expression of our light and is the atonement that we seek in each lifetime.

Being in atonement requires that our human nature or ego is aligned with our spiritual self. We must learn to be led through the partnership of our heart energy and our mind. When these two are in alignment we are led by unconditional love and fear is easily overcome. Fear is a central energy of the material plane and will be a persistent temptation. Remembering our spiritual core and allowing it to guide us will shed light on any darkness that we may encounter.

We do not have to be a spiritual avatar or attain a special level of mastery to achieve this level of being and living. All it requires is our willingness to be in continuous connection to Source, to have faith and to trust, which is the central aspect of our mastery journey. When we are "at one" we are always in a state of being our true self, expressing our divinity through our humanity. This is how we re-member, bring ourselves back to Source. Our soul's desire is to walk with spirit and be "at one", thus living in atonement and enjoying heaven on earth.

This is a reality we can create for ourselves and is how we manifest our heart's desires.

But there are challenges on this path, in the form of the ego, karma, soul groups, emotions and fear. These are our areas of separation, where we are disconnected from Source which we have the opportunity to alter through our journey of atonement through which we can re-member and reconnect. We make this path difficult through our belief in our imperfection and that in order to be 'at one' we must suffer and atone or make up for the many wrongs we have committed in the past. And we believe that it is through re-creating our karma and being forgiven by Source that we achieve atonement.

It is part of human nature to want another chance to 'get it right', to fix what we did wrong or to have a 'do over'. Take a moment to look at your life and consider how many things you would do differently if you had the chance. And this is what we do with our karma, we enter each lifetime wanting to do it again, to get it right or to have the other person 'get it right' in ways that validate us, the ways in which we contribute to their healing and the choices we make on their behalf. To do this we engage our soul group in creating the situations that remind us of what we have to fix in such a way that we will do everything we can to fix it. This is one way of achieving atonement but there is another, less challenging way that is available to us, one that is, more powerful and requires no suffering.

Once we forgive ourselves for whatever we believe we have done wrong, we have replaced our karma, fear and the ego's belief in our imperfection with unconditional love. This is our space of whole-ness, where we re-centered in our divinity instead of our separation. It is our willingness to see our error, which is the realization that we have never been, and can never be, disconnected from Source, that creates the path to wholeness. We do not have to atone for our karma, mistakes or limiting beliefs, for it is our belief in separation that creates it and how it manifests in our life. Forgiving ourselves releases the need to atone for our perceived wrongs and take our healing to new levels.

As we resonate at higher and higher levels of vibration we have access to new understandings and new perspectives on our individual journey, the role we play in the human family and our connection to Source. These understandings share a common Truth, that we are divine spiritual beings whose humanity is simply a phase that is part of a greater journey in consciousness. As spiritual beings we embody God's perfection, so there can be no wrong, no imperfection — and no need for atonement. Our karma reminds us of our need to remember who we are and to forgive ourselves, as our Creator forgives us.

This is our journey 'home', to reconnect to our own mastery and to remember that all is forgiven when we remember to forgive ourselves. And this is the purpose of our healing journey which is complete when we bring our material self into alignment with our divinity. The energetic paradigms of fear and pain will unravel when we align our material self, the ego, with the truth of our spiritual mastery, which brings us to enlightenment. We are children of God but more importantly, we are children of the Light and we are the light that brings healing to the world when we heal ourselves. And this healing is not about righting wrongs, revenge, fixing situations or denying ourselves joy because we believe that we have been imperfect. It is about reconnection, remembering, re-alignment and a renewal of what we have always known, that we already are what we have always wanted and the love and joy that we have been for.

From this point we are in our power, which is a powerful place to be.

Consider these principles for your personal mastery journey:

Do you have areas in which you feel separated from Source and have been working towards atonement by limiting yourself and your life?

Do you interpret atonement as your having to make up for your mistakes?

Who in your life is helping you with this process?

Are you ready for forgiveness and to believe that you are already perfect, whole and complete?

Can you accept that atonement simply means being 'at one' with your divine self and Source? If so, can you see yourself 'at one' with Source all of the time?

When we release the need for atonement, remembering that our relationship with our Source is never at risk, we are fully in our power. Being in our power helps us create a powerful reality and attracts powerful people and situations to us. We do not do this by overcoming our powerlessness through atonement with others, we do it by reminding our ego that we are, and have always been, powerful.

Being Powerful

Our journey into mastery requires that we acknowledge our power and learn to live from the perspective that we are powerful. No matter how powerless we may feel at any moment, no matter how out of control our life appears to be or how much we wish that we were braver, stronger, or more decisive, we are powerful spiritual beings and use our power to powerfully create our life, in the most powerful ways we can. Every situation and person in our life is a reflection of the amount of power we are allowing ourselves to connect to. Consider your life at this moment. Do you think you are living powerfully? What does that mean to you? In today's world we believe that powerful people are those who have money, fame, success and live a life that reflects their power. And that if we have power we can create those things. If we do not have them, it means that we are not powerful.

But there is a difference between spiritual and material power. We can have a great deal of material power and be very disconnected from our spiritual power. We all have unlimited spiritual power but can be unable to use it to create a powerful reality in the material world. Each of us is always powerful, even if our external reality does not appear to reflect that, according to how we define power. And our spiritual power, which is an inner resource, is always available to us, even if we are unaware of it and do not use it in very powerful ways.

Consider these principles about your spiritual power:
Whether you believe that you have power or not, you use your power every day. Everything that exists in your reality is there because you used your power to create it.

Take a moment to consider everything that you enjoy and appreciate in your reality — you used your power to create it.

Now take a moment to consider everything in your life that you do not like — you used your power to create that too.

Does your reality reflect powerful living?

How many times do you say or think that someone 'made you' do something? When do you feel that you are out of control or that you are powerless to change any aspect of your life?

Our power comes from within and is part of our spiritual heritage. While we may believe that power exists in the material world, it is actually only a reflection of our spiritual power. We can use our power consciously or unconsciously, with intention or from habit and create joy or pain, love or fear. Our power is part of us and whether we are aware of it or not, it is always available to us. It is a constant flow in our energy field and when we use it with intention and focus we energize our life and achieve powerful results. Living powerfully means applying our power consciously and with intention to every aspect of our reality, to ensure that what we create is exactly what we want.

Living powerfully also means using our power wisely and taking responsibility for all of our thoughts, being fully aware of how they create our reality. If we choose to think powerful thoughts, focusing on what we want in our life, we will create those things. If we fall into despair and hopelessness we are using our power to create a reality that reflects those thoughts. Being powerless is an illusion that is not the real truth for us but it is a truth that we can incorporate and live by. We are never powerless, although we can feel that way. We have simply forgotten how much power we have and how to use it to our highest benefit. Living in fear and doubt is also powerless living, while a more powerful alternative is living in abundance, joy, confidence and love.

The Universe's response to our thoughts is automatic and exacting, providing us with a continuous flow of manifestation based on every single thought, even the ones that we do not intend to manifest in our reality. The Universe is without judgment so it does not discern between positive and negative or expansive or limiting thoughts. There is no hierarchy of power within it so no person or thing is more or less powerful than another. Within the Universe everything is equally deserving in all things and in all ways. The Universe sees us as powerful and when we reflect this, we live powerfully and spread our light in the world to create a powerful life for ourselves, setting the template for that energy for all of humanity and creating that possibility for everyone.

Our journey into mastery is a testament to our power and how we are using it. Can we call ourselves masters and not be powerful? We are all masters and are all powerful. The illusion of powerlessness that we see in the material world is nothing more than a reflection of how we are connecting to and using our power, which can be changed at any moment. When we remember who we are and that our source of power is within us and not out in the material world, we step powerfully into our mastery and all things become possible. Our field of potential lights up and we expand our reality to include options beyond our imagining.

When we feel defeated or weak we are not powerless, we are simply allowing the illusion of the results of our powerless thinking become our truth. What is real and what is an illusion? The only truth is that we are powerful spiritual beings. Everything else is an illusion.

Consider these principles for your personal mastery journey:
How are you using your power in your life?
Do you feel weak, out of control and powerless?
What situation in your life at this moment is allowing you to feel powerless?
Which of your thoughts could you change to transform your life into one that reflects your unlimited and infinite spiritual power?

Being in our power allows us feel safe and protected, firm in the knowledge that nothing and no one can harm us. With powerful living we create boundaries, energetic separations that ensure that our energy is used in the most effective ways, to create our highest good. Boundaries also exclude from our reality those who would use or abuse our power. When used in the best way, boundaries help us maintain our foundation of power because they allow us to be in control of our energetic resources and stay focused on our purpose of being in joy, having peace, knowing love and living in abundance.

Setting Boundaries

As Lightworkers we tend to have very thin or nonexistent boundaries because we are aware of the role we play in the world's healing process and focus our energies on creating that outcome. We carry the light for the world, for humanity and our soul groups. We are the light that the world needs for its healing and even if the world is not ready for us, we return lifetime after lifetime to remind the world of its purpose of healing and transformation and the guidance that is available to them, from those who carry the light and from the spirit world. Yes, it is our purpose to bring healing to the world but we can do that without becoming martyrs to this process. We have martyred ourselves for humanity in countless ways and the time of the martyred healer is over. We can be powerful healers who lead by example instead of through our suffering, who help others by being the example of living at higher vibrations instead of taking on their dense energies and suffering with them or on their behalf. To do that we must understand how boundaries work and have strong boundaries that perform two purposes, to protect our own energetic resources and keep others out of our energy field.

We protect our energy by setting standards for how we will share it, consciously or unconsciously. Conscious sharing occurs when we are fully aware of where our energy is going, to whom and for what purpose. We are aware of the choices that we make to share our energy and pay attention to those we choose to do this with. When we are conscious of where our energy is going we can avoid becoming depleted because we are always aware of our energy levels and know how much we can give to others without compromising our own needs. And we give to others while being open to receiving and do not give without limits to those who are   incapable of returning anything to us. Conscious energy sharing is possible when we are grounded in our power and are aware of how much and how often we interact with others and how deeply we become involved in situations and with the people around us.

But while we often are aware of the need to do this, we do not always practice it because as soon as we are approached by someone who needs our energy, we rush in to share it. Or, when we believe that someone needs our help, we jump in, often before they ask us. Or if we empathically feel that there is discordant energy around us, we process it without wondering whether it is in our best interest to do so or whether we can actually handle the influx of lower vibrating energy or whether we should. These are some of the many ways in which we unconsciously share our energy with others and with the world.

Do you see yourself in this and see how you may be unconsciously sharing your energy with others? You probably do and have done so for such a long time that you are not aware of when or how you do it or of the toll that it puts on your energetic resources. Those times when you feel tired, irritated, when noises bother you and it is difficult to be around people are when your energetic resources are low and it is time to separate yourself from the world for a little while and renew them.

If we know that this kind of sharing is not always beneficial, why do we do it? One reason has to do with our healing mission. We are here as healers and we take our job seriously. So when we see energy that requires healing, we do our best to help, without considering that this is a lesson someone needs to resolve by themselves or that the job of healing should be done by someone who needs the opportunity to step in, recognize the situation and deal with it. We are so accustomed to playing the role of healer and transmuting energy that we do it automatically. That was once our responsibility but in the new paradigms, this has changed. It is time for everyone to find their power by doing their own healing and energy transformation, which they cannot do when we do the work for them. And if we assume that role, then we may have to spend many more lifetimes with them, which brings us to the second reason why should reconsider sharing our healing energy with others.

The second reason is a little more complex and involves our desire to speed the healing process along. We have been doing this work for many lifetimes and most of us are tired, we want to be finished, to go Home and release ourselves from interacting with the same people, lifetime after lifetime, without completing the desired levels of healing. For many of us this is a final lifetime on the earth plane and we want to complete it in the best way possible so we never have to return. With this in mind, as soon as we are aware that someone is ready to heal (or think that they are close to healing), we see this as a sign that we can release them from our path, end our soul contract and resolve our shared karma, so we rush in to ensure that this happens and give them all of the support they need.

After all, we have waited a long time for this moment and we do not want anything to go wrong so we can be released from this connection. In our rush to help them heal we ignore a few warning signs, including the one that tells us that the other person wants someone to do the healing work for them or they are only engaging us in this situation for us to become aware of our own need to heal and that this is an opportunity for our healing, not theirs. So we rush in, get sidetracked and then become stuck in the karma with them. And the other person is so willing to give us their healing issues or use our energy that they never stop to ask whether they should be more engaged in their own healing.

As illustrated in the story of the butterfly in the cocoon, which is recounted below, it is by completing the struggle of emergence that we grow our wings. But we often rush in to help because we do not want to watch someone struggle, or we have watched them struggle for a long time and we just want them to 'get it' this time so we give them a little push, in the form of our own energy, to send them in the direction of healing.

There is a certain sense of satisfaction that we receive from seeing people achieve enlightenment with our help but we forget that when we shoulder the burden for others we deprive them of the learning and the experience they may need for this part of their journey. And their enlightenment will be short lived because unless they do the work themselves, they do not really gain the understanding they need to apply it in their lives.

In the story of the cocoon and the butterfly a scientist was watching a butterfly emerge slowly from its cocoon. The butterfly struggled to release itself from the cocoon, got halfway out and stopped, appearing to be exhausted by its efforts. The scientist thought the butterfly was in trouble and wanted to help so he took a pair of scissors and gently cut open the rest of the cocoon, freeing the butterfly. He thought the butterfly would burst out of the cocoon and open its beautiful wings.

But that is not what happened. For a few hours the butterfly sat next to the cocoon, its body deformed and its wings bent. Then it died. By cutting open the cocoon and trying to help the butterfly, the scientist had actually interfered with its emerging process because the struggle involved in leaving the cocoon pushed fluids through the butterfly's body and into its wings, allowing them to become strong. With too much fluid in its body and not enough in its wings, the butterfly was unable to move, much less fly.

And this is what we do when we share our energy with others before considering whether it is something we should be doing or asking whether our efforts are actually of benefit to the other person. In becoming their on-demand healer we delay or prevent their growth, and sometimes their healing, from occurring and although we may help them through one situation, they do not learn enough from the experience to gain the knowledge to get through the next one. Essentially, we ask them to fly without allowing them to grow their own wings.

You know someone like this, they are the ones who come to you again and again with the same dramas, the same questions and the same situations that you have helped them through many times before. With your help, no matter how well-intentioned it is, they never learn what they need to in order to grow their own wings so they can fly powerfully under their own power.

Consider these principles for your personal mastery journey:

Is there someone in your life you are unconsciously sharing energy with?

Do you know someone that you wish would just 'get it' and move forward with their healing and are you tempted to help them without considering whether that is the best thing for them or for you?

Are your own energy resources depleted by your attempts to help others heal?

Do you need to set some stronger boundaries with yourself and with others so that you are not unconsciously sharing your energy?

Another use of our boundaries is to keep other people out of our energetic space. These are people who prey on us, looking for an opening in our defenses so they can swoop in and get as much energy from us as they can. The term 'energy vampire' is used to describe someone who uses others' energy for their own purposes. These people are just as powerful as everyone else but instead of relying on their own internal power resources, they prefer to use someone else's energy. These are the people who come to you for help with their problems and then count on you to clean their messes. They engage you in an argument and once you are energetically exhausted they walk away looking refreshed and energized. And they are, because they just received a big dose of your energy. They are the ones who are helpless, powerless and unable to manage their life on their own and who ask you to help them with something small and insignificant and before you know it, you are spending all of your time on their issues and have no time for yourself.

You also know them by how they seem to always be able to push your buttons, to irritate or annoy you or conversely, who seem to know exactly how to ask you for help so you drop whatever you are doing and help them with their issue of the moment. You have strong karmic ties and soul contracts with these people, centered in shared guilt and shame, and one of the lessons they have for you is to learn to set your boundaries to keep them out of your energetic field so you can share energy with them if you wish and if not, allow them to either call upon their own energetic resources or find someone else to get energy from. The boundaries you establish will teach them how to use their own energy instead of always relying on others.

Here's an example of how this works:

When Patty met John she knew she had met the man of her dreams. Tall, handsome and charming, he quickly won her heart. Patty was a successful businesswoman who had started a small company and built it into a multi-million dollar enterprise employing hundreds of people. She was active in her community, well respected and very competent. Although they had discussed the fact that she earned much more than John, he insisted that it did not bother him. Their marriage began happily but after a few years the problems began, starting with little insults that John made from time to time, growing into more heated discussions and finally arguments that lasted for days.

When she called for a reading Patty was stressed, unhappy and baffled by John's behavior. What had happened to the charming man she married? As soon as she mentioned his name, I saw an enormous vampire around her and told her that he was draining her energetically because he was jealous of her success and saw himself as a failure. Over the years of their marriage, Patty's business expanded but John's life did not expand in the same way. He started and quit several jobs, tried to start a business which failed, began to smoke marijuana, he was lost and his life had no direction. Jealous of Patty's success, he tried to find ways to undermine her, bringing her to his energetic level, so she would acknowledge his unhappiness and disillusionment. He wanted her to feel as bad as he did.

Patty did not want to end her marriage so we worked on setting energetic boundaries and building her inner strength so that she could recognize when her husband was setting her up for massive energy drains and learn how to deflect them. It was hard at first because John was insistent and as soon as she set a boundary he tried to bring it down. After a few months she sat down with him and had a frank conversation about her feelings and told him that she was ready to end the marriage if he did not change. At first John was argumentative but then the truth came out about how unhappy he was with his lack of success. They agreed to work together at fixing their marriage and to learn new ways of interacting with each other so that John could focus his efforts at improving his self esteem without dragging Patty's down.

This is an example of how a relationship with an energetic vampire can be transformed but sometimes the person is not agreeable to changing their tactics and in that case, the best solution is to walk away. Until they find their own energetic resources and are willing to use them to improve their life or solve their own problems, they will go from one person to the next, getting any amount of energy in any way they can.

Learning boundaries is an important aspect of mastery because without them we easily give our energy to anyone who asks for it or we give it to whom-ever we think needs it, without considering whether it is best for them or for us. Without boundaries we are always in danger of unconsciously sharing our energy with others, not mindful of what this is costing us energetically, or how we may be interfering with someone's lessons and life path.

Consider these principles for your personal mastery journey:
Are there areas of your life in which you need stronger boundaries?

128

Are there people in your life you are unconsciously sharing energy with because you think they need it or because they ask for it and you give without considering whether you should say no, giving them an opportunity to find their power to heal themselves?

Do you believe you can build stronger boundaries with these people or is it in your best interest (and in theirs) to walk away from the relationship?

What kinds of boundaries do you need to create to keep your energy focused on your own healing path?

What kinds of boundaries do you need to create to keep others out of your energetic space unless you consciously invite them in?

When we can release ourselves from atoning for past wrongs by being the martyr or helping others heal by being their energy source and learn to be powerful by claiming our power and setting boundaries, we are ready to end our karma. With karma life flows along the path of destiny. Karma is the path of destiny, our pre-ordered life path. Without karma, life becomes a process of creation, with no pre-determined paths or outcomes. Releasing karma is possible when we are ready to end our soul contracts and all of the lessons surrounding them, establishing a new paradigm for living.

Releasing Karma

The gift that we have at this time, as a result of the many levels of energy work that we have completed and the shifts in our energetic vibrations that have occurred, is that we can end our karma. This has not been possible before because we were not ready on an individual or collective level. Ending karma means that we are ready to forgive, that we have moved beyond the victor/victim roles that we have with our soul groups, that we are out of the energy of suffering and retaliation, and no longer hold the belief that we have to atone for things we have done in the past. Releasing karma means that we are resolving the soul level promises we have with others, the commitments that have bound us to them for lifetimes. And we also end any promises we have made to ourselves, all vows and curses that we believe have power over us and that have siphoned off our power for lifetimes. We can see the errors we committed by believing we were wrong in our actions or that others were wrong in theirs and be in the energy of acceptance of everything that has occurred between us.

Releasing karma also means that we are ready to change the dynamics of our soul group, which involves allowing them to continue on their path, in whatever direction they choose to take, without judgment or criticism of their choices. We are ready to acknowledge their power and the wisdom they are applying on their journey and know that they are learning their lessons, just as we have learned and are learning ours. And sometimes this means that we end our connection with some or all of our soul group members. Once we release karma we are in a neutral energy level with them and the only energies we express are unconditional love, acceptance and detachment. We acknowledge that we are powerless over others' choices and accept that whatever they choose to do is between them and Creator.

When we are ready to end karma, the process involves three steps.

In the first step we identify the karma, a process that occurs with the activation of the birth phase of our spiritual initiation. Here we have a glimpse of how our karma is initiated, who is involved, how we have interacted with them in the past, and the situations through which our karma plays out. Do we understand our role in the karma and are we willing to take responsibility for what we have created? Unless we are ready to take responsibility for our karma, we are not ready to release it. This is a choice point where we determine whether we are ready to practice compassion and forgiveness and take a giant leap into enlightenment, or proceed through the through the challenges of our karma, which is the second step.

In the second step, we must choose whether we are going to allow the karma to repeat itself or consciously end it. If we choose to repeat it, we accept that we have additional healing work to do and the karma has more to teach us. On a soul level we agree to allow the karma to be repeated, no matter how difficult it is, because we are not ready to let it go from the ego/emotional level. This can be a hard choice to make because we may be angry and resentful, wanting the other person to suffer as we have. Or we believe we deserve to suffer and are seeking atonement through our suffering. Can we forgive the unforgivable in others and ourselves? This choice will determine whether we are going to continue to live through our karma or be open to other alternatives.

If we choose to end it, we then we are ready for the third step of the process, unconditional forgiveness. This is the true focus of our mastery journey, the bridge between the third and higher dimensions and the great healer of all of our pain. If we can forgive the members of our soul group we can end the karma we share and extend this release to the karma that is a central component of the earth's energetic field.

Pause for a moment and let's go through a karma release exercise:

For step 1, think of a karmic tie that you have with someone you have a challenging relationship with. This could be a parent, sibling or other family member, someone who has abused, mistreated or betrayed you, a former partner or lover, a difficult co-worker or employer or anyone in your life who has made you fearful or powerless.

Do you understand your role in the karma and are you willing to take responsibility for what you have created and forgive this person unconditionally, no matter what they have done to your or has happened between you?

If your reply is 'no', then you are not yet ready to release the karma. If you are ready to take responsibility for your role in this karma, let go to step 2.

In step 2 you will decide whether you want to continue in a karmic cycle with this person. There are only two answers, yes or no. If the answer is 'yes', then you are not ready to release this karma because you want to give them 'one more chance' or to see if 'this time' things will be different. Or you simply are not ready to forgive them, and that is OK.

If you are willing to take responsibility for the karma and do not want to continue in your karmic cycle, then you are ready to end the karma and to allow yourself to interact with this person in different ways, or not at all. And if you are not sure and feel inclined to respond with a 'maybe', that counts as not being ready to release the cycle. You know that you are ready to release someone when you can do so without any hesitation. If you can release and are ready to do so, you move on to step three.

Your willingness to move into step three of the karma release process indicates that you are ready to forgive this person, which also means that you will disconnect the cords that connect you to them and end the karma between you forever. Note that releasing cords is not the same as removing someone permanently from your life, although that can happen when we do release work. Releasing or disconnecting cords simply closes an energetic connection point so that connection at that level is not possible. The energy between you must shift in order to create a new, karma-free connection point.

Within every karmic cycle activation there is the possibility for release and disconnection. If we have matured enough spiritually, by incorporating more of our spiritual learning into our material existence, and through becoming a more 'spiritual human,' we will be aware of the choice to forgive and know it is our best option in this situation. While it is tempting to continue with a karmic cycle, shifting the dynamics of our relationship happens with forgiveness and release. It takes all of our spiritual insight and awareness for this release to occur but if we do the rewards are great and we have taken another step on our journey to mastery.

There are three parts to unconditional forgiveness:

First, we create an act of forgiveness in which we formally forgive the people involved and ourselves for the karma. This is best done by writing down what is being forgiven and making a forgiveness intention.

Second, we release them and ourselves from the experience. We do this through our stating our intention to release them and ourselves, forever. This is also best done in writing, in the form of a letter to ourselves or in a journal. It is very useful to conduct this as a ceremony, where the letter is read aloud and then burned. The Appendix contains a copy of a Forgiveness letter.

Third, we are prepared to set our intention for our karma-free life in the energetic void that is created when karma is released. Without this step, we can unconsciously fall back into our karmic patterns. In this third step, we must be willing to move on and to know that the forgiveness we have extended has ended the karma. We cannot re-visit it or we will have to go through the process again. Unconditional forgiveness is 'without condition', without expectation of any kind of recognition, appreciation or acceptance. We forgive because we are willing to release ourselves from the emotional burden of carrying this karma and everything associated with it. Its release allows us to move into a higher vibration and choose from other possibilities for our life.

Releasing karmic bonds and ending soul contracts completes ties to soul connections that we have known for many lifetimes and creates the   opportunity for them to leave our lives forever, within the context of our karma, as   we shift away from the energetic vibration that our karma is grounded in.   When we resonate at the vibration of our karma, we attract the people,   situations and experiences that are aligned with it. When we raise our vibration, and the desire to end karma and the willingness to forgive does this, we shift out of the range of the karma and the people who resonate at its energetic level. Now we cannot connect to the karma and it cannot connect to us, as anything associated with that energetic level is no longer within our range of vibration and we cannot experience it.

Once karma has been released, and it only takes one person to be willing to release karma, our soul group must also raise their vibrations to match ours if they wish to connect us. As vibrational levels shift it is difficult to connect with anyone or anything that is at the former level, and that can include an entire soul group. Perhaps you are the one who agreed to shift your energy so you could make the others aware of a new vibration and new possibilities. If that is the case, as you are going through the process of transformation you may be so far out of their energetic range that they do not want to speak to you and in fact, your energy may make them so uncomfortable that they go out of their way to avoid you or they may fear you and your energy so much that they are rude, unkind or mean to you. But if they choose to shift their energetic vibration so that they can align with yours, then a new connection at a new vibrational level, which allows for new and different relationship energies, is possible.

Consider these principles for your personal mastery journey:

Can you identify the karma that you are ready to release?

Do you see the connections that exist between your karma and the people in your soul group?

Are you aware of the responsibility you have in the karma you share with others?

Can you release your karma knowing that you are also releasing this connection to your soul group?

Are you ready to forgive everything around this experience, no matter what it is? Can you forgive unconditionally, without expectations of acknowledgement, acceptance or gratitude?

What are your intentions for your new life paradigm, once you have released the karma?

Releasing karma makes room for new paradigms for living as we move from karma to creation. How do we create our reality without the restrictions that karma imposes? What do we ask for when anything is possible? This will be the challenge of our new paradigm as we move from the restriction of karma to the expansion of creation. When our biggest question will be "what do I want next" and not "what is going to happen to me now?"

From Karma to Creation

What path does our life follow after we release ourselves from karma? Once we are at that point in our spiritual evolution, it is something we   must consider. We have been accustomed to living with our karma for so long that we do not know what to do when it's over. We can feel lost, without direction and even afraid to take the next step. Perhaps it is because once we have cleared karma we are afraid to do anything that will re-create it. But that is only part of the story. Our karmic memory occurs at a soul level and every memory we have is based on the healing and fulfillment of soul group contracts, which we do when we live through our karma and its pain and suffering. Our soul group members have been with us for hundreds, even thousands of lifetimes, through eons of time. Now we have to create a new path for our life that does not include karma and healing.

What happens to our soul group?

They will either find new ways of relating to us or we will replace them with a different soul group.

What do we do without karma?

We will create from our power and in the energetic flow of the moment. That is a gift of ascension, acknowledging our power and becoming co-creators and we will learn to go from karma to creation.

When we are in the energy of karma our life is ruled by destiny, it is pre-determined according to the rules of our karmic cycles and contracts. No matter what we try to do or how we try to change, until we have released the karma it will be a constant presence in our life. Karma establishes our energetic vibrations so it will govern who we meet, the nature of our interactions, what the outcome will be and how every detail of our life will play out, based on what has occurred in the past and what we have come to heal. But without karma all of that changes. The problem that we face is what to do with our new, karma-free creative abilities. And what happened to the karma, did it disappear, is it still there, waiting for us to step into it again, and how can we avoid it?

The karma we are born with is part of our core lessons so it will always be there for us to choose as a potential option. In fact, until we resolve karma there is no other path for us to take as our energetic vibrations exist at the level of our karma and attract everything that resonates at its vibration. But once we have resolved the karma and are farther up our evolutionary spiral new choices become available and rather than step blindly into karma, we are more focused on choosing the terms and conditions of our reality through conscious intention and deliberate manifestation.

Beyond karma we will find an unlimited field of options for our live as creation becomes a possibility, which moves us from a reality that is governed by our destiny, karmic history and soul group interactions into a new paradigm of choice and creation. We can now become true co-creators at the level of Source and we follow our guidance to create the reality of our dreams. Karma no longer has the same attraction for us, although it is still an option, it is one of many instead of being the only one. And it becomes an increasingly less attractive option, the more we release and shift our vibrations out of its range.

In going from karma to forgiveness, we move from destiny to creation, from victim consciousness to spiritual mastery and from limitation to limitless possibilities. But this is meaningless for us if we are unable to recognize our new responsibility in the new earth, to co-create our reality as we want it to be, allowing our heart's desires to guide our manifestation. Knowing what we want is more important than ever and we learn this by listening to our heart, which speaks to us in the language of our dreams. When we were creating from karma our heart still spoke to us but we could not hear it above the voice of our karma, its pain and need for healing and transformation. Without karma, our heart's voice is loud and clear and we are ready to listen.

This is a new paradigm for humanity, confirmation that the new earth we have waited for is finally here and its energies are expanded beyond what we have been able to know until this point because we experience everything through the filter that our karma imposes on our individual and collective reality. In this expanded energy we are aware of the concept of limitlessness, of being without limits or limitations, where everything and anything we want to create is possible.

How does this affect our material reality? How do we proceed in relationships that have been marked by strong emotion, difficult challenges, powerlessness and lack of control? Although we can end our karma, we may still be required to interact with the challenging people in our lives. While ending contracts severs our karmic bonds, the physical ties may still exist and we may be interacting with the people we have cleared karma with. How do we handle that? Forgiveness creates new and different energetic connections, setting new connection points that others are free to step into. If not, they will be as uncomfortable with us as we are with them and there will be no opportunity or need for connection. Confrontation will not be necessary as they will simply fall out of our life and have no need to connect with us on any level. To them, we will become invisible because the energy that makes connection possible will no longer exist. We can let them go, knowing that they will be replaced with people we can connect with, and who are at our energetic vibration.

The restrictions of karma, hopelessness, powerlessness and lack, do not exist in this new paradigm but are still available for those who wish to choose them, along with the potential for so much more.

What happens to those who do not choose to release their karma and move into the new dynamic of creation? They will continue to live through their karma and that is neither good nor bad. It merely means that they are not yet ready to do their healing and release work so they will be given other opportunities to do so. Their challenges will point them in the direction of forgiveness and healing which they will be able to acknowledge when they are ready to do so and they will find the teachers who can help them accomplish that learning.

The end of karma creates the need for focused intention, as without karma to direct the flow of our energy, we can be scattered, confused and unsure of where to go. Without karma we become the creator (instead of following the path of destiny) and step into our role of Creator's creator on earth. We can look to the Universe for guidance and direction, but it will respond to our intention – which is our vision for what we want in our life and the energy we are willing to put behind it. If we are confused, the Universe patiently waits for us to make up our mind. There is no energy in heaven that will tell us what to do, which would be in violation of our free will. Although the Universe will support and guide us, it will not point us in any particular direction but it may, at our request, provide strong signs and clues as to which path best matches our intention. But this new and unfamiliar path can be rather frightening, even with the promise of unlimited abundance, boundless prosperity, joy, peace and unconditional love.

Everything on earth has a mission to create according to its purpose and ours is to bring the transformative power of light and love to the third dimension and bring humanity and the planet to ascension. Our participation in this creative mission begins at birth and continues throughout our lifetimes. We agreed, with Creator, that we would be the vessel for the creative energies with the purpose of fulfilling the destiny of ascension. All we need for our mission comes to us in an endless stream of energy from higher dimensions. Creation is interrupted when we are in the vibrations of fear and karma and manipulate the flow by inserting our expectations, doubt and judgments into the creative process. Then creation takes on a 'go/no go' view because we alternatively stop and go according to our levels of fear and doubt in each situation. To keep the flow 'flowing' and ourselves aligned in co-creation we must trust and believe in our creative power and create from love and in the present moment.

Our co-creative abilities are blocked by the ego, which points out the flaws in creation because it does not understand that the flow of creative energy is limitless and expansive and that all things happen in divine order and timing. It is convinced that the energy flow is a cosmic trick, a way for Creator to control humanity. Yet the relationship between creation and humanity is the same as that between us and our material home, the earth. The earth provides what we need in an unlimited supply, including the air we breathe, and we give the earth the love and light that it needs to ascend.

When we are fulfilling our purpose as Creator's creator, we are the vessel through which energy becomes form and everything resonates with our highest good and flows in an endless stream of abundance. Anything that is not flowing effortlessly is out of balance with creation. When we focus on being the light and love in the world that we came here to be and allow the flow of creation to bless us and humanity in all ways and in all things, we are fulfilling our mission as Creator's creator.

This is the time to allow our lights to shine brightly. The Universe is unwavering in its promise of unlimited abundance, boundless joy and unconditional love and waits for us to be ready and willing to receive. Unlimited blessings are available to anyone who is willing to live an unlimited life. By learning to be still in our confusion and opening ourselves to hear the voice of our heart, we can learn what is possible and this is the Truth we have been waiting to know. It is through the heart's guidance that we are given the blueprint for the reality of our dreams. The rejection of karma and our willingness to step into creation is the fulfillment of our promise to the Universe and it has waited for us to be ready at this moment and step into creation, opening us up to a reality that unfolds with blessings and the ultimate fulfillment of our journey towards ascension.

Consider these principles for your personal mastery journey:

Are you aware of some aspects of your karma that you have already healed and released?

Can you see how this decision has affected the people in your life? Are they uncomfortable around you, avoiding you or has your choice affected your relationship with them?

Are there people who have suddenly left your life or who you can no longer communicate with?

Can you create closure and let them go gently, with unconditional love, and allow them to learn what they need to on their journey?

Is there a particular karmic lesson you are not willing or unable to release?

How can you take the path of creation with this lesson, instead of being led by the karma?

What are the major areas in your life in which you are willing to become 'Creator's creator'?

As we release our old karmic attachments they will be replaced with relationships that include souls with whom we do not have any karma, creating a different kind of relationship, one that is very new to humanity. What would it be like to have a relationship with someone you do not share karma with? That is being experienced by many at this time, and as we heal and release our karma, we will be able to enjoy these relationships on a wider scale. We are moving from having relationships with 'soul mates', who mirror our soul wounds back to us, to relationships where we have no karma, with kindred spirits.

From Soulmates to Kindred Spirits

Few things in spiritual literature receive as much hype and are as misunderstood as soulmate energy. Everyone wants to be with their soulmate, to find that special person that they believe is the only one who can complete their life and with whom they can find true and lasting happiness. Because the soulmate concept has been so romanticized we are lured into thinking that finding our soulmate will lead to spiritual wholeness and complete emotional fulfillment. What we do not realize is that soulmate energy is based on karma and the true purpose of a soulmate relationship is to help us heal, to bring us to wholeness by showing us, in ways that we cannot ignore, where our karmic wounds and needs are centered. We are then placed in situations with people who exactly mirror our soul's energetic and emotional imprint, from whom we can learn these lessons and heal our wounds, thus resolving our karma.

Experiencing karma for the purpose of healing is the sole purpose of each lifetime. We are here to shift this energy through forgiveness, to change the paradigm of karma and to raise our energetic vibrations. Soulmate connections are the best way to do this because we connect to and interact with our soulmates in such a deep, compelling way. The bonds we share were created through strong emotions, violent trauma, deep wounds and promises we have made in lifetime after lifetime. These bonds also represent our deepest fears and needs and we easily become stuck in them as we repeat karmic cycles across our many lifetimes together.

What keeps us in these karmic relationships, no matter how difficult, is the familiarity of the emotional tie and our soul contract to heal it. Everyone has met another person whom they instantly liked or disliked. 'Falling in love' is an example of what can happen when we meet a soulmate. Their energy is compelling, overpowering and irresistible. Although we often experience this as a strong physical attraction to someone, the soulmate bond transcends the physical and exists on a spiritual level through a connection that exists within the soul energy we share. This energetic connection was created in another lifetime, one that may have been traumatic and involved betrayal, unrequited love, unresolved emotional issues or some type of unfinished business. We then reincarnate together to finish or complete the karma, only to find ourselves enmeshed in exactly the same drama that we previously experienced. And so the karma continues until someone develops the understanding and spiritual awareness required for forgiveness and release.

As we progress through our mastery journey and no longer need to experience karma, we are open to connecting with a new kind of soulmate, the kindred spirit, which has no karmic attachments and no emotional drama, only peace and unconditional love. Our bond with a kindred spirit is based on our higher energetic vibrations, which are beyond fear, emotional drama or unresolved emotional issues. This type of relationship is peaceful and non-threatening and it provides everyone with an opportunity for growth and healing in an atmosphere that does not require emotional crises to bring up hidden issues, because there are none to be revealed. The question is, are we ready to engage in these types of relationships? Will we feel connected if we are not involved in emotionally charged unions?

All of the dynamics of a soulmate relationship, including the drama, the need for emotional and experiential validation, unresolved issues, are no longer the basis for our connections with a kindred spirit. Instead, we connect through our shared interests and desires, spiritual understanding, level of soul growth and desire for a fulfilling, mutually beneficial relationship based on unconditional love, which we enter into as a whole and complete being. Most importantly, kindred spirit relationships do not need healing because we are ready for them when we are already healed, or no longer seek others to validate our growth or participate in our healing.

We are ready to join our kindred spirit when we are willing to release our need to be healed or to heal others through our connections with them. Because we unconsciously offer healing to our soulmates, we attract people who need healing, who we want to heal us or who want us to heal them. This is a difficult path that rarely results in a fulfilling, balanced and loving relationship. The kindred spirit dynamic asks us to release our need or willingness to heal others and to take on a different role in relationships. If we are not the healer, what role do we play? Can we be willing to simply give and receive love?

Are we able to be with someone who loves, honors and respects us for who we are, rather than for what we do for them?

These are not easy questions because participating in someone's healing gives us validation and purpose. If we feel accomplished and powerful as healers in relationships, we will need to find other avenues to satisfy those needs when our partners do not need our healing abilities. Being part of someone's healing is a powerful experience and if we need this experience to feel powerful, then no matter how wonderful our kindred spirit is, we may feel dissatisfied with them. In fact, in the face of their calm, balanced, peaceful energy, we may even find them a little boring.

We are ready for this new relationship dynamic when we resolve our karma and are ready to know what life is like with a partner who is willing to love us for who we are, appreciate our gifts, support us with kindness, consideration and unconditional love and to mirror our wholeness and healing instead of our pain. Are you ready for your kindred spirit?

Consider these principles for your personal mastery journey:

Are you looking for a soulmate, someone you believe will complete your life, validate you and be your partner?

What areas of healing do you need and how will your soulmate help you resolve them?

Have your relationships been challenging, with strong emotions and unresolved emotions?

Do you act as the healer in your relationships or have you attracted partners who you expect healing from?

Are you ready for a kindred spirit, someone who is already healed and ready to be in a fulfilling, drama free relationship with you?

What is your role in a relationship when you are not the healer?

Can you be in a relationship with someone who does not need your healing and is your energetic equal?

Are you prepared for a relationship that is not defined by drama or chaos but that is loving and fun?

Describe your kindred spirit, detailing the kind of relationship you desire to have with them, the things you will share besides the need to heal or be healed and the things you would like to do that you have perhaps never been able to do within a relationship. Kindred spirits can include friends, family, or romantic partners and are not limited to your most intimate relationships.

As we release our karma we also release its underlying energy of fear. Fear is a destructive energy that lowers our energetic vibrations, makes us doubt ourselves and our abilities, blocks our progress and prevents us from achieving our mastery. The story of our fear is long, complex and complicated. It has its beginnings in our initial separation from Source and has been the driving force of our many incarnations. As we step into our power we are able to face our fears and to understand their purpose and meaning. Releasing fear is required to resolve karma and be in the flow of unconditional love. But the reward for us, if we choose unconditional love over fear, is the ability to create a life and world that responds to our desire for peace, joy, abundance and unconditional love.

The Paradigm of Fear

Our karma tells the story of our fear, which arises from the point where we have disconnected ourselves from Source. Resolving our fear is the purpose of our journey through the material world, in response to our spiritual mandate of ascension. And in spite of all we believe about its complexity and importance, it is simply a journey of reconnection. Each level of spiritual understanding we achieve reflects a level of healing we have accomplished. So why is this journey so difficult? Our fear imprints are very strong and are carried over from lifetime to lifetime. They exist on both individual and collective levels and are imprinted in our emotional DNA. These imprints are the result of our unresolved emotional energy from previous lifetimes that can be described as an energetic scar which we carry in our emotional body. Every lifetime in which we try to heal ourselves or others through domination, manipulation, or other ego-centered behaviors creates another fear imprint. Each of these scars resonates with a fear so profound that they create more fear until we learn to dissolve them by finding our inner source of love.

Because they touch us at our deepest level and represent those areas where we feel we have committed our most grievous sins, or where others have sinned against us, our fears can feel overpowering until we understand the story they are trying to reveal and bring it to light. And because we try to heal our soul wounds with someone who is just as or more wounded than we are, we arrive at the conclusion that we will never be worthy of reconnection, never have the life we want, or never find joy. So we continue to live through our karmic cycles and our life never changes. Our fears, in all of their manifestations, will play out in every aspect of our life and determine the course of our life path until we are willing to face them and learn to allow our fears to transform into love.

The story of our fear is a long, traumatic and challenging one that can involve many situations such as, betrayal, distrust, lack of faith, powerlessness, being undeserving, abuse, hopelessness and rejection, and abandonment. It plays out lifetime after lifetime because we seek redemption through our karma and reconnection through atonement instead of release with forgiveness and unconditional love. And we have help from our soul group who will give us many opportunities to play out the story of our fear so that we can bring our soul's energy back into balance. Every place in our energetic imprints where fear resides is a place of imbalance with our divinity and a disconnection from our power and inner light.

For example, being rejected or abandoned by a loved one in one lifetime, especially at a time when this rejection meant death or starvation, or abandonment led to an early or painful death, results in a fear of any situation where this could happen again. Instead of creating proof that we are powerful, worthy of love and acceptance, we re-create abandonment and rejection situations in each lifetime, hoping that the person will not abandon or reject us and will validate us, our power and our desire to be loved.

So we will be born into a family that is cold and unloving, choose partners who reject us, or friends who betray us. We will create situations where we destroy the good in our life and have to pick up the pieces so we can find our power, shift our beliefs and create a strong sense of value from within to remember how loved, powerful, deserving and blessed we are.

At the core of this fear is the belief that nothing we do will ever be good enough to redeem ourselves in the eyes of God and we will be permanently separated from our spiritual Home. After all, if God loves us so much, why doesn't she rescue us, give us undeniable proof that we are loved and release us from our pain, or compel others to do so on her behalf? Each disappointment and rejection further reinforces the belief that we have done something so grievously wrong and terrible that even God will not forgive us. We are afraid that we will be deemed unworthy of unconditional love, will never be able to prove our worthiness and will then be condemned, alone, unloved and unwanted by our Creator. Each experience of rejection and betrayal serves to remind us of our unworthiness until we learn that we cannot heal fear with more fear.

In our roles as healers and light bearers we were often persecuted and misunderstood and this created some of the fear that we carry in our cellular bodies and emotional DNA. We take on the responsibility of healing humanity and approach it through our fear instead of love, by trying to overcome our weaknesses through pain instead of asserting our power to love. In our role of teacher we also assume the responsibility for the results we want to achieve and through our fear, view every doubt, criticism and judgment of others as justification of our fears. We then create judgments about ourselves based on the feedback we receive from others and are afraid to expand our consciousness farther, fearing that we will stand before our Creator expecting love and acceptance and instead, we will be rejected.

So we imagine God's judgment of us and accept it as truth, creating even more fear. After all, if the people in our life reject us, that makes us unworthy. In order to accept the truth of God's unconditional love and acceptance we must move beyond our self judgment. The fear of failure and of God's judgment represents our fear of being forever disconnected, unwanted and unable to return to our spiritual Home. Each experience of separation that we create serves to remind the ego of how much we are separated. This cycle repeats itself so we can resolve our fears but it usually serves to reinforce them.

Our early experience with an abusive, critical or dysfunctional family, a painful or humiliating incident, an attempt at healing someone that did not meet our expectations, or trying to meet someone else's expectations and failing to do so can set us up with a fear of failure that is nothing more than a re-creation of an expression of our fear so we can resolve it. Each of these situations shares a common thread involving our efforts at completing our reconnection which will always fail in this case because we try to use our outer world to resolve our inner conflict. We look for love, acceptance and validation from experiences we have deliberately created to give us the opposite result -- rejection, unworthiness and betrayal. Where can we find the love that will allow us to overcome our fear of failure? Is there proof that we are worthy of reconnection?

Within each lifetime, beginning with our birth, we look for proof that we are worthy of love and are often reminded, again and again, that the world has no love for us. With that belief we enter adulthood convinced that our fears are justified. And we are bombarded with the memory of everything that did not work out, where we failed, were humiliated or criticized, devalued and made to feel unworthy or worthless. And because we approach everything from our fear of failure, we create a self fulfilling prophecy and attracts situations in which we will fail. Instead of feeling confident and grounded, we are scared and confused, unsure of what to do or how to fulfill our desire for success, which is really a desire for love and acceptance.

This is shown in Mark's story:

Mark was a sensitive, loving child who learned to fear his critical, abusive father. Mark never knew when the next beating or cruel remark would come. Every day Mark hoped his father would say something nice to him and every day he was disappointed. He entered adulthood starved for love and attention, believing that nothing he ever did was good enough and afraid that he would never find love and acceptance. Although he was a talented and intelligent young man, Mark was unable to find and keep a job, had no romantic life, few friends and so many disappointments that he spiraled into a cycle of failure until he was ready to end his life. Believing himself to be incapable of success and with no vision for his future, Mark had given up and in his words, had become a "the failure his father always told him he would be." Unfortunately, his father had died several years before, without ever giving Mark the love and approval he wanted so he also felt he could never have closure on this issue.

During our coaching sessions Mark began to understand that his father saw himself as a failure and how the cruelty and beatings reflected his father's judgments of his own unworthiness and negative attitude towards life, that had begun in his childhood with the abuse and criticism he received from his own father. Mark's anger and resentment turned into compassion and he realized that his father had simply been passing on the fears and cycles of abuse and unworthiness that had been handed to him. While his father had not been able change it, Mark could do something different and break the cycle of fear, abuse, and judgment that had been the energy in his family for many years. With that knowledge Mark was able to see his life beyond his fear, understand how his beliefs were creating his life and work on changing them so he could learn to be more powerful, create a more fulfilling life and be happy.

When we have been criticized, abused or treated badly by others, we believe that this is what we deserve and we unconsciously carry that energy into everything we do. Our failure is assured because we set ourselves up to fail, since we cannot envision a different outcome. And this brings up an interesting point about our fears and the fear of failure. We fear failure but we do not create the elements necessary for success. We run away from the limitations of our fear but are not moving towards the expansive energy of love. When our success is defined by how much approval and validation we receive from others, we have set ourselves up for failure. Through the Law of Attraction, we are attracting people who will not give these things to us, because they do not have them to give, as we cannot ask others to give us what we do not believe we have.

Our starting point in our commitment to live beyond fear must be our belief in our own worthiness, no matter what our life looks like. Freedom from fear begins with an inner focus on our brilliant core of love. Our goals must be free of expectations, limitations, not dependent on others' actions, opinions or choices and should be relevant and important to us. This is a quantum leap in our thinking and it has profound implications – we must learn to be good enough for ourselves, to release our fear of failure and replace it with a vision of success and most importantly, connect with the unlimited wellspring of love and   acceptance that is within each of us.

Consider these principles for your personal mastery journey:

Think of something you have done that you believe is a failure. Now ask yourself these questions:

What kinds of fears do you have around this issue? Are you afraid of judgment, of not being loved or accepted, or not being good enough?

Is there someone in your life who has been a source of criticism, judgment or abuse? Do your fears reflect their attitude towards you?

What was your reaction to any judgment or criticism you received from the person you thought of in the previous question when they first began to criticize you and is that reaction different today?

Do you define success by what it means to you or have you created a definition of what it means to be successful in order to gain someone's approval?

Is your success dependent on anyone's opinion or input in any way?

Were you goals realistic, based on your knowledge, experience, skills and spiritual understanding at that time or did they reflect what you thought someone else wanted or expected?

Were you doing this because you wanted to, someone else wanted you to do it or you wanted to impress someone?

Was success in that situation really possible?

Can you find the blessings in your failure, what did you learn and how has that changed you?

And finally, was this experience really a failure, was it a lesson you needed to learn or the Universe's way of protecting you from something you needed to avoid?

Sometimes what we call a failure is actually a success. Consider Mary's story:

Mary was in love with Ron, who she thought was the answer to her prayers. Tall, handsome, smart and successful, he was everything she had hoped to find in a partner. And since she had been waiting for someone to come into her life for a long time, Mary thought Ron was her special gift from Heaven. Yes, he was a little controlling, sometimes he was mean and could make cruel remarks, but she was willing to overlook those things. When he proposed marriage, she immediately accepted. A few months before their wedding date Mary found out that Ron was having an affair. Devastated, she called off the wedding. For two years she grieved and stayed away from relationships, convinced that she was unlucky in love and would never find a man to replace Ron.

Then one day she happened to see a friend who also knew Ron. When the wedding was mentioned, Mary began to cry and talked of how sad she was that Ron was no longer in her life. The friend laughed and said it was actually a blessing in disguise because Ron had married the woman he had the affair with and had been arrested for spousal abuse after badly beating his wife. Mary realized that her failure was a form of divine intervention   and that she had been protected from Ron. She also realized that she needed to stop grieving, move on and start looking for a new relationship.

Before labeling our efforts a failure, if we review what we have learned, we can realize that our failure contains the blessings of success. Was it a situation that could have potentially been more difficult for us and our failure was actually a blessing in disguise? Did we learn that our relationship or that situation was out of balance and integrity? Were we trying to change someone so we could feel better about ourselves? What were we willing to overlook out of fear of being alone, unwanted and unloved? What kind of expectations did we have for this experience and were they reasonable? What fears were behind our efforts?

Nothing we do is a failure, as everything is a reflection of our energetic vibration and beliefs at that moment. There is a blessing in everything if we will look more closely at what we wanted or hoped to achieve, what we learned and how we benefited from the experience.

Consider these principles for your personal mastery journey:

When you think you have failed, do you punish yourself by thinking you could have acted differently?

Do you hope that someone will rescue you from your failures?

Are any of your actions done with the objective of healing or changing someone else?

Are you being realistic about yourself and others, your abilities, commitment to healing and level of spiritual understanding (especially of those you are trying to heal)?

Do you need validation from others to feel successful?

Do you quickly label your efforts a failure too quickly, before looking at them more deeply and looking for the blessings?

Can you find a blessing in each of your failures and see where you created what you wanted at that time and are now ready for something different?

Learning to identify the cycles of energy in our life is helpful in understanding how outcomes are created, depending on the vibration we are experiencing and how our lessons are presented to us. There are cycles of expansion, which are times when we embrace learning, followed by cycles of contraction, a pause in our forward movement during which we either process what we have learned and use the information on the next step of our journey or we go into doubt and fear, thinking that the pause means that the flow of energy has stopped and we are alone.

Fear is always our first response when the ego, which requires constant motion, stimulation, and results, dominates our thinking. But the moments of contraction are opportunities for us to assess how far we have come and to consider different options. Pausing to integrate our learning opens us to new possibilities, which we are not aware of when the ego is relentlessly pushing us forward into what appears to be new territory, but which actually mirrors what we have already done because our learning has not been integrated into our thinking. All of our energetic shifts occur first in our spiritual body and then trickle down to the ego. So by the time we are aware of the need to move beyond a fear, to transform an area of our life, we have the spiritual tools to accomplish this, we just need to convince the ego that it is possible.

Consider these principles for your personal mastery journey:

Can you name some of your deepest fears?

Do you see those fears repeated in your soul group, which includes your family, friends and other people you know?

Do you see how your fears separate you from your divinity and your power?

Do you recognize the cycles of expansion and contraction in your life?

What do you do in the contraction cycle? Do you worry and wonder whether you have done something wrong or integrate your learning?

Are you willing to live in your power so you can stop being afraid?

Within our journey of mastery, we must be willing to address and release our fears because they an expression of our separation from Source. These fears began with us, not with God. We assume our rejection and if we go to our inner light, we find that there is a spark of unconditional love and acceptance, of belonging and connection that has always been available to us when we could believe ourselves worthy of connecting with and   accepting it. Our willingness to be on this journey is an invitation to the revelation, expression and transformation of our fears. And they have one more thing to teach us, as our fears show where we are engaged in the energy of polarity, the struggle between light and dark that is central to earth's energetic vibrations and our ascension cycles.

The Lessons of Polarity

Polarity is the energy of the third dimension which we experience as dark and light, and then translate these aspects into judgments of good and bad, better and worse, richer and poorer, all of which are examples of polarity. We have lived this way for generations of lifetimes and eons of time and there is nothing wrong with polarity, as it is the core lesson the earth energy and the third dimension. Integrating polarity with the flow of divine energy is our life purpose. We have had to experience the full scope of polarity, both dark and light, in order to choose to either ascend into a higher vibration where there is no polarity or continue the journey of polarity. Each person will make that choice, according to their individual path and level of spiritual growth and understanding.

While we call the energies of polarity light and dark, they include the full spectrum of energies from the absence of dark, which is the pure light of unconditional love, to the absence of light, or the darkness of fear that is totally devoid of unconditional love. Most of us lie somewhere along the middle of this spectrum, somewhere between the light and dark, occasionally going too far into the dark and then making our way back into the light. We fear the light because we believe that through the many times we have fallen short of what we believe are God's expectations of us we do not deserve to be in it, so we stay closer to or in the dark.

The dark is a reminder of our failures, mistakes, indecision, poor choices and how we believe we have failed in our mission to go back to the light, back Home, back to our Source. But we have not failed at all as experiencing the darkness and bringing the light to it was our original mission. This was the divine plan of leaving the light so we could reconnect, to go as far into the darkness as necessary to understand and transform it.

This is why Lightworkers have gathered at this time, to help in the process of ending polarity, to release humanity from the magnetic pull of the dark and allow them to fearlessly see the light. This is done by the shifts we are making to the earth's energetic core, to the vortex of light that surrounds the earth, and opening the doorways to higher vibrations which we have done through our willingness to transmute energies and be an example of the light. Polarity's time is coming to an end because both we and the Earth are ascending into higher dimensions of being, accessing levels of energetic vibration that do not allow the presence of polarity's lower energies, which are based in fear.

So what do we do now and what does the end of polarity mean? More than we think because polarity, as the energy of the third dimension, exists in everything. So by ending polarity we end karma, judgment, fear and separation. And we bring them all together through connection, which is polarity's opposite.

Each step we make on our mastery journey takes us farther from polarity and towards connection. The end of polarity is the end of fear and its many forms and how they manifest on the earth. It is the beginning of oneness and unconditional love, expressed in the form of acceptance of all and recognition of our shared spiritual heritage and divinity. While we look forward to this change, the end of polarity has profound implications for how we think, speak, act and live.

The end of polarity is the end of separation and we are able to reconnect to Source on levels we have never experienced before.

It is the end of living through hope and taking responsibility for our creations, connection, manifestation and transformation.

It is the end of judgment, criticism and comparison and being aware of the importance of each individual's path as part of the collective journey.

It is the end of powerlessness which we experience when we move away from the light and the opportunity to be fully in our power. All of these things are possible if we choose them by allowing polarity to end and to remember that we are all One. What a wonderful opportunity for all of humanity to finally be able to recognize the divinity in all.

The end of polarity releases us from the victim paradigm that we have lived under for eons of humanity's experience on earth. Where we once felt we did not have choices, others 'made' us do things, we were 'forced' into ways of being or we lacked control, we now have the opportunity to reverse that thinking and enforce our spiritual birthright of joy, peace and unconditional love. As we know, when we transform our way of being we disconnect with any energies that are not on that level and open the potential for new energetic connections. We have a choice to do this and to respect each person's choice for their path. With the end of polarity we recognize the power in all and honor others' choices. We understand that we cannot be forced to do anything—and we cannot force others to do anything as well.

The end of polarity transforms the focus of the world and humanity. There are many examples of how polarity exists in the world. We describe others as richer or poorer than we are, better or worse off, with more or fewer gifts and attributes. We applaud the person who runs the fastest race and pity the loser. We celebrate the rich and famous and wish to be like them. Without polarity these judgments are without value. We recognize the inherent divinity in all and know that each person contributes their   part to the whole and each part is important. No person's contribution is greater or less than that of any other.

More importantly, without polarity our focus is on our connection instead of our differences and we see ourselves through our divinity rather than our humanity. This is a big step for us because nearly everything we think and do reflects an aspect of polarity. Are we ready to relinquish our need for heroes and role models, which exist within polarity, and celebrate our uniqueness as heroic individuals?

The end of polarity is also the end of karma, karmic cycles and soul contracts as these energies have run their course in our lives. Polarity defines these emotional interchanges as the way in which we seek revenge or   atonement for the harm others do to us or that we have done to them through our passages through the darkest of our fears. Without polarity there is no reason for karma because there is no energy to keep the karma in motion. This means that we stop living according to the belief in a forced destiny that is out of our control and begin manifesting through creation and the limitless and unlimited freedom of choice.

It is also the end of the belief that our lives are in God's control, where we take "Thy will be done" literally and believe that our Creator is also our task master. Now we are co-creators, accepting our power to create our reality in accordance with the partnership between human and divine, within us and between us and Creator.

The end of polarity is the beginning of living through unconditional love, where we are without judgment of ourselves and of others. But unconditional love begins in our own life and we must decide whether we are going to continue our love/hate relationship with ourselves, which is where we do the most damage. How can we accept the divinity and perfection of all if we do not believe that of ourselves? Since our outer reality is a mirror of what we think and believe about ourselves, any lack of love we experience is ours to heal from within because it is also what we are projecting onto the mirror of the world.

The end of polarity brings to a close the darkest energies that we have experienced in our history, war, genocide, discrimination and persecution of others because of race, gender, culture and national origin. Without polarity we recognize that we are the 'other' and they are us. Can we be the light we wish to see in the world and lead by our example and spiritual practice? We must if we are to participate in our mass exodus from polarity into connection.

Our ability to accept the end of polarity will determine the next step on our individual and collective path. As we become more connected our willingness to live within the dimension of unconditional love, where we practice our spiritual knowledge that allows us to step into the higher vibration of spiritual mastery and miraculous living, is the new reality.

It is a profound transformation that invites us to acknowledge our own divinity and learn to appreciate ourselves within our own magnificence. It is a new spiritual practice for all of us, one that requires us to "walk our talk" as divine humans. Our willingness to create the end of polarity, because we have created the space for this energy, is what will allow it to manifest and grow into the new consciousness, a new way of being for humanity. It is our graduation into new dimensions of being and proof that we re-member who we are and are now ready to be at Home on earth because the end of polarity is the beginning of heaven on earth.

Consider these principles for your personal mastery journey:
Can you see where polarity exists in your life?
Within your life, can you see where you step into the darkness of your fears and how you can shed light on them?

Do you see how polarity, your separation from Source, works in your life, how it affects your choices, what you believe is possible for you and how you may engage in self sabotage?

Are there areas in your life where you can raise your vibrations, by changing your thoughts and beliefs, to step out of polarity and bring yourself closer to connection and into higher dimensions?

We may be grateful to see the end of polarity if it means the end of separation, from ourselves and from Source, but with the end of polarity we step fully into our power. Now we understand and accept that we are in control of our lives, we are co-creators of our reality and the world. And with that power comes the responsibility for what happens on earth and for changing whatever is out of integrity with our divinity. We cannot wait for something or someone to rescue us, there is no hope for a better day other than the one we decide to create. We are the hope we have been waiting for, the one we are looking for who will have the courage to "do something" to change the world and unless we act, nothing happens. It is an expression of our power to accept responsibility for every situation that exists in the world today as well as the responsibility to change it. How can we acknowledge our power to change the world if we cannot also accept our role in creating the status quo?

Here we can replace hope, the belief that somehow things will be better, with unwavering certainty, knowing that we are in control of the unfolding reality of our life. When we are in the state of hopefulness we are sure that things will get better as soon as we get a lucky break, a second chance or a miracle. We wait for someone else to guide us, to tell us what to do next and transform the impossible into something we can live with. We hope that God hears our prayers because we are not always sure that God is available and listening. In the state of hope we forget that we are the most powerful person in our life. Hoping for the best is another way of saying that we are not powerful, wise, strong, knowing or able to create the life we want to live.

Stepping out of hope and into certainty is a little like riding a bicycle for the first time. It is awkward and scary and we fall a few times until we become familiar with the motion and balance it requires. But once we do, we never forget how to ride a bicycle. And once we move beyond hope and step into our power, our bicycle turns into a high performance race car. Acknowledging our power, our control over our individual and collective realities and knowing that we can live a life of dynamic, abundant and powerful creation is our reward. But then we can no longer blame anyone else for our situation and recognize that if there is a change to be made, it is up to us. Hope is replaced with trust and certainty, a peaceful, calm knowing that everything is in divine order and that we are the creator.

Each step on our spiritual journey takes us closer to our spiritual home, where we remember being powerful, at peace and loved. But our spiritual home is not a destination because it exists within us and we are always connected to it. We cannot hope our way into this understanding, it is a spiritual truth that we must accept and trust. If there is no hope then we must be powerful because there are no other alternatives available to us for our collective salvation. And this is where we connect to our spiritual mastery, our source of power and our willingness to be in control of creating the reality we live in. We can abandon hope because there are greater, more fulfilling possibilities available to us that will move us closer to heaven on earth, in our reality and for all of humanity.

Consider these principles for your personal mastery journey:

Can you name something you 'hope' will happen in your life?

Do you feel powerless about this situation?

Can you see that you have the power to control it and every other aspect of your life?

Is it possible for you to replace hope with trust and faith and then take action?

Action is required in place of hope but while we may be inspired to take action, our inspiration can be overshadowed by doubt.

Name one or two powerful things you can do to replace hope with action.

What kind of action will you take?

Will it be the right action?

Will you accomplish what you desire?

Have you set your intention for what you want your action to manifest in your life?

What does the action lead to and what happens next?

What will others think of your actions?

Will they agree with you?

What if they don't?

Do you believe that you are good, smart, capable and strong enough to do this?

How do you know?

What if you aren't?

Do you recognize these questions? Have you asked them of yourself? Nothing is wrong with them and they represent the way millions of people think but they are judgments and they are so much a part of our daily life that we do not even notice them. Judgments have two effects in our lives:

they create separation from Source and our unlimited potential, and

they limit the flow of energy and possibilities because through the filter of our judgments we see ourselves and every situation as imperfect, damaged and limited.

And we prevent ourselves from taking action because every choice arises from a desire to avoid making a mistake and as we worry, wonder, doubt, consider and re-consider, we do nothing. Then we say we're stuck but we are really in the throes of judgment. Can we learn to live without judgment of ourselves and others?

We can if we are willing to understand how much judgment is a part of our daily life, how it affects us, our thoughts and actions and then transform our thinking. Judgments are the simply the opinions we have about people, situations and issues which reflect the fear aspect of polarity. They create separation, through their implication that one thing is better than another. No matter how we make a judgment, whether it is positive, "this is the best thing that could happen", or negative, "this is the worst thing that could happen", we are creating polarity. A situation could indeed be wonderful, but it may be preparing us for something even better and by judging it in any way we are limiting ourselves from experiencing the next thing. Being in judgment limits our reality to a specific set of circumstances, conditions or situations. Once a judgment is created, our reality is defined by its terms and we cut ourselves off from the flow of energy that could bring new and different opportunities to us.

We judge ourselves very harshly, expecting perfection without the benefit of the underlying belief in our perfection. We judge every thought and word, action and step with impatience and criticism, believing that if we were perfect and connected, our lives would be different. But combining action with judgment is like putting faith and doubt together. They cancel each other out and we are standing still, unsure of what to do next.

And we have judgments about other people. We judge them by the color of their skin, their gender, their hair or eye color, where they went to college, the kind of job they have, their financial status, are they divorced, single or married, their accomplishments or lack thereof, their friends, their parents and family, where they live, work and more. This may be how we describe people yet each of those descriptions carries a judgment and that is where we tread into the territory of polarity.

Our judgments create the limitations that separate us from others and shed light on our fears. If we had no fears, there would be no judgments. We feel differently about someone who went to Harvard than someone who went to a junior college — how does this correspond to our fears about our self worth and how others value us? A doctor engenders more respect and consideration than a construction worker – do we fear that others will not take us seriously based on our status? In some areas, judgments are based on gender, skin color, age, religion or ethnicity. Wars, genocide and terrible suffering happen through judgments that one religion, culture, skin color or belief system is superior or inferior to another. What is it about them that we believe we should be afraid of?

This is where we separate ourselves from others and categorize them according to who we think they are based on the judgments that arise from our fears. Our mind automatically decides how we will respond to them before we have an opportunity to actually know the person, through an opinion that is generally based on where we see ourselves based on what we think they are (and how much we are threatened by that). Once a judgment is made, we have categorized that person as acceptable or unacceptable, as someone we want to know or not, based on a pre-conceived opinion that extends from our fears and beliefs. This extends to life situations and choices, as our judgments decide what we will seek out or reject, and these decisions are final, limiting our reality to the confines created by our judgments. Through them we assume the value, worth and potential of everything and everyone and they can limit our accomplishments, in unsuspecting ways, as one client discovered.

Roger was born into a wealthy family but when he was seven years old, his family lost everything in a bad financial deal made with a wealthy but dishonest family friend. The family was angry and bitter, blaming their misfortune on the "dishonest rich man" who stole the family's money. As an adult, Roger was successful in business but financially unstable because although he earned a great deal of money, it always seemed to slip through his fingers and he lived from paycheck to paycheck.

During a coaching session he referred to a news story about the arrest of a wealthy man and said that he deserved the arrest as his wealth probably came from cheating people out of their money. His judgments about wealth and money and their potential link to dishonesty created limitations that prevented him from enjoying the abundance he created in his life. Understanding his judgments about wealth helped him make peace with this aspect of his life and enabled him to enjoy greater and more lasting abundance.

Every situation that we are presented with passes through the filter of our judgments before we have an opportunity to consider a different option. Since our judgments are based on fear, they limit us in every way because with them we are on the fear or dark side of polarity. When we release judgment we go into the higher energies of detachment, acceptance, tolerance and connection. Within these higher energies we cannot have polarity because the higher energies remind us that we are connected, worthy, valuable, we are all one and we are all the same.

The end of judgment begins with our willingness to release ourselves from our own judgments, removing those beliefs that limit us and keep us in polarity and outside the flow of abundance in all things that resonate with our highest potential. As with all spiritual practices, we must start with ourselves, with acceptance and tolerance for who we are and remember that we are connected to our Source, as is everyone else. Can we release the polarity in our lives by releasing judgment and allow ourselves to reconnect to our divinity and perfection? And then extrapolate that to everyone in the world?

In a world that is infinitely and completely connected, there can be no judgment. In this place of connection we are reminded that our own path is limitless and abundant with possibilities. Whatever we want can be ours when we refrain from judging who we are, based on what we have done and where our path has already taken us, as well as judging those who have what we want (and envy is a form of judgment). This shifts our thinking from the past to the present, to focus on our dreams and vision for our own life.

On the level of humanity, releasing judgment removes every energy that creates discord and chaos and allows us to be in the space of connection, recognizing our inner perfection rather than our outer imperfection and differences, remembering our connection instead of creating reasons to be separated.

Consider these principles for your personal mastery journey:

Name a few areas in your life where you have judgments, either of others or of yourself.

Which of those judgments are yours and which of them were passed on to you through family or friends?

Do you see how those judgments create your opinions and beliefs of yourself, of others and of life and its possibilities?

Can you see where your judgments of yourself and others are limiting your life?

Do you feel less than, unworthy or undeserving in any area of your life because of your judgments?

Do you have judgments you would like to release and replace with acceptance?

The discussion of polarity has to include the issue of abandonment, which is central to our core issue of disconnection. This ancient belief began with the thought that we were abandoned by God in our path of separation, left alone to fend for ourselves, without spiritual support and guidance. Each lifetime is a re-creation of our belief in our spiritual abandonment experience in an attempt to heal and release it. This experience manifests in our relationships with others, where we could have people in our life who do not meet their commitments to us, or we were physically or emotionally abandoned by a parent early in life. We may experience abandonment as chronic illness, being alone or disconnected from those we love or want to be with.

Our abandonment story begins in each lifetime, with our physical birth, when we are removed from the safety of the womb, the umbilical cord is cut, separating us from the safety and protection of the mother and we are on our own. This is a mirror of our soul's birth in each lifetime, as leaves its spiritual home and comes to the Earth for another attempt at reconnection, a return to our spiritual roots. But from the ego's perspective, we have been abandoned by God and left here to struggle, alone and unprotected, cast into the darkness without the support of the light.

Despite this belief, the reality is that we volunteered for this journey and it is our sacred contract with Creator to help shift the earth's energy from polarity to love, from separation to connection. We do this in our lifetime as we continue with our search for our spiritual center that will take us Home. And this story is repeated throughout our lifetime because when we accept the abandonment belief we also accept polarity and then resign ourselves to thinking that we are not worthy of love and protection, we have done something terrible that will prevent us from ever re-connecting with our Source.

We seek to revive that relationship through our emotions, looking for others who will love and value us, show us that we are worthy of love and reunite us with our memory of unconditional love. But because we feel abandoned by our Source of love, we create polarity within our emotional relationships and they mirror our expectation of abandonment to us, rather than giving us the connection we are looking for. Until we resolve our abandonment issues within ourselves every aspect of our life will reflect our abandonment experience and the fears we have around it.

But the end of polarity removes our beliefs and fears of abandonment because without polarity we have no choice but to remember that we are connected to Source and to each other. This allow us to re-member, to rejoin as a collective family of humanity according to our divine blueprint, re-align ourselves with our divine nature, re-lease ourselves from ancient wounds and re-store ourselves to spiritual wholeness.

With the end of polarity we have an opportunity to remember unconditional love, to find it within ourselves and to reunite with our Source. Our ascension journey and the re-awakening of our inner remembrance that God could never and has not ever abandoned us leads us to the peace we seek and the release of polarity. Like the Bible's prodigal son, we abandon our home, seek our own path and then realize that every journey takes us back home again. With the end of polarity we find our way home and remember that we are the love we have been seeking and reclaim the mastery that has always been ours.

This is an inner healing journey and going within is the only way it can be accomplished. Once we find that love within ourselves, we will never feel abandoned again because we will have an inner core of love that will radiate out to the rest of our reality, attracting the fulfilling relationships, friends, partnerships and dreams that will remind us that with connection we know that we are loved beyond measure, protected from harm and can bask in the peace that comes from knowing that our Source is always with us.

Consider these principles for your personal mastery journey:

Do you feel that someone in your life has abandoned you?

Do you have a story about being abandoned by your parents, family, friends or people whom you trusted and depended on?

Do you feel alone, without support and without a strong spiritual guidance system?

How is your belief about abandonment reflected in your relationships and in other areas of your life?

Do you see how you can reconnect and find peace within yourself, comforted in knowing that you are never alone?

And so we come full circle in our journey from separation to integration, from total focus on the material to re-integration of the spiritual. With polarity we are out of the flow of co-creation, the energy that manifests from the point of unlimited possibilities and the miracle vibration. Choosing connection over polarity places us in the flow of Universal energy and out of the flow of karma. Any aspect of our life that is out of the vibration of joy and unconditional love indicates where we have chosen polarity and is transformed through the choice of connection. Every moment holds this choice and we unconsciously decide the path we take with each step on our journey. While we choose pain as our path to healing, the easier way is through connection, without experiencing the imbalance of polarity.

There is no divine mandate that says we have to suffer; instead, there is a divine mandate that says that we can enjoy life, appreciate the beauty of our earthly home and learn from joy instead of from pain. But each of us makes that choice from within and we must each use our free will to determine which choice we will make, depending on how we can heal our own polarity.

The only way to do this is by living through the light within. Each of us is an aspect of the Creator, a spark of divine consciousness that together creates the entire experience of God on earth. We have chosen polarity as our illusion of separation and now it is time for us to go Home, to remember that Creator spark within, reconnect with it and to make it the focus of our life.

As a human family we are ready for this moment, as we have had every possible experience of polarity and all of the pain associated with it. Every choice has unlimited options, those that we see and others that enter our consciousness when we set our focus on alternatives beyond the limitations of the polarity of our energetic vibration. At that moment we are aware of a vast array of possibilities for our path and we can choose the most joyful, peaceful and miraculous ones that will bring heaven on earth into our lives, releasing us from the vibration of polarity into reconnection and unconditional love. Each time one of us does this all of humanity benefits from the higher vibrations we create and the energy of polarity decreases exponentially. Releasing polarity is how we will create the higher vibrations that allow ascension to occur, move us into our spiritual mastery and bring heaven on earth.

Consider these principles for your personal mastery journey:

Can you name a few aspects of your life that exist in polarity, such as how you love, appreciate and value yourself?

Do you regret past decisions, think you made mistakes, and are you angry with yourself for choices you have made?

Do you feel like you are on an emotional roller coaster and your life is out of control? Can you identify where polarity exists in these situations? Are you willing to release it?

Can you see how every aspect of your thinking that is in conflict with your divinity and perfection is where polarity exists in your life?

Can you commit to releasing the polarity in your life? Can you begin with one aspect of your life you wish to change and focus on releasing its polarity by releasing all judgments, negative thinking, blame and regret around it?

We are at a crossroads in humanity's evolution, an opportunity for us to choose whether to live in polarity or step into a new dimension of being. Polarity, as we know it, represents the expression of the darker or lower vibrations of the Earth's energies. It is the either/or, better/worse or have/have not mentality that defines the third dimension. Each of those energies, when used in their lowest aspects, creates discord and represents areas where we are disconnected. But they also have a higher vibration that we can connect to as we raise our own vibrations. With each increase in our energetic vibration we are open to an energy's higher octave. We move from resentment to forgiveness, which is how we resolve our karma and leave the confines of third dimensional living.

We move from chaos and drama to peace, choosing to learn through joy instead of pain.

We move from fear to love, completing the reconnection cycle and taking us back to the energy of Home. And from the point of connection we are in the flow of transformation, ascension and miraculous living.

Transformation is the result of a shift in our energetic vibration, allowing new aspects of our field of potential to become our truth. Once we move out of the lower vibration of polarity we begin to recognize the potential for energetic transformation. Within higher vibrations we can live through the first Universal Law, the Law of Divine Oneness, where we recognize our common, divine Source and acknowledge this connection within us. This allows all aspects of polarity to move into their higher octaves. Although our ascension journey keeps us in the physical world, how it is expressed as our individual reality is something we choose.

Lightworkers came here to bring light to the world and the most recent cycle, whose purpose is the end of polarity, which began with Jesus' birth, has now come full circle. The world is ready for us but we are also ready for ourselves, to connect with our own divine energetic center and to create heaven on earth from the inside out. Our higher vibrations will manifest in our reality as new opportunities, choices and possibilities for our dreams, desires and miraculous living. Are you ready to experience the world at a new vibration, free of polarity?

Consider these principles for your personal mastery journey:
Can you identify any lower vibration emotions, thoughts, beliefs and feelings within you?
For each lower vibrating energy you identified, write down its opposite and use that as your focus for raising your energy to a higher vibration.
If you have begun to create transformation in your life, can you see the changes manifesting in yourself and in the people around you?
Do you understand that in order to change the world we must each be willing to create change and transformation in our life at an individual level?

Do you understand the Law of Divine Oneness, which states that we are all one, we are all connected to each other and we all originate from the same Source? Practice seeing everyone in your life through the lens of this law and recognize the divinity in each person. This is how you can begin to release the judgments that polarity imposes on you and bring yourself back into the flow of divine love and abundance.

Every aspect of transformation begins with our willingness to choose it. As we move through the experiences that lead us into mastery and ascension there are choice points at every step of the way. When we rise above the lower energies of fear we become aware of the options that arise from recognizing ourselves as divine, limitless beings who can access the doorways to new dimensions.

Do we have the courage to step through these doorways, knowing that when we do our lives will change forever?

Is it possible for us to accept our own divinity and perfection, knowing that the spark of divine Light exists within each one of us, no matter how much we have allowed our fears to hide it?

This is how we end polarity, by being aware that it is an option, in addition to the others we can choose from. We can choose polarity but we can also choose higher vibrations, such as connection. And when we choose connection, many things happen in our life, beginning with a shift in our energetic center, the core of the energetic vibration that we carry. As long as we are in the energies of fear and karma, our energy is concentrated in one of the lower chakras.

As we move into higher vibrations and create our place in dimensions beyond the third, we are able to move our energetic center to the heart chakra, which is where we connect to Source and re-establish our mastery. To do this we must understand how our energetic center works and what is required for its transformation.

Our Shifting Emotional Center

A critical element of our personal mastery journey is healing karma and learning to respond to the world with detachment instead of reacting from our emotions, where we hold and express our karmic history and energy. These are the lessons we accept within our soul contracts which become the path we follow on our journey in each lifetime, and determine how we relate to ourselves, to life and to others. Emotional responses are an aspect of our third dimensional experience and they are stored in our emotional center. Wherever these emotions are sourced or focused determines what kind of emotional energy we will use in our life path.

Our emotional center is located in one of the first three chakras, the body's energy centers, and each of these chakras contributes its unique energetic overlay to our emotional energy. As we heal our karma we allow our emotional center to move up to the heart chakra, where we are connected with Source, and allow our ego and spirit to connect.

The body has seven energy centers, or chakras, located at the base of the spine, navel, solar plexus, heart, throat, forehead and the top of the head. The body's energy travels through each of the seven chakras and they are balanced when the energy flows freely through them. But through the trauma and pain that is part of our life journey, our chakras become unbalanced and our emotional energy can become stuck in one of the three lower chakras, which relate to the material world and are the centers of structure and belonging, sexuality and survival, and ego and power, respectively. How we respond emotionally to our life situations indicates in which chakra our emotional energy is centered.

This is the central point of our emotional body as determined by our karma and the foundation for our emotional experiences. It also represents the theme of the karmic lessons that we will experience in our lifetime. And we enter each lifetime with a pre-determined emotional center, in one of the three lower chakras, which stems from our karmic history and soul group experiences.

Moving our energy from this center to the heart chakra is the focus of our healing journey, and it is either resolved or extended to be addressed in another lifetime.

For example, people who are first chakra centered are prone to experiences of betrayal and abandonment to which they can respond with fear or withdrawal, or they can try to manipulate others into providing the security and stability they crave.

Those who are second chakra centered experience lessons through addictions, sexuality and overcoming emotional and spiritual lack. Their emotional responses can include emotional and sexual manipulation.

Those who are third chakra centered have issues with power, self-esteem and can be ego dominant, which often expresses itself as needing to be in control. Their lesson are often in surrender which they react to by being overly controlling, which can lead to manipulation, being aggressively assertive and expressing anger when they feel threatened. They often feel powerless but take great care in hiding it from others.

How we respond to and connect with the world depends on which chakra our emotional center is centered in. It is also how the world responds to us because we will attract energies that correspond to our emotional center. Even though these experiences are not pleasant, they help us stay centered in a space that is known and familiar to us, no matter how uncomfortable we are there.

When we transform this energy and raise our vibrations our energy center will move up to the fourth or heart chakra. This is the beginning of the upper level chakras and is where we connect with Spirit, God or the Universe, the connection between the spiritual and material worlds. A fourth chakra based emotional center allows us, for the first time, to transcend the third dimension, release polarity, to complete ascension and connect to our mastery. This is a significant healing process in which we create situations that will allow us to assess, review and live through what may appear to be the worst of our emotional center lessons as we learn to let go, detach and release ourselves from our unbalanced emotional energies. There will be physical and emotional symptoms associated with this change, including disorientation, dizziness, having extreme emotional responses, being afraid and feeling out of touch with our emotions. These symptoms indicate that the emotional center has been upset and will require a period of adjustment to incorporate a higher vibration of emotional energy.

That does not mean that this shift will remove our emotions and emotional responses, we will still have them but they will be less upsetting, drastic and chaotic, and they will have less power over us. Detachment will be a stronger and more automatic option so we can learn the message of our lessons without having to fully experience them. In shifting our emotional center, we remove the unconscious control that our emotions have over us by shifting the focus from our emotional body to our spiritual body and become conscious of the emotional energy that we are sending out and receiving from others.

Once the emotional center has shifted to the heart chakra, it can open up to receive Spirit and allow the introduction of the spiritual energy into the material reality. The higher vibration and increased energy can be felt as being more joyful, happier, and at peace. Situations that once incited anger no longer have the same response. It is easier to detach from former emotional reactions and to be more objective about things that once may have evoked old, familiar feelings of anger, frustration or sadness.

There may be a decreased tolerance for violence or anger if the emotions had previously been centered in the first chakra. Feelings about sex and sexuality will change with a shift from second chakra centeredness and it may become less of an obsession or an overriding interest, becoming more balanced and manageable. Choices of intimate partners and friends may change as well. The shift from a third chakra focus, for example, results in fewer issues with power, self-esteem or the ego. With this energy balanced we will feel more in control of our life and emotions and less threatened by others, attracting people who honor our power and who respect us, rather than those who try to take our power away.

How do we know that our emotional center is shifting? It would be so easy to know when we've successfully moved through various parts of our transformation if we received evidence of our progress, like receiving a certificate of completion, or maybe having some sort of indicator on our body that shows us when we're 'done' with different aspects of our healing. Unfortunately, that does not happen. One way that we can tell that we are making progress is to observe what happens around us, the types of people that we attract, those that move away, the way we respond to them and the situations that we experience.

Are you seeing relationships end or are people who were once close to you leaving your life?

Are they being replaced with new or different people or situations?

Do you feel less tense, happier and more detached?

These are all indicators that you are successfully transforming different aspects of your emotional reality.

To help you determine where your emotional center is located and how you can shift it, we need to look more closely at each of the lower chakras and what happens when you have your emotional center focused in them. But first, here is an exercise that may help you discover where your emotions are centered.

Finding Your Emotional Center Exercise

The purpose of this exercise is to help you find your emotional center so you know where to focus your efforts on healing to allow your center to move to the heart chakra. In this exercise you will assess your relationships with different people in your life because everyone is a mirror of you. When you understand the energy of your connections, you will also understand where your emotional center is located.

To start, take a rectangular piece of paper and place it in front of you lengthwise, so that the longest edge is horizontal. Now, at the left side of the page, you will write down the names of the people you interact with in your life. They could be family members, friends, work relationships, partners, spouses, or anyone that you relate to in your personal and work life. A few examples are provided for you below, and you can add as many names as you feel are necessary.

Make five columns across the top of the page and write the following words in each of the columns:

First column: Anger, Abandonment, Fear, Betrayal

Second column: Frustration, Anxiety, Obsession, Sex

Third column: Doubt, Negativity, Powerlessness, Depression

Fourth column: Joy, Love, Powerful, Peace

The columns will correspond to your first four chakras. Your table should look something like the one shown below:

Name of person	Anger, Fear, Abandonment, Fear, Betrayal, Negative, Food and Sustenance	Frustration, Sex, Obses-sion, Anxiety Addictions	Negativity, Doubt, Powerlessness, Depression	Joy, Power-ful, Peace, Uncondi-tional Love, Detachment
	Chakra 1	Chakra 2	Chakra 3	Chakra 4
Mother				
Father				
Partner				
Son				
Daughter				
Friend				

For each name you have written in the left column, go across the table and put a checkmark in the box under the group of emotions that best describes your relationship with them or the emotions you feel towards them. You may have more than one column marked for some people on your list so do not worry if you cannot use just one set of emotions to describe someone.

If you feel you must pick one column for that person, try to pick the one that you feel describes the majority of your interactions. For example, is your emotional exchange primarily angry or negative or anxious? Do you have power struggles with this person? Are your emotional exchanges full of frustra-tion or are they negative and make you doubt yourself? Perhaps you are angry and have power struggles, or you feel abandoned and frustrated with this person.

When you are finished with this exercise, your matrix will have names going down the left column and each name will have one or more checkmarks in one of the columns across the page.

Now count the checkmarks in each column for Chakras 1, 2, 3 and 4. Does one column have more checkmarks than the rest? Which column is it? The column that has the most checkmarks indicates the placement of your current emotional center. Are you surprised with the results? Do you have any checkmarks in the fourth column?

You can repeat this exercise any time you wish to see where your emotional connections to different people exist. As you begin to move this energy it may be helpful to do this exercise again to see how your emotions are responding to your transformation. The goal is to have a majority of the checkmarks in column 4 so that you feel peace, joy, unconditional love and detachment with all of the people in your life. Even if you do not like them, you can be detached from your emotions so that you can feel acceptance for them and release the lower chakra emotions you were once connected through. This assists you in becoming aware of your personal power, raising your vibrations and your emotional energy center which shifts all of the dynamics of every relationship in your life.

Now that you know where your emotions are centered, read the descriptions for each of the chakras in the next section and the healing process associated with moving the energy in the next section. Remember that identifying the location of your emotional center is provides you with the information you need to raise   the energy to your heart chakra, where you can find peace and begin to create from your power instead of your pain. Transformation is possible once you know what energies you need to transform.

First Chakra Emotional Center

With a first chakra emotional center we are concerned with issues of belonging, of relating to others, of security and trust. Our most profound sense of connection is in the first chakra, including our connection with the Earth, our soul group, and biological family. We may experience first chakra lessons through distance or even separation from our mother or father, lack of physical, emotional or spiritual support from an early age and a family environment that was insecure or unstable. Our lessons from this chakra center may include abandonment, rejection, being ignored or isolated physically, emotionally or socially.

In past lives we may have been falsely accused and imprisoned, forced to leave our home, persecuted, reviled or ridiculed for our beliefs, separated from or rejected by those we loved. Security issues around this chakra also involve being a refugee, having a nomadic lifestyle, physical or social abandonment and homelessness.

These lessons manifest in different ways, from seeking the security of connection with others to how we take care of our physical body. Our relationship with food, which is how our physical body is sustained, is also part of the first chakra lessons. We can become obsessed with food and the feeling of protection and support we receive from it or alternatively, deprive ourselves of nourishment and become anorexic or bulimic. The need to belong to or to be part of a group may lead us to continue to build relationships with family members or people who have already rejected us, or others who do not have our best interests at heart. The need to join groups, from gangs to social clubs or organizations, even to being employed by a corporation, speaks to our need to know that we belong with and are accepted by others which is expressed with a first chakra emotional center.

Within this chakra experience is the question "Where do I belong and who takes care of me?" In our life path the lessons of our first chakra center could manifest as being betrayed, a sudden breakup of a relationship, the loss of a treasured friend, or of a valued job, all of which threaten our security and our place in the world.

Children who lose their parents or who are adopted have strong first chakra lessons. With this emotional center we are repeating past life experiences of rejection, of being separated from those we love, trauma associated with losing loved ones, being separated from our base of security or persecuted by those we thought should or would support us. All of these situations have a central purpose, to help us release the belief that without this sense of belonging to and being accepted by others, in a material sense, we are without an identity and are all alone. Our goal with these lessons is to transform them so we can remember our divine connection to create the sense of belonging that help us feel safe and secure from within, instead of seeking it outside of ourselves.

The first chakra lessons can be devastating because they threaten our physical and emotional survival and usually began at a time in our life when we were unable to defend or protect ourselves and were completely reliant on others for all of our security needs. Unless we allow ourselves to gain the spiritual knowledge that we need to overcome them, they can become life-long obstacles to our emotional and spiritual healing and growth as we seek connections with others to fulfill our need to know that we belong somewhere and proof that someone loves us enough to care for and about us. Our healing path goes from isolation, powerlessness and feeling abandoned, unloved and unsupported to finding our inner security that we can use to create an outer reality which reflects our inner knowing that we are always secure, protected, safe and loved wherever we are.

Moving the energy:

With a first chakra emotional center we have come to create our own sense of security in a way that does not depend on others. While that lesson is presented to us as a deep wound where we experience profound insecurity, a lack of nurturing and support and no one to care for us, it is not through finding someone who will give us those things that it is resolved. In fact, the opposite is true. The more we look to others to support, nurture and protect us, the more these things will be unavailable to us because we will choose people who cannot or will not give those things to us, as they do not have the inner core of security within themselves. The security and sense of belonging that we so desperately long for will appear when we stop looking for them in our outer reality and begin to create them within ourselves, as our outer reality cannot reflect something that is not already within us. Until we acknowledge this important concept we can experience profound isolation, rejection and loneliness from those we seek to connect with.

Healing the emotional lessons of the first chakra requires that we remember our powerful divine connection within which we are always safe, protected, nurtured, cared for and loved. No matter how disconnected we may appear to be in our outer reality, we must strengthen this inner connection in order for it to manifest in our life. Because the lessons of the first chakra are reflected in areas that are so important to our physical survival, they create a great deal of fear associated with emotional DNA memory of the pain of abandonment or rejection.

As we transform the first chakra energies into their heart-centered alternatives, we can disconnect from all relationships that were centered in the lack of acceptance and support and either reconnect with our soul group at a higher level or find new people to connect with. When our first chakra energy is grounded in the heart chakra paradigm of unconditional love we discover an unshakable sense of connection to Source, knowing that within it we are always protected and safe.

Our life moves from seeking ways to survive our pain, looking for others to validate our worthiness and finding someone who will care for us, to thriving with joy, a deep inner sense of security and the ability to live in the 'now,' the present moment, instead of re-living every painful emotional memory of the past that reminds us of our disconnection. For each negative or painful attribute associated with a first chakra emotional lesson, there is also a positive attribute that we will assimilate, once we are able to heal the emotional lessons and with this healing, find our own inner sense of security and belonging, which moves our emotional connection to the heart chakra, where we can experience the fullness of the belonging that we crave.

Consider these principles for your personal mastery journey:

Do you believe your emotional center is in your first chakra?

Do you have issues or fears around security, being provided for or having your needs met?

Did you have a loving, nurturing relationship with your mother or your family of origin? If not, do you understand the lessons of finding your own power and learning to survive and thrive without or in spite of your relationship with them?

Do you have a fear of abandonment, betrayal, of being alone or of having no one to depend on?

Were you adopted, a foster child or did not receive emotional nurturing as a child?

Do you look to others to meet your emotional and physical needs?

Can you see how you can meet your needs through your inner Source connection?

Second Chakra Emotional Center

When our emotional center is in the second chakra our lessons focus on self-worth, how we relate to people around sexuality and power, our creativity and intuition. The second chakra also determines how we relate to others and what we seek from others in order to survive on a physical and emotional level. While the first chakra deals with our basic survival, the second chakra deals with how we survive with others, including how we believe they love, value and accept us. If we are emotionally centered in the second chakra we are prone to using the energy of relationships to determine our self worth, to creating our own sense of self from the way that others see us. Addictions of any kind, including addictions to money, sex and food, indicate that the emotions are centered in the second chakra.

If our emotions were repressed during childhood, we use will use second chakra energy to try to resolve these issues, generally in a manner that repeats these early experiences. Financial issues, because they reflect our value or self worth, are also second chakra centered. Some sexual abuse issues are second chakra centered, although because they involve power and control, these types of issues are usually within the third chakra.

In past lives we may have been rejected for our beliefs, lived in extreme poverty, gone from "riches to rags," been rejected by a lover or partner, been an orphan or an illegitimate child, become a refugee through war or famine, been a political prisoner or social outcast, been a slave or servant, had a disfiguring disease such as leprosy or been cruel to others or insensitive to their suffering. We may have been abused sexually or used our sexual power to take advantage of, control or abuse others.

Within a second chakra center we have lost our identity, power and our inner sense of self and do not know who we are. Our tendency is to look to others for a definition of the self. We hope that others can show us the value, love, acceptance and worth that we want to have. There are several ways we do this: we give those things to others, hoping they will give them back to us, we try to become what we think others want or need us to be, or we try to connect with people who we believe have those attributes so we can receive this energy from them. It is easy for us to give our power away to those who we think will love or value us with a second chakra emotional center.

With second chakra lessons we can use our needs to manipulate others and become quite good at getting others to do what we want, with the thinking that they 'owe' us. But once we have exhausted our manipulations, giving and changing ourselves, which only attracts people who reflect those energies, we can move into depression and despair, and the belief that we are unworthy of love.

The issues presented by the second chakra put us face to face with how we see ourselves. Do we like ourselves? More importantly, do others like us? What can we do to have them like us enough so they will treat us well and we feel emotionally safe with them? The questions we ask of everyone are: "do you like me," "am I lovable," "am I worthy," and we ask them to prove it. But they cannot because if our self worth is an empty space, we cannot connect with others who have this space filled so we attract those whose self worth space is also empty.

Our quest to meet our need for self worth can take the form of addictions to people, money and things that, for a brief moment, give us the feeling of being accepted and having what we want. Because our sexual organs are in this chakra we can be fooled into believing that love and sex are the same thing, so we look for love and acceptance through sexual satisfaction. In fact, anything that gives us pleasure, no matter how brief, quickly becomes the vehicle for the fulfillment of our self worth. Since our fulfillment is brief, because it is externally sourced, we must have more and more of whatever we believe can fulfill us and we spiral into addictions.

The need to acquire money and the things that money can buy is an indication of our need to be valued. Addictions to food represent our need to be 'filled' and to feel full because our inner self worth resources are empty. Those who are obsessed with their appearance, who fear that a wrinkle, an extra pound or wearing the wrong clothes will make them socially unacceptable indicate a need to be what others expect so they can be valued. Because those with second chakra energy were once slaves or servants, they must transform their beliefs that their good comes from others, that they are valuable only when someone else says so, that they do not deserve to have their own space or value in the world. They can learn that their needs are important and deserve to be fulfilled and that they can have the most basic of life's gifts, especially freedom of choice, thought, speech and action.

Until we find our value within ourselves, through unconditional love, we will allow our addictions and beliefs and what they represent to become our source of acceptance and fulfillment. We will continue along this path until we recognize the need to create that sense of worth within ourselves, to learn to love ourselves so we can attract the love that we desire.

Moving the energy:

Healing a second chakra emotional center will allow us to create a solid, inner-sourced sense of self that mirrors love, self-worth and value to the world. We will have to accept the fact that we may have had difficult, painful or even devastating experiences that challenged our self worth and learn to let them go. Within these lessons is also a question of how we use addictions or depend on things outside of ourselves to satisfy our physical, emotional and spiritual needs. Any strong memories of or obsession with how others treated us, what they did to us or how much they hurt us must be resolved and released in order to heal the wounds represented by this emotional center.

Our lesson is to learn to find our value within, to love and accept ourselves unconditionally so that we become our source of fulfillment and then attract others who will love, accept and value us. We must learn to keep our focus on being ourselves and not on being what we think or believe others want us to be. Raising the energy of a second chakra emotional center requires that we accept responsibility for our own self worth, emotional well-being and use our intuition to guide us to emotional experiences that respond to our intent to heal, grow and that focus on our Highest Good.

For each negative attribute associated with a second chakra emotional lesson, there is also a positive attribute that we will assimilate, once we are able to heal the emotional lessons and with this healing, find our own inner sense of identity and worthiness, which moves our emotional connection to the heart chakra, where we can experience the acceptance that we crave.

Consider these principles for your personal mastery journey:

Do you find yourself obsessing over relationships that ended, things people did or said to you, or situations that you wish had turned out differently?

Are you addicted to food, sex, money or any other behaviors or activities that give you temporary satisfaction and then you feel bad about your addiction?

Do you believe you must earn others' approval, love and acceptance?

How is your self worth affected by people who do not like you or who treat you badly? Do you try to convince them that you are worthy of their love, honor and respect?

Do you find yourself trying to change who you are to accommodate someone else's needs?

Do you assume that people do not like you and then try your best to change their opinion?

Are you comfortable, happy and satisfied with yourself as you are right now?

Who are you when you are not trying to please or impress someone?

Do you feel that you have a strong sense of self and of your self worth?

Is freedom important to you?

How can increasing your sense of self positively impact your relationships and your life?

Third Chakra Emotional Center

The third chakra focuses on how we deal with the world. These lessons are centered in power, the ego and control. They may manifest in situations where we must stand up for our power, understand the difference between ego and spirit based control, how we view power and what we do to be powerful. Third chakra lessons show us where we give our power away, fear our power, are controlled or controlling and how we balance our needs with those of others.

In past lives we may have misused power, been controlling or controlled by others. We may have been part of a disenfranchised group that was powerless because of their age, gender, social or financial status. Or we may have been part of a group in power and abused the powerless. Rulers and politicians who have managed others through coercion and control and misused or abused their power are in this group, as are those who have used their power to betray others for personal gain. Sexual abuse and sexual crimes such as rape, because they involve power and control issues, are also third chakra based, for both the victim and the aggressor.

Third chakra lessons can, if we do not stay centered in our power, remove all of our confidence, our ability to see ourselves as powerful, challenge our control and bring us down to a level where we must realize that the source of our difficulties—and their solution—is within us. Fear is a strong factor in the third chakra as our experiences with powerlessness remind us of the damage that can result from being controlled, subservient to or abused by others. They also deal with all aspects of control – who controls us, who we control, what we are controlled by and what control means to us. Or they will involve that part of us that wants to be in control, to know the outcome, to live predictably. Sometimes, to do this, we will give our power to others because we feel they are more capable than we are or use our power to manipulate others into doing what we want them to do because we want to control our environment.

With this as our emotional center we will see ourselves as either powerless or powerful and act accordingly. If we feel powerless we may look to others to rescue or save us, or live life in a small way. Or we can bully others into seeing us as more powerful than we actually feel. If we are powerful, we may be able to use our power with wisdom or compassion, or force our will on others. How we use our power with this emotional center depends on the lessons in power and ego that we need to learn. Eventually, we will have to face our use of power in our life, whether we have abused or misused others' power or under-utilized our own.

With the third chakra emotional center we can fear power, especially if we abused power in previous lifetimes or were a victim of those who abused our power. Awareness of the pain that our power can create and not wanting to create more karma through the abuse of power can paralyze us into under-utilizing our power in different ways. We can be afraid to act and do nothing even at those times when action is required. Or we may go in the other direction and be overly generous with our power, willingly giving it to others whether they ask for it or not. We believe that others are as powerless as we feel so we do not ask whether we should be sharing our power with them. Power can become a source of embarrassment to us, something we do not want to own because we are too afraid that we will misuse it again to hurt others and suffer additional karma.

A lesser known aspect of the third chakra emotional center involves those who were present at Atlantis and witnessed its destruction. Many of them are present as Lightworkers in this lifetime to participate in yet another earth cycle of transformation. They have brought their memory of the Atlantean disaster to help in this transition, to ensure that it does not take the same path and that power is not misused, as it was in Atlantis.

But rather than embrace their power and use it to assist in the transformation process, they hide it because in Atlantis, their power was appropriated by those who had their own agenda and they were manipulated into believing they were contributing to Atlantis' transformation and ascension. So they unknowingly contributed to a process that eventually led Atlantis' destruction, which happened because instead of bringing heaven to earth, those in power were trying to use the earth's energy to copy that of the spiritual realm and eliminate spirit's presence.

But while they assisted in the process of raising the earth's vibrations to the highest level possible, which they believed was the path of ascension, they did not understand that the density of the earth's energy, without the interaction of spirit, was unable to withstand the levels of energetic vibration and the ensuing imbalance destroyed Atlantis.

Now Lightworkers are again being asked to hold elevated energetic vibrations and participate in a process of transformation which requires the sharing of their power once again. Their hesitation arises from the memory of what happened in Atlantis and their guilt at what they believe is the part they played in its destruction, which included the destruction of all of the progress towards ascension that had been made at that time. This memory is stored in the third chakra as a memory of power abuse or misuse and it prevents many Lightworkers from fully activating their power because they fear the consequences and that it will be misused.

Moving the energy:

Mastering third chakra lessons allows us to operate more freely in our world and to create ways of expressing our power with wisdom and compassion. We can remove our fear of being controlled and remember that as long as we have a powerful inner core, we will not attract people and situations that challenge our power and our reality will reflect our belief in how powerful we are, without the use of control or fears of being out of control. And we will attract people who appreciate our integrity and respect us, our power, and who we are, instead of those who are demanding, demeaning or controlling. We can also remove our fear that we will abuse power, which causes us to reject or withhold our   full power, so we live small, sheltered lives instead of being fully in our power and risking abusive behavior, ours or that of someone else.

This chakra lesson has invited interactions with many people who have taught us difficult lessons about how powerful we allow ourselves to be and once we master these lessons and learn to be comfortable in our own power, we are released from these connections.

Third chakra lessons teach us to live authentically, to act in integrity, to find a balanced way to use and express our power without fear that it will ever be used against us, taken away from us, that we will abuse it or give it away because we believe others are more capable of being powerful in our life. For each negative attribute associated with a third chakra emotional lesson, there is also a positive attribute that we will assimilate, once we are able to heal the emotional lessons and with this healing, find our own inner sense of power, which moves our emotional connection to the heart chakra, where we can experience ourselves as divine, powerful beings.

Consider these principles for your personal mastery journey:
Do you feel powerless or powerful in your life?

Is there someone in your life who bullies or abuses you with their power?

Do you give your power to others, because you feel they are more capable than you are or out of a sense of guilt in the face of what you see as their powerlessness?

Do you use your power to manipulate others into doing what you want them to do?

Do you act powerless with others because you are afraid of your power?

What is your relationship with control? Do you enjoy being in control or prefer to allow others to be in control?

Are you afraid of those in power because of what you believe they can do with their power?

Was one of your parents domineering or controlling?

Do you have a memory of being in Atlantis and present at its destruction?

Was your power misused and is that a reason for your reluctance to use your power in this lifetime?

Can you see yourself as powerful?

As we understand and heal our third chakra emotional center we release power that we have been afraid of and unwilling to acknowledge and use. How can you act more powerfully in your life, by integrating your power into every thought and action?

Every thought either expands our perception of ourselves or contracts it and is either moving energy forwards from the present moment into the future or backwards into our past. The times we feel stuck awaken us to the realization that the energy in our life is not moving. The process of moving energy is simply takes it from one level of vibration to another. With conscious, focused intention we do this with awareness so we always know where the energy in our life is going and how our life is unfolding, according to our intention, or unconsciously following our karma and energetic history.

Moving the Energy

Every person, event and situation exists to help us understand where our emotional center is located and move the energy from that point to the heart chakra, as we fulfill the healing terms of our soul contract. With lifetimes of trauma, our emotional energy becomes stuck in one of our lower chakras and our healing journey focuses on moving the energy to release the trauma so we can move closer to wholeness. This is both the purpose of each lifetime and its challenge, to understand where the trauma is centered and to transform it through healing and forgiveness.

Our journey into spiritual mastery brings this to the forefront because this is what stands between us and ascension. If this process seems to be more challenging at this time, it is. We have brought forward all of our emotional traumas to this lifetime so we could heal all of them and clear these energies from our own energy fields and in those of the earth. Whether our lessons involve belonging, gender and sexual issues, power and ego, or a combination of the three, our challenge is to resolve their ongoing trauma and raise our vibrations so we can be heart chakra centered. But how do we do that and how do we know that we have succeeded? And what happens after that?

It is the rise in our energetic vibration that triggers our emotional wounds, which happens when our energy has shifted and our trauma vibration is no longer supported. This is an opening to our emotional center, an opportunity to understand the energy and experience the lessons that will help us transform it. While we may interpret this as a moment of weakness it is actually a crossroads of transformation, a chance and a potential choice to step into our power and shift our energy. This is our cue to move our emotional energy and not hide, run from, bury or ignore it. It is not something to be ashamed of, or to feel that it is confirmation of our powerlessness. This is what we are here to do and our desire to move the energy is confirmation of our shifting vibrations and willingness to release this emotional energy.

How do we move the energy? As you read in the previous sections, our emotional center is in one of the three lower chakras, relating to belonging and connection, gender/sexual issues or ego and power. These emotional centers dictate how we respond to and connect with the world, what we attract in the way of people and situations to help us learn our lessons and how we will heal them.

First we must identify the patterns that we have been using to interact with the world, for this is where we are on autopilot, where we are reacting from our existing emotional center. Our emotional responses are so ingrained, so habitual, that we live through them in an unconscious and habitual way and then wonder why we feel alone and isolated, disconnected and powerless.

On the lower end of the spectrum, our emotional patterns can include fear, self sabotage, giving our power away, not using our power, running away, going into anger to feel powerful, or denial.

On the higher end of the spectrum our patterns can include detachment, self love, finding our courage, living through our spiritual truth, being powerful and accepting 'what is' with the mindset of transforming ourselves so that we no longer attract those situations. This is where our level of mastery is reflected, in how we respond to situations and what we do in the next moment.

Every person and situation mirrors our emotional energy center to us, so considering who and what are we attracting provides insight into how we can move the energy.

Are our friends loving and kind or do they challenge our power, or create drama and anxiety?

Are we comfortable with our family, partners, co-workers and neighbors or are they sources of discomfort and pain?

These people may be frustrating and annoying but they provide clues as to where our emotional energy is centered and their actions show us what we need to do to transform it

How do we respond when our emotional center is activated? This tells us how we are choosing to use our power.

Do we think we have done something wrong or are to blame in any situation where someone questions our actions? This indicates our level of self-love and also shows any guilt or shame energies we may be carrying.

Can we be detached and in our power at that moment or would we just prefer to run away and hide?

Do we fear the worst or can we be confident, knowing that our Highest Good is always reflected in every situation?

What about more difficult situations, such as when we are threatened by the loss of our financial security, or someone we love abandons us? How do we respond to those situations and how can we change the situation/response cycle so that we are always at peace, powerful and creating an unfolding reality that reflects our dreams as we step away from the expression of our pain and into the expression of our joy?

Then we change our response, setting an intention for transformation. It is not what others do to us that is important, it is how we respond to their actions. The people in our life are simply part of our life screenplay and contributors to our mastery journey. And at the core of our being we must remember that we attracted and even invited them and their actions into our life. What they bring out in us determines where we need to heal and move the energy.

Moving energy requires detachment, removing our connection to that particular emotion and response, replacing it with something of a higher vibration. While that is possible, we may be vested in our emotional center, wanting a certain kind of resolution, such as wanting someone to acknowledge or validate us, apologize, recognize us or respond to us in a particular way. All of these are attachments and they will keep us in the same emotional energies and cycles until we are able to detach. Are we ready to stop the fear responses and practice faith, trust and unconditional love? Are we ready to release our need for love and validation from others and develop self love so we can give them to ourselves and then have them constantly available to us?

Moving our energy center to the fourth chakra is done by recognizing the fear energy that we hold and setting an intention to release it, followed by the healing work, which includes forgiveness, learning detachment, being in the present moment and making a conscious decision to stand in our power. We are at our most powerful when we are in control of our emotions and are rid of the baggage of the past, when we are not responding to our life experiences from fear, but from a calm and focused center, when we are aware that every moment is part of our journey to mastery and understand the purpose of the lessons we are presented with (and remember that we created them with a specific healing purpose in mind). We will still feel emotions but will be able to choose how we respond to them. Fear will still be an option, as one of many choices available to us, instead of the only one we are aware of.

The emotions will still be there but we will experience them in a different way. Instead of fear we will have unconditional love; instead of powerlessness we will be centered in our power; instead of anger we will have detachment and acceptance; instead of doubt we will have faith and instead of grief, sadness and regret we will have joy. The foundation of all of these new emotions is unconditional love, the energy of the fourth chakra. And we will no longer attract the people, situations and experiences based on our lower chakra emotional imprints. Instead, we will attract those who resonate with our higher vibration so that our life experiences are centered in joy and abundance instead of fear and lack.

There is no reason for us to live anything but a life filled with joy, peace and unconditional love, once we do our healing work and stop resonating at a fear-based level. This is the gift of healing and transformation, to know who we are and to use that information to create our life as a miraculous journey of mastery.

Consider these principles for your personal mastery journey:

Do you see how the people, situations and events involved are assisting you in moving your emotional energy to your heart chakra?

Can you see what your cycle is, when your emotions are triggered?

Are you in the higher or lower end of the fear/love spectrum?

What can you do to change your cycle and transform the energy?

What is the blessing that others are trying to give you with their actions?

In what ways are they assisting you in creating your Highest Good?

What do you have to forgive to move your emotional energy?

Who are you willing to forgive, to move your emotional energy?

How can you be detached in every situation, becoming the observer so you can choose your emotional responses intentionally and consciously, instead of unconsciously?

Are you willing to do what is necessary in the form of your own healing work to move the energy?

What is your vision for your life once your energy is in the heart chakra?

Why does all of this happen? If we had lessons to learn and wounds to heal why don't we know what they are so we can focus on them, without wandering blindly for years, experiencing much pain and suffering? We do know, we just don't remember what our lessons are because they are part of our emotional DNA, the blueprint of our emotional body.

Emotional DNA is encoded deep within our physical, psychic and spiritual bodies and is the blueprint for our emotional body, just as our physical DNA is the blueprint for our physical body. And our physical and emotional DNA work together, as you will read in the next chapter, to ensure that we have the perfect physical and emotional body for our chosen life path. Within our emotional blueprint are all of the emotions we have ever experienced in all of our lifetimes, those that we have shared with our soul group, and the ones that were created from our karma and soul contracts. It is all within us, programmed within our emotional DNA, waiting for us to experience and transform it.

Your Emotional DNA

Have you noticed that you share behaviors with members of your family, even those you are not close to? Or that you are attracted to some people and not others? And your life path appears to follow a certain pattern, despite your best efforts? Or that there are certain emotions, emotional patterns or ways of feeling or responding that you see repeated within your family of origin and that you share with them?

Our ability to recall and repeat emotion is from the presence of our emotional DNA, the storehouse of emotions we have accumulated from all of our lifetimes. This is an aspect of our emotional body, in which we store the memory of every emotional energy and response we have ever had, as well as the realities we created from them. All of the karma and lessons we share with our soul group are also stored in our emotional DNA. This emotional history is our constant reminder of the energy we have to work with, heal and release in our current lifetime, as well as the energies of all of the different souls who have participated in this journey with us.

Our emotional DNA is an aspect of our human experience, and it is through our 'human-ness' that we feel emotions, such as love, joy, sadness and pain. Understanding and honoring the divinity of our humanity and its journey of healing and reconnection is part of the spiritual experience of life. Raising our energetic vibration so that we can create a balance between the spiritual and emotional energies, re-encoding our emotional DNA to higher vibrations is the foundation of our mastery journey.

Each lifetime carries over emotional residue from a previous one, which is an opportunity for us to complete something we believe we could have done better or differently. Or it can be a chance to retaliate against someone, to repay a debt or avenge a wrong. The reason we choose to incarnate is held within our contract with Source and our emotional DNA holds the information about where we separated, through fear, and how we can reconnect, through unconditional love. It is responsible for why we choose our soul group, life experiences, healing opportunities, who we will attract to help us carry out our contract and what some of our choices will be.

Our emotional DNA does not control our destiny; it merely contains the energetic foundation for our lifetime and the programmed responses that dictate how we will act within the scope of our karma. Whether we can do something differently, choose another path or access a higher vibration is what we have come to find out as part of our healing journey.

As we evolve and activate higher levels of vibration, our physical DNA is evolving from the two strands we are aware of to allow the activation of the twelve or more strands that actually exist. Scientists now recognize that in addition to the two strands they acknowledge, there are many more strands that are not active and which they call 'junk DNA'. But it is not junk, it is simply not being used as our energetic vibrations have not been high enough to activate it.

Our emotional DNA is intertwined within our physical DNA and we are unaware of it until our vibrations rise, which allows more of our physical DNA strands to activate and our emotional DNA begins to separate from its physical host. All of the emotional feelings, responses, reactions, beliefs and perceptions that we were once unaware of lose their energetic support and so the unconscious emotional responses we have been engaged in suddenly rise to our consciousness and we see where we need to balance our physical aspects, including the emotions, with the new vibrational levels we are embodying.

In fact, the closer we are to activation of additional DNA strands the more problems, doubts, fears and problems we seem to have. This is because without energetic support, which happens when we raise our vibrations, we are suddenly aware of the chaos, drama and suffering that our emotional DNA creates for us and then the means to heal and release it move to the forefront of our consciousness.

How do emotional and physical DNA work together? Any soul level promises or vows we take in a previous lifetime and all of their accompanying emotional experiences are imprinted in our emotional DNA, which then interacts with our physical DNA to create the physical characteristics that allow us to experience this promise. So the emotional DNA creates the energetic template which is translated into physical form where it can be expressed in a lifetime.

This is what Todd learned when he wanted to know why he chose a body that was, in his words, "short and unattractive." In a past life, Todd had been a talented and gifted writer and musician, as well as a very handsome man. Yet he squandered his talents, did not use his gifts wisely and although women were drawn to his good looks, he was cold-hearted, cruel and broke many hearts. In his next lifetime, he wanted to be physically unattractive to women so he did not treat them badly and his physical appearance was not a distraction that prevented him from using his gifts. To do that he specifically chose a body that would allow him to focus on his talents and gifts and would not be a deterrent to their expression or use.

His emotional DNA worked with his physical DNA to create a body he felt would help him with his lessons, as he believed it was his physical attractiveness that had caused him so many problems in his previous lifetime. Although he could have chosen a more attractive appearance he felt that he did not deserve it because of the pain he had once caused for others.

Gaining this knowledge did not make him grow taller or become more physically attractive, but it did help him become more willing to extend himself socially and to promote himself to others as a gifted musician and songwriter. He had been focused on studio work because he felt his appearance was a handicap and believed that his audiences would be more accepting of his music if they did not know what he looked like. Our work together gave him peace and confidence and allowed him to be more comfortable with his physical presence, which also translated into being more confident with his musical talent.

Consider these principles for your personal mastery journey:

Take a moment to consider the body that your physical and emotional DNA have created for you in this lifetime.

Are you tall or short, thin or fat, handsome/beautiful or unattractive?

Do you hate your body, find fault with it, wish it looked different or are you satisfied with it?

Do you allow your physical attributes to determine your feelings of value, self worth and abilities?

Do you have any impressions about your past life experiences that may be responsible for the physical body you have and the life experiences you are faced with?

In what ways did your family contribute to your feelings about your physical body?

What can you change about your beliefs and feelings about yourself to make peace with your physical body?

Each one of your physical attributes, including your gender and skin color, are part of the physical manifestation you have chosen to help you create the best expression of the lessons you wanted to learn and resolve. Even when you dislike your physical body or find fault with one or more of its attributes, you are activating one of your emotional DNA lessons. But your body is merely the physical vehicle for Spirit, the manifestation of its physical presence on earth and the only way in which Spirit can be part of the third dimension.

Our path to healing is smoother when we make peace with the body because when we are in conflict with our body we are ignoring the importance of the role it plays in our soul healing and blocking the flow of energy to our healing purpose.

Why are the emotions so important? We know the world of spirit as energy which is pure potential awaiting creation and the energies of the third dimension are emotional in nature. Mastery is ours when we can combine energy and emotion from the perspective of human and spirit. All of our emotional experiences are connected to our memory, actions and beliefs within a lifetime and our emotional DNA aggregates the emotions of all of our lifetimes. Each emotion we connect to or express represents an aspect of the emotional energy we resonate with, the thread of emotional experiences we have known and the level of emotional energy that we have come to heal and transform within us. The healing process helps us understand our emotions and how they are manifesting in our lives and then we can use our emotional/spiritual balance to create new pathways for our emotional DNA expression and transformation. This also heals the karma that is encoded in our emotional DNA so we no longer have to repeat it.

Without this process of introspection we are at the mercy of our emotional DNA instead of being in control of it. Imagine having every emotion you have ever experienced coming forward at the same time. This is what happens with unbalanced emotional responses and we watch helplessly while emotional cycles and patterns repeat and we do not know how to stop them. Without our conscious control and knowledge of the healing process, our emotional DNA responds from habit and fear and the beliefs and perceptions that were created from previous emotional experiences. These are expressed in cycles which we can stop once we understand their relationship with our emotional DNA.

When our soul is ready for transformation and our energy begins to shift our emotional DNA is activated and that process occurs as a situation that sets us up for healing. An opening for the co-creation of a new reality is established, where we ask the Universe to partner with us in this particular cycle. Although we do this unconsciously, we quickly become conscious of the results that manifest in our life. Whatever is contributing to our pain and suffering quickly becomes apparent and we are provided with the perfect situation that exposes every area where we can apply forgiveness, intention, conscious choosing, awareness and focus to heal and transform our emotional DNA and its expression in our life.

This doesn't mean that we have to remember every terrible thing that ever happened to us and re-live those emotions. Not at all. We simply have to be willing to have an awareness of our emotional history, how it manifests in our life, understand its role in our healing, what it attracts, and how it expresses itself through our lessons. It is time for us to create balance in all areas of our life and when we balance the power of our emotional energy with our conscious intention for a joyful, abundant, wonderful life, we are able to create loving, peaceful relationships and move out of the past that our emotional DNA carries into the present.

Emotional DNA plays an important part in how we create our reality. When we are faced with people, situations or experiences that recall past memories our emotional DNA is activated as are our karma and karmic patterns and all behaviors associated with them. Then we repeat behaviors, responses or actions, feel fear that appears to come from out of nowhere, and can sink into dark depressions that we cannot explain or resolve. It is the reason why certain patterns of emotions, such as abuse, depression, anger, or fear, occur in families. We choose the parents and families who will help us activate the emotional DNA aspects that we have come to heal around those issues. And at each phase of our physical and emotional development, beginning with conception, the emotional DNA that we need for our life path is being accessed and brought forward.

Our emotional DNA is created and supported by, contributes to and is enhanced by our karma. The emotional patterns that we need to respond when triggered by a karmic encounter are encoded in our emotional DNA, as are the choices that we have previously made within that karmic experience. We know this because we always respond to situations in the same way, unless we are consciously aware of our choices, our healing purpose and the emotional DNA healing that we are working on.

Consider these principles for your personal mastery journey:

Do you see patterns of behavior in your family, friends, soul group and the people you associate with?

Are you aware of the karma, patterns and cycles within your life?

Have you ever had reactions to people or situations that you could not control or did not understand?

Are your emotional responses in control of your life?

Can you see the connection between your emotional DNA, as expressed through your emotions, and the healing you have chosen to do in this lifetime?

Are you ready to consciously choose healing and transformation in your life, which also allows your emotional DNA to become activated?

Our emotional DNA is activated in two ways. The first happens at the moment of conception, when we choose which aspects of our emotional DNA that will become activated in that lifetime. With this choice, we select our parents and life details that will provide the appropriate sources to allow us to experience its best and worst aspects, setting us up for our healing journey. This choice has immediate results and is why, for example, some parents choose to abort a child or give it up for adoption or a miscarriage occurs and the child is not born at that time. With these situations there is an aspect of emotional DNA that must be healed and its activation occurs before the child is born.

There is also a transfer of the mother's emotional DNA to the child in the form of the emotional experiences she has from the moment of conception to the moment of birth. This is something I call the Maternal Energetic Emotional Transfer process and through it we have access to every emotional that our mother experiences during her pregnancy. How the mother feels about herself, her partner, the pregnancy and the child are included in this transfer and its resulting imprint on our emotional DNA. So a mother who is carrying an unwanted child, feels shame about the pregnancy, dislikes or has anger towards her partner, is creating those emotions in her child and they will be part of the child's emotional DNA. But that happens by design, not by accident because the child needs that emotional DNA pattern to work through its karma. Each child chooses its parents carefully, based on its healing path for a lifetime, that also includes any soul promises, vows or karma between it and both parents and the parents with each other.

Knowing this gave a client, John, a great deal of peace as he came to terms with his birth story which had created a belief that his mother did not want him. John's mother was a young teen when she became pregnant and was unable to care for or keep him, so he was given up for adoption at birth. The father of the child was an older, married man who would not and could not marry her, although he did love her very much.

Although he was adopted by a loving family who nurtured and loved him, John was deeply resentful of his mother's decision and blamed and judged her for it most of his life. He always felt like an outsider around other children and this carried into his adult years. John could not maintain relationships because he was so sure that his partner would abandon him that he either chose partners who would eventually leave him or he sabotaged the relationship so his partner left. He admitted that he believed his mother did not try hard enough to keep him.

But when we reviewed his soul contract, we discovered that his birth mother had a contract with his adoptive mother, from whom he had been taken during a previous lifetime. To satisfy their karmic debt, his birth mother had agreed to give him to his adoptive mother in this lifetime. With this understanding John was able to release his feelings of abandonment, forgive his birth mother, and create a loving relationship with her.

While may we have strong judgments about the choices and decisions our parents made during our childhood, they are part of the soul agreement and emotional DNA dynamic between the parents and the child. Through them our parents and family of origin create the perfect conditions to activate the portion of our emotional DNA that corresponds to our healing purpose with them. Then all of the emotions, wounds, thoughts, memories and feelings that are part of it move to the forefront and we are ready for the learning that will help us as we begin the healing journey that we have created for this lifetime.

In fact, our family is directly connected to our emotional DNA and our particular energetic vibrations trigger their corresponding emotional DNA patterns. This is why a parent can be very connected to one child while being resentful, jealous or have an intense dislike of another child. On the physical plane they are dealing with their children but much is happening on an energetic level. Enlightened parents would be aware of these vibrations and handle them with healing and forgiveness. Parents who are not enlightened would abuse, mistreat, harm or even kill the child whose energetic vibrations triggered their emotional DNA responses, which is why we are seeing increasing numbers of child murder or infanticide by parents or partners. The child activates specific past life memories of trauma and the person responds through their fear and emotional DNA associated with that incident.

The second phase of our emotional DNA activation happens during childhood and into adulthood, when our emotional DNA patterns and responses are established. Then our trigger can be as simple as someone saying something that angers us or we meet someone we have an attraction to, or encounter an unmet expectation, a disappointment, or end a job or relationship. Our initial response can be to go into a full scale panic and all of our fear-based emotional DNA responses are pushed to the forefront of our awareness. We have no idea of what to do or what is happening, our emotional survival is threatened and we are afraid. We cannot plan a strategic response because that takes too much time, so we react, doing the first thing that comes to our mind. At this point the destiny spectrum of our emotional DNA is activated and we are doing exactly what we have always done, repeating ancient patterns and are on the brink of either adding another layer to our karma and emotional DNA memory or releasing it.

If we are spiritually evolved, we use this activation phase to become proactive, asking questions such as "What is really happening?", or "Why did I choose to create this and what lesson did I need to learn from this experience?". We are aware of the emotions but are taking a position of detachment until we have a better understanding of what is happening and have had time to consider potential choices that will be revealed as we shift the emotions we have awakened and are expressing.

If we are not spiritually evolved, we use the activation phase to become depressed, angry, bitter, resentful, and feel powerless. We ask questions like "Why is this happening to me?" or "What did I do to deserve this?" and can go into blaming others for their actions and seeing ourselves as victims.

If we are able to step back and look at the situation more closely, we can respond instead of reacting, allowing ourselves to understand what the issues are and how they fit into our healing journey. Are our lessons about power, value, self-esteem, abundance or fear? We remember that everything contains a lesson and we look for the lesson in every experience, taking time to pause and reflect even when we think that running and hiding may be a possible (and perhaps even a preferred) option.

As we progress towards mastery we learn to recognize the habitual, fear-based responses that are encoded in our emotional DNA and pause before we choose our course of action. This gives us the energetic opening we need to move into a higher vibration which expands our awareness of the possibility of another option. Then another path can unfold, which contains the choices that move us beyond our karma and can create a new outcome for this situation, one that is much different from the destiny-driven programming provided by our emotional DNA. As long as we react through the emotional energy of our wounds we are repeating our pain and will have the same outcome each time. But with the intention to heal and the willingness to release our connection to fear we interrupt our emotional DNA cycle and invite new emotional paradigms into our reality.

The core of these choices is simple, we can either create new emotional pathways for ourselves or we can repeat the lessons of our emotional DNA, which means that we will attract more people, situations and experiences based on our emotional DNA vibrations at the level of our karma that will help us create another lesson to help us complete our healing.

With each emotional DNA cycle we are at a crossroads of healing, where the energetic support for the continuation of our karmic patterns and cycles is interrupted and we can make different choices. If we do not take these opportunities a new cycle will begin when we are ready to review our lifetime's healing purpose once again. There is no wrong way or wrong choice, or taking too much time to complete this process, as healing is our life purpose and when are ready to do it the perfect opportunities will be available to us.

As we progress through our journey into mastery everything on that path has a purpose, to create the healing, forgiveness and release that will bring us to enlightenment, evolution, peace and unconditional love.

Consider these principles for your personal mastery journey:

Are you aware of your emotional DNA patterns and cycles, do you know what emotions they involve?

Can you see these same emotions, patterns and cycles in your family, friends, partners and the people who are close to you?

Is something happening in your life that is triggering you at an emotional and karmic level?

Can you recognize the situation, pause and reflect on its meaning and then choose your response carefully, from a place of power instead of from fear?

Do you see where you have acted out of fear and repeated karmic cycles in your life?

Now that you know about the emotional DNA connection, what are other options or choices you could make in different areas of your life?

Do you dislike your body or any aspect of your physical appearance?

Can you make peace with your body and accept its role in your emotional DNA healing journey?

Are you prepared to view your life as a healing journey, knowing that each moment of your life has a message for you, one that will bring you closer to your mastery?

Emotional DNA healing is possible and it is another energy movement, from a vibration that reflects our karma and pain to a higher vibration that mirrors unconditional love. As we heal these energies we transform them into a higher level on the energetic spectrum and we release everything in our life that corresponds to their lower vibrations. Emotional energy is magnetic and it attracts everything that resonates with it. Healing changes the vibration of our emotional energy and then we can attract other experiences that resonate at a different energetic level.

Healing Emotional DNA

Awareness and understanding of our emotional DNA are the tools we need to heal it and once we are willing to understand the vibrations of our emotions we can be in control of the responses we choose instead of being a victim to everything that triggers us. Aligning with our power allows us to make other choices, and awareness and information bring relief to fulfill our desire for change. No one wants to continue doing what does not work or makes them unhappy. But knowledge is one thing and action is another. We can know what is out of balance and be grateful for that knowledge but doing something about it is the next step on our healing journey.

The focus of healing is to create new energetic vibrations that allow different outcomes, so the emotional DNA patterns are transformed because the energy that creates and supports them has shifted. Focusing on the results we want to create changes our energetic vibration, which introduces new energy for the thoughts, behaviors, beliefs and actions that are necessary to create a different outcome. All of our emotional responses are part of an energetic pattern which we change when we remove the energy that supports them and that allows us to create something else that is not a pattern but a conscious, intentional response focused on our highest good and the reality that we wish to have.

In relationships, for example, our emotional DNA and karma may cause us to choose the same kind of partner again and again. But hoping that the partner we are with will change if we wait long enough, becoming what we want and need them to be is not going to give us the desired results. By allowing ourselves to recognize where we need to heal, which in this case is shifting our energy so we attract a different type of partner, doing our own healing work, then setting our intention for the kind of relationship we want shifts our energy and we will no longer attract that type of partner because the energy that supports that level of being is no longer part of our energy field.

Focusing on the transformation we wish to create opens an energetic pathway that is outside the scope of our emotional DNA imprint. Our emotions are magnetic and attract similar vibrations to them, which manifests as everything we experience in our reality. The process of transformation allows us to change any aspect of our reality with intention or maintain the status quo, through habit. As we set our intention for what we want, different energetic vibrations are established and the process of energetic attraction is activated. In this way we are working from the present moment and creating the future, instead of re-creating the past and trying to force change on it. When we work from the point of the past, we always re-create it because we are within its energetic vibration.

Setting an intention for what we want in each moment allows us to discover what we are magnetizing, move the energy and shift our emotional DNA energies into a higher vibration because we are not feeding the existing energy. Whatever was able to connect through the old patterns can no longer do so because they are no longer present to connect to. Anything in our reality can be changed once we are willing to release the patterns and the emotional energy that supports them, and be prepared with new conscious, intentional choices for our reality.

Consider these principles for your personal mastery journey:

Are you aware of the emotional DNA patterns and responses that exist in your family and soul group?

Can you see how they repeat in your life?

Can you identify patterns of behavior, reactions that you always have or ways of responding to situations that are related to your emotional DNA?

What energetic vibrations do you need to raise or change in order to create change in your life?

Are you willing to release these patterns?

What are new ways of responding that you can use to change what is created in your life?

How do you think this could change your life?

Why do we have to struggle and suffer through life? Is the healing ever completed? If we are a divine spark of the infinite love of Creator, why can life be so hard? What have we done to cause the physical, emotional and mental suffering that we can experience in our life? And why do some people seem to have a wonderful life, enjoying money, fame, success, and happiness, while others suffer? If life is about suffering and pain, what is the point of being here? What is our life purpose? These questions all have one answer and it is a Universal truth that we know on a spiritual level but cannot easily grasp on a mind level.

The answer is that our life purpose is two-fold, to heal our wounds and then, after we do that, to create the life of our dreams, once we have released the things that block it. This is always possible for us but our belief in our separation, the disconnection from Source, the paradigms of pain and suffering that we have created are the "unfinished business" of our lifetimes and the reason we have to return and complete additional healing cycles. The secret of life is that it is a healing journey and this is also the purpose of our life.

The Purpose of Life

As we go through each lifetime our life's perspective is limited to what is happening within the current life path. From the perspective of our soul path, however, each lifetime represents a singular aspect of the healing journey which is the purpose of that lifetime. While we like to think that we are here to do something significant or important on a world scale and it may be something we believe is part of our mission, the truth is that our purpose is both more mundane and grander than we can imagine. On a mundane level, our life purpose is to heal our soul wounds. On a grand level, as we heal our soul wounds we also participate in the world's healing and the collective ascension.

Each time we return to earth we have a specific mission, to complete an aspect of our healing mission. This healing journey is the fulfillment of our soul contract, whose ultimate purpose is to reconnect to Source and our divinity, and to re-align our energy from polarity to connection. We are the ones who create the material aspect of life and make it about status, prestige, having more, and being the best.

But life is so much more than that. It is a process of clearing the past, becoming the ultimate fulfillment of our highest potential and to step into the divinity, peace and love that is our birthright and which we can achieve in each moment. That is a fancy way of saying that the only reason we return to the earth is to clear any fear-based energetic imprints that we left behind in a previous lifetime. While we may glamorize life in a material sense, its true purpose is to move energy from fear to love by resolving any aspect of a lifetime where we have disconnected ourselves from love.

The process of ascension, which follows healing and transformation, has occurred slowly by design so we could experience multiple aspects of separation and build a new paradigm for future generations, incorporating as many healing opportunities within it as possible and thus transform as much energy as possible. Our progress depends on our ability to recognize our mastery and find our power from within. And healing humanity's core wound, that it is "less than" God, is the focus of this journey.

As we have learned, each of us begins a lifetime with some aspect of earth energy, in the form of an emotional DNA encoding, as the focus of our healing mission. This may involve lessons in power, truth, acceptance or limitation, all of them reflecting some aspect of our belief in separation and in our powerlessness. We have undertaken these lessons many times and each one that is completed closes a healing cycle and brings us closer to our spiritual Truth. All of them are aspects of the fear polarity we have been resonating with and reflect our attempts to move closer to unconditional love.

While we enter a lifetime with only a vague memory of our soul contract, purpose and lifetimes of learning, we are not alone in our healing journey. We have many helpers, both in the spiritual world, in the form of our angels and guides, and on the earth plane, in the form of our soul group, to remind us of what we have come to do.

Our soul group, the souls who share our wounds and healing purpose, are traveling and learning with us. Together we will share experiences, playing different roles across the course of many lifetimes to resolve the shared aspects of our healing journey. Along with our individual soul groups, represented by our relationships, we are also part of the soul group of humanity, whose collective journey reflects a movement from fear to love, from pain into joy and from polarity into connection. All of them work with us to mirror our healing journey back to us so that we can learn to forgive. But too often we see this as confirmation of our unworthiness and we support this energy at its lowest vibrations instead of giving ourselves closure and ending our connection to it by raising our energetic vibrations. Then we are stuck in a cycle of repeating the past instead of healing it, setting the stage for another lifetime of healing to accomplish our mission.

Beginning each lifetime with the purpose of healing karma sets the energetic paradigm that encourages and even invites karmic experiences so we can heal them. These paradigms are the mindsets that we use to create karma and separation. Within our journey to spiritual mastery we have the opportunity to create new paradigms of connection, power, divinity and conscious living. So we take another healing journey into the paradigms that we have carried within us for lifetimes to shift their energy and create the transformation that releases them from our own and the earth's energetic fields.

The paradigms represent basic energies, all of them centered in a fear aspect of polarity that is our individual experience of separation. We each carry at least one of these paradigms as part of our emotional DNA, which is why we repeat lessons in every lifetime. It is also why we stay within our soul groups while we are in this healing process because we share emotional DNA patterns, energetic paradigms and soul wounds as well as everything we will require for their healing. While they are very powerful, these paradigms are nothing more than beliefs, truths that we think are the divine Truth but which are really core philosophies that we have adopted through the filter of our pain and suffering. The paradigms of separation, pain and suffering, of polarity and our powerlessness exist because we created them at a time when we were suffering, feeling powerless and disconnected from Source.

Consider these principles for your personal mastery journey:

Do you understand that your life purpose is one of healing? Can you see how this has created the life you have?

Are you aware of your own beliefs about your separation and powerlessness? How do these manifest in your life?

Can you think of one lesson or emotional DNA connection that you have with your soul group?

Do you know who is part of your soul group in this lifetime? Are you aware of those connections in your life now and in your past?

What are the paradigms that you have been living with? Do they involve lack, fear, powerlessness, sadness or grief, or any other situation which you now see as part of your healing mission?

Where are you experiencing these paradigms in your life?

And if you can see them as paradigms, do you know what you can do to transform them?

If the purpose of life is to heal ourselves and the world, why do we feel that we complete this journey alone? Who or what is here to help us on such an important journey and where are they when we need them the most? If Spirit is our partner, where is it when we feel lost, stuck and do not know where to turn? When we are ready to complete a healing cycle, we look for someone or something to help us with the process because we feel insignificant, unsure and incapable of the journey. In times of distress, we will cry out to Source or God to please help or save us. And we often do not receive the answer we want, not because God did not hear us but because we have the power to rescue ourselves, and God is waiting for us to use it. Asking God to rescue us is an impossible request because we have free will and because the Universe always views us as perfect, powerful and doing the right thing at the right time.

The questions we ask will either open us up to divine guidance or we will be put in the 'waiting room', as was my experience (and is described in a later chapter) during a particularly difficult part of my life. I had a dream in which I was demanding explanations as to why my life was so hard and God put me in a waiting room, where he said I needed to spend some time there until I worked things out. Note that I was not told that I could not or would never work things out, God had faith in my ability to figure out the solution to my problems, which I eventually did.

So we are not victims, tossed about helplessly by our karmic cycles. We are here as spiritual warriors, as emissaries of the divine and moreover, as individuated lights of God-energy to heal the human family's paradigm of separation. All we have to do is remember our life purpose, which is to raise our vibrations and acknowledge our mastery so we can heal and release the paradigms of suffering and woundedness, and move into mastery. Faced with the sometimes relentless challenges of our healing journey we tend to look at life as something that is happening to us, rather than what we are creating to uncover and heal our energetic paradigms and re-connect with our power.

But whatever happens to us is our creation that we manifested to highlight our need for healing and when we stay focused on the fact that we have a healing purpose and every experience, without exception, is part of that journey, our perspective changes. Asking the right questions, "What aspect of healing is this uncovering?" instead of "Why is this happening to me?" will help us see beyond the illusion of powerlessness we think is in front of us to the reality of the healing journey.

Since our need for healing brings out our greatest fears and put us into the fear aspect of polarity where we cannot see its opposite, unconditional love, our journey can seem dark indeed as we step into the abyss of our karma. It is only when we realize that we are reliving a story whose end will result in more pain and suffering that we remember the purpose of this journey, to bring every situation to healing, not to endlessly repeat it.

And so the cycles continue until we have an 'aha' moment where we realize that there is another way to do this, and another approach that we can take. The difference is in how we view ourselves as healers and how we complete our healing journey, through atonement or through mastery.

With atonement we believe that we have to re-live the pain we have caused ourselves and others, a belief that has been created through the repetition of our many karmic cycles. Then we return in each lifetime to offer ourselves as a sacrifice in order to make up or atone for what we have done before, trying to create healing and transformation by re-living the pain we have caused ourselves and others. Through this path we create great suffering that often remains unresolved and is carried into future lifetimes. This is the path of the unconscious mind that believes in its imperfection, error and separation. It enters each lifetime believing it is wrong, has been wronged and is unworthy of love and that through suffering it will be cleansed, perfected and healed.

This is also humanity's karmic struggle that plays out in the discord and chaos we know as an integral part of our humanity. There is another way   to experience karma, one that is less damaging, more powerful and requires no suffering, which we can choose to know as our healing path. It is possible once we have embraced unconditional forgiveness within our healing path. Once we forgive ourselves for whatever we believe we have done, we accept the forgiveness that is already ours from Source and it is complete. There is no more unfinished business at that level and we can move on.

This is a different, more conscious path that our mastery journey can follow. On this path we know the truth about our healing journey, how it is an opportunity for us to remember, forgive and within the moment of forgiveness, to reconnect to our divinity. In that instant karma is erased, healed and transformed into understanding. It is possible to engage in this process without falling into the abyss, revisiting every painful, difficult experience we have had in this or in previous lifetimes. But we have to stay conscious, remember the Truth of who we are and to be willing to allow ourselves to stay out of atonement and walk in grace. And when we are looking in the mirror of karma, to remember that we are looking at ourselves.

How we heal, who we heal with and how that journey is completed has been a complicated process where we have often looked for validation outside ourselves to confirm that we have accomplished our mission. If we can bring one person to enlightenment, heal even one other soul, we feel successful and worthy of redemption and reconnection. But as we learn more about our power and the power that everyone has, we are brought to the truth of Spirit, that everyone is on their own healing journey and where our experiences intersect is where each one of us can complete our healing. The only reason to experience karma is to complete healing and each person who is engaged in a karmic cycle is seeking that.

We heal others by becoming the healing they need, holding their energy, mirroring their wounds and then allowing them to heal through our efforts. This is what we have believed our role as healers to be, to bring others to healing by mirroring to them how painful and difficult their wounds are, atoning for what we did to them (or they did to us) by becoming their pain. Whether we do this through illness, self-denial, abandonment, experiencing betrayal, or allowing others to hurt us, our purpose is to heal them, to offer ourselves as a martyr and sacrifice to bring them to their healing center. But our real purpose is to heal and release ourselves, not others and our interactions with them do more to point out our own soul wounds than theirs. It is just easier to see others' wounds than it is to see our own.

In the spiritual world we have a group of spiritual beings who we can call on for assistance. These includes our angels and spirit guides who are part of our soul contract. They connect to us from a higher vibration and they remember our reasons for being here and the healing that we wished to accomplish when we began this journey. But until we are willing to move out of our choice to heal through our karma and emotions or to heal ourselves by healing others and open to a higher vibration we are not aware of their presence and unable to receive their guidance. Are we willing to make the switch, to choose a path of higher vibration to be able to see the pathway out of our own karmic cycles and give ourselves the gift of healing, no matter how much or how little those around us are healed or whole in body, mind, emotions and spirit? Can we use this time to focus on our own healing, growth and transformation, no matter what is going on with those in our soul group? Can we allow everyone to be responsible for their own healing?

While the participation we receive from our soul group may, at times, seem less benevolent that the loving assistance we receive from our spiritual helpers, these are our most valuable teachers and we know them well. In lifetime after lifetime we struggle with our collective karma and present each other with chances to atone for our perceived wrongdoing. With these human partners we undertake the healing journey through our karma, repeatedly inflicting wounds until we can arrive at compassion and forgiveness. But when we operate solely through our karma and its emotions we are blind to the other side, the spiritual resources that can help us recognize our karma, guide us into other modes of action and reveal where we can forgive and release.

Why do we have to do this? It's a question I am frequently asked and the answer is always the same, because the one who seeks spiritual understanding is the one who has raised their energy enough to connect with the potential to heal karma and bring closure to the soul group's karma. Then we have to wonder why the person who is generally the soul group's karmic scapegoat and the one who suffers the most in the soul group dynamics is presented as its healer. That has to do with the ego's desire to maintain the status quo, no matter how painful it is, despite the peace that comes with healing.

The one who is aware of the healing potential is the 'way shower' for their soul group and while they are not responsible for the healing, although they often take on the burden of that responsibility, they are the ones who can create these opportunities, often by becoming the martyr for their soul group, often by becoming the mirror of their pain and then asking them to act with greater compassion and understanding. A better way to do this is to powerfully create this pathway and then step aside, allowing the soul group members to accept or reject the healing as they can. When they have achieved a more powerful connection with their own spiritual guidance, they will be able to find their way through this doorway and release their commitment to the karma.

We can choose to heal through the mirror of our humanity and experience chaos or through the light of our divinity and take the path of peace, joy and unconditional love because this is a new option for us. And as we do this for ourselves, we also allow our soul group to find this healing. We have no idea what this path entails because we are the first to try it. It has taken many lifetimes to get to this place but here we are, with different options for our healing journey, to follow the path of karma or one of a higher vibration, using our spiritual guidance to help us recognize karma and find higher ground.

How does this work?

Think of the most difficult person in your life, ask your guides to show you their wounds and fears. Then ask to be shown the higher path to resolving your karma with them. Ask to be shown what needs to be forgiven in them and in you so that you can resolve this issue forever. Then apply whatever forgiveness you need so you can release yourself. Once you have broken the connection to the karma, your role in it is finished. Karma is like a dance and when one person stops dancing, the dance is over. It really is that easy, from a spiritual perspective, then we have to bring it down to a more human, mundane level and put it into practice in our life and in all of our relationships. Healing and resolution occur because when we set our intention for forgiveness and release, we remove the energetic connections to any energy that is less than unconditional love and we are then seeing ourselves and everyone through the light of spirit and in their powerful and perfect divinity.

Consider these principles for your personal mastery journey:

Do you communicate with your angels and guides when you need their help and guidance?

Can you identify members of your soul group in your friends, family and other people in your life?

Are you willing to acknowledge the help that you can receive from your spiritual helpers and allow them to guide you, especially in those times when you feel confused and helpless?

Do you recognize how your soul group is trying to help you with your healing and learning with every interaction?

Can you see how you are the "way shower" for your soul group, teaching them about the light, healing, forgiveness and unconditional love?

As a spiritual teacher and intuitive, the question I hear again and again from clients is "what is my purpose, why am I here?" and while the details of the answer are different for everyone, its basis is the same, the purpose of everyone's life is to heal, learn, release karma and transform their life from karma to creation as part of their journey to spiritual mastery. That seems like an easy task but we know how difficult it can be to learn from karma and then use that learning effectively the next time we experience a karmic interaction. But each of our lifetimes is a healing journey, another opportunity to experience the learning our life lessons have for us, to heal our soul wounds and transcend their pain into mastery, transforming our humanity into reconnection with our divine heritage and ascending into higher levels of energetic vibration.

Every aspect of our life will be focused on that purpose until we achieve it and then we can repeat it for the next round of lessons. It is the most important thing we can do, for ourselves, our soul group, humanity and the planet. Until the many permutations of karma are healed, forgiven and transformed, healing is the purpose of each person's journey.

That is why so many Lightworkers have gathered at this time, why the Indigos and Crystals are present and more highly evolved generations of children are being born. This is the end of an era for humanity, a time when healing and transformation are not only possible but so much has been put into place to ensure that it happens. As Lightworkers we are the pioneers in this process. We get to set the path and the standard, and it is indeed an honor. And we can start now so that the world heals and we allow heaven to join us on earth.

Those who feel they have another purpose are seeing what is possible beyond the healing. For healing is not the last step of this journey, it is the first step of the next one. We have waited lifetimes to heal and to live our passion, truth and to expand our consciousness. Our longing for something better is the voice of our soul telling us that it is possible, once we have completed this last step of the journey called the 'human being' into another one that we will begin as the 'actualized, spiritual human'.

For many of us, this is a final lifetime, a last visit to the earth plane. It is a completion of a soul cycle which was begun with the promise that one day it would be over. That time has arrived and it is both exhilarating and frightening, affirming and confusing. We are on the threshold of a new reality for all of humanity and our eons of healing work is what made it possible. As we close down this cycle we are reminded that each one of us creates the whole, that all are connected and there is the reward of peace, joy and unconditional love on each step of our healing journey.

It can be disappointing to realize that your life purpose is not to become the next Nobel prize winner, screen star, best selling author or celebrated public figure but that does not mean that you cannot become those things – you can, once you have fulfilled your purpose of healing. And you are a healer of yourself, of others, your soul group and of the world, as you receive healing from and give healing to everyone in your life. While this will be an ongoing paradigm for humanity, how we can apply healing is also changing. We must shift from 'doing the healing' to 'being healers'.

Healers and Healing

If you are a healer, and we are all healers of ourselves and others on many levels, which means you have undertaken the responsibility of using your gifts to bring transformation, growth and change to yourself, others and to the world, you have a multi-purpose life path. You are here to resolve your own karma and soul group dynamics, as well as contribute to the earth's transformation through the energetic vibrations that you carry. You have done this many times in the past and are present for this pivotal time in the earth's healing cycle to bring closure and complete the third dimensional experience. Because ascension involves opening to higher dimensions of being, those who can carry and transmit higher energetic vibrations are required to assist in the ascension process. This is the work of healers, which is the path many of you have taken in this lifetime.

The healer dimension of your life path is part of every lifetime, where you bring light to your soul group and to the world, which may or may not be appreciated by those you reach out to. Your work either receives thanks and praise or leaves you battered, drained and unappreciated. No matter what outcome you experience, you return in each lifetime to bring humanity and the earth closer to ascension. Healing energy is expressed in many different ways. Sometimes you are a victim and martyr, other times you are the epitome of success. There are times when you are a student and other times when you are a teacher. And this is why you are here today, although many of you do not want to be here or even feel that you do not belong here. As healers, your life path is focused on healing for ascension and you will do what you can to ensure that your task is completed.

We are at an important stage in humanity's evolution, a time of completion and closure, the end of separation and karma and the creation of new energies of reconnection, creation and being powerful. This is a cycle that exists within our own lives as well as for the earth itself. Every aspect of the material world is in a completion cycle at this time. And for some of us, this completion means saying goodbye to our soul partners and groups, a change in who we heal, how we use our healing energy and our healing commitments.

Healers have been engaged in healing for many lifetimes and many are here at this time to complete their healing contracts with their soul groups. Although we have been doing this with them for many lifetimes, this time is different, because in this lifetime we will have closure and an ending so that our part in the contract is over. Our belief is that this means that we will all heal and move on together but that is not happening as we expected. Our soul group members can be unwilling to release their karma and unable to raise their energetic vibrations enough to participate in the closing of our healing cycles with them so the soul growth happens for us but not for them.

Many healers are beginning to realize this and are conflicted in their feelings. Some feel guilty about their desire to move on because their soul group partners have not completed their healing. Some believe they have not worked hard enough, and others fear that they may have to come back to complete another round of healing with their soul group. There are some who are afraid for their soul group partners' karmic future if they do not heal but their fear for others is fueled by their own fear of having to return to help them in another lifetime.

Everyone has a choice in the matter of their healing, to heal or not. Either choice is right and reflects the person's level of spiritual growth and understanding. The question we must ask is not whether we are a 'good' healer, based on the results we think are achieved, but how we view our healing purpose. There are many ways that we heal others and ourselves and one aspect of healing that has changed for us is how we heal, by being of service or being a servant.

When we are of service we understand that the nature of what we do is to provide an energetic opening, insights into another way of being that others can accept or not, according to their level of spiritual growth and understanding. We can show them the light but they have to figure out how to incorporate it into their being and their path. We are here to serve others, to be a light for them, to participate in their lessons and to help heal humanity. But we are also here to serve ourselves, to heal our soul wounds, enable our soul's growth and are on our own path of reconnection, that is not dependent on anyone else's level of soul growth. Our challenge is to find a balance between serving ourselves and others so we can complete the tasks that we established within our contract in this lifetime and perhaps even go beyond that. Whose healing is more important and how do we approach our healing obligations and roles? Where is the balance in this process?

When we act as a servant in our healing role, we believe that we are responsible for both providing the information and ensuring that it is received and incorporated in someone's life path. This is frustrating and difficult for us and for them. For us, because we do not have any control over their healing and they quickly show us that they will do whatever they feel is right for them, despite our best efforts and we will feel blocked. For them, because we are trying to push them into a path we know is best, whether they are ready for it or not. We do not 'heal' anyone; we cannot do that for them. What we can do is provide the information at the right time, when they are in the right place and ready to receive it and they will incorporate in their healing journey when they feel the time is right for it.

With the perception of the healer as a servant, we believe we must be constantly available to others and create a positive outcome in all things. Then we become responsible for their healing. This is a noble effort that will ulti-mately fail because no one can heal someone else; that is a violation of their free will. And it takes our focus away from our own healing.

We have a long-held belief that healing others leads to our own healing and that is why we often find ourselves taking on others' pain and having poor boundaries relating to how much we will become involved in their lives. Without these boundaries we get so caught up in their healing that we do not have the time or energy for our own. And by taking on their issues, they become ours. The most damaging result of this, though, is that despite our good intentions all we are doing is affirming their powerlessness and their inability to experience, learn from and overcome their lessons.

When we take the other approach to healing, being of service, we remember that we are the light in the lives of others. We can then let them acknowledge their power, the value of their lessons and their responsibility for their reality. There will be many opportunities to help them and we can choose the way that honors their power and ability to heal themselves. By taking this path we give each person unconditional love and non-judgment and lead them into the light to allow them to find their own path to healing. They will make the choices serve their healing needs, that they are able to make and we have completed our role in serving them by pointing them to the light and allowing them to absorb what they can in that moment. The most loving way to serve others is to allow them the freedom to experience and learn from their own lessons in their own way.

Consider these principles for your personal mastery journey:
Do you recognize the healing role you play in others' lives?

Are you healing as a servant or by being of service?

Do you feel responsible for anyone's healing?

Are you frustrated with people who will not choose a more powerful healing path?

Are you afraid that you have not completed your work with them if they do not accept and embrace the healing you offer?

Can you recognize that everyone uses their power in the best way they can?

Do you know how to establish clear boundaries with those who present themselves to you for healing?

Those who choose to avoid healing have made a powerful choice for themselves, one that we cannot change. It is time for us to release our commitment to healing others as a servant and to acknowledge our role as healers in service to humanity. This does not involve who or how many we heal, but how we allow that to happen for the benefit of all, including ourselves. Finding the balance in these roles benefits everyone as each person is able to act within their power and create healing in their lives, according to their level of spiritual growth and understanding.

Releasing the 'doing' aspect of healing, which is what we do when we take on the role of servant, as opposed to 'being' a healer, in which we are of service, can be difficult. We have been the healer in our soul groups and with our karmic partners since the dawn of time and now we must step aside, let them move on and use the information we give them to the best of their abilities. Can we allow them the freedom to fully experience their karma, which we have often balanced or mitigated for them? Can we release our own fear of having to return for yet another lifetime if they do not heal and grow to the extent that we believe they should or know is a possibility for them?

When we release ourselves from 'being' others' healing, which means we try to do the healing work for them, we see where we have been holding ourselves back, limiting our own experience of embodying the higher octaves of Christ Consciousness, beyond that of being a martyr, and staying in energetic vibrations that we do not resonate with.

Contrary to what we believe, our own soul growth is not dependent on anyone else's and we do not have to stay behind with anyone, delaying our own movement, until they are able to complete their healing. The path of spiritual mastery requires that we see everyone as a master and not make judgments about what their mastery looks like. Everyone's path is uniquely focused on whatever lessons they have to learn and achieve. Each person is on their own mastery path, even the person we view as the least spiritually knowledgeable is on this path, progressing at their own rate, learning as much as they are capable of at this time. Although we try to help them move along faster, learn more, and incorporate more light, we cannot make the process happen any faster for them. So the question for us is not whether we are willing to be with some one until they finally achieve their healing, but to what extent we obligate ourselves to do their healing for them and stay in energies which may no longer resonate with us.

Are we able to accept that we have done all we can to help them with their lessons and we need to move on and allow them to find other teachers who will connect with them at their energetic level?

Can we say goodbye to our long-held healing commitments and not feel guilty about those we believe we are leaving behind?

This is a healing moment for our soul, to convince our human self that we are not responsible for others' choices or healing and release ourselves from lifetimes of assumed commitments to healing everyone and the world so we can eventually be healed and release from obligations to return to our soul group's karmic cycles.

We enter each lifetime with a significant amount of guilt over the healing we believe has not occurred for our soul group, some of which we may feel responsible for, and a commitment to change that dynamic. This is where we can become the "healer as servant" in our rush to speed up the healing so we can be complete and have closure. Although we approach our healing mission from this perspective, we cannot complete healing cycles by martyring ourselves for others. True healing is achieved through forgiveness of ourselves and others, and release. The longer we assume the role of martyr, the more we delay our ascension and theirs. By allowing everyone to be on their own path, without the benefit of our participation in their healing to the extent that we become the source of healing we believe they require, we empower them to do their own healing work.

As our energy shifts and we disconnect from them the more difficult this choice becomes since we believe that this is a path we would complete together in these final steps of our long shared soul journey and we now find that after all of our efforts, we may have to take the next steps on that journey alone.

While difficult, the choice is actually very obvious. The more we try to heal others, the more they pull away from us. As we complete our healing journey, we move into levels of energetic vibration that no longer allow us to be the martyred healer. And it is uncomfortable for us to be with those who still hold that energy or that expectation of us. The choice for us is to move fully into our new vibration and experience our reality from this new level. But we have strong ties to our healer status and the soul group connections that are part of our emotional DNA. In the scope of these ties it can be tempting for us to delay our growth because we feel their pain and fear. And we are afraid for them, of what will happen if they do not complete their healing to the extent that we believe they can or should. It is our natural tendency to help them because that is what we have always done. So we delay our own movement, hoping that by giving them more time or one more chance they will 'see the light' and our completion cycle can include their healing as well as ours.

This is a time for the completion of cycles, to move into higher levels of being, to accept new vibrations and to ascend. But not everyone is ready or willing to do the work that is required for their completion in our timetable. We will all face painful choices to allow those close to us to learn, heal and grow without our hand holding, to recognize their use of their power in the best and most perfect way possible and to let them find their own way out of their self-imposed darkness. Our choice has to be for ourselves, for what is best for our own soul growth. And we can disconnect energetically from others to allow them to choose the direction and timing of their healing and to ascend in their own way and in their own time. Sometimes when they know that we will stand by then while they contemplate this choice, we actually allow them to delay their healing because they know that we will not abandon them.

We can guide everyone to the light of their own understanding by gently disconnecting from our need to be the healer as a servant and martyr and release ourselves from the commitment to be their source of healing in this way or in any other way that puts demands on their healing. Then we will complete our cycles and allow them to finish theirs in a way that brings them to the full realization of their power and divinity, without sacrificing our own soul growth in the process. If this is happening to you, you can be at peace with your decision to move on for that is what is best for your soul and your journey will be at a new vibration, with new experiences, new learning and a new soul group as you release the one you have been the healer for and allow yourself to be a participant in one whose members do not require healing.

Consider these principles for your personal mastery journey:

Do you see the cycles of healing that are present within your soul group?

Can you see how and where you hold the light for others and direct their healing or assume responsibility for it?

What have you sacrificed in your own life and your path to allow others as many healing opportunities as they need?

How could you benefit by releasing someone in your life to find their own path to healing and move forward on your path?

Are you ready to release your guilt and fear that someone will not follow the 'right' path without your guidance and support?

Can you allow everyone around you to be powerful in their own way, removing judgments about how powerless you believe their way is?

Can you be content to "be the light" that shines for others by embodying the joy, abundance, peace and unconditional love that you wish for them,   in yourself?

What is really happening to us, on every level, is that we are afraid. We are afraid of doing the wrong thing or of not doing the right thing. We are afraid of going too far or not far enough. We are afraid of having to move backwards on our path but also afraid of moving ahead because we have no idea of what awaits us there. We are also afraid that we will not honor our soul contracts and have to return to finish them. We are afraid for those in our soul group who are not willing to do their healing work and this fear causes us to try to push them into healing they may not be ready for or are unwilling to do.

To find peace we must first find our fear so we can resolve it and then we no longer have to be afraid. Can we be brave enough to look beyond our fears so we can find their source and release them? Finding our fear is an important step on our path to spiritual mastery.

Where Is Your Fear?

Each of us has a dark place within us where our fear resides and we believe that this is where we are bad, undeserving and unworthy of blessings. But fear is not the darkness of a terrible place that we can never be released from, it is simply the absence of light, that place where we have allowed ourselves to be disconnected from Source. We fear an unknown future, basing our fears on a known past where something failed once and it will certainly fail again the next time we try it. We feel fear as a sense of discomfort or hesitation, even a sense of foreboding. But it is more than that. It is a reminder of events that have already happened in this and in previous lifetimes. Although we can connect our fears to events in the current lifetime, they represent energies we bring with us from other lifetimes, events and situations that have happened to us many times before.

Our fear is encoded within our emotional DNA, which has stored memories of experiences in different incarnations in the form of our emotional responses. So while we do not remember what happened, just how we felt about it, it is a constant reminder of a time in the past. All of these memories are transferred into each new lifetime, with the purpose of reconciling our emotional memory with our spiritual Truth, that all exists in perfection. We call these memories our fears and they represent areas where we have been disconnected our own perfection and divinity.

No matter what form our fears take, they all emanate from a core fear, of being abandoned or rejected by Source. They relate to a distortion of our memory of the reason for our lifetimes on earth. We read in the Bible that we were cast out of the Garden of Eden as punishment for our imperfection and our choice of humanity, destined to wander the earth and suffer for our sins. That story is not true because we are the ones who left heaven, our spiritual Home, of our own volition and who entered the realms of density and polarity so we could reconnect ourselves and humanity as part of our collective ascension.

This journey is a divine assignment, not a punishment. It is a sacred pact that we have made with Creator to participate in the earth's ascension journey, the shift from its third dimensional experience to higher dimensions. We are partners with the earth, not outcasts doomed to wander here forever, without hope of returning Home, for our ultimate task is to merge the two energies, spiritual and material, to complete this cycle and bring heaven on earth.

We also have an image of our Creator as an all-powerful, somewhat benevolent, often judgmental father figure who tries to help us see the error of our ways and who controls our access to heaven. Our belief that we have done something to betray Creator's trust and deserve to be punished is what keeps us from painlessly completing the process of reconnection. Our sense of powerlessness arises from this belief that we have done something wrong and need to be forgiven by Creator before we can begin to receive blessings in the way of forgiveness, assistance and support on our journey. Then when we take on the belief that we are powerless a step further and wonder why our benevolent Creator does not come to our rescue every time we have a problem. After all, we are told and believe that we were cast out at God's order and cannot control our own destiny, so why are we not rescued from the problems that we are powerless to prevent from happening?

This creates anger and adds another layer of separation between us and Creator. And we feel even more powerless because we are afraid to ask the question about our separation for fear of the answer that we may receive, that we really are unworthy, we were deliberately cast out and that God really does not love us. Even though we know this is not true, it is our deepest, most terrible fear and is based on the challenges of our life experience, it is hard for us to consider that it is a false belief.

Because we are afraid to ask this question of our Creator, we challenge everyone around us to act like we think God should and put the burden of rescuing us on them, making them responsible for making us feel better about ourselves, ensuring our happiness and validating us. Rather than looking within for reassurance of our worthiness, we look outside ourselves for someone to tell us that we are perfect, good and deserve to go Home, and we ask for their love, validation, acceptance and support.

When that does not happen we are angry with them and ourselves but we are really angry with God and another layer of density is added to our separation. When we can release our belief that we should be rescued by our Creator or those we put in that place of power and judgment, that we are powerless in this world, we do not have what it takes to create the life of our dreams and heaven on earth for ourselves, is when we will release our fears. But until we do that, we must deal with them.

Each lifetime is our way of reconnecting to Source but rather than taking a direct path to that outcome by expressing our light, we take an indirect pathway by living our greatest fears, the places where we cannot love ourselves and believe in our imperfection, and ask Source to love us anyway. If we can convince ourselves that we are worthy of love, by being rescued by our Creator, then we have proof that our disconnection does not exist. But Creator does not disconnect from us, we are the ones who disconnect from our spiritual center. And it is not the spiritual world that is moving closer to us, we are the ones who are moving closer to Spirit, by releasing our fear and disavowing our disconnection. We are never and can never be disconnected from Spirit.

Our true salvation comes from doing what needs to be done first, working on ourselves. How many people do we know, including ourselves, who do the same thing over and over again, such as connecting with the same kind of person, making the same decisions, creating the same kind of drama in their life and then being angry, unhappy or disappointed with the outcome? Instead of acknowledging their responsibility for their reality they are angry with God and wonder why their life is so challenging, why they are so unhappy and why God doesn't step in and stop the madness.

Until we understand the reason for this journey we feel alone, isolated, abandoned by our Creator and believe that we must suffer hopelessly and powerlessly. Our fear has become our life yet there is hope for us in the glimpses of mastery we can know when we see the Truth, that this is all part of the Divine Plan of ascension and reconnection and that the light we think has abandoned us is a constant presence within us.

Consider these questions for your personal mastery journey:

Is there someone in your life who you feel should be more supportive of you?

Do you know someone who you are trying hard to please or impress and feel that receiving this is very important to you?

What are you willing to do to gain their approval or acknowledgement?

Are you angry with those people in your life who are not supportive or appreciative of you?

Do you look outside yourself for validation?

Can you see where you may be angry with your Creator for your separation, the powerlessness you feel and your perceived lack of support?

Is there someone in your life who reflects that anger?

Your life journey contains many events, people and situations that support the ascension work you have come to do on earth. Can you see how they fit together and have led you to this moment of understanding?

Do you know what your fears are and how they block your path?

Where are your fears? Any place in your life where you feel stuck, powerless and ineffective, depressed, unhappy and confused, where you may know what to do but are unsure as to how to proceed is where you have fear. Each of these conditions is an aspect of your fear presenting itself for resolution and healing. While our fears may seem very powerful and they can be intimidating, resolution comes when we remember that they are simply areas where we have disconnected from through an emotional wound we created. They also represent areas where we can reconnect to Source or our central core of divinity. Fear is not from Spirit, it is an energy of the material world, an aspect of its density and polarity that we connect with because we carry its vibration . Fears are part of our soul group experience and karmic cycles. We incarnate to experience our fears so we can know what they are and make choices that remove us from the darkness of fear and into the light of understanding. Since they are so deeply ingrained within our cellular memory and emotional DNA, and whatever we are afraid of is very personal and relevant to us, we do not even know that we have them for they are part of our everyday thinking and of the thinking of everyone around us.

So stop for a moment and consider what your fears are. Do you have a deep, unknown fear that you cannot explain but is present in everything you do? Is there something that you wish you could do but are so afraid of that you cannot even begin? Do you see patterns of fear in those who are close to you?

This came up when I was reading for a client who was a very successful professional with a deep fear of public speaking, even though she had to speak before large groups as part of her job. While looking at her energetic field I saw an incident that had happened when she was nine years old and the emotions around it were still with her. She immediately knew what it was and was surprised that it still affected her because it had happened so long ago. But she remembered how traumatic and embarrassing it was at the time and could see how she had made the connection between that incident of public humiliation and her fear of being in front of large groups of people.

From a karmic perspective, she had several lifetimes in which she had to speak out and had been publicly humiliated, persecuted and punished for speaking. What happened to her at age nine, was not an isolated incident, but the presence of her fear coming to the forefront to prepare her for its healing. Once she was aware that what she believed was an isolated incident was actually a re-play of a fear whose presence was reminding her of what she had to overcome in her life, she was able to make peace with it. Then she could focus on releasing the fear at its source so she could speak in public with fearless confidence. Public speaking was no longer a source of embarrassment and humiliation but a way for her to interact with people in a powerful way.

Our fears may seem all encompassing, strong, omnipresent and so powerful that we cannot get beyond them. But whether they manifest as a fear of being out in the public, such as agoraphobia, or a fear of embarrassment, humiliation, persecution, ridicule or betrayal, they have their basis in an aspect of separation and are linked to our karma.

They block the flow of our expression, which is why they often manifest as something we are afraid to do, as in the client who was afraid of public speaking. And our fears in this lifetime, no matter what they are, have their basis in the past, another lifetime where the result of an action left a powerful memory that became a fear, a separation from our divine perfection that we would create opportunities to resolve in other lifetimes. There are no large or small fears, no important or unimportant ones. Each fear holds the space of separation and disconnection from the perfection of our true self.

Yet we created them as part of our healing journey so they have no power other than the power we give them. They are not from Creator or Spirit, they are from us, as part of our human experience and releasing them is part of our mastery journey. Because they emanate from us, we are the only ones who can resolve and release them. And once we do, we also release the blocks that make us feel powerless, confused, unsupported and stuck. Fear and karma are intertwined and karma is born from fear, it creates more fear, which creates more karma, and so on.

It is a vicious cycle that continues in an endless circle of pain until we release ourselves from the fear that we have created whose purpose is to remind us of our healing journey. We do not have to hang onto the fear, we can just let it go and as we do, remind ourselves that we are not being punished or condemned, there is no imperfection in the Universe and we have a special mission to accomplish and understanding fear is one of its aspects.

All of our lifetimes have led up to this wonderful moment, which is our opportunity to step into our mastery, and take the next step beyond fear into mastery, which shines the light of forgiveness, divine healing and unconditional love. This is a time to bring heaven on earth, to heal karma and remove fear from the earth's energetic dynamic, by releasing it from ours.

Consider these questions for your personal mastery journey:

Can you name two or more fears that you believe prevent you from living a fulfilling life?

Do you remember when you first created these fears?

Do you think you can release them?

What does your life look like if you do not have these fears?

Fear creates victims because when viewed through the lens of fear, we are powerless, out of control, pawns in the game of life and ruled by a destiny that someone else created for us. This is the victim paradigm, a belief in our power-lessness that is so strong, it creates a widening circle of victim consciousness that we embrace until we become what we fear the most, powerless,   ineffective, helpless and without hope.

The Victim Paradigm

Why has humanity struggled through eons of karma and the pain and chaos it causes? Why have we not been able to reconnect to Source before now if we have always had the ability to do so? Why is life such a struggle for us? All of those questions have one answer, the victim paradigm. At the moment of our separation we had a choice to remember that we were simply part of an experiment in reconnection and stay focused on that path. Instead, we created a story about being unloved, powerless, unwanted and undeserving of God's love. And the victim paradigm was created. The energies were set for humanity to experience life as powerless victims of the third dimension, destined to struggle endlessly against forces we thought were beyond our control. And with karma our victim story was magnified, a testimonial to the fact that we are surrounded by many forces who wish us harm.

Within our ascension journey we have an opportunity to transform the victim paradigm, to erase it from humanity's consciousness and replace it with the empowering memory of our Source connection, our co-creative abilities and the power we have as a spark of the light of God.

Nearly every lifetime starts with our victim story, our personal story of defeat, destruction, despair and depression, which we try to resolve by re-creating it and seeking a different solution for the pain through creating other outcomes. The details of the victim story are very real and serve as a reminder that despite our best efforts, we can be overcome by people or events and the life of our dreams can turn into a nightmare in the blink of an eye. No matter when the victim story first began, every detail is etched in our mind at the level of cellular memory and our emotional DNA, serving as a reminder of the pain and suffering that a lifetime can bring.

But this is not the intention of our victim experiences, which is to allow us to re-create our powerless scenarios so we can manifest a more powerful outcome. Every lesson in power begins with powerlessness and in our victim paradigm we have an array of our most powerless experiences to draw from so we can transform them into life affirming, expansive expressions of our power.

All of us go through different aspects of being a victim in our life, beginning with childhood when we are vulnerable and dependent, to adulthood where we try to achieve our dreams in the face of what can appear to be insurmountable challenges. We are faced with the choice of being a victim and believing in our limitations or rising above them to becoming a victor and stepping into our power. The victim paradigm is one that all of humanity must—and can—overcome and releasing it is part of our individual and collective spiritual journey.

Our victim story can begin in childhood when we remember incidents of being bullied by others, our parents were emotionally or physically unavailable or our needs were not met in some way. Or maybe something happened, such as an illness, abuse, a difficult home life, the death of our parents or siblings that created trauma and began to create the foundation for the victim paradigm's belief in powerlessness. On an unconscious level that paradigm becomes our life template and determines the course our path will take. Then we attract people and situations that relate to and even enhance our victim template because that is the energy we resonate with. When we wonder why people are not respectful, don't honor us or seem to go out of their way to block us at every turn, or why our life is hard, we are unhappy, unlucky or unfulfilled, the answer lies in our victim paradigm.

While we may feel very alone with our victim story, every person has one. Even the most accomplished person harbors a secret fear that they will become victim to some forgotten past incident, a newcomer who will overshadow them or be faced with a struggle that will reveal a weakness.

While we may not call ourselves a victim, our thoughts, beliefs and actions tell another story. A victim has many problems, disappointments, unmet expectations and unfulfilled dreams. They often think that others seem to be more lucky, gifted, blessed or connected than they are. A victim shares their victim stories with everyone because they want sympathy and to know that they are not alone in their unhappiness. They have probably received 'victim training' from their family, which can have generational patterns of victim beliefs. And they become a victim of their own victim story. Then they attract those who take advantage of them because victims attract tyrants, people who need to control, manipulate or dominate others to feel powerful, or they attract other victims.

When we are operating from the victim paradigm we send out a silent message to others that we are powerless and that they are more powerful than we are. When we need help we can find someone who answers that call but if we give our power to them in return for their help, we are pushing ourselves farther into the victim paradigm. Then our rescuer can become the person who controls us, so the savior becomes a tyrant and we step from one victim role to another. We can release the victim paradigm by reconnecting to our power through the memory of our Source connection but first we must understand the victim paradigm and be willing to release it even though we may be in a victim cycle as we are choosing our options.

Our spiritual journey can be compared to the Native American ceremony of soul retrieval, where a shaman takes the seeker on a journey to recapture the pieces of the soul that have been lost to past life traumas. In each lifetime we are provided with opportunities to heal ancient traumas that are buried within our soul memory and emotional DNA and to bring ourselves back to spiritual and emotional wholeness. These situations are revealed to us in the different ways we feel like a victim, the various trainings in 'victimhood' that we are offered by those who agree to create victim opportunities for us. The journey to wholeness begins with our ability to find our spiritual center, where we can begin to reconnect with our power and start the journey to reconnecting with our selves.

This is also the story of humanity's journey from its beginning until now, the time when we are shifting into new vibrations of being. As a human family we have the opportunity to step out of the victim paradigm and to remember our Source connection, divinity and our power. Our victim stories are based in fact, in this lifetime and in previous ones. There are situations where people abused us, took advantage of us or did not do what we believed they could or should have done. But within each of these victim stories is a karmic lesson, a soul contract, and a starting point for our journey to forgiveness, healing, transformation and closure. We have a choice to remain a victim and continue to suffer in powerlessness or to bring the wounded pieces of our soul together and become victors, spiritual masters who understand the greater picture and can choose healing over pain, the present moment over the past and a life of abundance and fulfillment over lack and sorrow.

While our focus is on our current lifetime, our spiritual journey encompasses many lifetimes and a wide range of life experiences. We have been kings, queens, peasants, priests and priestesses, mothers and fathers, sons and daughters, warriors, bakers, gardeners and horse trainers. We have been honest, powerful, generous and compassionate, as well as dishonest, powerless, greedy and manipulative. In the full spectrum of our lifetimes we have done many things, some we would be proud of today and others less so. For every lifetime in which we have abused our power, we have an opportunity to experience the abuse that we were responsible for and assume the role of the victim, then atone for it and heal and transform that energy.

When we have not used our power wisely or out of fear, we are given another lifetime which will provide us with many opportunities to step into our power. All of our lessons in power begin with an experience of victimhood. The fact that we can assess our life experiences in this way and feel pain, sorrow and compassion for the ways in which we may have once tormented others is a testament to our spiritual growth.

Clients are often surprised when their karmic readings reveal lifetimes in which they have misused power, were manipulative, and may have been cruel and unkind. It is hard for them to acknowledge that they could have been so non-spiritual in other lifetimes. But before we judge our behavior we must remember that there is learning in each lifetime and in the give and take of karmic cycles, we are both victim and tormenter, abuser and abused, until we learn all aspects of an experience and are willing to forgive and take the path to healing and replace the victim paradigm with something much more powerful, such as mastery. Julia's story is an example of this:

Julia wanted a karmic reading to understand her relationship with her daughter, who had always been a rebellious child was now a teenage mother. Julia had two other children who were well-behaved and easy to manage but this daughter was something else entirely. As we looked at her different lifetimes I saw where Julia had been a ruler, priest and a very wealthy man, all very powerful and authoritative. Her daughter had been someone who challenged her power and authority, and was usually right, but whom Julia saw as a threat to her ability to live her life the way she chose.

So in different lifetimes she had her daughter killed, imprisoned or banished. There was also a lifetime in which she had been her daughter's father and had not allowed her to marry the man she loved and instead, had forced him to marry someone else, to spite her. All of these lifetimes had created a very strong victim paradigm in both Julia and her daughter. Julia had learned that each lifetime with her daughter would involve a challenge to her power. Her daughter knew that each lifetime would present a challenge to her self, her happiness and often, her life.

So in the current lifetime Julia allowed her daughter to victimize her out of a sense of remorse and guilt for what she had done in previous lifetimes. She tried to heal her karma by atoning for what she had done and martyring herself to help her daughter resolve her anger. And the daughter, who was born with lifetimes of unresolved anger and a strong victim paradigm, became a victim of her anger and created a situation, by having a child at a young age, which forced her mother to acknowledge her, to focus on her needs and to care for her and her child. The pregnancy forced Julia, who had been preparing to begin a new career, to delay her plans so she could help her daughter and the baby.

Learning about the karma would have resolved this situation but because of the strong victim paradigm present in their karmic cycle, each of them had to resolve their victim paradigm by becoming more powerful. Instead, they each allowed the other to make them powerless and by doing so got stuck in the cycle. Eventually Julia would need to release her guilt and remorse, to stop trying to atone for what she had done and allow her daughter to find a more powerful path for her life. Her daughter would have to release her anger towards her mother, take responsibility for the path she had chosen in previous lifetimes, of being her mother's judge and guide to a more righteous, compassionate path, and find more powerful ways to live her life.

This is why our victim paradigm can be so difficult to change, because it deals with people and situations that we have been victimized by, are angry about or engage in self sabotage that prevents us from have a more expansive view of possible solutions to healing our victim energy.

Consider these questions for your personal mastery journey:

Do you see how the victim paradigm functions in your life?

Did you receive 'victim training' from your family and are they victims too?

What is your victim story, the place in your life where you are you powerless, feel out of control or afraid?

How can you turn your victim story into victory of the light over the darkness?

Can you accept that in some lifetimes you may have been a tyrant, abuser or misused your power and energy?

Are you able to understand that the challenges in your life may be a form of atonement that you have created to right any wrongs you have done in previous lifetimes and are you willing to forgive yourself unconditionally so you can release them?

Can you see how others may be attracted by your victim energy and supporting your victim story?

Are you willing to release your victimhood now so you can manifest your reality from your empowered, victorious self?

Without understanding, growth and healing, we are in an endless cycle of seeking retribution from those once caused us pain, as they are from us. Our past behavior cannot be judged as good or bad because it was part of our soul journey and reflected the choices we could make at that time. Each time the karma wheel turns in our direction we can make the choice of compassion, forgiveness and Light or more lessons in darkness, powerlessness and fear. As we seek balance between the light and dark we are atoning for those lifetimes that were spent learning about the darker side of our energy, our shadow side. Our mastery journey requires that we reconcile the dark with the light and return ourselves to balance and wholeness and embrace our shadow connection.

The Shadow Connection

We are a collection of many different aspects, each of them contributing to our unfolding path of reconnection to Source and re-membering our physical, emotional, spiritual and mental bodies into wholeness. Within the plane of polarity that is the third dimensional experience, each thing has its opposite, beginning with love and fear, which is one aspect of what we know as light and darkness. These are expressed in continuously shifting proportions, whose balance depends on the experiences we have chosen for our lifetime's journey of learning and understanding. There is a space in between our light and dark-ness which contains everything we need to know to propel us into the path of conscious, instead of unconscious, choosing. This is our shadow and although we can be afraid of what it contains, it is a powerful aspect of our being.

We are not, at any time, fully light or fully dark; rather, we exist in a place that is in between the two, where we experience life through the proportional balance of light and darkness that we carry. This is our shadow, which contains all of our pain, suffering and fear, as well as the knowledge, understanding and love that we need to bring enlightenment to our path. It is in the shadow that our transformation occurs and understanding our shadow connection is the key to understanding the purpose and meaning of our journey.

We see the shadow in many different ways, depending on our situation and our level of fear. Yet the shadow is the same, a constant presence whose balance of light and dark shifts according to the changes in our perception. Imagine how you would be grateful for the relief of a shady spot on a hot, sunny day. Yet on a cloudy, cool day that same shadow is cold and uninviting. The shadow is the same, but the context is different. And it is our judgment that stands in the way of our being able to appreciate the shadow.

Since we are on a journey of reconnection and movement from the darkness to the light, we believe that the dark is bad and light is good, so we run from the dark, afraid to face its lessons and blessings, in our unwillingness to acknowledge the aspects of ourselves which we believe make us unworthy of being in the light. We believe that unless we are all light we are not worthy of our divinity and the dark will overtake us. Yet there is no understanding in either of those polarities. As we incorporate mastery into our being we realize that it is just as impossible for us to see if a light is too bright as it is for us to see in total darkness. And it is that glimmer of light in the darkness that allows us to see the shadows, where we can begin to understand where we are, what we are doing and why. The shadow is our helper, our vehicle of understanding on the earth plane and without it our mastery journey is not possible.

Hidden in our shadow is the separation, the places here we believe we have disconnected from Source, our fear and the memory of where we have been less than perfect and not honored our commitment to express the light within. What lives within our shadow? Everything that we have ever experienced until this moment in time. Why is it so valuable? Because it is pure information which, without judgment, is simply a string of experiences, things that happened to us as a result of our choices in this and other lifetimes. The information is very useful but with it we begin to judge ourselves for being less than perfect, succumbing to our fears, acting out of anger and causing suffering for ourselves and others.

This is our imperfect and critical knowing and our judgment moves us farther from the light, creating more separation, because we believe we have stepped off of our path. But experience is the central theme of our path and with each one comes a lesson and a blessing, the chance for release and redemption. God never asks for atonement in any form other than our willingness to forgive ourselves as well as others. Our belief that we must suffer for our sins is an aspect of our judgment that we use to impose suffering on ourselves, delaying our reconnection until we accept ourselves as part of the light and learn to see the divine within us, no matter what our experiences may have been.

The shadow merely reveals our areas of pain to us so that we can choose another path. In a previous lifetime, for example, we may have had unlimited wealth and used it in ways that hurt and caused pain for others and ended that lifetime believing that wealth is bad. The current lifetime may be filled with financial struggle and we wish for unlimited wealth, believing that having money would solve all of our problems but our fear of abusing wealth, from a previous lifetime, limits us in this area. In this scenario, the shadow contains the information we need to understand why we are blocking the flow of wealth and abundance in this lifetime.

In the previous chapter we read about Julia and her daughter and the victimhood they shared from previous lifetimes together. Julia could not understand why her daughter was so angry and rebellious and her daughter was unable to move beyond her anger at her mother for the many lifetimes in which she was victimized and disenfranchised because of the truth she shared. The shadow is where the information they needed to resolve their karma and release their victim paradigm is held and if they could have accessed the shadow, they would have had fewer challenges with each other.

Without this understanding of the shadow and its information, our lifetimes can be spent running in circles and feeling stuck, not knowing why the energy does not move for us. Within the shadow is the information about what we have already learned which could prevent us from repeating that which we no longer need to experience.

Consider these questions for your personal mastery journey:

Are you aware of your shadow, the places in your life where you feel imperfect, wrong, angry or guilty?

Does your shadow make you feel powerless and unworthy?

Are you afraid of your shadow?

Are there people in your life who are helping you notice your shadow aspects?

Can you accept that by knowing the shadow you can find your healing path back to your inner light?

Have you experienced your shadow as you accept your mastery and are you willing to accept that by reconciling the energies of your shadow, what you dislike or fear, you become a master of them?

Instead of fearing the shadow we can bless it, learn from and embrace it because it is both our humanity and our divinity, representing all of the darkness we have agreed to heal and release so we can return ourselves to the light that we are. If we look at the shadow fearlessly, we find that it can actually be a blessing. It is not the shadow that we fear, it is our memories and experience of some of the shadow's aspects that keep us from looking at it more closely. Since the shadow's memory is part of our mental and emotional body what we fear are the possibilities that the shadow could hold. Ultimately, we fear our own imperfection, the knowing that we have been on the dark side, as the source of pain and fear for ourselves and others. Yet the shadow is just a thing that is powerless without the interpretation of our feelings, beliefs, thoughts and desires. The blessings of the shadow lie in its ability to reveal the path back to the light within us and use it to enable us to live in the light instead of the darkness.

We believe that the shadow is where we have been 'bad' and our 'good' resides in the light. But if we are willing to look within the shadow and shine light on it we can find strength to overcome it because knowledge is the shadow's gift and within this knowledge lies infinite possibilities for renewal. Instead of focusing on the light, we can use the light to uncover what is in the dark. This is the mystery of our healing — the gift that we seek from the light we actually find by examining the dark.

The shadow's purpose is to help us remember the aspects of darkness that we have used to reinforce our belief in our separation. Its light is revealed when we connect from a point of understanding, able to take the next step with crystal clarity once we know what we have done before, asking the questions that will provide us with new information and perspectives on how we have separated ourselves from our divinity and what we can do to renew that connection. When we look at the shadow from its light side the darkness is not as dark, whatever we have to heal is not quite as difficult, and we remember that we have help on this journey in the form of our spiritual team and our own willingness to heal. And the light helps us to be less critical, demanding and judgmental of ourselves so we can begin to learn without suffering.

The shadow holds all the energetic vibrations which correspond to every emotion we have generated across our lifetimes. Every fear-based emotion represents an interruption in the flow of our Source connection. As we move forward on our life path we must choose a response to every situation that is either grounded in love or fear. When we choose love, that aspect of the shadow is released and the flow of energy in our life is raised to a higher vibration. When we choose fear, the shadow releases the corresponding energy from our emotional history for us to experience once again. While the details and context may be changed to reflect the circumstances of our current lifetime, the energy is the same and we have another opportunity to experience it and this time, to choose love.

This is the shadow's healing gift to us as it and it desires healing as much as we do. With each choice we are able to alter our shadow's range of vibration, shifting the balance of dark and light, in accordance with our level of spiritual knowledge and understanding. Our objective is simply to find the balance between dark and light, fear and love, chaos and peace that allows for the movement of energy in our lives to be a continuous and uninterrupted flow of light, abundance, love and grace. This is our dance, in which we look for the balance between dark and light that allows us to learn, heal grow and ascend so we learn to make the decisions and choices that support our healing mission.

As we move through a lifetime we see our shadow reflected in everything — every thought and belief, every person and experience, every choice we make and even the potential realities we can see as available to us. They are all filtered through and limited by our shadow and how we choose to heal and transform it. This determines whether we see our shadow as a wonderful vehicle of understanding and a way to reconcile our experience of the polarity of fear, or as a black mark on our psyche, an example of our weakness and vulnerability to the temptation of fear. In this way we see our shadow as either working for us or against us, and we are either flowing with its learning or fighting it every step of the way.

In any lifetime where we have taken on too much darkness, which includes lifetimes where we have experienced any kind of trauma, our balance of light and dark is disrupted, the shadow takes on more darkness and it is harder to find the light within it. But it is still there — without the light we are unable to see the shadow. Each time we look for the light in the shadow, we take a step towards the light it contains and transform the shadow's energetic vibration. The shadow is our connection to both our Self and to Source, the missing link in our understanding of what we have chosen to experience and how we experience it. It is a doorway to our soul healing that provides us with both the questions we need to ask and their answers.

To better understand our shadow connection and what it means to us in terms of our healing we need to embrace it as a part of the whole, allow ourselves to be in the place of understanding with compassion and sympathy and then follow the light we find there. Where is the light in the shadow? It is present when we remove judgment, criticism and blame, when we recognize ourselves for every aspect of learning, understanding and growth that we have accomplished. We are not aware of the immense importance of each step on our journey and what we consider to be an insignificant learning experience may actually be the most important healing work we have ever done.

The light of understanding is in everything; we simply have to let it shine. No matter how small we think it is, the light is always seen and it is at the darkest of times that the smallest speck of light shines brightly. Through it we can create the balance that we seek that will bring peace to our chaos, embrace ourselves with love and acceptance and remember that we are bringing light to the world through everything that we are willing to do for ourselves and in every way that we are willing to acknowledge the light in our own lives and in ourselves.

Can we see that within the darkness of our experiences there is always the glimmer of light? Although we live in polarity, which is reflected in the opposites of the energies that exist on earth, we have the opportunity to experience neutrality or balance within our shadow. Yes, we are on a journey to the light and to reconnection, away from darkness and fear and into the energies of unconditional love. But it is our collective mission to bring heaven on earth, not earth to heaven.

If the shadow is good and the darkness is not bad, what is the purpose of this journey?

Are we not supposed to bring the light forward? Yes, but in order to balance the polarity of darkness and light, we cannot ignore or wish it away. Our mastery journey brings the shadow forward so we can find ways to reconcile ourselves with it, allow the energy to flow to and through it in an uninterrupted stream so we make more powerful, enlightened choices. The darkness will exist in some aspect of the Universe, as it is present everywhere. Do you know that it is the darkness of the sky that allows us to see the beauty of the stars, which are still present but are invisible in the light of day? And just as it takes darkness to perceive light, it also takes light to know that we are in the dark. When we are comfortable with our shadow, we are able to forgive ourselves and others, release ourselves from the darkness into the light and our healing is complete. And this completes an aspect of our ascension, preparing us for the next one.

Consider these questions for your personal mastery journey:

Do you see how your shadow is working with your healing purpose to help you find your light?

Are there aspects of your shadow that are blocking the flow of abundance, joy and love into your life?

Can you use the information that your shadow is giving you to find opportunities for transformation, healing and release?

Can you find the truth in what the shadow is telling you and then change what you believe about yourself, to reflect more light on your path?

Do you see how your shadow's vibrations are attracting everything in your life to you?

Are you ready for the transformation the shadow can provide you with?

Once we understand the shadow we are able to work with our darkness to expand the amount of light we allow into our life. This creates new life options and as we raise our energetic vibrations we also transform the levels of potential we can connect to from our field of potential. Each increase in our vibration opens doorways to new potential, new possibilities for us and our reality and a new pathway for our journey. In the field of potential is everything we can ever experience in our lifetime, limited only by the energetic vibrations we choose to express. The mastery journey expands our possibilities by expanding access to our field of potential.

The Field of Potential

From the spiritual perspective, our life exists on an energetic continuum that expresses the full spectrum of wholeness and perfection within each moment, based on our energetic vibrations and the unique place we occupy on our life journey in each moment. Our lives are perfect because we always express all of the potential that is available to us within each moment. We have not missed any opportunities or made any mistakes because we cannot choose options that are not available to us, as all of our options are limited to whatever we resonate with energetically in each moment. The choices we can make and the options that are encompassed within them are based on the combination of our needs, energy and the power we believe we have. And each choice we make reflects our fears and strengths, our willingness to embrace our power and divinity and the maximum energetic potential available to us from whatever is occupying our field of potential at that moment.

The field of potential is an energetic matrix containing everything we can manifest in a lifetime, which is the full range of our soul's promise for our mastery journey. But while the potential for something exists energetically, it manifests for us when we can connect to it, by being at its level of vibration. Access to any element in our field of potential is limited by the level of density that we carry through our humanity. So while we may have the potential for financial abundance, until we move ourselves into its vibration and release the density of the energy of lack and poverty, it will remain a potential that we cannot connect to.

If we ask for a fulfilling relationship, the partner of our dreams will be out of our reach until we clear the density of pain and sadness from our previous relationship experiences and raise our vibrations to the level of the loving, fulfilling, relationship we desire. And this is a tradeoff of sorts, where we must be willing to release the fears and limiting beliefs that keep us at an energetic vibration that is out of synch with what we wish for and want to manifest.

The field of potential is the starting point of our manifestation process, as it contains our dreams and heart's desire for what we want in our life. When we are ready to connect to another element in our field of potential, we disconnect from what we are currently manifesting and there is a gap in our energy flow, as we are no longer energetically connected to what we currently have but what we want to create is not quite within our reach. The steps we take to cross this gap determine how quickly we will connect to the next level of vibration and give form to the corresponding element from our field of potential.

If we believe that our dissatisfaction arises from having made a mistake, that we have chosen poorly and made wrong decisions, we will spend time in judgment and this lowers our vibration, delaying our ability to connect to the next level of our field of potential. If we understand that our dissatisfaction means we are ready to step into a new energetic dimension and have disconnected from the old energy, which is why it is no longer comfortable for us, we are prepared for the energy shift and the trip across the gap to the new elements in our field of potential occurs much more smoothly and quickly .

Consider these questions for your personal mastery journey:

Do you know what is in your field of potential? Think of one or more things you have always wanted to have, do or be. Do not judge whether they are possible, realistic or logical in this moment, just think about something you have always wanted. It is already in your field of potential, waiting for you to connect to it. What will it take in the form of healing or shifting your beliefs, to get there?

Do you have fears or judgments that prevent you from connecting to anything in your field of potential?

Has what you wanted been close to you at some point in your life but you were unable to bring it forward or connect to it?

Did you make choices at some point in your life that seemed to deliberately push your dreams or heart's desire away?

Are you regretful of your choices and if so, can you see how you are releasing your connection to the 'old' in your life and preparing to shift your vibrations to something else in your field of potential?

How can you raise your vibrations to manifest from higher levels of potential?

One way to speed this shift is to change our perspective on our choices. Every choice we make manifests something in our field of potential. Remember that while every possibility is present, it is not always available to us, as the availability of any potential depends on the choices we are willing to and can make. What we can choose depends on timing and vibration. It has to be the right time for that particular event to occur or choice to be made and we have to be at its vibration. The choices we made five, ten or more years ago were part of our field of potential at that time. Others may have been available but not within our energetic vibration, so we could not connect to them and were not even aware of them.

These options did not disappear completely, they remained available to us should we decide we wanted them at a later point in time. But as our vibrations shift so does what we want to connect to. An attractive option at age eighteen may not hold the same level of attraction at age forty. Do you remember when you could not wait to be twenty-one? Would you want to be twenty-one again and repeat everything you have learned since that time? Do you have the same dreams, needs and desires that you did then? Probably not. At this moment in your life you have different needs and desires and those are reflected in what you want to manifest from your field of potential.

But after a lifetime of disappointments we believe that we have lost our connection with our field of potential, that those things are no longer available to us because we believe that we get one chance or try at something and if we miss it, it is gone forever. There can be many permutations or varieties of an option that can appear at different times in our life, in different forms that correspond to our current energetic vibrations.

Consider Doreen's story as an example of how a lifetime dream can manifest because at age 72 she had her first experience of true love, something she had dreamed of, wanted and wished for her entire life. Doreen had plans to attend college and work at age eighteen but her parents thought that was inappropriate for a woman and wanted her to marry and have children instead, so she did. Her husband was controlling and emotionally distant and although Doreen did not love him she stayed in the marriage, took care of her family and always felt unfulfilled, like something was missing in her life.

Her husband died after thirty years and Doreen soon married another emotionally distant, controlling man because she was afraid of being alone and wanted the security of a marriage. After fifteen years her second husband died and she decided that she would not marry again. But she still wanted, hoped for and dreamed of having true love in her life.

She decided it was time to fulfill her lifelong dream of having a college degree so she enrolled in her local community college and began taking classes. Doreen loved school, was a good student and made new friends. She began to talk to a fellow student who was often in her study groups and they began to have lunch and spent long hours talking about many things. Doreen felt something with this man, an openness and connection that she had never felt before and she knew there was something different about this relationship.

A few months passed and one day he asked Doreen to dinner and she agreed. They began to date regularly and within a year were planning their wedding. For the first time in her life, Doreen was in love and had the relationship she had always dreamed of.

What changed in her life to allow this to happen? She decided that she would follow her heart and start living life the way she wanted to, learned to enjoy and even cherish her time alone and make friends and create a new life for herself. The option for true love was always in her field of potential but she had to be willing and ready to connect to it. Her greatest fear, of being alone, helped her attract partners who took care of her but who were also controlling because she did not want to be in control of her life. By releasing this fear and doing things that put her in control of her life Doreen was in a more powerful energetic position that allowed her to set her intention for true love and then wait for it to happen, and it did.

Besides the energetic requirements, there are other conditions we must satisfy when working with our field of potential. We must be willing to surrender our fears and release our resistance. Why would we have resistance to manifesting our dreams and how could we fear them? Resistance exists when the ego is at a lower energetic vibration than what we wish to manifest. The ego can create many reasons why we cannot or should not manifest something different and we must choose whether we will allow the ego's energy and fears to dominate or move beyond them into a higher vibration.

From the ego's past-based perspective, there is a price to pay for taking the risk to create change, beginning with the possibility of repeating past results and consequences. Within the ego lies the memory of all of our pain and power-lessness, every proof of our unworthiness and limitation and it constantly reminds us of our mistakes and failures and the emotional, mental, physical or spiritual price we paid for them. But while the ego remembers the pain, it does not always remember all of the details and instead, becomes fixated on one emotion, word, incident or event and uses that to judge every similar event in the future.

And it conveniently forgets that our life purpose is to learn lessons and heal karma, which is accomplished through our challenging life experiences. The ego lives in a very closed, single dimensional world where choices are made on an either/or basis, where a missed opportunity is gone forever and pain is always a possibility. It is through the ego that we see one choice as being better than another and regret 'lost' opportunities or missed chances. The ego has no understanding of the field of potential or energetic vibration and is only aware of what happened in the past and how that could possibly affect and limit the future.

We resolve ego issues when we understand them so let's look at the ego's 'price to pay' mentality in the appropriate perspective. The best example of this mentality is found in relationships, because they are where we have the greatest potential for pain, the most vulnerability and often the most difficult memories. The price of love is being vulnerable, repeating past choices, being hurt, abandoned or betrayed, and so on. Will the ego choose love over being alone? It may try but with lessons to learn and karma to resolve, the ego will focus on the pain and that energy will attract the person who will fulfill that lesson for it. So another lesson of pain occurs, the ego believes it was right and has another example to consider the next time we consider creating a relationship. No matter how many wonderful, fulfilling relationship connections exist in our field of potential, until we resolve the ego's thinking we cannot be at their vibration, connect to them or even consider them as options.

This is illustrated by Sally, who is fully aware that she limits her ability to be loved because she cannot allow herself to open her heart to anyone. She believes that being hurt is the price of love so while she secretly longs for the loving, fulfilling relationship that is in her field of potential, she limits her risk by never attracting someone she can fall in love with, is available to her or who loves her at a committed level.

And so she goes from one relationship to another, hoping that she will eventually find someone who will give her the love she wants and not break her heart in the process. In fact, that is one of her selection criteria, 'someone who will not break her heart'. But the men she attracts and chooses are married, commitment phobic, bitter divorcees, traumatized by their romantic past and are generally emotionally unavailable. Because she is attracting partners through her fears, instead of through her heart's desire for love, she is creating the same scenario with different partners, and the result is always the same. The ego is using her fear to shield her from vulnerability and blocking her from potential pain by attracting partners she cannot be fully connected with because they cannot or will not love her and make a commitment, thereby eliminating all risk that she will experience more pain. But that is exactly what she gets, more pain and heartbreak each time a relationship ends.

Sally's solution is simple, she must be willing to release the fear of pain that keeps her at the energetic vibration which manifests unavailable partners and believe that she is worthy of having the love she truly wants and that is in her field of potential. Then she will attract someone who mirrors her self love instead of her fear and pain.

It is through loving ourselves that we attract loving relationships. And that extends to more than romantic relationships. Our self love is reflected in every area of our life and includes acceptance, validation, friendship, trust and success. Do you know someone who blindly accepts others' bad behavior or who reinvents themselves to gain someone's acceptance and love? That is an example of someone who has no self love. And no matter what other options are available in their field of potential, they will attract people and situations that mirror their lack of self love.

To fully connect to the highest aspects of our field of potential, we must learn to love ourselves. This is our great lesson, the reason we undertake lifetimes and engage in karma, to learn to love ourselves enough to be open to receiving our heart's desire in every aspect of our life, fully partnering with our soul so we can be aware of our maximum potential from our field of potential.

Consider these questions for your personal mastery journey:

Are there dreams in your heart that are waiting for the right moment to manifest?

Can you see that this dream is possible for you simply because you want it?

How would you feel about yourself and your life if that dream was present in your life at this moment?

How would your life change if this dream was present in your life right now?

What would you have to do, release or allow to create space in your life for that dream?

What types of ego or fear-based thoughts have prevented you from manifesting your dreams? These could be messages you received in your childhood, beliefs you have created from your life experiences or   fears about your abilities.

Is there one step that you can take, including realizing that your dream is in your field of potential, that can help you manifest it now?

Our ascension journey awakens us to the many different possibilities that exist for each of us and for the world, all of them part of our individual and collective field of potential. One of those options is to remove the belief that the price of spiritual learning is great pain and difficulty. We can accomplish our spiritual learning in any way we want; in fact, it is when we have moved forward on our spiritual path that other, painless options are available to us. We will learn just as much and even more quickly, when we choose the painless options and free ourselves from trudging through difficulty to arrive at our destination. The destination, our spiritual evolution and ascension, is the same whether we choose the path with the painful price or the easy, painless path. The choice is ours to make and to take.

Can you take your most beloved, outrageous, deeply desired dream, find it within your field of potential and tell the Universe that this is what you want? Then have faith that it will come to you, open your heart and mind to this possibility, be willing to receive it and be prepared   to watch your dream come true—without a price other than you having faith in your ability to create the reality of your dreams?

Do you love yourself enough to create the possibility for this? When we love ourselves we give ourselves the gift of re-membering the love of Creator in our life and that makes everything possible. While Creator's love never stops flowing to us, we can never fully connect with it and all of its limitless blessings until we learn to love ourselves.

Learning to Love

Although we are created from love and we exist because of love, learning to love is our most challenging life lesson. Our mastery journey is our return to love. Not the romantic love we can experience with another, but the soul-awakening love we find within ourselves. This is a simple truth, the love we can spend our life seeking from others shines brightly within us. Then why do we spend so much time looking for love in the world? Our core soul wounds arise from the rejection we experience when we are denied the love we ask for. While this core of love is our birthright, love from others is not and it is something everyone must learn. The core principle of love is that the love we want in life take physical form in our outer world when it begins within us. Another core principle of love is this -- we will never find someone who loves us more than we love ourselves because the mirror of our reality can never reflect more love energy to us than what we have within us.

And there is a price associated with loving ourselves but it does not have anything to do with pain and hurt. The price of loving ourselves is living with honesty and integrity, knowing our truth and accepting who we are, unconditionally. It requires a profound belief in the spiritual truth that we are love, we deserve to have love and to be loved. The progression to love begins with love of self, which leads to love of others which then allows love from others. Self love is reflected through our willingness to be in our power so no one can ever destroy our confidence, self-esteem or truth because the love we have for ourselves is not dependent on who loves us or how much love we receive from someone else. To master love we must first become masters at loving ourselves.

Every situation and relationship in our life mirrors how much we love ourselves. Once we love ourselves unconditionally, we attract all kinds of love that reflects our unconditional self-love back to us. So the message is quite simple, love yourself and the love you seek will find you and it will be reflected in every area of your life, whose many different aspects all reflect how much you love yourself. Are you tired, disappointed, hurt, depressed, sad and lonely?

How much do you love yourself? Once you are able to love yourself unconditionally, you will attract the love and every situation that brings you joy, connections, peace and every other outcome you desire. And there will be no price attached to it, no pain, disillusionment, betrayal or disappointment.

If we know love in spirit, what happens to us in the material world? We have to convince the ego about love and it is not swayed by the promise of knowing joy, being in love and receiving love in return. If those experiences are not in the ego's memory it will view them as a liability instead of a blessing. To the ego the price of allowing love, on any level, is vulnerability, and deep within our cellular memory and emotional DNA are the memories of the many times we suffered when we were vulnerable. But Spirit is aware of these things and this is where the partnership between Spirit and ego, between material and spiritual, that is part of our ascension journey, becomes important.

The ego wants to remind us of our pain to protect us from repeating it but it does this by reminding us of where love was denied to us. That is the ego's interpretation of our rejection. The truth is that we are rejected in our search for love when we want to receive it from others because we have little or no love for ourselves. We cannot approach the world with an empty love basket and ask that it be filled, although that is what we do time after time. We receive love, measure for measure, based on how much we are willing to fill our own love basket with self love. Then the world will gladly and exuberantly give us the all love we seek and more.

Spirit holds out the shining truth for us, that the love is always there but it is within us. Although we stubbornly ask the world for love, Spirit quietly and gently guides us towards our inner source while reminding us that our path will always lead us to this place, no matter how long we take to arrive at this truth. It knows that learning to love from within is what we need to connect to the new relationship, success, abundance or whatever we wish to manifest in our outer world. And we need Spirit's input to do this because the ego will resist the manifestation of our dreams, no matter how much we cherish them. But Spirit knows that if we are focused on our dreams with faith and trust, they will happen. Spirit also knows that our belief in what we deserve is closely connected to the amount of love we have for ourselves.

The painful experiences we draw to ourselves that mirror our lack of self love are on our path so that we can learn to turn within to find the love we continually seek from the world and others. All love begins from within, as it is created from the core of love that shines within us and waits for us to connect to it. The world cannot mirror more love to us than we are shining out to it. As we continue our mastery journey and move into ascension we will learn to love ourselves in our humanity with the same love that is available through our divinity.

Consider these questions for your personal mastery journey:
Have you considered whether you love yourself or not?

Do you have a place in your life where you could be more loving with yourself?

Do you see how your fears about love or your expectations of it have limited its flow in your life?

Is there a person or situation in your life that is reflecting your lack of self-love back to you?

Where do you fear being hurt or vulnerable and are you willing to release these fears?

What do you think the price of your dreams is?

What aspect of creating your dreams makes you uncomfortable?

How can you move out of your comfort zone to make your dreams about love, or anything else you want, a reality?

Our self love is evident through what we manifest for ourselves, because everything we allow ourselves to have, based on what we believe we are worthy of and deserve, flows from our level of self love. Each of us has a dream for our life, a scenario where we are doing exactly what we want and are happy and fulfilled in every way. But if there is no proof in our past experience to let us know that this can be true, we believe that there is no way it can happen for us, that we will have to give up something else to have what we want or once we have it, it will go away, is only available to the lucky few or someone will take it away from us.

With this perspective we can't envision life as a vast potential of options and choices. For us, life is not an 'and' view, where anything and everything is simultaneously possible, it is 'either/or', where life is a series of tradeoffs, and the acquisition of one thing means the loss of another. With self love we give ourselves an option that includes the concept of 'and', meaning that we can have what we want and everything that goes with it, and it will all fall into place with divine order and timing. When we can love ourselves enough to step into this level of flow our life unfolds in miraculous ways. Through our self love we can live through the true concept of abundance, in that there is always more than enough for everyone, including us, all of the time.

Take a moment and write down your dream life, the life that you wish you had right now. Where would you live, what would you be doing, who would you be with? What would you feel and how would others respond to you? Giving yourself the time to consider what you want and setting an intention for it to happen is another aspect of self love. Putting your dreams in writing brings them from the unconscious into the conscious mind. Be honest with yourself, write without judging or criticizing, allow the energy to flow through you and tap into your heart which holds the dreams that are possible for you, even if they are not happening or do not seem possible right now.

As you consider your dream life, are you wondering how hard it will be? Are you afraid that you either cannot have it or that it will be disappointing in some way? Do you wonder how difficult certain aspects may be or how hard you will have to work to achieve them? Are you familiar with expressions such as 'no pain, no gain' or 'if it doesn't kill you it makes you stronger'? We can say those words with a knowing laugh because we are aware that most of our learning comes through painful experiences. In fact, we often don't believe that we have learned a lesson if there was not some kind of painful component attached to it.

If we truly believe that we are deliberately attracting painful lessons because we hold the belief that pain is the price we must pay for our spiritual growth and learning. We can learn a great deal, in fact more than we ever have, without painful lessons, by changing what we believe about the price of our spiritual growth and loving ourselves enough to accept that we are worthy of effortless and joyful learning. Can we love ourselves enough to release the need for pain and sorrow and allow our learning to be effortless, guided and easy?

As the mirror of our beliefs, our reality reflects what we feel about ourselves and ultimately, how much we love ourselves. When we love ourselves we deliberately avoid everything that resonates with pain and in fact, with self love we no longer attract it. There is no spiritual law that says that spiritual learning has to be painful. Pain is how the ego expresses its lack of self love and when we incorporate the balance of Spirit into our choices, our inner core of self love shines out to the world. And loving ourselves means that we are constantly focused on the best, most wonderful, pain-free outcome for ourselves and know that we have a choice between love and pain.

From the ego's perspective, if we do what we want, someone may suffer or be inconvenienced. And this becomes important because if we do not love ourselves we are always seeking love from others. So we do our best to fulfill our obligations to them and do what we think will create the love we want from them, no matter how inconvenient it is to us. Or we are disappointed when events do not turn out as we hope they will because without self love we have a very limited view of our life options.

Self love is where we connect to our mastery. While there may not be an example of the benefits of self love within our human experience, Spirit holds this energy for us, loving us until we are willing to connect to this love by learning to love ourselves. All of the love we want from others is contained within us, in the calm and quiet space where Spirit keeps the flame of unconditional love burning brightly. We cannot become masters until we achieve mastery in our search for love and know that we will find it within ourselves first, before we ever find it in the world around us.

Consider these questions for your personal mastery journey:
Do you hold any beliefs about your dreams that limit their manifestation?
As you write down the details of your dream life, is there a voice within you that reminds you that they are not possible, will never happen or that manifesting them is beyond your abilities?
What kind of pain have you experienced through the lessons you have learned?
Can you find the link between your level of self love and the pain you have experienced?
Do you have a belief that you must suffer in order to learn your lessons?

Is it possible for you to love yourself enough to consider painless choices?

Is there a link between your memories of past pain or your belief that lessons are or must be painful that creates challenges for you?

How can you love yourself enough to give yourself the gift of effortless, joyful learning?

Faith is another way we can learn to love ourselves, which is how we express our trust in the Universe. Everything that we create in our reality is a reflection of our self love. Think about that for a moment. When we love ourselves, we manifest the best, most joyful, peaceful, abundant and blessed reality. Everything else mirrors our lack of self love. The price of this kind of manifestation is faith in ourselves and in a benevolent Universe that is waiting to respond to our every need. All we have to do is ask from the wellspring of love that we have for ourselves, without the limitations imposed by pain, because this is where we show the Universe that we believe we deserve to have all of the good and wonderful things that we desire.

That takes the full responsibility of creating any outcome away from us and puts half of it where it belongs, with the Universe, which responds to love and faith, not fear and doubt. Are we ready to have everything we want? That is a frightening concept because it puts us in control and then if we don't have what we want, we know who is responsible.

We form our opinion whether we deserve to have blessings from our past experiences and our level of self love. But what if that was changing? What if we could move into a perspective where every decision was made from the present moment and radiated with our self love and we chose to explore our limitless options, without judgment, because we loved ourselves enough to use every opportunity to expand into our highest potential?

What if we looked at each choice or decision from the perspective of self love and we made our choices based on how much we wanted to expand and bless our lives? This mindset would change the options in our field of potential and expand our lives beyond our imagining. Instead of looking at life as a series of limited and exclusive options, where choosing one thing meant that we could not choose something else, we could choose anything and then change our minds at will, releasing anything that did not resonate with our level of self love and living life as an adventure of unfolding experiences.

This would not mean that we would spend our time hopping from one thing to another because we would make each choice fully mindful of what we wanted to create in our life at that moment. Any option that did not resonate with that intention simply would not be attractive to us. So we could confidently end one situation that was out of integrity with our new energetic vibrations, knowing that in doing so, we would attract something else that did. And since the new one would come with divine timing and perfection, we would not worry about when it would arrive and would feel unthreatened by the gap in the flow between asking and receiving.

How does loving ourselves affect the world? As we look around us we see conflict, pain and misery in many parts of the world. We are told that we are winning the battle of light over dark but feel as though we are losing the world in the process. Does peace exist in the world's field of potential? We all wish for peace to exist everywhere. We pray for peace, hold vigils for peace and even fight for peace. We are told that peace comes at a price, is often arrived at through conflict and it demands 'eternal vigilance'. But the price of peace is not conflict, as we have been led to believe, it is unconditional love and that begins within each one of us.

Each of us is responsible for mastering our fears and the ego and for loving ourselves enough to believe that we deserve to live in a peaceful, joyful and loving world. We do this through expanding love, not by destroying the ego, which is an important aspect of the earth's energy. Whether we want peace in our own reality or for our global family, in order to have it we must first be willing to give unconditional love to ourselves, which expands it to everyone else. Our ascension journey is providing us with opportunities to learn and practice this concept so that we can help bring peace to the world.

Is it easier to fight for peace than to simply love and accept others? Finding peace through conflict teaches us that peace comes at a terrible price. But that is an illusion, for obtaining peace through conflict only happens when the other party is overcome or beaten down. Fighting gives us a sense of purpose; it vindicates the wrongs that have been done to us and allows us to feel that we are doing something to validate our struggle for peace. This is karma at work and an example of lower chakra based energy.

When we fight for peace we feel united within a common purpose which is to end conflict by showing others the error of their ways. But this is judgment and it serves to create resentment and bitterness and is an opportunity for future conflict, further recycling the karma that exists between us. We can create peace but first we need to define what peace means to us and to be able to create it in our own reality. When we love ourselves peace becomes an option.

Each of us must choose a definition of peace, understanding what it means for us on a personal level. Does it mean having personal freedom, emotional security or financial abundance? Does it describe the kinds of relationships we have with others or is it simply the absence of conflict in our reality? Peace arises from self love because with it we will not feel threatened by others every time we have a challenging interaction. It is when we are ready and willing to love and accept ourselves unconditionally that we can be in a space of non-judgment, from which we love and accept others and have them love and accept us in return, which allows peace to flow from within us to the world around us.

Learning to love, beginning with ourselves, allows us to mirror love to the world and this makes world peace possible. For where unconditional love exists peace is the only possible outcome. Conflict disappears when we are at peace within ourselves and we can then experience the "peace that passes all understanding." Acting from a place of unconditional love allows peace to flow to us, through us and creates a vibration of peace for everyone around us. At that moment we can see others through the eyes of God and know that we are all connected, are all the same and are all part of the human family.

Does this sound like a fairy tale? It should not because this is the reality that our ascension path and our journey of personal mastery are helping us create. Divine consciousness is unfolding within us to help us see the illusion that fear creates and to be willing to experience love.

Once we remove ourselves from the belief in consequences, penalties and limited choices, of fear, separation, and judgment, we move into the reality of unlimited potential, where everything is possible and each choice is grounded in self love, mindfully setting our intention for the best outcome. And when we follow this process, beginning from self love, every outcome can expand into its highest potential because it reflects our self love. Each decision becomes an opportunity for us to explore a new reality and to move forward on our spiritual path in the energy of love.

Each choice is made with the intention of joy, peace, unconditional love and abundance so that we create exactly what we want in our reality and extend that to everyone else. Creating something we want so others cannot or won't have it is not an expression of self love or of love for others. Unconditional love is our starting point so we are not looking to the world or to others for validation, confirmation or fulfillment. We already have those things because we love ourselves and expand that love everywhere. There is no fear regarding timing or the fulfillment of our desires because we live in the present moment, in which all things are possible. Once we create the freedom that comes with self love, love from others can become part of our reality and we have a glimpse of the gateway to heaven on earth. This is the highest expression of our mastery.

Consider these questions for your personal mastery journey:
Do you see how loving yourself contributes to expanding love in the world?
Are there things you can do to increase the love you have for yourself?
Can you look at every relationship in your life and make a comparison between the love you received from it and the love you had for yourself?
What limiting beliefs do you have to release to see yourself as lovable?
Can you find a place of peace within yourself where you see the flow of energy as it moves in your life and then, love every aspect of it and of you?
Is it possible for you to appreciate divine timing as an example of the love that supports and protects you and wants the very best for you?

To step through the doorway of unconditional love we must learn acceptance, which is where all judgment of everyone and everything is removed. With acceptance we see everyone as being in their own power, at the vibration that is right for them, doing the things that their spiritual growth and understanding allow them to do. Acceptance is humanity's greatest lesson and it is the price of unconditional love.

Acceptance

Imagine that you are on a vacation with someone, taking a trip that you have planned together and are very excited about. You look forward to making the most of this opportunity to spend time together, having fun and learning new things. As you begin this trip everything goes according to plan but at some point on the journey, something begins to change. Your travel companion begins to lag behind, they no longer want to participate in the things you previously did together and they create excuses to spend as little time with you as possible. You are concerned by their behavior and soon realize that you will not finish this journey together, that something happened somewhere along the way and you are no longer traveling on the same path. Although you do everything you can to help this person see the value of continuing the journey with you, they simply move farther away until it is difficult for you to connect with them on any level.

You are sad as this is someone you care about and are close to. Although you are ready to give up a great deal to help them change their mind, they are adamant; they have made their choice and you are not part of it. You have a choice too, to continue to send energy their way, hoping they will change their mind and in doing so, to stand still and wait for them to choose to be with you again. Or you can move on without them, accepting the choice they have made and knowing that although you do not understand it, it is the right choice for them. This is painful and upsetting because you are not sure what happened along the way to create this situation but you must choose another path for yourself as they move farther and farther away from you.

This scenario is presented as an example of what is happening to many people as we approach the final stages of the ascension process and lessons are being completed in many different aspects of our lives. There will be surprises as those we thought would be part of our life journey in the future will not be there and others who we never dreamed would be willing to walk this path are there to walk beside us.

These choices are being made on a subtle level and from an energetic standpoint that may initially look like the world and everyone in it have turned against us. We wonder what we are doing wrong but this is part of the lesson, to learn to see others as they are and to accept them as being in their power, doing whatever is right for their path, in the vibrational frequency that is right for them. Our role is not to judge or condemn them but to accept their choice, no matter how it appears to affect us. This is our lesson in acceptance and it is one of the keys on our mastery journey.

Our first lesson in acceptance comes in the form of experiences which teach us that everyone does what is right for them and we choose whether we will allow their choices to affect us emotionally and energetically. If our connection level is emotional we will take everything personally and become involved with the lower vibrating energies of the emotions we are feeling. This is where we become angry, frustrated, hurt and obsessed with someone's behavior and try to change them, their beliefs and actions and convince them that they are wrong. We believe that our personal happiness depends on our ability to create an outcome with them that meets our needs and expectations at all costs.

From the perspective of our anger and pain we are unable to see that we have healing to gain in this situation and it is our lesson in acceptance, where we are being challenged to let go of the expectations and needs that we have made this person or situation responsible for. Lessons in acceptance prepare us to move into a higher vibration so we can experience a different reality that we cannot be aware of when we are angry, hurt, disappointed or sad. Of course, we can continue to strive for the outcome we want and manipulate the situation until we achieve it but then we are faced with a battle of wills, which no one wins. Letting go, no matter how much we want to hang on, is a lesson in acceptance, of recognizing everyone's sovereignty and accepting that their path and all of its choices is right for them, even if it does not include us or our desired outcome.

Our second lesson of acceptance is to accept ourselves, our choices and decisions, the life experiences that we create and all of their outcomes. But we must go beyond accepting ourselves through the belief in our imperfections, settling for who we are within the belief that we won't get any better. We have to accept ourselves as perfect in every way, as divine, spiritual beings whose experience of humanity has the simple purpose of healing and transformation. So we are not misfits, spiritual novices or accidents of nature. We have a purpose, a path and although we are always in control of every aspect, this control only extends to the details of our own life. What others choose is beyond our control and we cannot judge our success or failures through the lens of their responses. Just as it is our willingness to accept responsibility for our life path and everything in it, without exception, that reconnects us with our co-creative abilities, where we work with the Universe to create our personal heaven on earth, it is an option that is also available to everyone.

And this is where we can get stuck because by accepting responsibility for everything we cannot blame anyone for anything that happens to us. We are the cause and we create every outcome and effect. Can we acknowledge that every situation we think is a problem, every person who has hurt us in some way, everything that we view as a failure or a mistake was created through our specific, if unconscious, intention?

This is hard to accept and yet, it is the source of our emotional and spiritual freedom because by accepting our power and the results of the choices we make, we create an opening for partnership between the ego and Spirit and reconnect to our divine nature, becoming masters of our humanity and consciously allowing Spirit to become our guide. And the blessing of self acceptance is the ability to transform every challenge into opportunities for joy. With acceptance we act beyond the emotional energies of our ego and human nature and are in direct communication with Spirit.

When we rise above the emotions and choose to be in acceptance, we know that whatever is happening is perfect, there is nothing wrong and our emotional response is a sign that we need to detach, look at our own fears and find our healing in this situation. In all of these experiences we are both teacher and student, we have something to learn from whatever interactions we have with someone and they have something to learn from us.

The truth that Spirit is trying to teach us in these situations is that our life path is not limited by others and that others' actions and choices cannot affect us unless we allow them to. Acceptance represents our most powerful position because it removes us from judgment and from the emotional energies that are our first response when we are afraid of being alone, abandoned or rejected by someone who matters to us. Our wounded self is afraid of what may happen to us if we have to go through that experience. But on a core level we are afraid that if we do not have that mirror of validation in our life, we will have to acknowledge our fear that we are unworthy of love. So we do all we can to keep these people and situations in our life because we believe they are our source of love.

Acceptance is a higher vibration of agreement. While we may not like what someone has done, being in agreement allows us to offset the pain of our disappointment and hurt feelings through justification. But this is based on our judgment and opinion. With agreement we can conditionally accept others' choices and take refuge in our powerlessness in the face of their actions. We can say things like "I can live with that" or "It's your choice but I don't think it's the right one" which are judgments through which we passively voice our displeasure.

With acceptance we celebrate that each of us is on an individual mastery journey and rejoice in the knowing that others' choices have no impact on what we can choose for ourselves. Acceptance releases us from feeling responsible for anyone's choices or the results of their actions. With acceptance we can look at any situation and simply acknowledge that it is right for that person, without adding our beliefs or opinions about it, which do not have any influence anyway and which are not important. Acceptance has its basis in unconditional love, which is totally non-judgmental and non-critical, moving beyond emotion, perception, belief, opinion and expectation and experiencing everyone and everything with detachment.

Is acceptance possible in today's world, where many of our relationships involve commitments, obligations to and complicated connections with others?

What if our life partner decides to leave us, our company no longer wants our services or our family decides to stop speaking to us?

Do we just accept and move on as best we can?

What about the emotions, security, commitment and effort we have put into these relationships?

Do they matter?

Does anyone appreciate anything about us or what we have done for them?

As we ask these questions what we become aware of is our fear, realizing that we are less worried about what someone has done than what their actions will do to us, how they will affect our life and what will happen to us. While we have the power to make choices that affect and govern our own reality, we are afraid of being excluded from others' choices. Choosing our reality is a powerful option but not one that we necessarily want to do alone. So while we know that we cannot ask others to make choices in their lives that benefit us, we hope that they will include us and our feelings in their choices. But the reality of acceptance is the realization that everyone does what is right for them and while we are sometimes included in these decisions, we can also be excluded from them, sometimes deliberately, and at other times unintentionally.

So the partner who wants to leave should be allowed to go.

If you dislike your boss or your job, quit before you are forced to do so.

If you have issues with your family, work on what they mean to you so that you can create powerful boundaries within your relationships with them.

The blessing of acceptance is that we are in our own power and while others may do things that challenge us, the amount of drama, chaos and disruption that their choices can create in our life is very limited.

In fact every situation that is a lesson in acceptance shares a common theme, which is centered in the aspects of fear energy that we each carry and is a call to love ourselves first. When we are challenged to accept someone's choices, especially those that we believe affect our life in a disruptive, painful, unexpected or inconvenient way, it is because somewhere along our shared path we have given them our power, have allowed them and their path to become more important than ours and have placed our happiness, peace of mind, joy and security in their hands. Their rejection is our lesson in acceptance and a chance to reconnect with our power.

An example of this comes from a client I worked with. Diane was married to a successful, financially secure man, had two young children and lived in a large, beautiful house. Prior to having children she had a successful career but now chose to stay home with her children. Her marriage was comfortable but unhappy and her husband worked long hours and was seldom at home. One day her husband announced that he had found someone else and was leaving her. She was devastated and angry with him for making a decision that would drastically alter her lifestyle and break up the family. During the difficult divorce process Diane tried to get as many of the marital assets as possible, to make her husband 'pay' for what he had done to her, their children and their family.

Eventually the divorce was completed and Diane had to return to work and take control of her life, providing for herself and her children, which her husband had done when they were married. It was difficult for her but, in her words, she had no choice. And as she re-started her career and turned her focus towards her future, she began to find joy and remembered how she had once enjoyed working and being responsible for her life.

Whether Diane thought it was right or wrong for her husband to make the choice that he made, her opinion was not going to change his mind. He moved out of their house on the day he told her he wanted a divorce and there was no option for discussion, she had to accept it.

And she had not been particularly happy in her marriage even though she did not want it to end. Was her husband happy? When I asked that question during a coaching session she hesitated in responding but later admitted that she had never asked him because she did not want to open that discussion. She sensed that he was unhappy but was afraid that if she asked him then she might find out that he wanted to leave. It was easier for her to pretend that everything was fine than to know the truth. But she eventually found out in a way that did not leave her with any options other than to accept his decision. Diane said she was ashamed to admit that she was willing to live with a certain amount of unhappiness rather than face her fears of being alone. And she truthfully acknowledged that while she had mostly enjoyed her husband's control over her life she was also unhappy and felt unfulfilled.

The important point here is that she eventually had to face her fear of being alone and learn to accept his choice and its outcome for her life. Her lesson of acceptance included acknowledging her responsibility for giving her power away, of being afraid to face the truth of her marriage and her unhappiness. Diane admitted that she knew that her marriage would eventually end. She had hoped that she would be more prepared when the end came but she was also angry that he made a choice that presented her with no options. Diane had to choose how she was going to use her power and energy, either by being angry, hurt and resentful over a situation that she could not change or accept what had happened and allow the healing that would bring her the peace, security and joy that she wanted and to accept responsibility for creating her new life.

What if we know that what the other person is doing is wrong? How can we accept that? But who is it wrong for, them or us? Do we feel it is wrong because this choice inconveniences us in some way? Can we honestly decide whether something is wrong for someone else? And if we do think their behavior is wrong, what are we going to do about it, what can we do and to what level will we impose ourselves, opinions and energy in their lives to force the changes to their actions or thinking that we believe they should make?

On a human level we make many judgments about others' choices but on a spiritual level, we know that their choices are part of their path and everyone is on their own life journey. We always interpret, judge and respond to others' choices according to how we believe they affect us. And our response is determined by our fears, desires and expectations of the person or situation. It is our choice to be angry, afraid and resentful or to find the lessons in acceptance we are presented with. We can decide that the other person is making a mistake with their choices or behavior, that they are being unfair or betraying our trust or love, but is that our decision to make?

When we put our self worth in someone else's hands everything they do puts it into question. Had we been a better person, loved them more, been more of what they wanted, would they have made a choice that honored the sacrifices we made on their behalf? We ask these questions and yet our lessons of acceptance tell us that it is not about us; others' choices are made in spite of us and what we do. It is more difficult to appreciate and believe in our worthiness when we believe that it depends on someone's actions.

After all, if we were good, loving, successful, or deserving, they would not act that way – they would stay, love us more, be kinder, see our value and give us what we needed. Through their actions we begin to question ourselves and try to prove them wrong instead of recognizing that what they are doing is an expression of their life path. Once we allow another's expression of their needs and desires to become personal, we have incorporated it in our path and allowed it to connect to and resonate with all of our fears. By making their choices personal, we put our integrity into question instead of accepting responsibility for our role in the situation and acknowledge that we have delegated the details of our life to someone else.

Our lesson of acceptance becomes one of learning that everyone acts in their own self interest, no matter what we do, and accept that on their path, they will always do what they think is best for them, their soul's growth, healing and transformation, which is all they can do.

Consider these questions for your personal mastery journey:

Think about someone who has done something that you did not like or that was contrary to what you wanted. How did their choice make you feel?

Can you see the role this situation played in your healing and soul growth?

Have you ever loved someone who did not or could not love you in the same way?

Have you ever wanted to be in a relationship with someone who did not want to be in a relationship with you?

Did you ever work hard for a promotion or a reward that you did not receive?

Have you ever wanted to create an opportunity for yourself that others appeared to block?

What do you think about those people, that they are difficult, that everyone is working against you, standing in your way or deliberately trying to hurt you?

What do you do in these situations? Do you become angry, sad, depressed, work harder, try different strategies to arrive at what you want until you either get something close to what you have asked for or do not have the energy or willingness to try any longer?

Do you see your lessons in acceptance in these situations and understand what you have to learn in them?

How can acceptance help you find peace and gain closure in these situations?

How does acceptance fit into your mastery journey?

How can we be in acceptance when someone does something that hurts us? In the example of Diane, which was presented earlier in this chapter, she knew that her marriage was unstable but was afraid to discuss it with her husband. So while she was hurt and angry at his decision to leave her, it was not a total surprise. Diane was responsible for not having the courage to face her fears and talk to her husband about their marriage. In other situations, we may be unhappy but willing to live with our unhappiness because we are afraid of change. Have you ever had a job you disliked but stayed with because of the salary, length of your commute, or fear of looking for another job? Then when you lose your job you are angry, but could you have avoided the situation by taking the initiative to look for a new job before it became a necessity?

Our willingness to accept the status quo, which is often settling for what we have even if we are not happy, is often based on our fears – we are more likely to accept an unhappy situation if we are too afraid to change it. Accepting that the situation is not right for us and finding the courage to invite change allows us to embrace opportunities that allow a more fulfilling situation to unfold. Is it more difficult to accept a situation when it brings up our fears?

This is particularly true in romantic relationships, where lessons of acceptance challenge our fears of being alone, rejected, abandoned, disappointed, humiliated or invalidated. One client was very depressed because she was in love with someone who was not as committed to their relationship as she was. Although she was trying hard to prove her love and commitment by being a kind and faithful partner, he was unkind, unfaithful and critical of everything she did. She had a choice to accept him as he was and live with his behavior or leave the relationship.

Before she could make this choice, though, she had to be fully in acceptance that his behavior had nothing to do with her. This was how he behaved in relationships. Once she realized that it did not matter how nice she was or how much she did for this man, she was not going to change him or get him to meet her needs in the relationship, she could make the choice to accept him as he was and decide to stay or give herself closure and move on.

By being in acceptance she stopped blaming him for what he was doing and herself for not being able to change him. She understood that their vibrational connection was at a healing level and that she had been focusing on healing him, to help shift his energy, rather than focusing on the healing that was present for her, which was to learn to love and accept herself. She also saw where she had been manipulating him to give her the love, acceptance and approval that she wanted in a relationship and to finally accept that he was not capable of giving it to her in that way as he was giving her all he could. Once she acknowledged her healing and incorporated into her life, she was able to leave that relationship and find a partner who was loving, kind and ready to commit to her in a way that met her needs.

As masters we must learn to accept everyone and everything as an expression of unconditional love. This does not mean that we must tolerate bad behavior from others. When we realize that everyone chooses their behavior and actions and what does not resonate with what we want in our life we have to be willing to walk away. Acceptance has no judgment, criticism, expectations, opinions or beliefs of anyone or anything. Within acceptance we realize that everyone is being themselves and situations simply flow according to the energetic vibrations and lessons of the relationship. Rather than plant our feet and force others to change to meet our needs and expectations, we have another option, to get out of the way and choose to interact with what vibrates at a more compatible frequency.

This reveals how we perceive healing, whether we are doing healing for others as their servant or martyr or being a healer by embodying the highest possible frequency that we can resonate with and manifest our path from that level. Each time we need confirmation of our path through validation from someone or something, we are expressing a lack of integrity with our higher vibrations and we will receive a lesson that will bring us back to acceptance.

Why can't others see the potential in themselves that we are aware of? When we accept the role of doing healing for others we see them in their highest light, in the perfection of their soul's energy, instead of how they are expressing that energy through their ego. We try to help them heal and 'get better' by showing them their highest potential and then wait for them to agree with us by becoming that level of potential. Although we may not do it intentionally, we are trying to show them how much they are limiting themselves by creating situations where they have to become 'more than' they are at that moment to help them realize the level of potential we want them to achieve.

By helping them to view themselves as we know they can be or as we want to see them, we believe that they will build the connection to this higher aspect for themselves. Then we hope they will express their gratitude by giving us the love and validation we want. When we become this type of healing for others our intention is to help them find, embrace and express the light that we know is right for them because we feel it is right for us. And when they do not agree with us, we blame and judge ourselves and take it personally. Then we work even harder to show them the error of their ways.

Here we must recognize that we have no insight into someone's true path, which is a matter between them and Creator. It is not possible for us to know how many lifetimes it has taken someone to arrive at the place where they are now or to know how much progress they are making. We cannot know the details of their soul contract in this lifetime or how they have chosen to express that contract. What we may see as insignificant spiritual awareness may actually be the greatest understanding and growth they have ever achieved in any lifetime. What we see as small steps in spiritual understanding may be giant leaps in their universal consciousness.

When we judge others we are assuming that we know everything about them and take on the responsibility of showing them their 'true' path, which is something we cannot know. In this way we elevate ourselves and our under-standing, thinking we are always the teacher when in reality, we are both student and teacher in every situation, giving and receiving learning and healing. Every situation is a healing opportunity for us too. We are guilty of spiritual arrogance when we assume that we know what is best for someone else and ignore the healing and learning that they have for us. Everyone has their way of seeing, accepting and incorporating healing and learning into their life and we must respect that as healers, teachers and students of mastery.

As we move along our path to mastery, we learn to accept others and remove all judgments, criticisms and expectations that we have of them on every level. It is when we are at this point, which is the zero point in polarity, that we are completely neutral and in the energy of unconditional love. This is so freeing and yet so difficult for us to do.

Imagine not having any judgments or expectations of anyone, of being able to acknowledge everyone as the divine spiritual being they are, not limited by how we feel about them or what we think of them, their actions, beliefs or how they are using their energy and potential. As healers, we must accept that each person is completely within the energetic space and vibration that is right for them at that time, including us. As students and teachers, we can recognize lessons in acceptance as opportunities to express unconditional love from a point of complete non-judgment. When we are in acceptance we can allow our Highest Good and blessings to unfold. And then we can allow that to happen for everyone else.

Acceptance is a test of our mastery commitment. With acceptance we are very clear about every situation, see everything as it is and remove our judgments about it. We can then allow everything to unfold, understand our role in every relationship and see the perfection in the lessons we are presented with. There is no judgment or criticism of any situation as good or bad, beneficial or detrimental, easy or hard. And here is the blessing for us, with acceptance we see every interaction in its perfection, all of the energetic vibrations that exist, the synergy of our meetings, interactions and events, the perfection of Divine Timing, and how they all work together to create a situation that meets the healing and growth needs of everyone.

We can then allow others to be who they are, on their own path, doing whatever they need to do in fulfillment of their mastery journey and then decide whether it is something we want to connect with or not. Sometimes others need to deliberately reject us and our participation in their choices because they need time to do their own healing work and they need for us to remove our energy and support. We have to be the light, not ensure that others accept, use, acknowledge or embody the level of light we believe they could or should carry.

Our role as healers has shifted from 'doing' healing to 'being' healers and embodying the healing we want or expect from others in our own lives. So the happier, more successful and fulfilled we are, the more we are being the healing that we are trying to teach or give to others. This is a new way to heal and with it we do not need anyone's validation or acknowledgement, nor do we have anything to give them that they cannot create for themselves. We accept their path and the expression of their energetic vibrations and if there is no point of connection we are not obligated to create one.

Without the pressure to heal others, we can allow our blessings to manifest because we are on our own path, not someone else's. Every time we try to change someone or believe we have to work hard to create an outcome for or with them we are off of our path. The harder we work at trying to heal someone else the more we are out of integrity with our Self and into lessons in acceptance. And we do this deliberately, so we can see where we have scattered our energy and gather it back to us so we can be back in the energy of effortlessness, which is the path of mastery.

Remember that karma is the path of imperfection, the belief in separation, judgment, rejection and abandonment. It is one of many energetic paths available to us. One of those paths is to be in the state of receiving blessings. Can we allow ourselves to be blessed to the full extent that we deserve? Not to the extent that we believe we deserve, but the full extent of the Universe's limitless ability to bless us. We can when we recapture our scattered energy, allowing others to be in their own energy and walking their own path. Then our focus shifts to the best and highest use of our power and our intention leads us in the direction we want to go, without the distractions that arise when we try to get others to walk that path with us.

At this point we can get out of our own way and acknowledge our own divinity and the Truth of our being, that we are children of the Creator, sparks of the Divine Light and we are loved, valued, appreciated and recognized by Creator. When we accept that belief and incorporate it into the depths of our being, we will see it mirrored in every aspect of our life.

Consider these questions for your personal mastery journey:

Is there someone in your life who needs your support for their growth and when they have received enough of your energy you lose contact, only to have them re-surface for their next energy dose when their life has fallen apart again?

How much of your energy goes to support others' healing journeys and how often do you get set up to handle their healing crises?

Is there someone you are seeing in their highest energy and not as they are? Can you accept them as they are at this moment and simply let them be in their own energy?

Can you do this without feeling responsible for their soul growth or guilty about focusing on your own path?

What does your life path look like when you are not healing others?

Can you learn to 'be' healing instead of 'doing' healing?

Everyone has a choice as to how their life unfolds; everyone is choosing from among the choices that they see as possible for them. A choice will remain a spark of potential that awaits creation until it can be recognized by the person who is at the energetic vibration to be able to choose it. Choices are powerful things because through the choices we are aware of and the ones we make, we know where we are on our path. Life is a series of choices that we make, according to our level of spiritual growth and understanding.

Living Through Choice

The process of transformation and ascension that we are experiencing now is the end of humanity's third dimensional cycle and everyone will have the opportunity to choose how they complete their ascension process. They will either choose to move into higher dimensions or not, depending on their level of spiritual growth and understanding. How and when each person faces this choice and what they decide to do is unique to them and part of their path. We each have a choice as to how much we are willing to accept transformation and mastery, when it will happen to us and where we will travel with it. The power to choose is the gift of our free will and every aspect of our reality reflects the choices we make. We are responsible for our lives, our choices and their results.

Everything we do is a choice -- even a decision to do nothing is a choice. We have chosen every aspect of our life journey, beginning with our choice to enter this lifetime and participate in this stage of the ascension process. You may not remember that choice (and you may wonder why, if you had a choice, you chose to come here now and to experience what you are experiencing) but you made it, nonetheless. You chose the parents who would bring you into this lifetime, where you lived, how you grew up, and who you married, partnered with, even who you abandoned or rejected or were abandoned or rejected by. You chose your children, your lifestyle, your job and your friends. Your date, time and place of death will occur in the way you choose them. While we are generally unaware of the majority of these choices, we make them every minute of every day.

And the reality we live in is simply the result of the choices that we make on our path. We judge our choices by the results we obtain and then blame ourselves when our life does not turn out as we hoped it would. Instead of being angry or disappointed with the results we have to live with, it would be more effective to look at the choices we made along the way, within the energetic vibration and mindset we had when we made them. Each choice we make reflects our energetic vibration at that moment and we cannot be aware of a choice that requires a different vibration than the one we are at. For example, if we choose to marry someone at a time when we are feeling powerless and needy, we will not be aware of a choice to begin a career, move to another city, or get an education, as those choices require a vibration of fearlessness, self love and self awareness that we do not have at that time.

So we will choose to marry that person because it is the only choice we are aware of. We cannot judge this choice as wrong at a later point in time, when we are no longer needy and powerless, because the choice we made was part of our journey from being needy to being powerful, from being fearful to being fearless. The growth, learning and healing we experienced was made possible by each choice we made on that path.

Our energetic vibration determines the types of choices that are available to us and that we can be aware of and as we change our vibration we also change our range of choices, each with its own possibilities and outcomes. We cannot know the outcome of our choices in advance because the potential outcomes change with each shift in our energetic vibration and the outcome is the result of every choice. Each level of understanding and wholeness we complete leads to a different set of choices within our field of potential, each with their own outcome.

The Universe contains an infinite set of choices and each one is a possibility. But at each moment we only see the ones that we are capable of seeing through the filter of our energetic vibrations, beliefs and perceptions, which exist to limit our choices to the ones that pertain to that part of our journey and our healing commitment. It would be very hard to make choices if we were aware of all potential outcomes, so we are limited to the ones that exist within our range of vibration, and that correspond to our growth and learning needs in that life stage.

Think of a choice that you made when you were young, now consider whether you would make that choice today. There is a good chance that you would make an entirely different choice because your beliefs and perceptions have changed, you have more experience and have gained knowledge from all of the choices you have made since that time. Now you make different choices only because you are aware of the results of the choices you made in the past. And because you are in a different vibration you also have different choices available to you.

Consider these questions for your personal mastery journey:

Think of a choice you made whose results or consequences have greatly impacted your life.

Do you remember how you felt about yourself, your options, and the choice itself at that time?

Can you remember how many options you thought you had or were aware of at that time?

Are aware of how that choice has changed you and in what way?

Do you use the learning you made with that choice to make different choices now?

Did someone in your life influence the choice you made and do they still influence your choices today?

Can you see how you have made the journey from powerlessness into your power, or from being in fear to being fearless?

Do we make our choices under our own power and guidance? We may think that we do but we unconsciously include the wishes and opinions of our soul group in most of our choices, because their energy is within our cellular memory and is a silent, unseen participant in every choice we make. In addition to carrying our soul group's energetic vibration which we have been absorbing in this lifetime from the time of conception, we also carry all of the energies that we have accumulated during our many lifetimes with them. This vibration influences our decisions by establishing the foundation for the beliefs and perceptions that we will need to heal and transform, which also helps us create the manifestations of our fears. This influence continues throughout our life, until we make a choice to change those energies.

How do our soul group energies affect us and our choices? Here are a few examples:

If you do not choose to relocate for a new job because you want to stay close to your family, then your soul group has influenced your choice.

If you choose to move as far away from your family, friends or partner as possible, your soul group has influenced your choice.

If you decide to not marry someone because your family disapproves of them, you have allowed your soul group to influence your choice.

And if you marry the person anyway, out of spite or a need to prove yourself, you have still allowed your soul group to influence your choice.

If you choose a particular job or career path because everyone in your family has that profession then your soul group has influenced your choice.

And conversely, if you choose a different path because you do not want to follow the same career as everyone in your family, they have also influenced your choice.

These examples are provided to underscore the fact that our choices are affected by our soul group in ways we may not be aware of. We think we are making our own choices, independent of other influences, but every aspect of our soul group energy is an unseen component of our choices because our soul group mirrors the healing we have agreed to complete in our lifetime. We may later regret our choices based on their outcome, but at the time they were made, the energies we used to connect to the choices available in our field of potential were strongly influenced by our soul group.

Every choice we make reflects our energetic vibrations, healing path and the lessons our soul group prepared us for. Yet, and this is important to recognize, a different choice may not have been possible because that particular choice and its associated outcomes were necessary for our soul's growth and healing. It was not until after that choice was made that other choices became possible.

The most obvious choice is the one we make because it leads to the next step we need to take. At every moment in time, we make the right choices, based on the information we have, the outcome we need, the karmic healing and soul contract we have agreed to fulfill, and the lessons we must learn.

How many choices do we have within any given situation? The number of potential choices is limitless, but the ones we are aware of are those that are within the range of our energetic vibrations at that moment, each representing an aspect of potential and an opportunity for learning, healing, growth and transformation. Our challenge is to respond to the array of choices with intention and clarity, removing fear and emotions, raising our energetic vibration so we can be aware of the highest possible choices we can resonate with. Every aspect of fear that we allow ourselves to have places corresponding limits on the choices we are faced with. The choices we regret making are probably those we made in fear, which greatly narrowed the range of choices and, since healing fear is our life purpose, our fear actually created the choices that we were aware of. There are no wrong choices as each one we make reflects the possibilities that we can envision for ourselves at that moment. When we can expand the vision for our potential, we can be open to other choices and move from learning into mastery.

As we move into the vibration of miracles as part of our ascension journey we will begin to see more possibilities and opportunities, and a vastly different range of choices. Some of these may be challenging, others may be easy, and all are part of our spiritual growth. Each step on our path brings its own blessings and lessons. None of them is ever 'wrong' and each of them reflects the wisdom and growth that we have attained at that moment. We will become more comfortable with this process if we remember to live in the present moment and allow ourselves to experience the full range of possibilities that are available to us at that moment. At any other moment, we will perceive different choices.

If we can learn to respond to each situation with peace and joy instead of fear, and to take a step back, detach from the situation and ask whether there are other potential choices available, we will be aware of a wider array of possibilities so that with each step on our path will know when we are choosing powerfully and fully aware of how we are choosing. This allows new paths to open for our mastery journey and the availability of potential choices we would never have considered.

Consider these questions for your personal mastery journey:

Are you aware of any choices you have made in your life that were influenced by your soul group, either that you made because of them or in spite of them (or to spite them)?

Have you made a past choice that you regret today? Are you aware of other options that may have been available to you at that time?

Do you believe that you could have made a different choice then?

Have you made similar choices at other times in your life? Can you see a cycle or pattern in your choices?

For each choice that you regret making, can you see that it is the outcome you regret and not the choice you made?

What other outcomes were possible with that choice?

What other choices, that you were not aware of at the time, may have been available?

Understanding the concept of choice helps us understand a critical aspect of our path, that we are in control of the unfoldment of our reality and the result of each choice and what we learn from it changes what we attract and how everything in our life manifests from that point on. We can choose between seeing things from a spiritual perspective, which is recognizing the energy of everything and consciously choosing which vibrational path we will pursue, or the material perspective, where we become grounded in the emotional energy of people and situations and make choices based on our emotions and judgments of our self worth and value.

Our path to spiritual mastery will reveal the reasons and energies behind our past choices and give us clarity and confidence to make different choices in this moment. And with every choice, the path we take is governed by our free will and which truth we live in, spiritual truth or material truth.

The Truth We Live In

When we live through our spiritual authority, which acknowledges that we hold our own power and through it control the reality we live in, transformation is possible. The life we are living at this moment reflects the best and perfect use of our energies and the truths we know. Each new level of understanding allows us to access different energetic vibrations, expands our awareness to include different ways of being and moves us into the possibility of different life potentials. As we gain confidence with our spiritual mastery we see small glimmers of new possibilities and we hear our heart whispering of new dreams and possibilities. We begin to realize that there is more to life than what we have been able to know or experience and that perhaps there is a greater truth that we have not been able to know until this moment.

Now we can explore options that we may have never considered, create realities that were once distant dreams and free ourselves of the pain and sadness of our past. Acknowledging our spiritual authority, the stepping stone to mastery, is how we access our divine presence, which reveals a new truth, our spiritual Truth, through which we realize our mission in the world, understand our gifts and talents and embrace the possibility of a joyful, love-filled, peaceful, abundant life. But knowing our spiritual Truth reveals that we have lived a double life and what we have long held as truth was perhaps not true at all.

There are two types of truth, the Truth, as in spiritual truth and the truth, as in material truth. Spiritual truth holds no judgments or criticisms, is completely detached from any outcome and holds one belief, we are a divine presence, perfect in every way. Material truth is where we have judgments, criticisms, are attached to outcomes and expectations, and believe that we are imperfect beings seeking a level of perfection that we will never be able to achieve because of our inherent imperfection. Material truth is what holds us in our karmic experiences, our feelings of inadequacy, powerlessness, unworthiness and fear. Spiritual Truth is guided by spirit whereas material truth is the realm of the ego.

How do you know which truth you live in? Try this test.

First, take a look at your life from the material truth:

Name one choice in your life that you regret.

Think of one person that you wish had treated you differently.

Consider the path you could have taken if you had been more confident, trusting, or self aware.

Think of one decision you did not make and how your life may have turned out if you had taken it. For example, if you had married someone else, pursued a different career path, moved to a different place or did or had the courage to make a choice you have always avoided.

Think of one dream you had for your life that you abandoned.

Do you feel sad, angry and powerless? Do you feel that these choices or decisions, or the path you took, have limited your life in some way? Let's go one step farther and look at the people in your life, both past and present. How many of them live with regret and sadness, how many have unfulfilled dreams and unmet expectations? If these beliefs exist within your family, this is part of your soul group heritage which you have incorporated into your truth.

Now look at your life through the spiritual Truth:

For the choice you regret, what did it teach you and how have you used this information to make other choices?

For the person who did not treat you well, could they have treated you differently or did their actions reflect the most perfect expression of who they were at that moment?

For the path you could have taken, are you more confident today because you understand how your lack of confidence prevented you from making other choices? Did that experience enable you to have more self confidence in yourself now?

For the decision you did not make, can you really know how your life would have been had you made a different choice?

For each thing that did not work out as you anticipated, were you being protected from something else or did you need to experience the path you took so you could empower yourself to make a different choice at another time?

For the dream you abandoned, is it truly gone or is it waiting for you to be powerful, confident and emotionally and spiritually mature enough to see it through to fulfillment?

What is better, to pursue the dream and not have the inner resources to fulfill it or to wait until the right time so you can envision an even greater outcome for it?

The spiritual Truth takes us beyond judgment, into limitless possibilities, in which nothing is ever lost, gone forever or impossible. Those are the ego's thoughts and part of the limitations of our material truth. Within spiritual Truth we know that everything happens in perfection, which includes divine timing, right action, greatest learning and optimal results. We can spend a lifetime regretting a decision only to realize that it was a 'reverse blessing', where we were blocked from doing something that was not in our highest good and being prevented from an experience that would ultimately have caused us more pain than necessary. Accepting that is difficult because it is our nature to look longingly at what we think were lost opportunities or the chances we did not take, believing that our current reality would be so much different and better if we had taken that path. But if we did not take it at the time it were presented, we were not ready and the timing was not right, we would not have been able to take action in the best possible way and the results would not have been what we wanted.

With the material truth we see these situations as limitations and we agonize over missed opportunities, our bad luck or timing, the 'one that got away' and punish ourselves for our inability to 'do better'. With the spiritual Truth we accept one truth from which everything else flows, that we are perfect in every way, always expressing our divinity and fulfilling our healing purpose. It is our choice as to which truth we live, spiritual Truth or the material truth. Which one will you choose for yourself? The choice you make determines whether you live your life in joy and peace or in regret, sadness and limitation.

With our awareness of the spiritual Truth comes a realization that all of the other kinds of truths we have believed as true, truths which exist on a material level and reflect the lack of love, acceptance, tolerance, faith and trust that we have learned from others and from our life experiences are actually not true. This is a powerful realization because it allows us to question what truth we are living through and how it is reflected in our reality.

If the spiritual Truth is what has been true for us all along, why has it taken us so long to understand it? After all, we are spiritual beings having a human experience, so the spiritual truth should be obvious to us. And it is, hidden behind the veil of our ego-driven beliefs, perceptions, understandings and the heritage of our material truth. Our human journey is about transcending the veil, lifting the illusion and creating a bridge between the spiritual and material worlds. We came here to do this work and now that we are on this path we can begin to accept the spiritual Truth and learn to live it, instead of the material truth that has been the guiding force of our lifetimes of existence.

Although the spiritual Truth is much more pleasant and fulfilling than the material truth, it is very difficult for us to believe that it can be our truth. There are many examples of the limitations of material truth in our life and not many of spiritual Truth. Our reality, which we believe is true, often reflects the fear, lack of abundance and spiritual poverty that we accept as truth. And when we live with a truth that is focused on lack and fear every aspect of our reality reflects that truth back to us. Material truth tells us that we must struggle and suffer, are imperfect, limited in our abilities, powerless and that we are disconnected from Source because of our imperfection. These are the beliefs we must overcome to create the reality that Spirit tells us is the real Truth.

How do we change a truth that has been the fundamental basis of our reality and of humanity's path in general? Turning from material to spiritual truth can be as easy as turning the page of a book or waking from an endless nightmare of fear to the dawn of a bright and promising new day. We can start by remembering that spiritual Truth reflects the will of Creator in our life, that we have love, peace, joy and abundance in all things. This Truth flows to us from the Universe but when it arrives on the material plane it becomes distorted as it is filtered through our fears, which reflect what we believe to be true about ourselves, a truth that is based on our material world experience.

This material experience causes us to ask questions like "Why does God allow this to happen" or believe that "I am not worthy of more".

Through our free will we accept material truth as being our truth but free will can also open our eyes to the beauty of spiritual Truth, empowering us as spiritual beings with authority to create the reality that we desire, for ourselves and for the world. What we then learn is that there is only one truth, and that is spiritual Truth. The material world, which is everything we can see, hear, feel, taste and touch is the illusion that we perceive through the filter of the ego and represents a tiny reflection of the beauty, joy, unconditional love and peace that are ours by simply acknowledging ourselves as part of a loving Creator whose will has always been for us to accept and live through the Truth, once we are able to accept it.

We can choose the spiritual Truth but it is a new and unknown path. None of the familiar markers are there and no one on our material path can offer enlightenment. It can be scary until we realize that the known path, the material truth, is the path of karma and destiny. It is what we have always done and represents what we have always chosen. The spiritual Truth is a new path into a higher dimension, one where karma does not exist. Are we brave enough to choose it or if not, to allow it to choose us?

When our soul knows that we are ready to accept our spiritual Truth it helps us along the way by opening our eyes to the illusion of the material world and its limited truth. In that moment the life that was once appealing is no longer interesting; things we once wanted or were willing to suffer or sacrifice for are no longer worth the effort. A common element among our material truths is the way in which they contradict the spiritual truth of who we are. How do we know when we are accepting a material truth instead of a spiritual truth? Our material truths remind us of our powerlessness, they compel us to seek approval and validation from others, focus on what is missing and what we are not capable of or do not deserve.

They are the echo of what we have heard from others, even those things that we cannot remember. This awakening is usually not a period of elation, joy or even satisfaction. Instead, we feel dissatisfied, uneasy and know that some-thing different is out there for us, we are just not sure what it is. We no longer know where to put our faith, belief and trust. What is the Truth and what is the illusion? How can we know the truth when all of our reality is simply an illusion that reflects our beliefs? Different aspects of our material truth can end and we find ourselves alone, unsupported, wondering what happened to our world. It is not a punishment; it is an opening into living a greater truth, one that will allow us to create the reality that goes beyond what we can know from our mind's perspective when it is focused on our material truth.

When we have the courage to challenge our material truths we can ask ourselves "Is this true" every time we hear a voice that reminds us of our fear, of what we cannot or dare not do or what is not possible. Each situation we look at with fear or dread because we feel that we are not enough or there is not enough love, abundance and joy for us, is an opportunity to challenge our material beliefs, asking whether they are really true, finding the source of those truths and replacing them with the knowledge that our potential is limitless. Our spiritual Truth reminds us that we are worthy of everything our heart desires and it waits patiently for us to embrace this as our Truth and use it as the source of our power in the material world.

We are here to create space for heaven in the material world, to become the miracles we wish to manifest and to raise ourselves out of the vibration of fear and limitation into the sphere of unlimited potential. That process starts with our acceptance of our spiritual Truth, replacing our material truths that have held us back for lifetimes of existence with the knowledge of our divinity. By being willing to ask that question we open the door to a higher vibration, a new way of being and allowing our spiritual Truth to become the foundation for our reality.

Now that we are ready to face the truth, how do we apply it in our life? How do we shift the illusion so it reflects our highest levels of truth? How do we know what the illusion is if our perception of it changes with every thought?

With each step on our path to mastery we have new insights and information that assist us on our journey of reconnection to our power and to Source. As we receive this information we are more aware of the illusion of the material world and the reality of the presence of the spiritual world. We see where we are limited by the belief that the material world is all there is. And our new challenge is to change these beliefs, open ourselves up to new possibilities and accept new truths beyond those that we can experience in the material world.

But with this change we become aware of the conflict between our spiritual Truth, which speaks of limitless and boundless potential and the material truth, which is focused on fear and limitation. Every place in our life where we feel we are undeserving, unlucky, unable to create joy, abundance or love is a place where we have adopted the material truth and are out of integrity with our spiritual Truth. We know that because we experience these beliefs through the limitations that exist in our life. What do we do with that information and find the courage to make changes?

The Universe has a wonderful way of showing us where we are stuck in an aspect of our material truth (which means we have limited ourselves in some way) and where we need to open our eyes to a new truth. In the moment of our awakening from our illusion we feel powerless but if we go one step farther and are open to expansion, the energy begins to flow and we can let go of what is begging for release. Applying our spiritual Truth to every area of our life means acknowledging the perfection of each moment, our ability to learn from our lessons, heal our soul wounds and from that point, claiming the empowerment that comes from our learning the Truth.

Transformation follows faith and trust, when we know that the Truth exists even if we do not have proof of it at that time in the form of a physical result that we can see, hear and touch. When everything in our life contradicts our spiritual Truth we are challenged to transform every aspect of our reality. But we really only have to change one thing -- all we have to do is accept the spiritual Truth of who we are and the illusion of the ego-based material truth will shatter, to be transformed into a reality that reflects the new Truth we wish to use as the foundation of our life path.

This is so exciting and empowering that we want to share it with others. So we try to tell them about our journey and open their eyes to their own spiritual Truth. The results can range from exciting to disastrous. Some may be happy to learn about a new truth and embrace the knowledge. Others may not be ready to hear about our new truth because then they are challenged to change their concept of the truth. They may tell us we are 'different', that they can no longer interact with us in the same way; that we scare them or they will avoid us. We are no longer standing in the same aspect of truth and we do scare them because if they follow us then they must examine their lives and ask themselves whether they are living in the spiritual or material truth.

And if we have been in victim consciousness, our friends may be victims too and can't share our new sense of power for it challenges them to rise above being a victim and become powerful. So instead of sharing our joy they can find it challenging and if they are not able to resonate with our new energy, the connection with them is gone.

Knowing and applying our Truth to our life sometimes means that we have to create new friendships, careers and life paths. But we can do it because our spiritual Truth is empowering and through it we work in direct partnership as co-creators with the Universe, in life affirming ways that create wonderful, fulfilling opportunities that are available to us with our new energetic vibrations. Those who are ready can embrace this path. Those who are not will run in another direction.

Transformation brings its own challenges and once we are aware of the illusion we must find a new Truth, creating a gap between our old illusion and the new reality that we have yet to create. During this time we can feel socially isolated, unsupported and unsure of what to believe. This is a period of adjustment that passes and then we will find like-minded people who we can share our Truth with and receive acknowledgement and honor in return because they have found and connected to their own Truth.

These are members of our new soul group or family and each has been on their own path of finding, acknowledging, accepting and connecting with their Truth. The transformation happens as quickly or slowly as it needs to but the end is always the same, we accept and acknowledge our divine spiritual heritage and know that we are co-creators with the Universe to design a reality that flows with abundance, peace, joy and unconditional love, for ourselves and for all of humanity. It happens quickly when we recognize our need for transformation. It happens slowly when we have not yet integrated our free will with our divinity and are still living in the illusion of the material truth.

Consider these questions for your personal mastery journey:
Can you identify a material truth in your life? Something that you believe is true but is limiting your life in some way?

Can you transform that material truth into a higher vibration, a spiritual Truth that is available to you instead?

Is there someone in your life who cannot accept your new Truth? Can you let them be in their own energy instead of trying to convince them to accept yours? Are you afraid of the transformation that may occur for you when you step into your spiritual Truth? Think of one dream or wish that you had and focus on that as what you want to manifest with your spiritual Truth.

Are you ready for a life of limitless possibilities, abundance and joy? This is what accepting your Truth will help you manifest in your life.

The true blessing of spiritual Truth is that it allows us to dream big, to see everything as possible, to know that we are limitless and expansive, and to live life fully and in joy. Can you imagine that kind of life for yourself? It is possible when we decide that we will live through our intention and the assumption that we are protected and provided instead of hoping that everything will turn out and assuming a reality based on our fears.

Assumption and Intention

The knowledge that we create every aspect of our reality gives us a sense of power and purpose, until we realize that we really are in control, even when all of the events of our life can make us believe that we are not. What happens when, despite our best intentions, life goes in crazy directions and we feel helpless and unsure of which path to take? How can we be masters or consider mastery when we cannot seem to control our own reality? Can we really be in control of what manifests in our reality and if so, why are there times when what we manifest is exactly the opposite of what we want? The process of manifestation is set in motion by our intention and while our intention may be to have joy and fulfillment, it is what we assume about our possibilities that determines their outcome.

Through intention we give energy form and structure, setting its direction and creating a potential outcome. And the energy responds to us in ways that consider all of the beliefs that we have attached to the outcome, which includes all of our assumptions. If we assume that we will have what we want, we are adding to the outcome. But if we assume that this situation will be like all of the things that have happened previously in our life, that is to say, that it will turn out badly too, then we are taking away from the energy and the outcome will reflect this assumption, instead of something more powerful.

There are two kinds of assumptions, one is based on the past, which includes everything we have already experienced, the other is based in the present moment, where each moment unfolds before us according to the intention we hold in that moment. This is another test point on our ascension journey and a test of our mastery. Are we willing to put aside every belief we have about how life 'should be' or 'has always been' and allow each moment to be the best and most perfect expression of our energetic vibration?

Of course we are, until we are faced with the fear of not knowing how life will unfold because we have no foundation for knowing or understanding how to guide the ego through its fears. While living through the highest intentions is our goal, it is through our assumptions that life becomes a painful, challenging healing journey of karmic cycles we can never seem to move beyond. Our many lessons exist because we assumed them into being, as our assumptions carry as much energy as our intention.

With mastery we can avoid that path and change how we create our reality, going from past assumption into present intention. Our new life purpose becomes one of moving beyond assuming a probable future based on the past and intending a higher vibration for this moment. That sounds easy enough and it is, but we have a little work to do before we can proceed.

Before we learn to live our lives through intention, purposefully and consciously creating the reality that we want for ourselves, we must do some inner housekeeping to remove the barriers that prevent us from doing that at our current state of spiritual evolution. These barriers are the beliefs and perceptions that we have put into our lives to protect us from pain, disappointment and chaos. Although they exist to protect rather than hurt us, they appear as soon as we set our intention for transformation and their whispered warnings arise to remind us that change creates pain and discomfort arise, reminding us of past experiences. When we understand that these assumptions are grounded in the past we can stop re-creating our past and begin living in the present moment, where we create our reality through the power of our intention. But first we must understand how we have been living through assumption.

What do we assume in life? If we really look at our lives, we will see that much of what we do is based on assumption because much of what we do is based on what we have learned from our past experiences. This process is not accidental as our brain is programmed to remember the past so it can help protect us in the future but when used unconsciously, it applies the experiences of the past to every aspect of our reality and creates a present that mirrors the past.

Assumption is the polar opposite of intention and through it we connect to an energy that already exists and expect it to continue in the same way. Intention, its opposite, is the direct application of our energy to an intended outcome. No matter what has happened in the past, intention is focused on the present moment and what we wish to have happen there.

Assumption leads us to believe that everything in life will have the same outcome, which will be similar to one that we have already experienced. And in some ways this is good. We assume that our car will always start when we turn the key (that's an assumption I always make), that others will stop at red lights as they are supposed to, that the sun will always rise every day and it will rise in the same place. But we have other examples that are more challenging, which can relate to anything in our life—we assume we will be betrayed when we have the experience of wanting someone's approval and they reject us in a humiliating way. Or we will assume that our efforts are not rewarded when we work hard at our job and ask for a raise a manager turns us down. We will assume that we are incompetent if we try a new activity and are embarrassed by our performance. And we will assume that we are a failure if we start a new business and it fails.

Each of these experiences can lead us to believe that if we put ourselves in a position to extend ourselves in some way, emotionally, physically, mentally or spiritually, we will fail or some aspect of the results will not meet our expectations. Every failure can result in an assumption that this will always happen each time we try to move forward. And without conscious awareness that we have created assumptions based on experience instead of through our spiritual Truth, we can wonder why we feel blocked or stuck in our lives.

Assumptions are not limited to what we experience in our own lives. We are bombarded by messages that allow us to create assumptions about how we should live, the kind of education we should pursue, our career aspirations, the clothes we should wear and the results we will derive from them. For example, magazine ads tell us that if we use a certain kind of shampoo we will have the same glossy, shiny hair as the model in the picture. So we buy the shampoo, assuming the ad is true but our hair does not look any better than it did before. Or, we pursue a university degree assuming that it will lead us to a fabulous job at a great salary only to discover that finding a job is difficult, even with a college degree and the salary offered may be far less than what we assumed it would be.

We also have assumptions about how we should be treated by others and by the world. We assume that everyone has our best interest at heart, until we experience someone who is only out for themselves and doesn't care what happens to us. We assume that if we do our best at work we will always have a job until we experience a sudden and unexpected layoff or job loss. We assume that families love and respect each other until we experience rejection from a family member or our interactions with them are anything but loving. We assume that society is well-organized and is there to protect us, until we experience otherwise. As babies, we assume that someone will take care of us and as children we assume that we will be safe and protected.

All of the assumptions that we have about being taken care of and provided for are tested and when the result is chaos and pain, we create an opposite assumption, that we won't be taken care of, that no one will support us and that we are alone. Then we extrapolate that to include a belief that the Universe will not support us either and so we forget about our connection to Source and our own power.

Consider these questions for your personal mastery journey:

What are some assumptions you have about yourself, based on your childhood experiences?

Is there someone in your life who holds assumptions (negative or positive) about you, your potential and your abilities?

What assumptions do you have about your potential and possibilities?

Are there any opportunities you have not considered because you assume that you will not be able to succeed in those situations?

How many of your assumptions about yourself are based on what others have told you?

How many of your assumptions about your life and potential are based on the past?

Do you assume failure before you consider the possibility of success?

As soon as we begin to assume, based on our past experiences, we put limits on the Universe and that creates boundaries for our reality. Assumptions limit our ability to create because they are based on fear and not on an inner knowing that we are powerful and are always in control. Living by assumption is like watching the first part and then the very end of a movie and creating a theory about what happened in the middle. We hope that we will get the end result we want but we do not do those things that will allow it to happen. When we live by assumption we do not allow for creation because we believe that we already know what is going to happen—after all, didn't it turn out that way before?

And when we begin to look at our assumptions we see how they create the experience of our reality, as they become the tools we use to direct the energy in our lives. The greatest of these illusions is that of separation, that we are separated from Source and live in a world of either/or, better/worse, richer/poorer and depending on which side of the separation we are on, we see ourselves as limited and powerless. We assume that some people can be rich while others must be poor, that there is good and evil, that we must have war to create peace, that God or Creator is greater than humanity, that there is such a great chasm between the spiritual and material worlds that we can never be in both and they will never be equal. We are not always aware of these beliefs because they are very subtle but they are an important component of our human thinking.

But as we continue to grow and move into wholeness we are able to see through the veil, beyond the illusion of the earth plane into the vast multi-dimensional universal continuum that we are also part of, where there is no duality. We know that all of humanity is connected to each other and to Spirit, that the material and spiritual world are interconnected. Once we arrive at this point, the assumptions that feed the concept of duality simply disappear and we are left with the knowing that we are all one, all equal and that there is no duality so there can be no assumptions about anything other than the power we each hold as divine beings.

This puts us in the powerful position of intention, but first we must work through the illusion because it is created through our assumptions and we must understand our connection to the illusion and the important role we play in its creation. We are masters of illusion and we create the illusion of our reality through our assumptions.

The illusion is a powerful vehicle because it feeds on our fears and anxieties about ourselves and our place in the world and it supports and is supported by our assumptions. It exists on an individual and a global scale. Globally, so much discord exists because of the assumptions that we make about other people and cultures. One thousand years ago, wars were fought over religion and land. Today, wars are still being fought over religion and land because the illusion of duality is still seen as the truth for much of humanity and the assumptions that are made from the belief in separation carry over from generation to generation. As long as we assume that others are different, that we are right and they are wrong, that ours is the better way and we must convert them to our beliefs, we will continue to feed the illusion and the assumptions that it creates. And we will continue to live in a personal and global world plagued by discord.

It is not easy to break through the veil and see beyond the illusion because we must then accept that we are living our lives within a reality that is not real. It is based on assumptions that have either been handed to us or that we have created for ourselves, based on our past experiences. With that knowledge we can distinguish between what we will choose as a reality and what assumptions we will use to create it, based on our intentions. Yes, we are powerful manifestors but if we are operating within the confines of assumption from the past, then we are not creating, we are unconsciously recycling past outcomes. That process creates its own chaos as we must then decide what we are to do next.

How do we live without assumption or how do we use assumption to support our intention for our experience of the highest vibrations? This is one of the blessings of our ascension journey for once we are able to see beyond our limiting illusions we are no longer bound by them and we can create life as we intend it in this moment rather than assuming it into being from our past.

Consider these questions for your personal mastery journey:

Can you see examples of duality and polarity in your life? Where do you believe that you are separated from your joy, abundance, peace and love?

What role does the illusion play in your life and where can you see beyond the illusion into a higher dimension of being?

Are you limited in some area of your life by the illusion that certain things are not possible, available or accessible to you?

Can you take one area of limitation and focus on removing that illusion and all of your assumptions about it, so you can have the experience of living at your highest potential?

Have you assumed some areas of your life into being and are struggling with limitation? Are you willing to release them and co-create your life on a universal level instead of the level of your assumptions?

Any feelings of being powerless, unhappy, unloved or dissatisfied are the results of the assumptions about reality that we have accepted as truth. Can we, as a human family, see through the veil, dispel the illusion and create the reality that we want to live in? The power is ours and the Universe stands ready to support and help us when we are ready to begin. Where do we have assumptions? One of the biggest areas in which we all assume is in the area of love.

One of life's greatest gifts is that warm feeling that comes from being loved. Humans have a basic need for love and small babies who are not loved may eventually die. It is true that a child who is not loved and who experiences neglect will not develop along normal guidelines. Love is something that we will spend a lifetime seeking and once we find it, or think we have found it, we will do whatever it takes to keep it alive. The knowledge that love may be there, around the next corner, in the next encounter, is what allows us to continue to look for it, no matter how many times the search has turned out badly in the past. The memory of a love, any love, no matter how brief, can sustain us for a lifetime. Because love is all about feeling, it is tightly   intertwined with our emotions and how we feel about ourselves. And mixed in with those emotions are many assumptions about what we will be, have and do when we have love in our life. We also have many assumptions about how those who love us will (or should) treat us.

While I don't want to dampen anyone's enthusiasm about looking for love, I must point out that it is our assumptions about love and what it may bring us that fuel most of our desire for it. Without our belief in separation, our grief at the loss of our Source connection and our belief that God does not love us, we would not spend so much time and effort looking for love from others.

We assume that love will make us happy,   feel better, enrich our lives, show us that we are worthy of being loved. And this is not just about romantic love, it includes every interaction that involves acceptance, being valued, feeling worthy and knowing that another person wants to be connected to us or through our interaction with them, on all levels, show us that we are valued. We receive or look for these many different aspects of love from our families, friends, co-workers, employers, the woman at the coffee shop—everyone we are in contact with gives us some measure of love, which, depending on the source, we view as various degrees of acceptance. We don't assume that everyone should love

301

us in the same way (like the woman in the coffee shop), but we do derive a sense of validation and comfort from knowing that through their display of affection and acceptance, someone loves us.

Consider these questions for your personal mastery journey:
Make a list of the various people who you feel value, accept and love you in some way.

For each person on your list, name the emotion that you feel when you think about them and in what ways they enrich your life and the kinds of emotion you feel about them or from them.

Do you have any assumptions about any of the people on your list and how they feel or think about you?

Is there someone in your life that you wish would love your, or be kinder or more respectful to you? Because you do not receive this from them, do you assume that they do not love you?

Can you make peace with the assumptions you have about this person and your relationship with them, knowing that they are doing the best they are capable of?

For each name on the list you make, write down how that person reflects the love you have for yourself.

And, once we believe that someone loves and accepts us, we take the next step into assumption and that is where complications are created. We assume that because someone is our friend, family, lover, or partner, they will show their love and affection for us in a particular way. We know we are assuming when we begin a thought with "because they love me they should …" or "if they loved me they would …". Our assumption is that if we are loving and kind to people they are supposed to return our feelings by being kind, thoughtful, considerate and nice to us, even if that has not been our experience with them or others like them in the past. And if they do not, we hold ourselves as the one who is wrong and unworthy of love.

So we create rigid assumptions that are accompanied by strong self-judgment. Our assumptions come with expectations and we wait for them to be met. If we can't find this in one person we will go to the next, until we find someone who convinces us that we are completely unworthy and unlovable and we stop trying, tired, discouraged, afraid and convinced that love does not exist in the world, or for us. With our assumptions and their associated expectations we begin our search for validation from a place of unworthiness and then look for someone to prove us wrong.

What is so challenging about assumptions? There are two things we need to know about assumptions in order to transform our thinking from assumption to intention. First, assumption is based on the hope that our worst fears will not manifest. While we assume that we will receive love in the way we want it from others, we quietly fear that we will not. And our fears are based on the truth that is part of our past. In the past we have not received the love we want and we hope that by choosing another person or giving the same person another opportunity, the past will not become prologue to the future. But we know in our hearts that the past will be repeated in the present, because this is how it has always been. Unfortunately, our fears are often well founded and what we fear usually comes to pass, not because it is mandated by the Universe, but because we manifested it by focusing on it and allowing it to become the foundation for our intention.

The second aspect of assumption that we should understand is that it reflects our ego's perspective, which is always based on the past. The ego knows that we are not worthy or deserving of the love, respect and acceptance that we want. Its greatest fear is that we will have proof of that and when we do, when we approach all of our relationships from the point of assumption.

Taking a spirit-based approach moves us from assumption to intention, where we intend to have love, joy and acceptance and we support our intention with the assumption that they will happen as we intended in the best and highest way. With intention we create the energy for those things to occur for us and they will because we are in harmony with those energies in the present moment, creating a reality that reflects our desires in the moment.

Assumption by itself is a powerless way to manifest. But when partnered with intention, it becomes our most powerful manifesting tool. With assumption we are attached to people, situations, events, experiences, the past and our fears and all of the judgments we have about them. With intention we are fully in the present moment, without judgment and set the energy for each step on our journey. We transform our thinking by removing hope and replacing it with an expression of what we wish to manifest. The process goes like this:

"I hope they will like me." becomes "My intention is to be surrounded by loving, kind people who like me and show that in their actions and I know that I will."

"I assume I will get this job and like it." becomes "My intention is to have work that is fulfilling and contributes to the success and abundance I want and deserve and I know it will happen."

"I hope that I will have a relationship someday." becomes "My intention is for a fulfilling relationship with a partner who loves, honors and respects me and I know it is happening in this moment."

"I assume that today will be filled with the same bad luck I had yesterday." becomes "My intention is that this day will be a flow of abundant blessings and it is happening in this moment."

Can you do this in your own life? Start by writing down every situation where you are assuming that others will fill the gaps in your life, will contribute their energy to the places where you feel unfulfilled, uncertain, and unloved. Add to your list all that you hope will happen to change your life situation. Then set your intention to have all of the love, respect, certainty, success and abundance that you want. Now assume that it will happen just as you have set your intention for it to happen. When you do this you are transforming the energy in your life and releasing yourself from the judgments of the past, from the powerlessness of hope into the detachment of the present moment where whatever happens next depends on what you are thinking and doing right now. Now you are stepping into your power and remembering who is in control of your reality.

And one final note, for each person who does not give you the love and acceptance you want, learn to practice acceptance and assume that whatever they are giving you is the best and the most they have to give, because it is. We assume that others treat us badly out of meanness, disrespect and disregard for our feelings. And while that may be true of some people, for the vast majority it is not. They simply give us what they have to give and there is no more.

When we assume that we are receiving the highest and best expression of another's energy in each moment, we can release ourselves from the belief that we are unworthy of better treatment and find people who will interact with us in more emotionally and energetically fulfilling ways. As we ascend into higher vibrations we release the past and all judgments and assumptions we have created from it that, without the presence of conscious intention, determine the reality in each moment. We can set ourselves on the course of creating the life of our heart's desire by intending it into being and assuming that it will be that way.

If our assumptions assist in the creation of our reality by supporting or destroying our manifestation efforts, why not use that power to assume the very best for ourselves? What if we could assume that we would be happy instead of focusing on not being unhappy? Can we assume that we will have an abundance of love in our lives instead of focusing on not being without love, or not being hurt by those we love? By assuming the positive, life-affirming aspects in our reality, can we bypass the painful experiences? The answer is yes, absolutely. All we have to do is to learn to start assuming that we have what we want, instead of assuming that we will end up with what we don't want.

As we move through our ascension journey and are provided with experiences to move our lives into a different reality, we can be surprised at the extent to which we have past-based assumptions and it can be quite disheartening to find out that we have created a great deal of our reality from them. At one point these assumptions were acceptable and suddenly they are not. What do we do next? Do we create new assumptions or do we take another step and learn to live without assumption? The message of our transformation is clear, to learn to create a reality that exists from moment to moment, from miracle to miracle, extending our concept of our world to incorporate the unlimited potential that is always available to us, one that assumes the highest and best outcome and knows that it will happen. This is the realm of intentional knowing.

The higher aspect of assumption is intentional knowing, which is the conviction that all will unfold according to our intention. At that point we know that we have the power to choose a different outcome and experience it in every moment. Living through intentional knowing is being firmly grounded in the certainty of our own power, of our connection with Source and with the freedom that comes with knowing that all is well in our world. We stop looking to the illusion of the outer world for confirmation of our value and remember that the reality flows from the inside out – we create it with our thoughts and beliefs.

Once we use assumption to support our intention in life affirming ways the entire Universe stands at our bidding, ready to fulfill our heart's desires because we are ready to look beyond the veil of assumption and access the vast potential that can be created from knowing who we are and what we are capable of when we are fully grounded in our power. Then we can dream big, allowing our most cherished desires to become possible because nothing, including our assumptions, stands in their way.

Dream Big

Once we accept our spiritual Truth and put the past into perspective, clearing out the cobwebs of the material truth's illusions that define our current reality, we are ready to live a life that we want to live, doing anything and everything that we want to do and fulfilling our dreams. Does this sound too good to be true? Or are we skeptical because we have tried this many times and it never worked for us before? What is going to be different this time? Can we give ourselves permission to dream big?

'Dream big' is a catchy phrase that tells us if we have big enough dreams, we can have everything that we want. There are two parts to creating a reality by dreaming big. The first part is to have the big dreams to set the energy in motion and the second part is to have the big thoughts that support the energy to manifest that reality. And that is what we do not always learn about dreaming big — if we have big dreams, we must match them with big thoughts. What generally prevents our dreams from manifesting is not that we don't have big enough dreams, it is that our small thoughts prevent us from manifesting our dreams. We may dream big but we think small.

When we 'think small' we bring elements such as doubt and fear into our thoughts. As soon as a shred of doubt begins to enter into our energetic space, we can lose our momentum and our big dreams can suddenly evaporate before our eyes. It only takes one small doubt, one tiny bit of fear, one critic (even an internal critic) to undo all of the work that we have done towards creating our dream. Why is that? Is it because we are weak or undeserving (which is what we may think) or is the process so fragile that it can be easily undone?

It's neither of those. We deserve to have our dreams come true and the process is not that fragile. When we dream big we create situations that challenge our belief systems, where we have stored the memories of many unmet expectations and unfulfilled dreams, gathered across many lifetimes. As soon as we open the door to the possibility of another potential dream, we bring up all of those memories and our mind, if we do not monitor our thoughts, will bombard us with thoughts of why our dreams didn't come true in the past and how many ways things either won't work out at all or won't work out the way we would like them to.

Sometimes, when we begin to focus on our dreams, pay attention to our thoughts and create what we want in life, things just flow. Suddenly, we're riding a wave of potential and everything is good. That happens some of the time. At other times, we begin to ride that wave of potential and everything comes to a sudden stop. Nothing works and we feel like we have gone back to the beginning and have to start over again. What we thought was going to be a fast ride forward down easy street turns out to be a slow and painful ride backwards through every fear and anxiety that we have about what we want to create that rises to meet us. Nothing is wrong, but it's time to face ourselves on the path of transformation.

When we start to dream big and allow ourselves to take our lives in another direction, we move the energy around us. In other words, we 'stir the pot' so to speak, and everything that has been hiding from us (or that we have been hiding from) rises to the surface. And sometimes it isn't very pretty. When we begin to move the energy we get to look at many things in our lives that we didn't notice before and because we are in transformation mode, we look at them in a different way.

The purpose of this exercise is not to stop us in our tracks, as it sometimes does, but to give us a final opportunity to review the issues, to ensure that we are complete with them, tie up any loose ends and let them go. Too often, though, we let what feels like a blast from the past stop us, thinking that we have gotten as far as we can and that's all there is. But that is not the case at all. Remember that when we move the energy in our lives we bring up all of the past issues that exist for us. It's all part of the process. Since we have been shifting our energy and thus our perspective, we have a chance to look at these issues in a different way.

Dreaming big is a life-changing process and facing our fears is part of it. We have to ask ourselves whether we believe we deserve to have what we want, whether we are ready to face change, how we are going to re-structure our lives to accommodate our dreams and what our next steps are.

We also have to learn to walk in faith and trust, knowing that our deepest desires are appropriate for us and what we go through when we stir the energy is part of a process of removing the obstacles from the path to fulfillment. The flow is always there and we are always in it, we merely have to face and overcome our fears and then we can continue on our path to making our dreams part of our reality. And as with everything on our path, we can do this in our life but not for others, no matter how much we want them to share our experience.

Just as we cannot heal anyone else, we cannot change their life or make it better or different for them. We can help them by creating the energetic space where they can learn to dream big for themselves. Our control extends as far as our own reality and each person has free will. We can help others by showing them other options but we cannot make them walk that path, no matter how attractive or beneficial we think it is. By being powerful for ourselves we create a vortex of power that they can learn to create in their own lives. By believing in their power, in the perfection of their lives, in their ability to create what they want, they can learn to create that energetic space for themselves. But we cannot do it for them.

If you have ever watched a baby who learns how to walk, you know that they choose the moment in which they take that first step. And it happens when they are ready for it. We can't make them do it at any other time; it is something that they have to learn to do for themselves. And in the same way we cannot teach someone how to create joy, peace, love or abundance for themselves,   but we can believe in them so strongly that they can begin to believe that they can do it for themselves. When they do it is their choice.

Our teacher Jesus was able to heal people because he saw them as healed and he believed it for them so strongly that they could believe it for themselves. This is how we can help others to learn how to dream big—by seeing them as perfect and capable and by looking beyond what appears to be the error of their ways and our judgment of their choices or decisions and seeing them as living in absolute perfection. Because it is when we can accept others completely as they are, without judgment that we can see them in their power. We help others dream big by acknowledging their power and perfection, and we empower them by being in our own power and perfection. When we empower those around us we share with them the greatest lessons that we have learned through our ascension journey, that we are powerful beyond measure and despite all appearances to the contrary, once we learn to dream big, we claim our power, shift our energy and will never be tempted to think small again.

What does it mean to dream big? It is the desire to be more, to expand our current reality and stretch the boundaries of our thinking, but not in the material sense. It is the voice of our soul telling us that that we are finished with the learning we are experiencing in the present moment and we need to grow so we can move beyond it. Our soul sends out the call and our heart responds with whispers that we can have a bigger dream. Since our reality can never be bigger than our thoughts allow it to, in order to expand our reality we must engage the mind to think bigger thoughts to meet the size of our dreams. How we perceive ourselves, our capabilities, our limitations and potential creates the boundaries in which we live. If we are living a life that is restricted, it is because our thoughts are restricting us. When we decide to expand our thought processes, we expand our boundaries and this allows our dreams to grow.

Stretching these boundaries creates growing pains, similar to those we experienced when we first left our home to start our own life. While this may have been exciting it was also frightening and filled with unknown elements. Each time we stretch the boundaries of our thinking we place ourselves in that space where the future is unknown and where we may not have the comfort of knowing what will happen next.

Too often our boundaries serve to limit us and our potential because they are based on our past experiences and belief systems. New experiences are created when we dream big, stretching our potential to allow what we never thought was possible, to have a life that we may not have ever considered as being available to us.

Consider these questions for your personal mastery journey:
Is there one area of your life where you have been thinking small?
Can you name some boundaries in your thinking that contribute to your small thinking?
How can you change your thinking from small to big?
Can you pick one aspect of your life and dream the biggest dream you can think of?

What does your big dream look like?

Are you willing to allow your thinking to expand, matching your big dream so you can create it?

In what kinds of ways does your life change when you dream big?

Are there situations in your life that will change when you dream big?

Is there someone in your life who will not understand or accept your big dreams? Can you accept this and dream big anyway?

Are you ready to surrender to this process, to allow the flow of energy to move in your life so your big dreams can manifest?

Dreaming big stretches our boundaries beyond what we think is possible, surrendering our fear and allowing the Universe to share its vision for our reality with us. This is the Universe's wish for us, that we allow the impossible to become possible, live in joy and abundance so that each day is a celebration of unlimited abundance and possibilities. We are always under the guidance of a benevolent Universe that watches over us and waits for us to invite it on our ascension journey so we can become co-creators of our big dreams. Don't wait for the Universe to give you permission to dream big; participation in the third dimension is by invitation only – you must invite the Universe to partner with you on your path and when you do, the biggest, most outrageous dreams become possible.

And we can take this one step further and dream big for the world, so that we can put our energy towards manifesting peace, joy and love for humanity and our planet. That is not to say that we can alter someone's free will and create peace where others do not want it, but we can create the possibility of peace so that it becomes an option. Remember that a single light, however small, dispels the darkness. Dreaming big for the world will help create that light so that there is less darkness. This is our mastery call, to create for the world what we want to create for ourselves.

If we can dream big for the world we can offset all of the negativity that we hear about every day and create a new reality, one that contains the possibility of peace and abundance for everyone. We can't wait for good news to start feeling good about what is going on in the world, because the overriding energy of the third dimension is fear. We see many examples of it on television and in the newspapers. When we add our own concerns to what we hear about all we are doing is building on that fear energy and creating even more of it.

No matter how far we get into ascension there will be examples of both light and darkness on this planet. What we are now able to do is to provide ourselves and others with choices as to how much darkness we and they wish to live in and with. When we focus on the darkness, in this case, by agreeing that the world is a terrible place, is in a terrible state, and the situation is hopeless, we merely perpetuate the darkness and fear. At some point we must stop participating in the fear and begin to change the tide of the energy that governs humanity. We do this when we dream big for ourselves and for the world.

While things may not appear to be wonderful in the world, at this moment they are what we have created them to be. In order to change them we will have to start focusing our energy in different directions, by creating the possibility of a different reality for the world through our ability to dream big and this sets the energy in motion. And we can help with that change right now by dreaming big for the world, believing in the good in people, believing that there is enough for everyone, that peace is an option, that love is the answer, that we are all connected and by focusing on bringing in and spreading the light. We have created the world as it is and we can change it, by being willing to dream big for the world.

Consider these questions for your personal mastery journey:
How can you dream big for the world each day?
What can you do to dispel fear and darkness in the world around you by beginning with your own life?
Can you spend a few minutes each day bringing light to humanity?

Is it possible for us to change the world? How can we create the transformation that millions before us have been unable to do? What can one person do in the face of so much negativity and fear? Each of us has free will and we can choose to be in fear or in the light. When one person chooses the light they create an energetic imprint that exponentially magnifies the light so it is available to many others. Our free will is our gift from Source and we can use it in any way that we wish. When our wish is for light, peace and love, we have the ability to create great change in the world. Through our free will we have the gift of mastery over the third dimension. And how we use that gift creates the balance of light and darkness, the level of joy and sadness, the amount of love and fear that is present in the world.

Our Free Will

We think of free will as our punishment for being human. It stands accused as the reason for our separation, the thing that keeps us in karmic cycles and stands between us and Source. Our free will is responsible for our self sabotage, judgment and karma. It has become the enemy in our ascension journey, our challenge to mastery and what we must conquer to reconnect with our divinity. But this is wrong. Free will is not the enemy, it is a gift and is the source of our power on earth. Our free will allows us to do whatever we want as masters of the third dimension and we can use it for good or evil, to create joy or pain, peace or chaos.

At the moment of our initial separation free will was bestowed upon us as a gift to allow us to use the energy of the earth and to eventually choose to return Home, to our spiritual roots. Because we can use our free will in any way and we are responsible for every outcome and situation that we create with it.

When our free will is consciously partnered with our spiritual guidance and the memory that we are a manifestation of God, it allows us to be powerful co-creators of heaven on earth. When it is used unconsciously and under the sole power of the ego, its use reflects the worst of our fears, creating destruction, chaos, and pain. We have experienced every aspect of the use of free will by the ego and are now ready to use it in partnership with Spirit.

Our free will directs our energy and how it will manifest and all of these different aspects, the ego, spirit and Source, must be present for free will to function in the highest and best way. When used in connection with our mastery, free will allows us to express the highest aspects of our divinity and create heaven on earth.

The best example that illustrates how free will works in our lives is by using the analogy of a car. The body of the car is our physical body, our Higher Self is the engine and steering wheel and our free will represents the driver. Without an engine the car does not run, and without a steering wheel the car cannot be directed in a particular direction. But, without the driver to start the car, place their foot on the accelerator, put their hands on the steering wheel and physically drive it, it is useless as well.

So it is the combination of our Creator energy, in the form of our Higher Self and our free will that drives our 'vehicle' to where we wish to go. The engine and steering wheel have no say in where the car goes -- they are totally dependent on the will of the driver. The driver needs the steering wheel to control the car, the accelerator to make the car move and the engine to power it. In essence, they are all dependent on each other. The car doesn't care if we drive down the street or into a wall -- it has no opinion as to where it goes. That decision is up to the driver and where she decides to go is where the car will travel.

So with our free will we can go wherever we want to as slowly or as quickly as we want to get there. But many of us either forget that we are in control of the vehicle, that it responds to our direction or we have our car on cruise control, moving in the same direction, at the same rate of speed, rarely slowing down or stopping, holding onto the steering wheel for dear life and hoping that we do not crash and burn. Too afraid to use our free will because we remember how we have used it to create havoc in our life, we take the safer route and do not use it at all or on a limited basis.

Consider these questions for your personal mastery journey:

Can you name an area in your life where your free will has created chaos in your life?

Do you see how your free will has worked with the energy of fear in your life?

Do you believe that free will is a challenge to your spiritual mastery?

Are there areas in your life where you are on 'cruise control', afraid to make a move in any direction and just moving forward with no particular direction?

Has your free will been in conflict with your spiritual guidance or Higher Self?

Do you believe that your free will is the 'enemy' and that it limits your choices and your journey of mastery?

We tend to think of our free will as the reason we have chaos, drama, lack and fear in our lives, instead of its true purpose, which is to allow us to create what we want on the earth and in our reality. Free will is how we have dominion over the third dimension, as we are in control here, in charge of what happens in our own lives and in our world. When we are not in partnership with Spirit we take on the responsibility of Creator from the ego's perspective and forget that the highest and best use of free will is when we are co-creators with Spirit.

We have the final word in what happens in the third dimension and that is according to our original plan for the human and earth ascension cycle. We do not receive direct assistance in the form of intervention that saves us from ourselves because that violates Universal law and from the perspective of the Universe we do not need it — we have all of the energy, power and tools we need to create heaven on earth, know exactly what we are doing and each decision and choice is perfect. Free will is humanity's greatest gift and its biggest challenge because it simultaneously sets us free and holds us back, it encourages and defeats us and is the one thing that prevents us from manifesting what we desire most in life because free will, when partnered with the ego, causes us to resist and be in fear instead of surrendering to the flow of the energy with which we create our reality.

Instead of seeing free will in a positive light, we use it as an excuse for our missteps, mistakes, missed opportunities and misguided choices. We see free will as a point of weakness that stands in the way of our divinity and spiritual mastery instead of what it truly is, a powerful expression of our humanity that we can combine with our divinity to create a new paradigm that is integrated and balanced. Would you view your free will differently if you knew that it is the only source of power in the third dimension? Free will is what manages, creates with and directs the energy of the third dimension. Spirit has no power here, except by our invitation and intentional and conscious partnership.

We are not here to carry out the orders of Creator on earth, we are as masters here to create the earth as a blend of the spiritual and material, to guide ourselves and the earth to ascension, to balance the assumptions of the ego with the intention of Spirit, to create a balanced energetic vibration, not the domination of one energy over the other.

We already have that with polarity and we have been tasked with transforming these energies as part of our healing path of reconnection. Our free will allows us to do that because we always have a choice as to what we will do, how we respond to transformation, whether or not we learn and resolve lessons and how easy or difficult this path is. Because with our free will comes a very important choice, whether we take the path of most or least resistance, which we can also call the difficult path or the easy path.

One challenge of our spiritual journey is making the process of growth and learning easier. We know that the journey can be hard, many of us have struggled and suffered through it most of our lifetimes. But how hard does it have to be? Does it have to be difficult at all? We have come here to bring heaven on earth and that process can involve 'going through hell' first. That is our path of maximal resistance.

But there is a path of least resistance, where we can learn and grow without pain and chaos, which is a blessing that arrives when we remember our spiritual Truth. The easier path is available to us even in the fulfillment of our soul contracts but we must be willing to choose it. Many of our past lives have involved fighting and struggling to bring change, to be heard and to spread the light to those who were not ready for it. So we came prepared to fight for our cause, to spread the light in any way we could, to get the   job done, no matter what it took.

Our free will allows us to choose either path to accomplish our spiritual healing and growth. And the choice is not always apparent when we are in the throes of our challenging lessons. To know the easier path we must be unafraid, have no emotional investment in the outcome and be willing to release our 'no pain, no gain' mentality. Our choice often involves the more difficult path, either because of our belief that challenge must be met with another challenge, or we believe that other options are not available to us.

But the greater reason is that we are not aware of the easier, less challenging options because many of our lessons recall our fears and doubts and make us feel powerless. So we react out of fear instead of responding from faith, use our fear to answer challenges with more physical and mental power instead of engaging our spiritual resources. Armed with our fear-based power we do the first thing that we can think of without asking whether there is an easier way. The powerlessness we fear becomes the energy of our choices and we know that powerless choices yield powerless results.

Since the easier path is not part of our memory we do not believe it exists. It becomes obvious when we can practice detachment, are not invested in the outcome that the ego wants to have, are willing to let go of the process and trust that we will be guided to a perfect outcome.

That sounds so easy, why would anyone choose the hard path? Because the easy path takes trust and faith, the highest and best use of our free will, a willingness to forgive and to surrender — not as in giving up, instead, separating our ego from the process and allowing the Universe to guide us, balancing our ego's desire for immediate results with our spiritual understanding of divine timing, completing lessons and the path of transformation. We must be willing to release our need to be right and be in the energy of acceptance.

As we approach a lesson if we can remember that we have the option to choose which path we will take through it, both paths become obvious to us. Both will require effort and our willingness to learn but the hard path will take us through it on an ego level; the easier path will take the spiritual route. Whatever we choose is what is right for us — sometimes we need to take the hard path because we cannot remove ourselves from the emotional energy the lessons recall in us and we need to address the situation through our emotional energy.

Healing our emotional DNA and the karma associated with it is an important part of this process. When we remove our emotional responses and their associated feelings of anger, disappointment, hurt, unmet expectations and sadness all of our lessons take on new meaning. They become opportunities for learning instead of proof that we are not good enough, unlovable, unworthy or undeserving of what we want. We are no longer a powerless victim but a student of mastery and powerful living and each situation is another opportunity to practice how powerful we can be. We stop resisting and start receiving the blessings that are available as part of each lesson. Then we can find peace without chaos, love without hurt and joy without pain.

The path of emotions is the more difficult path because when we are emotionally charged an easier choice is not always obvious. Our emotions put us in the ego's energy and there is a completely different dynamic involved. The ego wants to be right, in control, to take charge and to win. With the ego we will take a difficult lesson through to the bitter end and the easier path of surrender becomes a sign of weakness or defeat. Can we release our attachment to the emotions and the outcome we want to achieve at all costs and simply accept and forgive?

That's hard to do when we are on an emotional, ego-based mission, in which we want to be vindicated and someone has pushed us to our last nerve. There are questions we can ask to determine whether our ego has taken over, such as:

Why is this so important to me?

Do I really want to do this?

How far am I willing to take this?

Is there a less challenging path available?

Am I willing to let this go?

Do I need to forgive this person or situation and can I do that?

How do we know which path is which? Sometimes it is not obvious but one way to tell whether we are on the more difficult path is by what is happening to us and our reactions. Our level of emotional investment comes into play, whether or not we are aware of it, and it has the power to affect what we experience, how much pain we will accept, how long we are willing to stay in the experience and the outcome that we can anticipate.

Every situation that we participate in has a level of emotional investment. Whether we want someone to love us, to be successful in our career, get along with our friends or be accepted by our family, we are looking for a certain emotional outcome from the situation and we will work hard to ensure that we achieve our payoff, which can be love, appreciation, value, acceptance, to be heard, or to be acknowledged. What are some of the payoffs you want in your life?

When our level of emotional investment is high, we create a situation where we are so attached to the outcome that we will do anything to ensure that we meet our goal. The need to be 'right' is our primary focus. Our free will takes over and becomes insistent on the outcome it wants to have. And we resist anything that does not give us that result. We use all of our energy to focus on a particular outcome without considering whether it is best, right, or appropriate.

With a high level of emotional investment our path can be extremely difficult because we want to 'make things happen' or to be right and with such a strong attachment to the outcome we don't see any other possibilities, we are not able to step back, let go and allow events to unfold in the way that is divinely perfect. This is the more difficult path, where we want to win at all costs, no matter what the cost is. Until we realize that it is our emotional investment that keeps us in the situation, we will continue to fight for the outcome that will make us feel better about ourselves, the situation, our life, our power and our value.

Consider these questions for your personal mastery journey:
Can you name a situation in your life in which you were or are attached to an outcome?

Is there a situation in which you wanted to win at all costs?

Have you ever wanted someone to acknowledge you were right or worthy and what were you willing to do to create that outcome?

Is there person or situation in your life that you are emotionally invested in?

Do you understand the energies you have around your emotional investments?

Can you see how you have used your free will to create certain outcomes, to 'win at all costs' and what was the cost to you in terms of your time, energy and emotions?

Are you aware of the fears that are behind your attachments and why you have these fears?

With emotional investment we are on a difficult path and although we feel that we are controlling the outcome, what we are doing is using our free will, together with the ego's perspective and trying to ease our fears while trying to avoid pain as much as possible. Yet we are supporting the creation of the most painful outcome. Are we even aware of our level of emotional investment? Not as long as we are drive by our fears. But when we can be detached from our emotions, we have a better perspective on how our fears and emotions work together to create the challenging path. And if we need more information, we will create lessons to reveal that to us.

The more we resist a situation, the greater our level of emotional investment. As we stop resisting, we are able to detach from the emotions. And when we can let go of our attachment to a desired outcome we allow the Universe to bring us something more wonderful than we can imagine, limit or remove the influence of our emotional investment and set our course for the easier path of least resistance.

Once we understand the ego's perspective and know why we are so vested in the difficult path, the easy path becomes an option. Of course, if we choose the difficult path anyway, we will arrive at the same level of learning and growth. It may take a little longer and we may be worn out at the end but we will eventually arrive at the end of the lesson. The path of least resistance is always an option for us, and we don't get any additional points or blessings by making our life difficult. We can choose the hard path and we have to remember why we chose it. Or we can choose the easy path and learn our lessons without sacrificing our peace and joy.

So our biggest and most important lesson with the path of least resistance is allowing ourselves to take the easy route, to let go and release the belief that we gain or learn more if an experience is difficult. The path of least resistance is the doorway into effortless living, peace and joy, no matter how difficult our lessons are. Can we step back and ask whether something fits our energy and contributes to our life in a positive way before we fall headfirst into a difficult situation? Then can we let go of it?

In our role as healers and Lightworkers we take on many challenges. On a soul level we know that we are capable of great courage and commitment but on a human level we take these to an extreme. This is especially true when a situation involves anyone we are closely connected to. Our healing connection often propels us into taking on the role of managing the situation and creating the best possible results, often at the expense of our own peace and serenity. We can choose to fight or we can choose to let go. No matter how clearly we can see a different solution, we can choose the path of least resistance for ourselves but not for others.

But it isn't that easy, especially when we are emotionally committed to someone or are invested in a particular outcome that involves a specific response. Then we get into full healing mode, doing all we can to make things work. It's strange that we often work harder and hold on more tightly when the lesson is about releasing and letting go. That is when the path becomes hard the less we are willing to let go, the harder the lesson becomes. Then we challenge the Universe to give us our way, plant our feet on the path of maximal resistance, dig in our heels and prepare for a showdown. Who do you think will win? But it isn't about winning, although that is sometimes how we feel. It is about creating the best and most wonderful outcome for ourselves, which is not always what we think it should be. Can we surrender, which means to stop fighting, and see what else is possible?

We don't need to be fully involved in everyone's healing and sometimes acknowledging that we can't help someone is a lesson in the highest use of our free will. When a situation does not resonate with our energetic vibrations or contains a lesson we have completed or do not need to be part of, it becomes a constant struggle that drains our energy. Lessons are meant to be life enriching, where we learn something that helps us along our spiritual journey. Being able to release what doesn't fit, isn't right for us, or is simply too hard puts us on the easier path. What we resist holds important lessons for us and is often an indicator of where we need to let go, become a co-creator, let ourselves take the easier path of least resistance and create peace and serenity on our journey.

So often the person we are trying to heal is the one we think needs the most healing because they 'push our buttons', which provides insight into our places of resistance and thus the lessons we must learn. How we respond determines which path we will take because we can fight them and think they are just trying to make our life difficult or remember that every person and situation has a gift for us. It is hard to pause and make that choice when our buttons are pushed because we are angry, afraid, our feelings are hurt, we are disappointed, betrayed, sad or in pain.

Each of these situations alerts us to a 'point of pain', an area where our soul has a contract to heal and grow. As we address these points of pain we complete healing cycles and are ready to move on. Or we can see these situations as challenges to our power or stumbling blocks and confirmation that we are wrong, less than perfect, undeserving of love or joy.

I often tell clients that there are no shortcuts through the process and it's true, we can't avoid lessons or learning. What we can do is to be aware of and open to the learning that they have for us, which is available when we are willing to take the easier path, the one that is free of our expectations, judgments and emotional attachments. Every situation where our buttons are pushed is an opportunity for us to experience quantum leaps on our healing journey. Are we able to resist the urge to take the emotional path and see what Spirit is offering us instead? Can we stop resisting and allow ourselves to be in a state of appreciation for the gift of healing, even if it means that our buttons are pushed to their limit in the process?

If we are looking for an easier ride through life, we won't find it on the spiritual path and it can be such a disappointing realization. There will always be lessons to learn and choices to make. Each situation has a blessing which may be wrapped in a very painful experience. These painful experiences arise as situations where our buttons are pushed and we have to deal with people, situations and emotions that bring us face to face with every fear and doubt we can imagine. But what we do find on the spiritual path, when we are willing to examine ourselves at the core and then stop resisting the lessons, is peace and joy.

What pushes your buttons? What are you resisting? Where could you practice surrender and what prevents you from doing that? Use that information to uncover a lesson, then move beyond the emotions and find the blessing of learning, which will bring you peace, joy and the unconditional love that you are looking for as you set out on the path of least resistance.

Consider these questions for your personal mastery journey:

Is there someone you are trying to heal or want to heal?

Do you see how invested you are in their healing?

What is the lesson for you in this situation?

What are the blessings you can receive by letting this go?

Where are you resisting this lesson and release and what does the resistance mean to you?

Are you willing to examine your motives in their healing?

What have you learned in this situation that benefits your mastery journey?

Is there someone in your life who 'pushes your buttons'?

What is the lesson for you in this situation?

What is it about this situation or person that you recognize in yourself, as a source of limitation, pain or fear?

What can you do to release yourself and them and find freedom from this situation?

Whatever path we choose, easy or difficult, the destination is the same, a new place on our spiritual journey with a new understanding of ourselves, our connection and our path. We learn new truths that we can incorporate into our understanding of our place in the Universe. Anything that does not resonate with your perfection, worth and value is not the truth. Change your truth and you will begin to create the reality of your dreams, one that is filled with peace, joy and unconditional love.

This also requires a shift in what we know of reality. Initially, we believe all we see around us as real. But since we know it is an illusion, is there a reality and if so, what is real? This is the stepping off point in our mastery journey, finding the 'real' in reality.

The Real in Reality

The world we know and experience is a snapshot that reflects our perceptions of what we believe the world should look and feel like in that moment. And the snapshot changes with each shift in our energetic vibrations and beliefs. While we describe our reality by what we can see, hear, feel and touch and believe that it is solid, constant and true, it is all merely energy that ebbs and flows according to our vibrations. Is there a reality at all? That depends on what we call 'reality' and our expectations of it. The truth about reality is that it only exists within the moment we are aware of it and it changes within each moment, as we move from one thought to the next.

The world is an illusion of the collective consciousness and our individual world is the illusion of our individual consciousness. Since each of us contributes to the whole, the world as we know it is merely a collection of consciousness and an illusion that is created from that consciousness.

But reality feels very real to us and it is, in that moment. How can it not be real? And if it is not real, then what is 'real'? If we know that the world is an illusion, what is reality? How do we create the illusion of 'realness' and what do we do to find the stability and grounding that we need? Is what we see with our eyes real or is it an illusion of reality that we have created for ourselves? If so, how can we tell the difference between reality and illusion? And if there is no reality, then what are we?

Reality is simply a mirror of our inner world, reflecting back to us all of the thoughts, beliefs and perceptions we have in that moment. This is our reality generator, which can be compared to a machine, fed by our thoughts and beliefs, which is constantly churning out our reality. Our thoughts are simply sending out an endless stream of instructions to the Universal energy around us, which responds by creating a reality according to the instructions it receives. Does this alter the way you think about your reality?

We know what is real because it has a physical and emotional presence. Our homes, jobs, cities and neighborhoods and the people around us look real.

And it certainly feels real when we are unhappy or physically ill or in fear, or when we do not have enough money to pay our bills or do not have a job. But what we use to judge our perception of reality is the emotions. In fact, much of what we know about our reality is created from our emotions. This is how we define our reality, through the combination of what we see and feel in a given point in time. Yet we also know that situations can change in a moment and become something very different. A destitute person can suddenly win the lottery, a sick person can have a spontaneous recovery, a new love can appear and erase our sadness.

These things appear to change our reality but what they do is change the circumstances so we can have a different perspective and shift our energy, which immediately changes reality we create from that point forward, until the next energy shift. What is real about reality is our response to it and since that changes according to our emotions, the only way we can know what is real is through how we feel about it in that moment.

This can be seen in a client's story. Dana owned a beautiful home in the mountains, a designer showcase with gorgeous furniture, spectacular views, fitted with every luxurious amenity. To anyone else this was a dream house but to Dana it was a prison. As part of her divorce she had to agree to live in that home with her children and stay there until they were out of school, even though she really wanted to live elsewhere. The home's peaceful country setting was too isolated and limited Dana's professional and social options. She quickly forgot how she had carefully chosen every detail, meticulously planned each room and lovingly chosen its custom furnishings with her now ex-husband. With her new perception she hated the home she once cherished and would have preferred to live in a tiny apartment.

As much as we want to believe that our reality is solid and grounded, it is nothing more than a reflection of the thoughts, emotions, beliefs and perceptions that we have in each moment. Dana, the client in the story, was no longer the satisfied, happy woman who was living in her dream home with her loving family. Everything in her home reminded her of a life she no longer had and since she was forced to live there and could not move, she began to hate the home and everything in it. Nothing about the home had changed, except the way she thought and felt about it. This is an example of how our reality changes according to our thoughts and emotions.

Our view of reality is either material or spiritual and this determines whether we think we are at the mercy of the world or the master of our destiny. If our view of the world and our reality is from a material perspective, everything that happens will create opportunities for us to shift back and forth, from joy to despair. We see each event as a separate entity, unable to see the whole and all of the connections.

This is where we are powerless, where what is happening controls how we view ourselves and the world around us. An event that creates drama or chaos has the power to end our dreams, make us believe we are helpless, throw us into depression and stop us in our tracks. But if one thing changes for the better, we are suddenly happy again and all is well in our world. Do we want to live life constantly on the edge like this? We can, but it is difficult and emotionally draining. The spiritual perspective gives us another view of reality.

From a spiritual perspective, the world is simply a flow of energy which contains an unlimited array of potential realities and takes shape according to the thought forms that are directed towards it. Imagine thinking about have an apple and seeing it materialize before your eyes. Does that seem too fantastic to be true? What if you think about having an apple and someone walks by and offers you one? The same principle is at work, the apple that you thought of just appeared before your eyes. This is the kind of manifestation that is possible with a spiritual perspective of reality.

The Universal energy is non-specific and non-judgmental, it is both 'nothing' and 'everything', meaning that it has no form until one is assigned to it and that form can take any shape. The energy does not choose what it will be and is nothing, meaning it represents 'no-thing' until it receives our instructions. Within every moment we are giving this energy form with our thoughts and beliefs and it is responding by creating according to what it is receiving.

This is why reality is an illusion because it is nothing more than energy which can be shifted and transformed into anything we desire. So we must truly watch what we ask for because our desires are being broadcast unconsciously through our thoughts and beliefs in every moment and they are creating our reality. Here is a story that shows how quickly reality can be transformed:

I received a call from a client who was frantic because he had just learned he was going to lose his job. He was so upset he could barely talk and said that this was the worst thing that could happen to him. All of his hard work and dedication meant nothing to the company that was now ready to end his employment. I advised him to calm down and to create something wonderful out of the situation by focusing on creating the best possible outcome.

Two hours later he called back with news that he had found a position in a different department that allowed him to use his skills in a more creative and supportive environment. He was overjoyed at this turn of events and his energy was much different than it had been two hours earlier, even though he was in the same building and at the same company.

The reality had shifted because he had changed his perspective from viewing the situation as disastrous to one with potential. And he acknowledged that he really disliked the previous job and the manager he worked with and had hoped that something would change. While he had created the job change he wanted it was initially upsetting because he was afraid he would not find another job but with a shift in perspective, from being in his fear to connecting with the potential in the situation, he manifested exactly what he wanted, a job with a supportive manager who appreciated his creative skills.

We look for content in reality, for real-ness and stability but it is about context, which reflects meaning and emotion. This context has many sources, including our thoughts beliefs, the opinions and beliefs of others, expectations, fears, doubts and dreams, all of which are connected to our emotions. We send out information in the form of thoughts that create a reality and then we judge what we have created through the meaning we attach to the results we obtain. So we are in a constant state of simultaneously creating and then judging what we have created based on how we feel about it and how others respond or react to it. All of these elements participate in the creation of our reality and it is a process that, like breathing, we are unaware of unless we focus on it.

Without conscious intervention, in the form of intentional oversight of our thoughts, emotions and judgments, we are creating a habitual reality, based on the ego's fears, our karma, the past we have already experienced, our conscious and unconscious attachments to others' input and what we believe about right and wrong and good and bad. Using what we know about others and what we think they will say or do to create our reality helps us to ensure that we are creating a reality they will agree with and approve of. Our reality, then, is not always completely ours as it contains aspects that are based on others' opinions.

Have you ever stopped yourself from doing something because you knew it would be criticized by someone?

Have you ever wanted to do something but knew that going in that direction would mean that you had to explain your actions to someone who would be angry or judgmental? Did this stop you from acting on your desires?

A few years ago I bought an old chair at an antique store. It definitely was not the most attractive chair in the store and everyone else had ignored it but it was perfect for a project I had in mind, so I bought it for ten dollars.

My friends asked me why I had purchased such an ugly chair and wondered what I was thinking. But I cleaned it up and then painted it with brilliant stripes of blue, green, yellow and red. The plain, ugly chair was now a work of art. Everyone who saw it wanted to know where they could get one just like it. Imagine their surprise when I told them it was the ugly wooden chair they had previously laughed at. What I manifested from the chair was something that reflected my dreams, passion and creativity. But I had to hold my vision and move beyond the ridicule and criticism I received from others to allow that vision to become real.

It is the dreams that we are willing to support, in spite of what others say, that make our reality joyful and fulfilling. It is our intention, focus and passion that allow us to command the energy to move in the direction of our dreams and desires. But we unconsciously use others' emotional responses to fine tune or alter our reality, ultimately creating a reality that is safe, criticism-proof and acceptable to them. Our fine tuning includes the two types of feedback we receive from others, actual and implied.

Actual feedback is the kind we actually receive, which is what others say, how they act or what they do. This feedback is interpreted as it is received, and we assess whether we have received the acknowledgement, validation or acceptance that we wanted from this person. All of this feedback is stored in our memory and each time that type of situation arises or we interact with that person we use our stored memories to create our reality.

Then we step into the area of implied feedback, which is the response we think we will receive, based on what we have experienced with others in the past, our relationship with them, their previous criticism or judgment of us and how much we value or want their acceptance or praise. The truth we believe about implied feedback is just as powerful as anything we have learned from experience and we use it to judge the worthiness and value of our dreams and whether we will act on them or not.

All of this contributes to the reality we are willing to allow ourselves to have, based on how much we value ourselves or others and whether we have the courage to stand up for our dreams or let them go unfulfilled. With conscious intention we can create a reality whose content and context are focused on what we desire for ourselves. And our journey to mastery requires this because when our soul reminds us of our heart's desires, we have to decide which reality we will create to fulfill it and whether we have the courage to boldly create our dreams, no matter what we think or fear others will say or how they may respond.

Consider these questions for your personal mastery journey:

Are you consciously aware of the reality you are creating? Or are you unconsciously churning out thoughts that are creating your reality and wondering how those things appeared in your life?

Name three things in your reality that you would like to change and as you are writing them down, pay attention to the thoughts that are created as you think of them. Do your thoughts support your new reality?

How do these thoughts and beliefs, real or imagined, limit the reality you are willing to create?

Can you think of a way that you use implied feedback to stop you from creating an aspect of your reality?

What actual feedback have you received from others that causes you to pause and reconsider your actions?

Are you willing to change your thoughts to change your reality?

Are you willing to change your beliefs, about yourself and what you believe others think about you and what you do, to change your reality?

Are you willing to ignore the judgments and criticism, real or imagined, of others to create what you want in your reality?

Name at least one person you believe is critical of you or of your life.

How many choices do you make or change based on your beliefs about what this person may say about them?

Can you see how aspects of your reality are manifested in response to others' opinions?

Are you willing to create one thing in your reality that reflects your heart's desires, without fear of judgment or criticism from someone else?

What if we are not happy with our reality? What creates this feeling of not being fulfilled and what can we do about it? What do we do when we believe that something is missing in our reality? This places us in the reality gap, the space between wanting and having. While we all have moments where we wish that things were different in our lives we do not consider these wishes until something within us changes, which happens when our energy shifts just enough to create an opening to allow the glimmer of a different reality to appear for our consideration. Our soul is telling us what is possible for us and that is enough for us to consider other options.

What is populating our reality needs to be replaced with something else. And we have two choices, we can fear the energetic vacuum that we are in and immediately fill it with something familiar from our past or we can choose, in that moment, to look for other options, even if we are not yet aware of what they are.

Each moment represents the collective energy of everything that we have ever been, done and experienced and from that moment, we create the next moment, based on what we believe is possible. So within every moment we are assessing the past and using it to extrapolate the future. That is why it is difficult for us to move in another direction—we are continuously creating the future from the past. But learning to create our reality from the now, by living exclusively in the present moment, changes everything.

The only thing that is real in our lives is whatever is contained in a single moment, which we have learned to call the 'now.' It's a popular concept that sounds great on paper but is more difficult to do in practice. Creating reality from the now means ignoring everything that we have learned from the past and walking into an unknown future with faith and trust in a benevolent Universe. It requires that we ignore the warning signals and memories of past pain that our brain has meticulously stored for us and believe that despite what the past was, this moment will be different.

But when we live in the now, our reality becomes a wonderful adventure full of exciting possibilities that surpasses anything that we could create from what we know of the past. A reality that exists in the present moment is full of uncertainty that is not born of fear, but of promise and anticipation; when anything is possible, everything can happen.

It contains an infinite number of potential realities, any one of which can become a new reality for us. If we are looking for a job, for example, and are fully in the present moment, we are open to any potential reality and trust that the one which encompasses the most wonderful benefits for us will manifest. It may come to us in unexpected ways—perhaps through the friend of a friend, or at a chance meeting at a coffee shop—but it will be perfect for us in every way.

Creating reality in the 'now' means living without expectations, the certainty of how things should or can be, and open ourselves to the unlimited possibilities that the next moment holds. If we are willing to step into each moment believing that it is full of miraculous opportunities waiting for us to connect to them, our reality can change in an instant and any one of those miracles become our new reality. Until we become aware of the present moment, we are unaware of how much we live in the past and project our future from what we have known. We can find comfort in the knowledge that everything we think of as real is actually just an illusion, a projection of our thoughts by remembering that as an illusion, it can be changed at any moment, when we are willing to change our thoughts.

And until we change those thoughts we are operating within our cycles of birth and death, karma and forgiveness, and within our definition of what we need to feel complete, fulfilled and whole. Do we know what our definitions of completion and closure are? We should, because they determine when we allow ourselves to release our commitments and responsibilities, fulfill any promises we have made and move into new expressions of our power. Our commitment to the cycles of completion determines where we are on every step of our journey and until we feel complete with every experience and every person in them, we will stay within them until we are.

Completion and Closure

Each of us plays an important role in the energetic changes that are happening at this time and the work we are doing in our own lives resonates exponentially in the world. As we acknowledge the importance of each step that we take towards transformation we also step into our role as energetic healers, teachers and vehicles of transformation. We have agreed to bring the new earth into being, to set its energies and to create heaven on earth through our mastery commitment. This is a cycle of completion, the last phase of a journey we began eons ago within a spiritual/material partnership whose purpose was reconnection and transformation. Its fulfillment has required millions of steps, taken by millions of people, across millions of lifetimes.

Our role in this process is so important that without us and our willingness to participate there is no partnership, transformation or ascension. We have inched our way through the progress we have made and can now know life for what it is, cycles of closure, completion, transformation and healing which lead to new opportunities and possibilities, different outcomes and other choices.

These cycles are happening with the earth as well, as we are completing an astrological age of 25,600 years and an even longer galactic cycle, as well as an earth cycle that we do not fully understand because its completion is also the completion of humanity's cycle. Some say this is the end of the earth but it can be better described as the end of an era, of the earth as we have always known it, the end of separation between the human and its divine nature, the end of the veil between the spiritual and material worlds, and the end of karma.

It is not necessary for us to understand these things with our logical, human minds, we must understand them from a spiritual perspective and trust in the perfection of a divinely ordered Universe. Although we are all connected through these cycles, the nature of our paths is different according to what our soul needs to experience and the cycles that each of us has come here to complete.

Each lifetime offers many pathways to the healing and transformation that is its purpose. How we choose our path is as important as the path we choose. Our healing comes when we can make a choice based on our highest potential and release the energies that are not in alignment with that, to allow new energies to be considered. We have to end the old before the new can manifest and the purpose of the cycles of completion is to be complete with 'old' energies and have closure with them to make room for new paradigms.

Every aspect of our lessons, experiences and relationships contains completion cycles that require release and closure. Each of them is a mini completion cycle that allows us to learn how the new energy feels and to accept or reject it, which creates the path we will take in that moment and whether we can carry our new learning into the next moment. While we may have been hoping for a single lesson, a single test of our learning, that is not consistent with our ascension process, which is an upward spiral, and not a straight line.

Each lesson we complete, learning we achieve, understanding we gain and mastery level we accomplish allows us to rise to another point on this spiral and from there we have a new perspective on our lessons. Our linear thinking is a product of our third dimensional illusion of reality. And it does not allow for the cyclical nature of our lives, in which we experience birth, growth, transformation and death, each death giving rise to the beginning of a new cycle, as was discussed in the chapter on Spiritual Initiation.

We can understand how these cycles work by expanding our concept of our natural life cycles to see how they happen within every moment of our own life. There is a birth with each beginning, a trial, a period of learning and growth which holds the lesson, leading to transformation once we have achieved the learning. Then the old dies away, the cycle is complete and we are ready for the next cycle. Everything that happens to us, every situation we encounter, every person we interact with, no matter how briefly, is part a cycle. And these individual cycles are part of the lifetime we have agreed to undergo as part of our soul's cycle of learning, growth, healing and transformation. This is true for everyone — we are all working through cycles and being presented with opportunities to complete them.

With each completed cycle we become more aware of our power, we have more information to help us through the next cycle and we move farther up the spiral of evolution into our ascension journey. And we may find ourselves alone on this part of the journey, without the souls we have contracted to do learning with. What happens to them if we leave them behind? What is our role in their completion cycle and to what extent do we have to help them when they can't seem to help themselves?

That is a difficult choice for us to make, one that we will face many times during this lifetime. As we complete our cycles and ascend into higher levels of energetic vibration we may also complete cycles with those we thought would be partners on our path. It may not be our choice; they may choose that for themselves. Part of our cycle may be the realization that we can no longer extend healing to everyone and the call to move forward will be too strong for us to choose to stay behind. Our work with them is finished and that cycle is complete. They will find other teachers and other lessons to help them with their completion work.

And so within each cycle we will create new definitions for closure, validation and endings. We will have to re-define what it means to be complete in a situation and with others. Learning acceptance and surrender is part of the completion process. When a relationship ends or a situation no longer has any vibrational connection for us we want closure with it, to have an opportunity to arrive at an ending that we are comfortable with, one that validates our input, experience, sacrifice and participation. We say that we want to be complete with it, to have closure and to be finished and that means different things to us.

As healers of our soul groups we want to ensure that everyone is complete with their healing and that our work is finished within our definition of closure, which includes the ending and resolution of our karma with them in a way that we are at peace with. Secretly, we want a clear ending and closure that ensures it's over and they are as complete as we want to be. But that is not always possible and sometimes getting closure means completing our cycle without receiving the validation we want.

Can we say goodbye and not feel guilty about those we believe we are leaving behind? Will our fear of having to repeat karmic cycles keep us involved in relationships that are actually complete but with which we are still waiting for confirmation of closure from someone?

Our definition of closure includes feeling good about what we have done and some sort of validation for the time, energy, effort and emotion that we contributed. The ending is meaningful, well-defined, known and final. But this is what we want through our fear of karmic retribution or to know that we have done all we could and are off the hook, so to speak. In essence, we are waiting for someone to tell us we have closure but we need to move beyond that point and give it to ourselves because closure is how we complete our life and healing cycles. We don't need anyone's permission to move on, or for anyone to tell us that it is time for us to leave.

In order to understand closure we must look at the information contained in our cycles. Are we healing others, being healed, learning about acceptance, power or transforming ourselves? Do we have to learn about energy or power and staying in a vibration that no longer matches ours? Completions indicate that we are finished with learning and healing at that level and have created an opening that allows us to move fully into our new vibration and experience our reality from this new level. Closure comes when we release our energy from the situation and know that all has happened in divine order, even if it was not in the way we hoped would happen.

Our strong soul group connections can interfere with closure because while we may be finished with a cycle and release our energetic support that has sustained a connection, we can feel their pain and fear and be tempted to delay our closure and keep those connections open until we have their permission or feel that they are ready for this connection to be finished. Our natural tendency, learned over countless lifetimes together, is to help our soul group because that is what we have always done. So we delay our own movement, hoping that by giving them one more chance they will 'see the light' and our completion cycle can include their healing as well as ours and we can have closure which includes the satisfaction of being part of their healing.

There are two aspects to the closure that we experience in completion cycles, emotional closure and spiritual closure. Emotional closure happens when we are complete with our emotions, we believe we have done all we could and are satisfied with the outcome and the responses we receive from others. Since our emotional closure is dependent on others' responses, it is not always possible to have. And our willingness to stay within an experience long after a cycle has been completed can depend on our need for emotional closure.

Here are some questions we ask ourselves when we want emotional closure:

Do I feel appreciated and loved for what I have done for them?

Are they empowered enough to willingly release me?

Am I empowered enough to willingly release them?

Did I get what I wanted from this connection?

Can I release the connection, situation and this person without regret, judgment or fear?

Moving beyond emotional closure requires detachment because while we may have done all we could in a situation, the person may not be willing to release us and we did not get what we wanted. We may believe that someone else was capable of doing more or behaving differently. Our options are to wait for them to acknowledge our efforts and release us, to show us we are right about their abilities or to simply let go and move on, removing our expectations and acknowledging that they have no more to offer us in terms of emotional validation. With any completion cycle we seek the termination of our soul commitments, contracts and karmic obligations all of which have strong emotional connections that seek fulfillment in any completion cycle, before we feel comfortable with giving ourselves closure.

Spiritual closure can happen if we detach from the emotional energies and all of our expectations. All of the things we have learned about in previous chapters, such as acceptance, choice, release, assumption and intention, assist us in creating spiritual and emotional closure. And we can have this spiritual perspective on closure when we extend unconditional forgiveness, releasing all energies, expectations, judgments and connections and allow ourselves to shift into higher dimensions of being without fear that we have unfinished business with others. In spiritual closure someone's response, validation or agreement does not matter. We look at the situation through our soul's eyes and see the perfection of their path and know that all is well. Spiritual closure comes from the heart while emotional closure feeds the ego.

Completion of cycles is necessary for ascension and the shifting of our individual and collective consciousness. But while this is an opportunity everyone can access, many are not ready or willing to do the work that is required for closure to occur. We will all face painful choices to allow those close to us to learn, heal and grow without our hand holding. Our choice has to be for ourselves, for what is best for our own soul growth. And we can disconnect energetically from others to allow them to find their own power, to direct their healing and to ascend in their own way and in their own time.

We can guide everyone to the light of their own understanding by gently disconnecting from our need to heal others and release ourselves from the need for emotional closure. Then we will complete our cycles and allow them to finish theirs in ways that brings them to the full realization of their power and divinity, without sacrificing our own soul growth in the process.

Did we complete the work we committed to? How do we know and where does the validation come from? There are situations where we do not receive validation of our contribution yet it was important, no matter how large or small we think it was. We are both teacher and student in every situation and we participate in all aspects of a lesson. Every experience has something to teach us about our journey. And it is our definition of completion that allows us to have it or not.

Our expectations, self image, self-worth or any other aspect of ourselves is involved in the process, anything that does not validate that will create the feeling of being incomplete. And it is through this feeling that we wait for closure because we are waiting for the validation we want to make ourselves feel better. It is what we want out of most situations and although it is our dark secret that we share with no one, it alone determines whether we are complete and can have closure with any person or situation.

We can be finished with something and yet not be complete with it. This happens when we have decided that something is too hard, too painful, too difficult or we want it to be over. So we disconnect our energy from it and think that this is the end. But when our expectations have not been met, when we leave a situation out of anger or frustration, we have created another level of energetic connection that starts another cycle for there has been no completion, learning or closure. It will come up again for us so we can approach it from a different perspective, each new lesson providing us with another opportunity to complete this cycle of learning so we can release the energy and move on.

Once we shift these energies we can change the timeline, transforming our response to a particular energetic vibration in every situation.

Changing the timelines is like creating a new and different outcome for a particular situation, an alternative to repeating karmic patterns. A timeline is an energetic continuum whose energy flows in a specific direction and is at a specific vibration, which reflects our beliefs, karma and energetic vibration. Each timeline creates a specific reality that has its own cycle of healing, learning and transformation. Through our timelines we repeat karmic patterns, encountering the same kind of people, creating the same experiences and making the same choices, over and over again. They are very obvious in relationships, where we may meet and connect with different partners but obtain similar results because they all share an energetic signature. This is not a sign that we are unlucky in love; it is a timeline reflecting our beliefs, karma, lessons and energy around relationships.

Timelines include the energies of our lifetimes of karma and emotional DNA imprints. They represent the energy that we put out in the Universe which then attracts everything with a similar energetic vibration and pattern, creating a snapshot for our reality. As we express our desire for completion and healing we attract everything our timelines represent, bringing them fully into our awareness so we can make different choices and step into a new timeline. That is why a desire to heal often creates a situation that appears to get worse before it gets better. We must experience the timeline's energies and know what they are before we can change them.

Changing timelines is possible as we complete cycles and this is how we raise our vibrations to create new and different realities. Cycles are completed and healed through forgiveness of ourselves and others, reconnection to our divinity, acceptance of our power, and our willingness to go through the completion process and to give ourselves closure. Resolution, peace and satisfaction are available to us as we allow ourselves to shift our energies so we can create our reality instead of living through our ancient timelines and their karma and lessons. Now we can choose how we will direct our energy and use our co-creative abilities in ways that serve our ascension, becoming masters on the human and spiritual levels.

The cycle of completion we are entering is the end of the era of the 'human human' and the beginning of the 'spiritual human'. This was part of the timeline for humanity and ascension is its endpoint, as well as the new beginning for the next cycle. And we are at this point in our evolution because we have collectively chosen to raise our vibrations and become open to new and higher energetic levels. This is an opening to many alternatives to end karma, create closure with soul group relationships, allow new soul group connections and manifest with intention instead of karma. This is a quantum advance in how we interact with and manage energy that allows us to consciously choose our completion cycles, how they will unfold and where we will focus our energy. But as with all of these experiences, our control is limited to our path, timelines and outcomes and the choices we make within them.

At these higher vibrations we accept that we are managers of our energy, setting its course and direction and where we will place its focus. We can choose how we will participate in our own healing, whether we will help others heal, who is part of that process and when it is finished. The cycles of completion occur when we are ready for them and closure occurs when our intention for it has been realized. It is our intention that creates the template for the completion process and we are in control of every step of this journey. Intention is the foundation for the conscious and deliberate use of our energy to manifest our reality, into the past for healing or grounded in the present moment, to create miracles.

We can wait for direction and guidance from the Universe but at this energetic level we have the knowledge and discernment to make our own wise choices. Although we have always had the ability to choose, at this place in our collective timeline we have finally figured out where the power is centered (within us) and that we possess the ability to use it wisely and purposefully. Our ability to manifest our personal heaven on earth has never been greater. We are complete with ourselves, our karmic ties, our healing commitments and soul contracts. These are exciting times, full of promise and new beginnings, which are created from the endings we allow to happen.

Completion is our reward when we have finished the full spectrum of healing within a situation, when we have learned from the experience, made the connections within our healing journey, allowed ourselves enough time to fully process the information, completed any forgiveness work we had to do and then given ourselves permission to move on. This permission is possible when we have recognized the lessons and are aware of how they interface with our healing mission, the growth we needed, what we had to release and how we let it go.

As we become complete with experiences, we can become complete with lifetimes too. Every experience is a mirror of our soul's journey, so within each lifetime we can gain an understanding of what we have been working through for different lifetimes, as it will show up in the lessons and the people we invite into our reality. It is all part of a singular purpose, to help us complete cycles of soul growth and, at this time, to complete eons of experience and finally release old paradigms to allow a new reality to become the truth for us. A lifetime does not necessarily end with a physical death, although that is one way to end it. When a cycle has been completed and we are finished with the lessons we brought into a lifetime, we can create a new soul contract and a new path for our life, thus creating a new timeline.

Many of us are completing cycles with our soul groups and karmic patterns for the first time in our many lifetimes here. And we have the support of the ongoing energy shifts, collapsing and expanding vortexes, and access to higher vibrations to help us with this process. Are we willing to end lifetimes of sadness, pain and drama and transform our experience of life and of living into fulfilling, spiritually and emotionally whole realities? Now that we are able to complete these cycles, what happens next? What do we do after we have completed cycles?

The choice of who or what shares our life once our cycles have completed is not entirely up to us. Anything that is not resonating at the level of our energetic vibration and the new paradigms we have created for our reality simply has no place within them. Since all of the requirements of connection, which include shared experience, similar energetic vibrations and a corresponding life paradigm and timeline, will not be present, there is no connection or possibility of interaction at that level. Our feelings for them will not be positive or negative, they will be neutral.

With compassion and unconditional love as our primary energies we can stay detached and separate because there is no desire or reason for connection or interaction since those commitments have been fulfilled, the experiences are no longer part of our emotional DNA, and our contract for healing is fulfilled. We will feel the same level of connection to our former soul group as we do with a total stranger on the other side of the world that we do not know and have no interaction with.

So this is the new paradigm for us, once we have completed cycles. We will be in a place of complete acceptance, where we allow everyone to be in their own energy and know that those who match ours will be able to walk beside us. And those who are not will simply be either a neutral presence in our life or will not be there at all. With the completion of our healing cycles we can create new and different relationships and situations, with people and circumstances that resonate at our new and different energetic levels and we do not have to do anything to create them, they will appear when the timing is right so that our new reality matches our intention to create a life of peace, joy, unconditional love and effortless living.

Step consciously into the completion cycle you are creating, knowing that each ending creates an opportunity for a brilliant new beginning and the manifestation of your dreams

Consider these questions for your personal mastery journey:

Can you find the completion cycles you are currently experiencing in your life?
Are there people you are afraid or unwilling to let go of?
Do you feel responsible for their healing and transformation?
Can you release them to do their own healing or find other teachers?
What does your completed life look and feel like to you?
Are there areas of your life where you are seeking closure?
How do you define closure and what does it mean in the context of your self worth, the validation you seek and the people in your life?
Are you able to see yourself as fulfilled in your mission of your own transformation?

With completion and closure we are at a crossroads of transformation. So often we have found ourselves nearing the end of a cycle only to dive back in for one more opportunity to satisfy the ego's desire for emotional closure. This period of indecision is over because we can accept others' choices with detachment, knowing they are making the right choice for themselves.

But that places us in a unique position, where we have to make new and different choices. We can no longer blame others for the choices we didn't make or the path we didn't follow, there is no one in our life who holds us back or stands in our way. What do we do next? When we are at the crossroads of transformation, each moment is important, each step leads us to a new destination and the entire Universe waits for us to choose what we want to do next.

The Crossroads of Transformation

When I lived in Australia I used the public transport system because I simply could not master driving on the other side of the road and car. One day while waiting at the bus stop I watched a woman run across the street to catch the bus. In her hurry she tripped over the curb and flew forward, unable to stop herself. A woman stepped into her path and caught her, preventing what would have been a bad fall. It is a scene that has stayed with me because it showed how one moment can make a difference in our life. When we are at a crossroads of transformation, each moment counts.

What happened between those two women at the bus stop in that defining moment shows how what appears to be a disaster can be transformed through divine intervention. A single moment can make a difference that transforms our life in many different ways. When we tell the Universe we are ready for transformation, anything can happen. We are open to change, willing to let go and wanting something different. Transformation always comes, sometimes in small ways that seem insignificant, sometimes in big ways that appear over-whelming and change our lives forever. And it sometimes happens through the efforts of other people. We have to be open and paying attention because what happens in the next minute can be the transformation we were looking for.

Everyone standing at the bus stop saw what happened and we were all impacted by the woman's willingness to help a stranger. I am sure that young woman will never forget the kindness of the woman who prevented her fall and perhaps she needed a reminder of the goodness of people, the willingness of someone to be of service to her and the protection of the Universe as part of her moment of transformation. Transformation prepares the way for blessings that can come in any form. By paying attention, being in the present moment and trusting that each moment is important, we allow the Universe to work on our behalf. If we are so focused on our situation, wondering where help will come from, whether it will come at all or feeling powerless, we are walking with our heads down and can miss some wonderful opportunities that may be right in front of us.

We tend to think of being at a crossroads in our life as times when we must make choices that have an important or long term impact, such as a choice to marry, have a child, or choose a career path. Or different milestones such as a graduation, marriage, the death of a significant loved one or an important ending or beginning in our own life. Each of these situations marks important life transitions but they are not the only times when transformation occurs. In fact, if we wait for these significant events to mark the crossroads in our life we are missing many opportunities to transform our reality. Because we are in a constant process of change and every day we are at the crossroads of transformation on some level, where each option we are faced with has multiple choices attached to it, each one leading to a different outcome.

Which path is right? They all are, depending on what we need to accomplish, want to learn and are ready for. Sometimes we can be so focused on taking the right path and so determined to not take the wrong path that we stand still. What feels right for us at one point may, upon review, seem like the worst possible path we could have taken. After what can seem like so many dead ends, how do we know which path is right? What is right and best for us at one moment is not always the same in another. And we know that because we have the outcome of our previous decisions and choices to use as bench-marks.

Our path will not be a straight line from birth to death, lesson to resolution, from karma to release. It will twist and turn, wind through different experiences with the goal of ensuring that we learn all of our soul contract's lessons. Instead of judging our experiences, we gain insight, move towards enlightenment and increase our range of options by reviewing what we learned, how and why we chose that particular option and what our expectations were at that time. Then we have information we can use for the next decision. Another crossroads of transformation will appear when we are ready for it and we can choose differently the next time.

Sometimes our crossroads of transformation are introduced with the need to make choices about our priorities. We need to determine who or what is most important or is deserving of our time and attention. Do we remember to include our self in that decision? Sometimes that is our lesson and the transformation process involves learning to take care of ourselves, to decide whose needs we will focus on, who comes first, whose healing is more important and where our energies are directed.

Putting ourselves first is selfish and self-serving, as many of us have been taught to believe. So we often put others' needs and desires first and take care of our own when we have the time. Our belief that giving to others will benefit us in the end is only partially true. We are here to be of service to others and we can best do that when our own needs are provided for and our energy levels are high because we are not continuously depleting them by giving our energy away. But there is a difference between putting others' needs before ours and being of service to them.

We can feel guilty asking the question "What is best for me" when others appear to have greater needs. There will always be someone around us who needs our time and energy. Making ourselves a priority with each decision, asking "What is best for me" before acting on behalf of someone else keeps our energy levels high and allows us to be of service to others without doing their work for them. And that is the lesson of priorities, allowing others to do their own healing work, being a shining light that teaches them how to light their own inner flame.

We are the pioneers in the ascension journey. Lightworkers have created the path to healing and reconnection to Source that will be taken by others who will use what we have created to find their way to the peace and joy that is heaven on earth. Our task is to empower them with information but they have to do their own work, as we did.

This is a journey that requires commitment and willingness, surrender and faith. We can make the process appear effortless to others but they have no idea what we went through to get to where we are. In time, they will understand and know how challenging the path can be, as well as how rewarding and enlightening it is. And while it may be tempting to give our energy away, we have to set priorities, take care of our own needs and know that the best way to teach is to allow another to learn in their own time. As we choose our path, we can remember to make choices that empower us. We are more powerful healers and teachers when we operate from a place of being fully in our power.

It can feel at times like we make decisions that take us backwards, re-visiting experiences and going over old ground that we thought we had already covered. Perhaps we did but we may have needed to learn another aspect of that lesson. We can't be in a hurry with this process, there is no time-line or deadline, and the journey has no end. As we approach each crossroads of transformation we can take our time, review our options, expand our vision of our power and possibilities and then choose something that will serve our highest good at that moment. When we are ready for a different turn on our path, to move in another direction, we will have an opportunity to choose again.

It is our nature to judge things as more and less important than others. While there are things that do have greater relevance, in the Universe all choices are important and nothing has more or less energy than another. For example, the choice as to whether or not to stop at a coffee shop one morning could seem insignificant. However, perhaps someone you have wanted to meet also makes that same choice and this 'chance' meeting changes the course of your life. This is a crossroads of transformation moment and if we are paying attention we will be present in that moment. We hear many stories of how someone missed a flight that later crashed, or purchased a last-minute lottery ticket that was the winner. So a choice that we may have judged as unimportant becomes a very significant life transition point. To fully appreciate each opportunity that arises we must be aware of the potential of each situation and be fully open to anything, without judgments or attachments.

Every day of our life contains many crossroads of transformation that play out through every choice we make, every thought we think or action we take, empowering the next step of our journey. Since the future is being written as we think and speak, our transformation is constantly unfolding. How can we differentiate the really important choices from the ones we think are less important? We can start by believing that all choices are important. But that is not the most critical element. What is really important is to know when we are at the threshold where transformation in the form of a significant life change, the realization of a dream, or getting what we want, can occur. How do we know that we are ready for transformation and when is it happening?

The call to transform arrives quietly, usually as a feeling of confusion, doubt, or uncertainty. Life is no longer satisfying and change looks very attractive. But where do we start? Knowing where to begin, when everything is unclear and unsettled can feel intimidating. This is the moment in which we can feel most alone but the Universe has guided us to our crossroads of transformation and invited us to walk through the doorway of our potential. Do we have the courage to step into our power and begin living the life we want to live, one that brings us the abundance, prosperity, peace and love that we desire? It is the unsettled, confused feeling that is our trigger and when we mistake it for something else we move from being on the threshold of transformation and change to falling back into despair and hopelessness.

This is where we make an important choice, to believe that we are powerless and have made bad choices or to see that we have completed a cycle and have released the energetic connection to our life as we have known it. Do we take on a victim role and feel that we are at the mercy of other forces that can include other people, our past or our shortcomings? Or do we let that all go and ask to see what is behind door number 2?

Consider these questions for your personal mastery journey:

Can you remember a time when you have been at a crossroads of transformation?

Do you remember the choice you made in that moment?

What were you thinking, afraid of, or considering as you made that choice?

Did another person's needs or desires influence your choice?

How can you put yourself first in your life?

Do you have the courage to see what is behind "Door Number 2" in your life?

What if you gave yourself permission to choose what is best for you?

Are you willing to be present each moment so you can be aware of your transformative moments?

What would your life look like if you were willing to take the path of your dreams in every situation?

Can we take a chance on ourselves? Can we risk being who we could be, can be and really are? Can we see beyond the current reality, which is really only a small blip on the continuum of our potential, and have faith in ourselves and our dreams? This is the challenge of transformation, to remain steadfast in our awareness of what is being pointed out to us as examples of our fear and move into an awareness of abundance, prosperity, unconditional love and joy. And it is our path to wholeness in body, mind, emotions and spirit.

The Path to Wholeness

Our spiritual experience of life is a healing journey, where we commit to leaving the security and comfort of our Home and act as emissaries for our individual and collective healing. Each of us, during the course of our lifetimes, has participated in the creation of the discordant energies on the planet and we return to participate in the process of healing the specific and unique energetic vibration of separation that we have created. This is what our return to wholeness is about, transforming everything that represents the separation of human from divine. We return to wholeness by bringing forward our wounds and experiences of separation from our Self and our Source, caused by lifetimes of pain, sorrow, disillusionment, expectations and the belief in the limitations of spirit and the power of ego. As we accept responsibility for our role in separation we also recapture our scattered energies and create our opportunity to return our 'selves' to our original, natural, whole state or blueprint.

This is called being re-membered or brought back into connection within the body of Spirit. Through this process we re-join ourselves and the family of humanity with its spiritual roots and allow ascension to occur. Everyone on the planet is participating in both healing journeys, their own and that of the earth. Each lifetime in which we have reinforced the belief in separation creates an opportunity for another human experience in which we can learn wholeness.

We are not less whole through our humanity, or more whole in our spirituality. Each has had its place in our lifetimes of soul learning. This is a journey of balance, where we allow body, mind, emotions and spirit to find a common center so that each operates in full consideration of and participation with the other. This is our divine trinity (the body and mind are considered as one) and all of its aspects must be in alignment. We often think that through this journey we must become more spiritual and that is a definition that has caused us to believe that humanity is a lower aspect, wrong or imperfect and we must overcome our humanity to become spiritual. But we are already spiritual and each of us expresses our spiritual nature to the extent that the level of our soul growth allows us to.

People who act without compassion towards others are called 'inhumane' but that really means that they are acting fully within their humanity, without the benefit of Spirit. Without this connection they cannot access the energies of compassion and unconditional love and behave in ways we consider obnoxious, cruel or even reprehensible. This behavior is fully in the fear spectrum that is one potential of the earth's energy and it is because we have incorporated so much light and love into our humanity that we find this behavior appalling.

Since we are seeking balance between the spiritual and material, any energy that is out of balance, either too material or too spiritual, does not feel right. But there nothing wrong with the human side of us and when we experience problems it is because the human is operating without the balancing energies of Spirit. Each step we take towards integrating our spiritual nature into our humanity allows the presence of unconditional love and adds another level of balance between these two energies which makes us whole. Wholeness involves appreciating all of our aspects, body, mind, emotions and spirit, recognizing that each is important and contributes to the whole.

The body is not bad or imperfect and it has two purposes, to be a vessel for spirit and to interact with the earth. The body simply fulfills spirit's requirement for a physical presence on the third dimensional earth. And the body functions in accordance with the mind — it does what the mind tells it to do. Without the mind, the body is merely a collection of tissue and bone, a form that cannot function, as we see in people whose mind has been damaged and who are in a persistent vegetative state.

When the body is out of balance we can follow a quest for physical perfection which can take any of many paths, from obsession with our physical appearance to excessive material consumption, as we look for new and different ways to find the best material expression of our physical perfection. So we become addicted to plastic surgery, the gym, or to shopping, in our search to prove to ourselves that we are perfect on the outside, to counteract our perceived inner imperfection.

Our physical body is perfect and what we see as imperfect is a reflection of our inner fear and unhappiness, our judgments about what our ego believes we are instead of what our Spirit knows as our truth. We are perfect in every way and when we fully embrace that knowing our body will not have to confirm our belief in our imperfection and can express its perfection through its acceptance of wholeness.

The mind is not bad, destructive or even defective in its functioning. The mind's purpose is to ensure that the body operates efficiently and effectively, providing memory and the ability to interact and reason within the third dimension. It fulfills its purpose in an exacting and even mechanical way. The mind, however, is limited to its own history, memory and limitations without the higher perspective that Spirit provides. Without the body the mind is useless and without Spirit the mind functions within its pre-programmed cycles of memory and karmic history. When it works with Spirit the mind expands beyond its third dimensional limits and accesses higher level of awareness instead of the ego-driven, human level which can cause great pain and suffering for ourselves and the world.

By trying to create the perfect mind, without Spirit, we over-develop the ego so we can think our way into joy. Without the enlightenment provided by Spirit, the ego has free rein to experience its own energies, which are rooted at the level of fear. But since the mind and emotions created the problem, when we follow this course we simply become more enmeshed in our wounded soul energies. The mind does what it is designed to do, ensure the functioning of the body, protects us through its memory of potentially harmful situations and moves us along our life path in a linear manner.

Without Spirit the mind cannot access a higher vibration and that is why, when the focus is on mind development to the exclusion of Spirit, we repeat patterns and cycles, staying enmeshed in our dramas and traumas. Then we turn to war, domination, abuse of power and intimidation to alter our reality because those are the tools the mind uses when fear is its vibration. This is where the ego feels comfortable, within its illusion of a limited, controlled reality because left to its own devices it can perceive nothing else.

It is the lonely mind that tells you your life will not change, you will never have, do or be what you want, and it is the mind that gets stuck in completion cycles, constantly repeating the past, which is its reference point. Without Spirit, the mind lacks balance, compassion, access to spiritual truth and a higher vibration. Since our journey is one of integrating all of our aspects into wholeness in body, mind and spirit, we must learn to calm the mind, make peace with the ego and enable it to view Spirit not as the enemy but as a source of the higher vibrational energies it needs to shift into mastery and embrace ascension as the next step in humanity's evolution. The mind has another important function, it communicates with the emotions, which are the energy of the third dimension and another aspect of our divine trinity.

The emotions, like our free will, appear to be our enemy at times. We feel that we must be in control of and conquer our emotions but they are nothing more than the energy of the third dimension. They require the body and mind for articulation, using the body's physical presence as the vehicle through which they can be generated and the mind, which is the manifestor of the third dimension, for their expression. Without the body and mind, the emotions are simply energy that cannot be seen, heard or felt. The third dimension is the home of emotional energy and it is the only dimension in which the full range of emotional energy can be known.

Emotions are the outlet for our emotional DNA, cellular memory, karmic history and are the reason for and purpose of our healing mission. They represent all of the energies that we will align with in any lifetime, for healing and transformation. As guardians of our soul lessons in the third dimension, they give expression to our emotional, energetic, spiritual, and psychic healing. Our free will manifests through our emotions and they create our reality.

Our emotional energy, which resides in our emotional body, is uniquely ours. No two people have the same emotions. No two people can feel emotions in the same way and each person will interpret experiences and situations through the filter of their emotions. And although we lump emotions together as one entity that exists within the physical body, we have many emotional bodies that include:

The physical body and its cellular memory and emotional DNA,

The heart chakra through which we feel emotions

The mind, which manifests from the emotions, and

The collective emotional body which is the collective energetic matrix of the earth

There are two aspects to the heart chakra:

The high heart is our ascended heart, where we have opened our heart to Spirit and tempered our third dimensional emotional energy with the higher dimensions of Spirit. The high heart is detached, emotionally neutral and expresses unconditional love in all of its manifestations, which include joy, peace, acceptance and compassion.

The low heart is our emotional heart, which feels and expresses our emotions from an ego/third dimensional perspective. The low heart resides in the ego and is attached, has expectations, judgments and is fear-based.

Which heart energy do you use to connect with others and express your emotional energy?

Emotions emanate from the past, from our own emotional storehouse that includes our emotional DNA and cellular memory as well as all of our past experiences. And from the past they create a fixed reference point, as our emotions always lead us back to what we know or have known from all of our past experiences. Our soul group mirrors our emotional energy, which is why we attract and are attracted to people who 'feel' the same way we do. Emotions are also habitual and emotional responses are merely habits that we unconsciously respond from in every moment. Together with the mind, they are the creators of our reality because the emotional energy is what we create from in the third dimension.

Each of us has a storehouse of emotions that includes all of the emotional responses that we can have, and unless we shift our energy we cannot have new emotional responses to any situation. These emotions will dictate how our life unfolds because we will attract only that which is at the same vibration as our own emotions. This is their magnetizing property—they will attract people and situations that energetically match, support and validate them.

Emotions always seek validation and our mind creates our reality based on our emotions. So without a shift in consciousness or transformation, which is created through our connection with Spirit, our emotions will always be in a validation cycle, seeking from others what we do not believe we have within ourselves.

Although our life is a spiritual journey to wholeness, we cannot become whole by focusing on our spiritual side, to the exclusion of the mind, emotions and body. Spirit requires the body, mind and emotions for expression. Without them Spirit has no form through which it can participate in the third dimension. Spirit is the bridge that allows the third dimension to access higher levels of consciousness. It brings the third dimension into higher levels of being, allowing energetic conversations to occur between all dimensions. Spirit is hard for us to understand because it is without form, structure, physical attributes or any other aspect that allows us to 'see' it with our third dimensional senses. And yet it exists all around and through us; we are it and it is us.

Spirit interacts with us on many levels and is part of many aspects of our journey of mastery and ascension. It plays a critical role in our healing as it partners with us in the creation of the soul contracts and activates the scenarios for our healing when it is time for us to begin a healing cycle. Then it protects us from harm and even going against our free will in times when it is necessary to ensure that we complete our mission. It provides energetic support for our lessons, through connection with our angels and spirit guides and holds the energy for our soul lessons in the third dimension, creating the situations that will assist in our emotional, energetic, spiritual, and psychic healing. But it also holds the energy for our wholeness, which is our return to our divinity and our healed aspects.

Spirit also partners with our free will and intention to manifest at higher levels and is the life force we incarnate with in every lifetime – Spirit gives us life and is life.

Spirit is the life force that is present in all life forms, including the earth, and makes life possible. When we die, Spirit leaves our physical body and this completes our presence on earth for this lifetime.

To be whole we require a balance of Spirit with our other trinity aspects. If we are too spiritual and try to focus our energy too much in that realm, we are not grounded on the earth and cannot effectively function here. We are also risk becoming spiritually arrogant and discounting the value of our material presence and of the earth in general. Then we develop the attitude that Spirit is 'good' and material is 'bad' and now we are in judgment, creating another cycle of learning and completion. Instead of achieving wholeness, we have created another level of separation and we are alienating ourselves from the very purpose of our lifetime. While we need Spirit in our journey to wholeness, that does not make it more important than any other aspect of our self and denies the gifts and value of our other aspects.

Understanding wholeness requires that we can accept ourselves as perfect. Wholeness cannot exist without perfection. And without wholeness we are stuck in the density of separation and cannot achieve ascension. But we have to distinguish between material perfection, which focuses on a limited set of physical attributes, and spiritual perfection, which is our natural state in which we are always perfect in every moment and in every way. We are born perfect, we move from one aspect of perfection to another and everything about us exists in the total perfection of who we are. The lie of a standard of physical perfection that we see in images found in print and media, which is often what limits our ability to believe in our own perfection, is revealed as we discover the truth, that they are retouched, tweaked and altered so their perfection is merely an illusion created with the help of sophisticated technology.

So we have to look within to find the perfection we have been trying to create in our outer world. What will we find when we have the courage to look within? Will we be disappointed in what is there or will we find anything at all? The only way to find perfection is to accept it as being our Truth and this keeps us from falling into the cycles of judgment and separation that arise when we begin to criticize and judge ourselves. We even embody perfection in our separation, which is one aspect of our earthly presence. If we are confused we have good reason because we have been living dual lives, so to speak. Within one aspect of our life we are here to bring the memory of perfection to earth so it can ascend and in the other, to hold the energy of separation so it can be released and transformed.

The earth, in its third dimensional paradigm, is the plane of duality and we are a mirror of both the separation and of God's infinite love, mercy and blessings. No wonder we go back and forth from separation to connection and are confused about our purpose, what we are supposed to do and who we are. That is why it is so hard to embrace ourselves as perfect, when we are struggling with duality, our emotions, mind, body and wondering how Spirit could ever want to hang out with us when we don't particularly want to hang out with ourselves. But there is nothing wrong with us, no matter how terribly imperfect we may think we are. Can we embrace our innate perfection so we can be in the mindset that allows and even encourages the integration of ourselves and from that point allow the continuation of our journey to wholeness?

Did our journey take longer than we imagined? Considering how far into the darkness we have gone and how much light we have brought to the world, we have made great progress. And there was never a time limit for this process, although we have been within this timeline for our many eons of existence. It would happen when humanity was ready for it. Our task, as we struggle with the last remaining remnants of darkness, is to remember that this is a journey to wholeness, where our material reality is being prepared to merge with its spiritual complement. And whatever progress we make at any point on that journey is perfect. It has taken all we have, physically, emotionally, mentally and spiritually, to get here, which is why when we embrace our perfection and see ourselves as whole we make the journey so much easier.

Consider these questions for your personal mastery journey:

What aspects of your divine trinity, body, mind, emotions and spirit, do you feel you are uncomfortable with?

Do you believe that your body is imperfect in any way?

Can you find perfection in your body, knowing that it is the vessel for Spirit? Does this change how you view your body?

How much of your mind's thinking is based in the past? Can you see which of your thoughts are past-based?

Now that you know that your mind's function is to interact with the earth's energy, do you view your ability to manifest differently?

Understanding that the emotions are the energy of the third dimension, do you feel differently about them and their role in your life?

Can you make a conscious decision to choose the emotions you wish to experience?

Knowing that Spirit needs your body, mind and emotions to interact with you and the world, are you ready to create a different relationship with these aspects?

How can you incorporate more of Spirit into your life and stay balanced within the other aspects of your divine trinity, the body, mind and emotions?

Each aspect of our being, body, mind and spirit, is necessary to our growth, healing and transformation, our presence on earth and our ascension. So we can honor all aspects of our being and appreciate them for what they are and how they help us create heaven on earth. Each of them is equally important and our ascension happens when we recognize and honor all of them. When we judge any aspect of ourselves, body, mind, emotions or spirit, we step out of wholeness and into separation, from ourselves and from Spirit. This separation dishonors the divine spark of God light that each of us carries within us. We need each of these aspects of our being to be whole and when we focus on one and neglect the others we limit ourselves and our ability to fulfill our purpose.

Because the only purpose of each lifetime is to become whole, with one part not being more important than another, all aspects of our self are inter-related and synergistic and waiting for us to re-member them into wholeness, bringing the parts of ourselves together into a balanced, energetically limitless spiritual human beings working in conjunction with the Universe. When we are whole we are able to co-create more powerfully because we do so from an integrated perspective.

Balance is the key to wholeness and we have a world of evidence to show us what being out of balance creates. Through our history as humans we have examples of how limited we can become when we ignore our wholeness to focus on a single aspect, forgetting that each of our aspects contributes to the whole.

With a focus on the body we become self-absorbed and our attention is solely on the physical aspects and energies in our life.

With a focus on the mind we become intellectuals, ruled by ego and logic with limited access to higher level energies such as compassion.

Our focus on the emotions creates drama and chaos, where our emotions rule us and we are powerless against them so we go from one emotional extreme to another, unable to find our calm center from which we can know detachment, peace and love.

With a focus on Spirit we ignore our humanity and believe ourselves equal to God but from the ego's perspective and we become spiritually self absorbed, arrogant and feel we are better than others.

And with a singular focus on any aspect of ourselves, we are in judgment and continue the energy of polarity and separation. Our journey to wholeness requires that we honor all aspects of ourselves because our mission is to become spiritual humans, incorporating spirituality into the third dimension to raise ourselves beyond humanity to embrace the   integration of all energies beyond the third dimension. This can be done in our lifetime and indeed, we are doing it now. We are the trinity in action, body, mind, emotions and spirit, and it is through the energetic synergy of the trinity in balance that we complete the ascension process.

One of our limitations is our ego's fear that it will be overcome by Spirit and die in the process. That is not the case for our journey into wholeness is one of integration, not domination. It is the lack of trust in Spirit and ignorance of our spiritual heritage that creates this belief. The human energy, when focused on itself, believes its power comes from domination, fear and external power. The energy of Spirit adds balance, brings us back into our center, and carries the highest vibration, unconditional love.

Through the integration of all of the aspects we become spiritual humans. Just as our body contains all of the aspects necessary to function as it needs to, it functions at its highest potential when it integrates all other aspects of our being. Without Spirit, neither the body nor the mind can embody our soul purpose, to complete our mission of bringing heaven on earth. Spirit remembers the soul contract and how we have tried to complete it in the past, providing us with valuable insights into how to ensure our success in this lifetime.

That is why our connection to Spirit is so important because it alone remembers why we are here, the purpose of our journey and how we can fulfill our mission. And our journey into wholeness brings us to our objective, to interject the energy of Spirit into the human experience so we are balanced, body, mind, emotions and spirit and co-creators with the Universe of heaven on earth, spiritual masters operating in the miracle vibration.

Consider these questions for your personal mastery journey:
Can you see where you may be unbalanced in your view of yourself or of others?
Which aspects of your divine trinity, body, mind, emotions and spirit, are not integrated?
How does this manifest in your life?
If you feel stuck in your life, is there an aspect of your divine trinity that you can bring into balance so you can create movement in your life?
Is there an area of your life where you can integrate Spirit to bring it into alignment with your healing purpose?
Are you ready to commit to being balanced in all your aspects so you can complete your journey to wholeness?

Now that we understand the role of the aspects of our divine trinity and how each contributes to our life journey, we can look at this path in a new way. Is life hard? It was never meant to be. Have we become so focused on the destination that we have forgotten about the journey? Each of us is on a path that is part of a journey Home, to our spiritual roots. And we need to remember that the path, the journey and the destination are all connected and all lead to the same place.

The Path and the Journey

Before our birth we determined a path that we would follow during our time on earth, one which would provide us with the best opportunities to fulfill the terms of our spiritual contract. This path represented an aspect of healing and growth that our soul could achieve in our lifetime. Within the path were details of the lessons we would learn and karma we would heal to achieve our contract's objectives. The journey consisted of the series of life experiences that we would undertake in order to make this all happen and could include a number of different paths. All of this had a single purpose, to reach our ultimate destination of reconnection and then ascend into higher levels of consciousness to create a balance between the spiritual and material worlds.

Each lifetime is part of our overall journey of connection and ascension. Although we are usually only aware of what is happening with our current lifetime, the paths we take in different lifetimes are often very similar. I have found this to be true after doing thousands of karmic readings for clients and have been amazed at the parallels between their current lifetimes and those that present themselves when I look at their karmic path. These lifetimes represent an energetic signature that becomes the theme of a lifetime. Although the way we express lessons may differ from one lifetime to the next, the energetic signature is the same. Our journey begins where it left off in previous lifetimes and the path we select for any lifetime is one we are sure is achievable and we are confident in our ability to complete it quickly and successfully.

But our spiritual nature forgets how painful life can be, the density of the third dimensional energy, how difficult some experiences are to overcome, how hard it is to forgive and how strong our emotional attachments to people and things can become. From a spiritual perspective, the journey is easy but we are doing spiritual work in human form and the human experience sometimes gets in the way. So while we start our journey with every intention of completing it, different things can slow us down until we are stopped in our tracks. Our path, which once seemed so easily attainable, has become too challenging and we're stuck, lost and unable to move in any direction.

Was the path too difficult? Did we go in the wrong direction? Can we start over? Starting over is a nice thought but not always an available choice when we're feeling stuck. In any case, we usually must get through whatever we have created and is in front of us before we can do anything else. We become stuck when we see the destination as the objective of our human experience, instead of remembering that the true objective is the lesson and learning and the information we need to advance is always on our path, we just have to find it. There are lessons and blessings in everything, when we are looking for them. And each step gives us some spark of enlightenment that we can use to take us to the   next step when we are looking forward, not back into the past. Even though we may have quantum leaps in consciousness, our path moves along one step at a time and as we learn, heal and grow, detours, sidebars and alternative paths become possible.

All of the elements we need for healing on a particular path are available to us. As we increase our understanding our awareness also increases and we are able to know and understand ourselves as spiritual beings having a human experience, the healing nature of our lifetime and that our true purpose is ascension, the mystery of life is solved. Each individual life experience contains all of the elements we need to help us achieve our objectives when we stop focusing on the destination and look for the answers within the journey.

Instead of repeating difficult and painful experiences we can complete our soul's growth with fewer lessons, rather than endlessly repeating them in the hope that the next time we will be more informed, aware, consistent and efficient. When we focus on the pain, judgment and fear that we experience in our lessons we step into a repetitive cycle and our journey can spiral out of control. This can take us off of our path and into a sort of spiritual vacuum where we feel we have lost our connection, are powerless and can no longer imagine our destination, much less achieve it.

Getting ourselves back on our path requires that we change our focus from the destination to the journey and learn to view our experiences at their most basic level, which is our soul's growth and healing our karma. By shifting our focus from what is happening to why it is happening, our point of reference is grounded in our spiritual understanding instead of our emotional experience. Emotions are part of our humanity and they can either help us on our journey or get in our way. They get in our way when we use them to judge and criticize ourselves and others; they help us when we use them as tools to understand our role as creators in the third dimension, our karmic history and then make different choices.

The contributions of our life partners and soul group, the people with whom we share our emotional history and connections, are with us on this journey because we gave them an exclusive, special invitation to join us, no matter how difficult, illogical or painful their contribution may be. Viewing lessons with detachment and seeing these interactions from our spiritual understanding helps us process these experiences, accept the learning and move on. Our emotional understanding focuses on how bad we feel, how painful the experience was or we judge ourselves as unworthy of love based on how much or how little others love us. Through the mirror of our reality we will create the same kinds of experiences with everyone in our life and how we understand those experiences can help us create different and less painful experiences for ourselves.

The same thing applies to the situations we encounter. We often repeat life situations, where we are alone or facing financial difficulty, losing a job or a relationship or involved in some kind of drama, until we accept how we have specifically selected the path that would include these situations, take responsibility for them and then move into understanding what they have to teach us. Our spiritual understanding views these situations as lessons in how effectively we use our power. When viewed through our emotional understanding we see ourselves as unlucky, undeserving or powerless. Then we are in an energetic vacuum where time seems to stand still and nothing appears to be happening and yet, this is a powerful point of transformation, as I discovered when God put me in the 'waiting room'.

Several years ago, while going through a difficult part of my life, I dreamed that I went to see God in his office. I sat at his desk and complained about my life, how difficult it was, how unhappy I was and how I felt that he was not helping me at all. God listened patiently for a few minutes and then got up and asked me to follow him. I was so excited, thinking that I was going to be given a magic key or some special gift that would take me out of my misery. Instead, God put me in a waiting room and asked me to sit there for a while and think about my situation until I could learn to find its blessings and realize the real source of my power.

I woke up from this dream crying, feeling that God had abandoned me. A few days later I found a small book in a store and it opened to a chapter that described the meaning and purpose of God's waiting room. I had the answers I needed to understand the power of the waiting room and why I was put there, so I could change my perspective on my life because until I did I was missing the entire point of the experience.

The waiting room was my opportunity to reflect on how I had created the energetic vacuum that I was in, that place where I was confused and felt powerless to change my situation. Because I approached God with my complaints and from my powerlessness, I was not going to get the relief and rescue I wanted. No one was going to rescue me until I took responsibility for my life, found my power and manifested a different outcome. Until I found the blessings of the path that I had created for myself I was stuck there until I could find a way to reconnect with my power and create a new way out.

The waiting room is a difficult place to be but one that we put ourselves in when we lose sight of our path and focus only on what has happened to us on our journey and instead of remembering why we are on it. When we are in a spiritual vacuum we forget that we are spiritual beings and lose touch with our power, our connections and the help that is available to us.

Consider these questions for your personal mastery journey:

Have you ever found yourself in the 'waiting room'?

Did you feel abandoned by Spirit, lost, alone and afraid?

What did you do to resolve your feelings and regain your power?

Could you feel powerful in this situation or did you wait for someone to rescue you?

Were you willing to give your power to someone else so they would get you out of this situation?

Can you see the options that were available to you at that time?

If faced with a similar situation now, what would you do differently?

Are you afraid of finding yourself in that situation again?

How can you avoid being in the 'waiting room' in your life?

This is a place where we feel lost, alone and afraid. Our journey has stopped (or so we think) and we are confused, stuck and seeking a guiding light to point out our next steps. We look for someone or something to show us the way or the way out, or to let us know that we are moving in the right direction. Instead of going within for the answers, we hope that someone will rescue us or let us know that we will be fine once the situation is over, and then take our hand and guide us to that place. While this is happening we can feel like we are dying and this is a kind of death. It is a challenge to the ego's need to create the experience of fear and powerlessness in our life and the ego believes it is in a   life or death situation.

And in a way it is. In order to get out of the waiting room we must create a space for the guidance that comes with spiritual understanding and that means the ego has to relinquish some of its control. In this place where we are experiencing our greatest fears, we have to choose between fear and love, internal power or the ego's control, expansion into our ascension or contraction back into the past. Since the ego is always afraid of dying and being eliminated, it will do its best to convince us of the hopelessness of our situation. But we have already had, at some point in this process, a glimpse of what is possible so we can choose a different reality for ourselves, one that takes us out of the waiting room and into a new potential. Our struggle may appear to be with a circumstance, person or situation, but it is all happening within us and is really a battle between the ego's desire to lead the way and our soul's orchestration of our healing journey.

Which side will we allow to win?

The waiting room is often the final step in that period of initiation, another crossroads of transformation on our path. As always, there are many different choices. We can close our eyes and hope that it will be over soon or we can go within to find our own inner source of help and guidance and then move forward with confidence, knowing that we are in control of our reality and that there is a place for both ego and Spirit on our journey.

Sometimes we use the energetic vacuum of the waiting room to remind us of how powerful we are. But that only works if we do not stay in the vacuum so long that we become discouraged and begin to believe in our powerlessness. Too often, it serves to reinforce the belief that we are alone and helpless. The vacuum has its own timeline which can feel very long, when we forget who is in charge of the process and who can control the amount of time we spend in this place of emptiness which is merely a stepping stone on our journey, a place where we can arrive at spiritual clarity. When we are in the waiting room and ask for help, it can come in many ways, but we have to be willing to step out of the fear of our emotions and trust that help is given when we ask for it. And when we do receive the answer, we are prepared to do the work to move ourselves out of the vacuum of the waiting room and into an expanded mindset and expansive reality.

But our life journey is not a single path and we develop multiple variations of lessons, any one of which is a potential for our life, depending on what we choose to learn on the journey, the lessons we have to experience, and the soul group members we are learning with. These different variations come into play when we choose how we will experience our journey, either emotionally or spiritually.

When we choose an emotional experience of our journey, we are dealing through the ego, the outer reality and the world within the limits of the third dimension. Then the peace, joy and abundance that we could experience in our life become dependent on the outcome of our emotional interactions with others. If they are happy and satisfying, then our journey is easy and we feel complete. But if they are difficult, our journey is a roller coaster, rising and falling according to the drama of the moment. And the options available to us are limited to the extent that others are willing to validate us emotionally in ways that make us feel whole and complete. The emotional journey requires that we learn to focus on the inner world, our own healing and connect to our own power for validation. It is also a chance to learn forgiveness as we will experience situations that require us to learn how to forgive ourselves and others.

Choosing to experience our journey from a spiritual perspective is how we manifest the completion of our soul's intention for healing and ascension. And it is a choice that can take multiple lifetimes to make. This choice helps us find the connections between the lessons and our experiences and change our journey from karma to creation, from following our pre-ordained destiny to using our co-creative powers to manifest our life with focused intention. Until we can make bold choices that balance our material and spiritual aspects, our life journey is merely a repetition of the past where our ego constantly challenges the soul's desire for healing and rejects its active participation in the process. In the end, all paths eventually lead us back to Spirit as it represents the reconnection we have been seeking all along and then we are Home, not in the spirit world but in our own heaven on earth.

Before we get to heaven on earth life can take many twists and turns, often taking us farther from our destination than we could have imagined possible. It is those times when we look at our lives and wonder "How did I get here?" If we were doing the right things, how did everything spin out of control? We ask questions and receive no reply, not because there is no answer but because we are either not asking the right questions or forgetting who is in charge of turning the situation around. If we are not prepared to do things differently from that point forward, if we do not honor our dreams and our passion, we will find ourselves in the same situations over and over again, feeling lost and confused, an aimless, rudderless ship trying to navigate the waters of our destiny without the guiding light of our soul's knowledge.

This doesn't mean that we are failing in our spiritual growth. We could be choosing the path that looks 'safe', that is in alignment with the limitations imposed by our fears or that is what we have always known. The path filled with drama, pain and unhappiness is what we have come to change. When we are tired of those things we will be ready to choose something else. That takes a measure of trust and it also means that we must make choices that are totally unfamiliar to us and whose outcome we are unsure of.

There is a turning point that we reach, that point where we ask the right and best question, that is the deciding point for change. But we must step away from our fear, out of what is comfortable or known, and do something different. And that is one of the stepping stones on the journey, learning to detach, seek guidance, look for the spiritual alternative and make unfamiliar, but more powerful choices.

There are no accidents or mistakes on our journey. Each situation is something that we created to help us arrive at our destination. The most challenging situations have the greatest lessons to teach us and we can learn them quickly if we can view our entire journey from a spiritual perspective, use our emotional experiences to help us make different choices, remember our power and let go of fear and doubt.

What is the destination? It can seem so difficult and complicated and impossible to achieve.

The destination of our spiritual journey is to reconnect with our Self,   to find the balance between the spiritual and the material and then manifest our reality from that point. That is the purpose of each of our lessons. The end of our journey does not occur, as religion teaches us, when die and hopefully go to heaven. Each of us has to learn to create heaven on earth for ourselves which is achieved by balancing our spiritual and material aspects. That can be achieved within a lifetime and it is an internal process, not an external one. Once we have heaven in our heart, we can manifest it in our life.

Our destination is internal and we reach it when we know the joy and unconditional love that is the energy of the spiritual realm. We can achieve that destination in a single lesson or in a hundred lessons. How long it   takes is not important and the Universe is infinitely patient with us. We are the ones who become frustrated with ourselves when life becomes too painful or difficult. And we judge ourselves for not working fast or hard enough. Our spiritual quest is internal but experienced through our interactions in the outer world and   when we reach our destination, we will know by how we feel on the inside, not by what we have in the material plane.

Discovering the synergies between the path and the journey means understanding how each experience participates in the overall purpose of what we came here to learn, heal and achieve. With a brilliant dawn of insight we can realize that life is not supposed to be hard, painful, sad and challenging. Those are aspects of our journey because we are driven by the ego and the emotions, focused on the fear that imprisons us rather than the love and power that can set us free and try to dominate our lessons by forcing an outcome instead of being in their flow.

Then we settle into the comfortable and liberating knowledge that life can be easier, the answer is always within us and that lessons are always about power, forgiveness and love. Once we have learned this truth about life we have fulfilled our contract and can choose other paths and destinations. Each journey provides us with new understanding and another opportunity to create the joy, unconditional love and boundless abundance that is our spiritual heritage. This is what heaven on earth is all about.

We can fulfill our spiritual contract within a lifetime and in fact, many of us are doing that now. When our contract is completed we are free to do other things with our life, move even farther along our path and even choose a different kind of journey. Proof of this is seen when we experience endings in our longest, most challenging relationships. At first we question ourselves—did we do something wrong? Then we question others' commitment, dedication and love. But in the end we learn that this is an ending whose time has come and is proof of the completion of our contract.

Aspects of our emotional life end when a contract is fulfilled and in some cases, so does our physical life. Some people do choose to cross over when they have completed a contract, content to be finished with this journey and not interested in creating a new life path. But we have many examples of the other choices that people are making, such as changing careers, reinventing themselves, or choosing new options for their life.

It is not an accident that so many people today are choosing different lifestyles or deciding to make drastic changes in how they express their gifts and talents, whether that choice is voluntary or enforced. They have fulfilled their soul contract in one area and can choose to go in other directions. Once we understand the relationship between our spiritual path and the journey we undertake to fulfill it, and apply our spiritual and emotional knowledge in the form of the choices we make, learning our lessons becomes a journey of growth and understanding and our path moves into new, unexplored and adventure filled territory. Then life becomes a series of unfolding miracles and blessings that we create from a position of power.

Our path and the journey can be a wonderful adventure of joy and fulfillment as we step into our roles of co-creators, partners with Spirit, in creating our life. This is a new paradigm for us and it represents another area of learning and growth on our journey.

Consider these questions for your personal mastery journey:

Can you see the relationship between your journey and the one or more paths you have chosen to accomplish it?

Are you aware of the role your ego plays in the choices you make?

Is your ego fighting for survival and how can you resolve the ego's need to stay in its fear vibration with your soul's desire for healing and resolution of this life lesson?

What choices can you make to reconnect with your power and find new ways of expressing your lessons in more joyful ways?

Do you know how you can express your personal heaven on earth in your life?

Can you see that the endings that are happening in your life are confirmation of your own growth and healing?

What types of life challenges are you facing that represent an ending of one aspect of your path and a new beginning in another direction?

Can you use these endings in powerful ways to create a new life path?

Are you able to refrain from viewing certain results as mistakes and see how whatever is blocked is an opportunity to change direction?

How often do you take the 'safe' path and what are some bold steps you can take to fulfill your most cherished dreams for your life?

And now we have come to a new crossroads of transformation where we understand that we are not less than any aspect of the Universe. We are here by design, not by accident and we are not helpless victims spinning out of control, living a pre-determined reality. We are co-creators with the Universe and as such hold the power to create the reality of our choosing. The earth is our playground and we determine what happens here when we acknowledge our divinity and co-creative powers.

The Process of Co-Creation

Our spiritual journey can unfold in two ways: it can be a journey of overcoming obstacles, where we constantly battle our fears and feelings of inadequacy or it can be a journey of enlightenment, where each new experience allows us to enrich our lives with a greater appreciation of our power and spiritual understanding. And we can experience our journey as a battle between our free will and Spirit or as a flow of co-creation, where we understand that we express our highest aspects when we look to Spirit for guidance and support, and are able to integrate that into our thinking and being, in conjunction with accessing our power and managing our reality through it.

To understand co-creation as a life choice we must release the belief that Spirit will tell us what to do and will always guide us in the 'right' direction. While we will be guided in a direction, that guidance includes our soul's desire for healing so our experiences are merely vehicles for the expression of our soul wounds. The choice of how our life unfolds depends on our attitude and willingness to surrender the ego's need for validation of its power and energies with our belief in how easy or challenging our life should be. This is where we choose the easy or the hard path and the difference lies in how much spiritual energy we integrate into our journey.

Each new lesson or challenge either reinforces our belief in our powerlessness and belief that we are alone on this journey or awakens us to the possibility of the effortlessness that is possible through powerful co-creation. And an important aspect of co-creation is surrender, which we must see in a new context. In its traditional meaning, we think of surrendering as 'giving up' or admitting defeat. But in our mastery context, to surrender means that we stop fighting, take the path of least resistance, acknowledge our spiritual support and work with it instead of ignoring it or fighting its participation in our life. Surrender is the highest expression of our mastery because through it we step into our power, acknowledge that we live in a reality of our own making and are open to the expression of the highest aspects of our field of potential.

Most of us choose the difficult path because we believe that life is supposed to be hard and the more we suffer the greater our reward at the end of our journey. But that is an old view of the process of spiritual growth. The key to creating an easier journey lies in connecting to our spiritual resources, which includes our guides and angels as well as our intuition and inner wisdom, so we can use the process of co-creation to manifest our life, step by step, with conscious intention of where we wish to go, while leaving space for the Universe to bless us with the unexpected.

When we undertook our spiritual contract we chose a team of helpers whose guidance would provide us with the information that needed to fulfill it in the most perfect way. Our purpose was to use these connections to help us remember what we knew we would forget as soon as we entered the material plane. Most importantly, we forgot that our contract is between ourselves and Source. Our contract with ourselves is to complete our healing. Our contract with Source is to raise our energetic vibrations and prepare ourselves, humanity and the earth for new paradigms. With this in mind we become co-creators, focused on the ultimate goal within each moment so we don't lose sight of our purpose by getting lost in our stuff or baggage.

As we learned in the chapter on The Path to Wholeness, participation in the third dimension is by invitation only, so Spirit has no power to work with us or to interfere in our lives unless we allow its participation. That is why when we cry out to God to rescue us, as I learned in my waiting room experience, there is no answer. We see the Universe as Creator and then wait for it to create on our behalf. But its role is that of co-creator with us, in a powerful partnership that manifests exclusively from the energy that we extend to it.

Somewhere along the way we adopted the belief that God created both us and world and is in total control of what happens in it. But we created the world with God, so that we could engage in the experience of ascension. This is a cosmic truth that is the greatest misunderstanding of the ages and through it we have been misled, dominated, abused and overpowered by those who prey upon our belief in our powerlessness and separation and convinced us that they had all of the power and the solutions, as well as the Source connection.

When we call upon our spiritual guidance and our Source connection for assistance in the most powerful way, which is to help us remember the purpose of our lessons and find powerful ways to resolve them, we are co-creating our spiritual journey. The degree to which we can do this to manage our life experiences depends on many factors, but there are three most important ones. First is where we look for help. Many of us look for powerful people to let us know that we are on the right path or are moving in the right direction. If we can't find anyone to validate us or our experiences, by resolving, making them easier or better yet, making them go away, we believe that we must be on the wrong path. By going within we indicate our willingness to surrender our will to Divine Will and will find the answers we need to make the next choice of decision and they will come from within us.

Then, we must look at how we use our experiences to validate our journey. When our life is difficult we believe that we are not worthy of anything better. After all, if the Universe loves us unconditionally, wouldn't it provide the best possible life experience for us? It does by responding to the energies we put forward based on our soul contract for healing. The Universe helps us on every step of the way, but not by removing our lessons and releasing us from our self-imposed healing commitments.

It works with and through us, but not for us.

It responds to the energy, in the form of the words, thoughts and beliefs that we put out.

It matches the energy, thought for thought and word for word, that we extend and delivers the results accordingly.

It does not and cannot create anything more than what we are asking for. Co-creation is always available to us and we can co-create our healing by staying connected to our inner guidance and remembering that it is a constant presence on our journey.

Third, we believe that we are co-creating our life when the best, most wonderful and powerful things appear for us. But we are always co-creating our life. How wonderful and fulfilling our life is depends on what we are co-creating with, ego or Spirit and the energies we are using, fear or love. If our thoughts and beliefs are fear-based, we cannot expect to manifest anything but that which resonates with our fears. The Universe will respond to us from our lowest point of energetic vibration. So no matter what we are asking for, if we are resonating at some level of fear, that is the energy we will create from.

And our Source connection is not as powerful when we are in fear. The Universe operates from a point of unconditional love, which is the absence of fear. It also sees us as being perfect, powerful and in control. When we are afraid and ask for help from a point of fear and a belief in our imperfection and powerlessness, our energetic vibration is low, we are co-creating from the ego and whatever we manifest will reflect this energy. If we want to manifest more powerfully, we have to become more powerful.

Here's an example of how this process works. Imagine that you have written a play and are also its director. Each of the actors in the play is going to perform their part according to what you have written. If they didn't you would be unhappy with their performance. The actors' roles are limited to the information that is on the script you have given them. Would you expect them to recite lines from a different play?

Yet that is what we do when we complain about the reality that we are dissatisfied with. We forget that we wrote the play and if we want to have different results we must change our input by re-writing the script. Our primary input is our emotional energy, which, as we have learned, is the energy of the third dimension. Emotions are our most powerful third dimension energetic resource and through them we create havoc or joy. When we underestimate the power of our emotions we ignore an important aspect of co-creation.

Our emotions set the level of our energetic vibration that then factors into every outcome we create. Every emotion we are carrying is a co-creator with us and acts as an energetic magnet, attracting a similar energy, no matter what we set our intention for. Our anger does not create peace, it creates more angry situations. Our resentment or bitterness do not create fulfillment, they create more resentment and bitterness. Our sadness does not create joy, it creates more sadness. Our current emotional state is the energetic point from which we co-create.

Spirit is our partner but it is not going to change our vibrations so we can create more powerfully. Instead, it is simply going to help us create from whatever energetic vibration we are currently at. Whatever dissatisfaction we have with our reality is the reflection of our emotional state mirrored back to us.

We are always co-creating our life, with a balance of love and fear and ego and Spirit. When these energies are balanced we draw from the highest aspects of all of our resources, spiritual and material. When fear and ego dominate, we are at a lower energetic vibration and take on all the responsibility for creation, leaving no room for Spirit. And what we manifest reflects that, although we tend to blame Spirit for not helping us create a better, more fulfilling outcome. Co-creation is not about the good and wonderful things that happen to us, it is about everything that happens to us. The Universe responds to our every thought, belief, word and action. The power that we use with them is what delivers the results. When we use all of our energetic resources in powerful ways everything becomes a flow of miracles, where we have a balanced flow of asking and receiving. And it manifests in everyday things, as illustrated in the following example.

It was autumn, time to plant flower bulbs that would bloom the following spring. My favorite garden shop had some beautiful hyacinth bulbs and I chose a few for my garden. There were many other bulbs there and I thought that I would like some of them too but my budget was limited. As I was deciding between either buying more hyacinth bulbs or some tulips and daffodils and wishing I could have them all, the shop owner approached me with a big bag and said I could have all of the bulbs I wanted for free, since he had to clean them out and wanted to give them to someone who would use them. So I got all of the garden bulbs I wanted, including the hyacinth bulbs and they were free. That is the process of co-creation through power at work.

When we co-create through power we simply ask for what we want, without wondering whether we will get it, how it will come to us, whether we can afford it, whether it will last, or any of the many different arguments that we can think of to limit what we receive. The co-creation process goes into action with every thought that we have. If we are experiencing poverty, drama and chaos, we are co-creating that in our lives by being at that energetic frequency and our reality is mirroring our thoughts of poverty, drama and chaos. . Our thoughts are more than random bits of information that pass through our mind. Like our emotions, they are powerful energy forms that we use to create our reality. When they are combined with the energy of our emotions, they are powerful indeed. When we are upset, sad or afraid, that energy is added to our thoughts. Have you ever noticed that when things go bad they only seem to get worse? And things begin to improve once we change our focus from being upset about a situation to creating a solution. When our emotional energy shifts we change the energy that we are adding to our thoughts, which produces a different outcome.

Emotions such as anger, fear, sadness or despair are stronger than those of joy and love simply because they have a strong resonance with the third dimension and our ego. And on an emotional level we probably have more memories of being sad and feeling powerless than of feeling joyful and powerful. There is more fuel for our difficult emotions than there is for the more uplifting ones and they are all part of our co-creative process.

Consider these questions for your personal mastery journey:

What thoughts are you thinking in this moment?

What emotions are you feeling in this moment?

Putting your thoughts and emotions together, can you see a situation in your life that they have helped you co-create?

Is this situation an example of your power of or your powerlessness?

Are you aware of other situations like this that you have created using your emotions and thoughts?

Can you be aware of your thoughts and emotions for the next five minutes or more and see how they create your reality? If you practice this daily you will learn how to manage your thoughts and emotions so you are aware of how you are using them to co-create your life.

Have you ever asked for something and did not receive it? While you were disappointed, maybe you really had not expected to receive it at all so the disappointment was not too bad. When we do not believe that we deserve something or don't think we can have it but we ask for it anyway, we send confusing messages to the Universe. On one hand we are sending out the energy for what we want and at the same time, sending out energy that we do not want, deserve or believe we can have it. The creative power of our thoughts is unlimited and all thoughts create equally. So asking for what we want has the same power as not believing we will receive it. And nothing happens because of the conflicting messages.

Out of the thousands of thoughts we have each day, how many of them are consciously creating what we want, how many are limiting our creation, and how many are unconsciously creating more of what we want to change? Abundance is created through thought and it is another area where our thoughts and emotions send mixed messages. What we have an abundance of depends on four things: what we currently have, what we want, what we ask for and the beliefs we have around the entire process.

Once our energy shifts other aspects of life become available to us because we are ready to connect to them from our field of potential. We are always blessed with abundance, which is not limited to the wonderful, amazing blessings that we can have. There is abundance in all things, it is a Universal law and like all of these laws, it is non-judgmental. So there is an abundance of lack as well as an abundance of wealth. There is no difference between them. Abundance is simply abundance. As I have said and written many times, the Universe doesn't care if we want a glass of water because we are thirsty or a new home because we need a place to live. It is all equal in the eyes of the Universe. So if we ask for abundance because we don't have anything and think we're asking for a blessing, we need to re-consider our thoughts and energy because we will get more of what we already have if that is what we are focused on.

Any dissatisfaction with our existing reality simply means that we are ready for something else, not that we have done something wrong or are unlucky. There is no answer when we ask the Universe why it hasn't blessed us with something else because it is our responsibility to create our reality, in partnership with the Universe. And it works through the principle of co-creation, where it responds to the energy of our thoughts and emotions and what we are asking for.

How we ask is as important as what we ask for. Do we ask with authority or do we beg and plead? Do we ask from our mastery or from our victimhood? What we do next is equally important. Do we wait for the best result or act on what manifests first? When doors open, we must be willing to walk through them. And we are at our most powerful state when we ask with authority, we affirm our co-creative ability, expect abundance in all we ask for and are willing to act on the information we receive. In the process of co-creation, the Universe works with us to create heaven on earth for each of us, to the extent that we allow it to.

As long as we see ourselves as insignificant, powerless and out of control we will use all of the power of the Universe, which is entirely at our disposal, to create a reality which reflects that. Once understand the power of our thoughts and how intention, emotion and beliefs all work together to create our reality, creating abundance, joy, unconditional love and peace will be easy.

Consider these questions for your personal mastery journey:
Are you thoughts aligned with what you want in your reality?
Are you aware of thoughts that limit you in any way?
Are your beliefs in alignment with what you are asking for or are you negating your manifestation by asking without believing that what you are asking for is possible for you?
Can you see how you may be blocking what you want to manifest?
How can you align your beliefs with what you want to create in your life?
Do you believe you deserve to have and can have everything you are asking for in this moment?

When we understand and learn how to work with the process of co-creation, our lives can be an effortless flow of abundance, peace, joy and love. We are always working with Source energy in every aspect of our lives so we are always co-creating. If our life is in chaos, full of drama, and every step forward is difficult, our co-creation efforts have been rather one-sided, meaning that we have not used our connections and our power to create a path that is easy and flowing effortlessly. We can step into co-creating by making a few changes.

First we start by acknowledging that we feel powerless because we have forgotten our power. Our ability to co-create does not depend on whether we think we have power or are in a powerful situation because we always have power. Our most powerful reality is manifested and supported in a continuous flow when we are constantly connected to the infinite reservoir of power that we have within us. Once we come to terms with the issue of whether or not we have power then we can focus on how we have created the reality we are experiencing and use our power to resolve it.

It is helpful to do some internal checking here and have a dialogue with ourselves. Were we acting out of fear or a belief in our powerlessness? Did we ask for what we truly wanted or accept less than we knew we deserved? Are our beliefs in alignment with what we want to manifest? Finally, are we asking for guidance in the best way, as powerful co-creators (and not beg or plead for help), to make the changes that will help us move forward in a more powerful, peaceful, joyful and abundant direction?

The Universe is infinitely patient with us and for many of us, the simple act of acknowledging our power is the foundation of our lessons. Rather than starting out from a place of power, lessons in reclaiming our power always involve situations that make us powerless. As we move through this lesson and are able to reclaim our power we complete this cycle of healing. Then we can step more powerfully into our co-creative abilities and create the powerful life we want, which reflects our divine heritage of abundance, peace, joy and unconditional love.

As a final thought on this topic, we are also responsible for co-creating the world we live in. Each of us contributes our energy to the unfolding reality that we see in the world. There is no difference between the small world we call our reality and the larger world that is the planet and all of humanity. Take a moment, as you are reading this to consider that the thoughts that you have, right now, about you, your life and your reality are being magnified around the world. Each of us has this ability and each of us uses it every day, whether we are aware of it or not.

How does it work?

Have you ever had a bad day and it seems that everyone you meet has decided that this is the day they will pick on you? Clerks are rude, your friends don't have time for you, you're late to everything, or you spill your coffee on your new outfit. You are simply co-creating your bad day in the world and everyone around you is picking up on your energy and mirroring it back to you. Now imagine this power being magnified through the thoughts of every person on the planet. What would happen if everyone focused on peace, love and joy? What kind of world would we live in?

Once we are aware of this power, we must also embrace the tremendous responsibility that comes with it. It can no longer be 'someone else's fault' that the world is in chaos, that there is hatred, discrimination and poverty. We may not have materially participated in the problems but we do participate in them energetically. And if we believe that things can't get better, that we cannot make a difference, that we are helpless and powerless, we are participating in the problems at an energetic level and change is prevented from happening. The power for change is and has always been with us because we are co-creators.

We co-create the world as we co-create our own reality, so our focus does not have to shift from our reality to making the world a better place. All we have to do is acknowledge our co-creative power and use it to manifest our own heaven on earth, which allows that energy to be magnified around the world. Think of what the world would be like if each of us did that for five minutes, an hour, a day, or all of the time. We would not have to work at getting rid of the darkness—the darkness only exists to magnify the light. So when we shine our light the darkness is absorbed into it and all becomes light. Each time we are willing to create love, joy, peace, abundance and compassion for ourselves we can remember that we are also creating it for the world.

What does this power look like? We are surrounded by energy that looks like countless particles of light, in constant motion, surrounded by vast empty space. The particles of light are the energy which is waiting for us to give it form. The empty spaces are what the energy will expand into . These energy particles move towards us as we set our intention for manifestation and then move away to form whatever we called into being with our thoughts or words. The energy recognizes our power and responds with whatever we wish to create.

Working with energy is how we use our power to create our reality. We do it every day, consciously and unconsciously. From the kindness someone shows us to the traffic ticket we receive, from the partners and friends we attract to our financial status, everything that happens in our life is a result of what we direct the energy around us to do. When we are not aware of this power we can use the energy in a very misdirected way, creating many things that we don't want. We do that for several reasons: we don't understand our power, we don't know how to work with the energy or we don't know how the energy works.

We are the first generation to be introduced to our power and to have the knowledge of working with the universal energy. It's no wonder that we are not aware of how to use it, since there have been few teachers until now. And we must overcome many lifetimes of believing that we are powerless, our lives are out of our control, our destiny is pre-determined and that luck is how abundance is created and that is something that happens to other people. Once we accept that we have power and learn how to use it, we can use the energy around us wisely, creating what is best and right for us.

Since we have had few teachers to show us how to use the energy, we do not understand how it works and this is how we get ourselves into trouble. The energy is completely non-discriminating and non-judgmental, meaning it has no opinions, thoughts or feelings about how we use it. We can use it to create wealth or poverty, loving or disastrous relationships, joy or sorrow. It does not ask "why" or whether this is what we want, it merely responds to our thoughts, words and beliefs. Once we accept the constant and continuous presence of our power we can learn to work with and manage the energy so that our power is reflected in a reality that blesses us abundantly with everything we consciously ask for.

Our power can be used actively or passively. With passive use, we either focus all of our energy on what we don't want, such as saying things like 'I don't want to be poor', or I don't want to lose my job', or 'I'm afraid I'll never find someone to share my life with'. Or we ask for what we want and then spend all of our time convincing ourselves that it won't happen, we won't receive it or we don't deserve it. Or we give our power to someone else and hope they can create what we believe we are not capable of creating. From the passive perspective, our power is a mystery to us, since we are not aware that we are using it to create the opposite of what we want. We are unaware of the connection between our power and our reality, our thoughts and what they create in our world.

With active use of our power we are aware of its presence and are connected to it. Our connection to it feels like a helpful presence that easily manifests according to our instructions. It gives us comfort and reminds us of our co-creative abilities. We know that our power requires responsibility and accountability so we use it with discretion, aware that every thought and word connects with the Universal energy and sets it in motion.

Consider these questions for your personal mastery journey:

How are you using your power, actively or passively?

Are you aware that every thought and word sets your power in motion?

Do you give your power to others and hope they will create the best outcome for you?

Are you connected to your power in a way that reminds you of your co-creative abilities?

Do you consciously use your power every day to create the life you want?

Living in the past is a passive use of our power. Whatever we regret, wish we had done differently, better, or not at all, what we resent or wish had not happened focuses our energy in the past and brings it forward into our current reality. And we may have an opportunity to repeat the experience, with the same outcome, until we learn to focus on the present moment, on what we are capable of today, and forgive ourselves for not being powerful, strong, wise, compassionate or loving enough in the past. The past is the storehouse of regret, chances not taken, mistakes and unused potential. There is no power in the past, which is why it represents a passive use of our power.

Unlimited potential, powerful intentions, new opportunities and transformation are all part of the present moment. It is what we do in this moment that creates the possibilities for the next one. We cannot change the past and there is nothing powerful for us there. This means that we are challenged to stop focusing on the past if we expect the present and future to be different. Our most powerful moment is the present, where we have complete freedom to create whatever we want.

When we work with the universal energy in a balanced way we use our past experience as a learning tool that helps us avoid obstacles as we create the future. Once we learn that touching a hot stove can burn our finger, we check to see whether a stove is hot before we indiscriminately put our hand on it. In the same way, we take the information from the lessons we have learned in the past and use them as guideposts to move farther along our spiritual path. This utilizes the past in a useful way, to help us create a different reality that does not involve repeating experiences that we do not want to repeat. We can actively use our power when addressing the past as a guideline to know where we need to step forward more powerfully, to be more sure of ourselves and to trust in our power to powerfully co-create our reality.

Consider how the past plays a role in your present reality:

Do you see aspects of your life today that mirrors how it was five, ten or more years ago?

Are you doing things today that you once said you would not repeat and find that you are doing just that?

Are there situations in the past you wish you could repeat, so you can make different choices?

Are you stuck in the past, wishing that you could change it?

When those opportunities arise, are you making other choices or repeating the past?

There is really no right or wrong way to use our power, any way we use it reflects our level of spiritual growth and understanding. We can measure how we have used our power through the results that we obtain. The beneficial results, those that we enjoy and bring us what we want, are obtained through the same power as those that are less beneficial, the results that bring us more of what we want to change or wish would go away. The issue is not how much power we have—as we all have the same source of power—but how we use it.

Realizing that we have as much power as anyone else on the planet is difficult for many to accept. Does that mean that we have as much power as the world's wealthiest people, presidents and rulers and corporate CEOs? Yes, we do. They have used theirs to create what they want and we can use ours to create what we want. But not if we are trying to create what someone else has because we believe that it will make us happier or we will be better off than we are at this moment.

We use our power in the right or best way when we use it with conscious intention. Our intention must be conscious, meaning that we are aware of exactly what we are asking for because then we direct the energy in the best possible way. And we can then focus our full power on it and increase our chances of success. The more we focus our intention on what we want, the better our chances of having it appear in our life. For example, if we want a loving, fulfilling relationship, we should ask for that. And not focus on the relationship our friend has, creating love to show the person who left us for someone else that we are worthy of love, to prove to our parents that we can find someone or any of the other justifications we may attach to wanting a relationship.

The less powerful use of our power happens when we do not acknowledge how much power we do have. Or we think others have more power than we do because they appear to be happier, wealthier or more successful than we are. Or we do not have the beliefs to support what we wish to manifest. The results we receive will reflect our acknowledgement and use of our power. Feeling powerless does not mean that we do not have any power, just that we are not connected to it and using it consciously and with intention. When we use all of our power, we can manifest spectacular results. The less connected we are to our power, the more powerless our results will be.

Consider these questions for your personal mastery journey:
Can you acknowledge how much power you have?
Do you believe that you have as much power as anyone else in the world?
Are you aware of times when you were feeling powerless?
Are you willing to see yourself as a powerful person, with access to unlimited power?
What kind of changes would you make in your life if you used your power in a powerful way?

As we acknowledge our power and accept Spirit as our co-creator, we manifest a reality that reflects the highest aspects of our energies. Although we have the power to create a more abundant, joyful and powerful reality, for ourselves and for the world, there is one aspect of our journey that never changes—we take it one step at a time, from one breath to the next. Our most powerful place is in the present moment because it is within each moment that the next is created. And with that knowledge comes the simple understanding that life exists from one breath to the next. Where is the present moment? The moment in which we are breathing because it is the only moment we have available to us.

From One Breath to the Next

Can we see that the present moment is the only one that exists for us? The past has been completed and the future depends on what we do in this moment, which creates what happens in the next one. The future is, in fact, merely the next moment after this one. Living in the present moment is like breathing. Just as we live in this moment and the next, we live from one breath to the next. While the body can exist for long periods of time without food or water, it can live for only a few minutes without breathing. Our first breath occurs the moment we enter the world and our last breath occurs at the moment we die. The one constant presence in our lives is our breath. We cannot take all of our required breaths during the day in the first five minutes in the morning. We cannot take one breath and skip the next ones. We cannot breathe on behalf of someone else nor can they do that for us.

Quite simply, if we do not breathe we die. So the present moment, the moment in which we are fully aware and powerful, is the one in which we are breathing because no matter how far into the future we can plan, our lives exist solely within each breath. We live from one breath to the next and our survival in any moment depends on our ability to take the next breath.

There are many aspects of our physical bodies that require no thought or effort. Imagine what life would be like if we had to remind our heart to beat, the correct muscles to work when we wanted to stand up or walk, our eyes to see when we wanted to look at the world around us, our ears to hear, our blood to flow, or our lungs to take the next breath. All of these things are done automatically for us. If we had to take care of them we would not have time to focus on anything else.

Breathing, which is the most important element to our physical survival, is taken care of for us, from the unconscious, rhythmic activity of our lungs to the plentiful supply of air that we require. This unconscious effortless is also present in the way we can allow Spirit to work with us to manifest all of our needs as our co-Creator.

The important functions of our physical body have been designed to operate without our attention so we could focus on other aspects of our journey. This is an example of how the material world can manifest effortlessly for us. And yet we still worry about what is going to happen from one day to the next. When our focus is on the past or the future and not on the present moment, which is where we are taking the next breath, we are ignoring the example of how Spirit can work effortlessly in partnership with us. Unconditional love is in the air we breathe, it is provided to us effortlessly by the Earth and the Universe, and the elements that work together to ensure that we have always have an abundance of air to breathe and by the body, which remembers to take each breath on our behalf.

How much time do we spend worrying about where our next breath of air will come from? None at all, because this is how effortless our physical reality is. Just as we do not think about whether we will remember to take the next breath or worry that there will be enough air for us to breathe, so we can release the worry about whether all of our needs will be met when we acknowledge how Creator provides us with what we need, in unlimited abundance, as we remove our focus from worry, doubt and fear to acceptance that there is always enough.

And as we take our next breath, and the one after that, we can remember that it is being provided for us in unlimited abundance by a Creator who loves us beyond measure. We can breathe with intention and peace of mind, fully and completely, knowing that the love of the Creator is in each breath we take and that just as the air we breathe is provided effortlessly, so is every other need met for us when we remember that our life is a spiritual journey occurring in a material plane where everything we want is acquired through conscious intention and effortless manifestation. We may be waiting on the Universe to bring us what we desire but in reality, the Universe is waiting for us to set our intention for manifestation.

Whatever is going on in our life that is not working as we wish, whatever lack exists in our reality, anything that is not bringing us joy is not God's fault. And we can ask Source to help us, solve our problems and send us blessings, and we will feel like change is not happening because changing our life is not God's responsibility; it is ours. We already have everything that we could possibly want as it is present in what we have in our lives at this moment. Everything we desire is ours by divine right as a child of God but we have to ask for it by setting our intention to co-create it. Our only limits in receiving are held within our ability to acknowledge and connect with what we believe we deserve to have. And God waits for us to acknowledge this so we can recognize and accept our blessings.

It is not God's way to withhold blessings or to make us suffer. All good things come from God or Source but their manifestation begins with and is the result of our ability to think, believe and act powerfully. The Universe works through us and with us and cannot create something in our reality that we have not already asked for. Our wishes are not daydreams or idle thoughts; they represent the desires of our heart. Whatever we wish for is what is possible for us and can be part of our reality. And once we are ready to accept our blessings heaven and earth will move to help us manifest them. But God waits for us to begin that process and each breath we take is an affirmation of our desire to be present, loving, fulfilled, joyful, living in our purpose and on purpose.

Everything in our reality is a material reflection of our spiritual power. When our reality seems to spin out of control it is not because God has abandoned or forgotten us, it is because we have forgotten who we are – we have forgotten to breathe. Have you noticed that when you are worried or afraid you become a 'shallow breather', taking small, quick breaths and not breathing fully and deeply? If this is true of you, where in your life are you taking shallow breaths, not allowing yourself to fully express and expand into your power and live on purpose?

Our true power lies in remembering that we are and have always been in control of our reality. When we live powerfully we are connected with the Universe and everything is possible for us. When we feel powerless it is because we are not living life through our Source connection and are not using our power. There are no victims from God's perspective, only those who have forgotten who they are and the power they already have. When we are scared by something we hold our breath and in the same way when we are in a state of blame or powerlessness, we are also not breathing in the fullness of life and all of its potential and possibilities. Maybe we think that by limiting our breath we will get the attention we want, that someone will come into our life and rescue us.

A friend of mine has often shared a story of how she would hold her breath as a child when she did not get her way. Sometimes she held it so long she would pass out. Then one day her mother, tired of dealing with this, threw a glass of cold water in her face which, of course, made her breathe again. She was so shocked that she never held her breath again. When we hold our breath or do not use our power, we receive the equivalent of a glass of cold water to the face in the form of something that reminds us that we have to activate our creative abilities, take control of our reality, use our power and begin to act and live with purpose.

It is our divine destiny to create abundance doing meaningful work that we are passionate about. It is our divine destiny to have loving, fulfilling relation-ships in which we are cherished, respected and honored. It is our divine destiny to have our every desire met on every level. We are never victims; we are always in control. There is no mystery to manifesting what we want because that is what we are capable of and came here to do. When we work with the Universe as powerful co-creators, we can do great things for ourselves and for the world but God waits for us to acknowledge our power and until we do, will wait patiently for us to begin to breathe again.

Consider these questions for your personal mastery journey:

To become present in your life and to learn how to be in the 'now', in the present moment, focus on your breath and breathing. You will notice that this helps you relax and stay focused. Remember that the moment in which you are breathing is the present moment.

Do you worry about what will happen in the next days, months or years? If you do, take yourself back to your breath and remember that this is the present moment for you, and the only one you are living and breathing in.

Can you acknowledge that the effortlessness with which you take each breath is the same way you can manifest your reality as a powerful co-creator?

Do you blame the Universe when your life appears to be out of control?

Do you stop breathing, or creating, in those moments?

Are you able to shift your victim-based thinking to remember that in the eyes of Creator you are never a victim?

Instead of asking God to rescue you, can you ask to be shown the role your lessons play in your life and how to use them to best serve your healing purpose?

Are you able to acknowledge your destiny as receiving the fulfillment of your every desire?

And now we are at the point where we are creating the new earth. The new earth is an inner world, a new paradigm for human 'beings' that allows full participation with Spirit, acknowledgement of ourselves as powerful co-creators, the fulfillment of all that we desire and the creation of heaven on earth. Are we ready for the new earth? I hope so because we have created it and it is here right now.

Welcome to the New Earth

We are here, at the crossroads between the human and spiritual worlds, with the doorway to the new earth before us. Though it has been, at times a distant, faint memory, we have always known that we would eventually arrive here, in this moment and at this crossroads of the connection between the spiritual and material worlds. It has been the purpose and destination of our journey as the family of humanity, as spiritual beings having a human experience. This has been our soul (and sole) purpose of healing, growth and reconnection, of doing our work so we could return to our spiritual home. But this time is different, rather than return home to begin our journey again, we have changed the earth's vibration of the earth to re-create 'home' here. This path is one that has been shared and repeated by all of humanity, each of us a spark of the Light, going out and returning, lifetime after time. At this special time we have opened the gates of Heaven to create heaven on earth and this new earth is now available to us.

The doorway opened without fanfare, a big announcement or tangible confirmation. We have anticipated that its arrival would be announced by the appearance of angels, ascended masters, or perhaps a visitation from extra terrestrials, confirming our ability to access other dimensions. But the need for this kind of confirmation or validation is part of our old paradigm of doubting our abilities and Source connection. The new earth is not a gift from the spirit world, it is our gift to ourselves. We created this opening through our own efforts and the spirit world is not coming closer to us, we have been moving closer to Spirit. The new earth is not going to be visible from a material or five sensory perspective. We experience it through our 'extra' senses, our inner knowing and our willingness to accept our spiritual mastery.

The new earth represents our spiritual graduation and we know it's here, we can feel it and we see examples of it all around us, in the disintegration of the foundation of the third dimension. All of the old energies of fear, greed, manipulation, domination and polarity are, literally, coming to 'light' and while it may feel like the world is falling apart, with the opening of the new earth portals the energies that support our old paradigms have no power. Any lower vibration energy that enabled and even encouraged them has now shifted. This will be an ongoing process of dissolution because as we have experienced in our own life, the old energies have to be uncovered and released so the new ones can be accepted and integrated.

The creation of the new earth and the dissolution of the old realities will be felt as a series of expansions and contractions, as part of the old reality contracts and begins to fall away, the new earth energies will expand to fill the vacuum that is created. The birthing process begins with a contraction, a realization that something is not right or an event that forces us to accept that transformation is required. From a personal perspective, this could be a sense of dissatisfaction with our life, the end of a relationship, a job loss, an accident or other traumatic event or an illness. Our life as we know it stops and we have to regroup, reconsider, re-assess our priorities and make changes. From a more global perspective, we will see (and are already seeing) institutions whose activities are based on greed, manipulation, self-serving policies and domination of others fall because their true nature is uncovered and people are no longer accepting of these kinds of activities.

The contraction is painful because of its emotional attachments and it is challenging because it represents a shift, an ending and a point of transformation It is also an opening to an expansion of energies, if we choose to consider new possibilities and use our spiritual understanding to assess the lessons, create new options and choose to respond powerfully and release fear. Or it is followed by another contraction if we choose the path of fear, disillusionment and powerlessness. Each contraction is followed by an opportunity for expansion and eventually the contractions stop when we find powerful new options for our life. When we move through the contraction into expansion, we create an opening for the new earth in our life and are born into a new paradigm. This creates room for the new energies and a higher vibration. And the cycle will repeat itself until our levels of ascension and mastery are achieved, individually and collectively.

The promise of the new earth and its new paradigms for being and access to higher vibrations and dimensions, is ours when we are willing to accept its blessings, release our judgments, and be open to possibilities beyond those we can imagine. The periods of contraction show us where we are limiting our options, the expansion provides us with a view of what is possible, if we choose to abandon our judgments and attachments, surrender fear and allow the impossible to become possible.

Within this powerful space, however, the choices we make take on a greater importance because we have moved beyond karma and destiny into a new era of unlimited choice and instant manifestation. Our free will has always allowed us to choose our path but we did so within the influence of our karma and destiny. These two forces often blinded us to other possibilities until we had accumulated enough life experiences and soul healing to choose to forgive and release our soul journey partners. With the completion of this cycle we are fully within our power, free from the distractions of the unconscious drive to resolve karma and ready to create new levels of reality. Life then moves from karma to creation, where our perspective operates at a higher level, where we can view the karma from a detached perspective and see other choices.

Do we want to engage with that person or situation, or is our Highest Good better served if we move on to another level of experience, releasing the timeline of that reality so we can experience a different, more expansive one? Does this experience limit or expand our potential? Is this the path of karma or creation? And most importantly, does this serve us in our desire for fulfillment, love, peace, joy and abundance? The new earth has many choices, each of them full of wonderful new possibilities that are free of pain, drama, fear and chaos.

With every step on our path we can make the choice for the new earth or to be in another reality. It is our ability to know that the new earth is a choice for us that opens us to its presence and potential. Following the path of karma will always be a choice but it is there to remind us that all potential realities exist for us, we simply have to choose which one we will reside in. The difference between the third dimension and the new earth will be obvious and the more we choose a higher vibration the less appealing karma will be.

Entry into the new earth is limited solely by our ability to choose it and this choice will be available to everyone. It is a demanding choice for once we choose the new earth there is no turning back to our old realities. And why would we want to? In the new earth we have freedom, we are in the miracle vibration, we can manifest the life we want (as we do now but on a much different level) and create an effortless flow of abundant blessings. The new earth is experiential, we create it from the inside out. Our spiritual knowledge and understanding will be the tools that we use to create the new earth in our own lives.

Before we get excited about being able to make a quantum leap into other dimensions of being and leaving the third dimension behind, the process will not be that quick or in some ways, that easy. We may step back and forth between dimensions until we feel comfortable with our power and the potential it affords us. Sometimes we need to move backwards a few steps to obtain closure and to convince ourselves that we are making the right choice. Sometimes our fear of creating more karma with our soul group prevents us from fully disconnecting from them until we feel that we are finished with those lessons.

Everything is always in divine order, there is no better or worse reality than the one we have in this moment, just as there is no good or bad in any situation. We make the choices we are able to connect with and when we have learned from them we are in a position to make other choices. If we allow the new earth to be one of our choices, however, we will get glimpses of this new paradigm and slowly integrate it until we are comfortable enough to be fully be present in its energy, without the fear that we have not done all we could for others or have unfinished business that we may have to return to complete.

The new earth has its challenges too, in the form of living in integrity, being in our Truth, acknowledging our dreams, honoring our gifts, living through our highest potential and following our guidance. One of our challenges will be to look at life's choices from the position of "What's right and best for me" and not feel guilty or think we are being selfish about the choices we make. Although we have longed to go home, our mission was to create that here on earth and now we have.

It will take time for us to become familiar with our new home and find our way around. There will still be lessons, as that is part of our earthly experience, but how difficult they are and how long we stay in them becomes a matter of conscious and intentional choice. We can learn to live by enlightened choice instead of through fear, through creation instead of destiny and radiate the peace, joy and unconditional love that we feel within to the world. The world that has known us as Light workers will know us as Light beacons in the new dimensions, because we will no longer be martyred healers but will shine our light brightly to help others remember their own brilliant spark of divine love and they will have the example of what is possible for them by what we do, how we live and how we interact with others.

The new earth introduces new ways to be connected to our power that have not been possible on the material plane. We have many memories of being separated from and denied access to our power and yet this issue is no longer relevant to us. The use of power will be the foundation of many of the lessons we experience in the new earth, as they are now, beginning with the knowledge that everyone is powerful and our Source of power is the same for and available to all. It will become increasingly clear that the use of power in violation of universal laws will create consequences that happen much more quickly than before. We will have nearly instant confirmation of how we are using our power, to either enhance or to disrupt our life and will quickly experience the consequences or blessings (although consequences are blessings too). Lessons in power will serve to help us reconnect and use our power in ways that remind us that we are children of God, that each of us is a spark of divine consciousness and we must love ourselves as we are loved by our Creator.

Many of our third dimensional lessons in power have focused on claiming it, reversing lifetimes where we have given our power to others, it was taken away or we were afraid to use it. The new earth's lessons begin from the standpoint of our absolute knowing that we are powerful. This is how we step into miracle mastery, manifesting the life of our dreams by remembering that at any moment we are one powerful, conscious and intentional thought away from heaven on earth.

We have the responsibility of bringing the new earth to fruition in the most powerful way possible, in a manner that honors everyone. The days of one group asserting their power over another, of using control and domination to force their will on others, are over. Each of us is part of the unfolding process of change into new paradigms and no one is any more or less responsible for ensuring that we create its foundation and then use each moment, each lesson and each opportunity to affirm that the new earth is our new paradigm for living. There is much responsibility in the new earth and our willingness to create balance between the spiritual and material worlds anchors this energy. We are now at the moment we have been waiting for and we are the architects of this new reality.

The mind looks for confirmation of the arrival of the new earth from those who we believe should tell us that it is here. Will the announcement come from the angels, the archangels, the ascended masters, extra-terrestrials or from God? That is the mind at work, wanting to know by seeing something it can believe in. But the new earth is a special combination of the spiritual and material worlds and the new earth is not 'out there', it is within us. We are the new earth.

The new earth is not a place or location, it is not a special city that enlightened ones will travel to and find peace and joy within its gates. We cannot find the new earth within the material world and say 'we are here' because it is our ability to transform the material world that gives birth to the new earth. As we move from material to spiritual thinking and being we also have to move from the need for material confirmation into spiritual knowing. The new earth is a lesson in trust and power—can we trust and believe in something we cannot see and are we able to understand the power that comes with this knowing?

We have blessed ourselves and the planet with the energy of the new earth and the real possibility of transformation into spiritual humans for those who seek it with an open heart. And we have also taken on many responsibilities with its formation, including holding the energy for it across many lifetimes, trusting that it is now here and learning to think of ourselves as powerful enough to change the world, because we can and we have. Just as we have to believe in the presence of miracles before they manifest for us, we also have to believe that the new earth exists even though we can't physically see it. But we can feel it and have confirmation of its presence through the transformation that we and the world are experiencing.

After all of the work we have done it would be nice to receive confirmation but that is another one of the lessons we have to learn, we no longer need confirmation as co-creators of this powerful new energy. Our need for someone or something to let us know that we have made progress shows where we are afraid that we are not enough. Our willingness to have faith, trust and believe in the presence of the new earth reminds us that we are powerful enough to create a new reality for ourselves and for the planet. We have completed our task of ascending into higher dimensions and now we are there. Now we have to learn to move away from needing the Universe to tell us everything is OK to trusting and believing that we have succeeded. We are co-creating the new earth one belief, thought and miracle at a time. Each of us represents a piece of the new earth, we are its promise and potential, so as we believe and trust that it is here we begin manifesting our life as powerful co-creators and spiritual humans living in higher dimensions.

With the new earth comes the availability of new levels of enlightenment, of being in the miracle vibration where life can be an effortless flow, of spiritual mastery, where we can stop working at our spirituality and begin living it. As the old paradigms fall away, the new earth will be a place of refuge, a place of peace for those who are confused, disenchanted and disillusioned by the old realities. The light of the new earth will be very attractive to those who are looking for peace and they will find it. Our task is to take the 'work' out of Light work and to shine, happy to be home and ready to step into our roles of co-creators of heaven on earth for ourselves and for the earth.

Welcome the new earth into your life. It is a new vibration for you and for the planet. It is a manifestation of your willingness to ascending into higher dimensions of being. You will feel its presence in your life as a sense of excitement, peace and joy, a knowing that you have arrived. This is a new beginning, where you go from here can be made one choice at a time, with each choice to follow your Truth opening limitless possibilities for you. Our work has been accomplished and we have ascended, acknowledging our equal partnership with Source and are now fully partnered and living in heaven on earth.

Consider these questions for your personal mastery journey:

The new earth is a movement from victim-based thinking to mastery. How can you integrate this into your life?

Do you think of yourself as a master? Can you integrate mastery thinking into your life, seeing yourself as powerful and divine, living your mastery?

Can you find examples of the new earth, through healing and releasing fear in your life?

Each of us is responsible for creating the new earth. How can you create this new paradigm in your life?

Are there people who have made you feel powerless or situations in which you were dominated by others? Can you release them as part of your movement into the new earth?

And as we create the new earth, we also create a new paradigm for all aspects of humanity. We will see how our relationships with others become more powerful and fulfilling, but more importantly, it is in our relationship with ourselves that we will see the greatest change. Now we can embrace our Christ Consciousness, through which we express our divinity and our mastery. But this is not the martyred Christ Consciousness we have known, this is a new Christ Consciousness, the ascension vibration through which we express, proclaim and live through our mastery.

The New Christ Consciousness

Attaining Christ Consciousness is the goal of our spiritual journey. This is the point in our journey where we have fulfilled our spiritual mission, shine our inner Light and transform our journey from one of karmic fulfillment to creation and reconnection to Source. Christ Consciousness is a state of inner being, the full realization of our divine purpose on Earth. For many generations the paradigm of Christ Consciousness has been viewed as one of martyrdom, carrying the sins of an unconscious, ungrateful and unhealed world and being a vessel for atonement. The new Christ Consciousness arrives with mastery, joy, abundance and it is expressed through enlightened consciousness and self-realization.

The role of martyr has been assumed by many Lightworkers throughout the ages. They have carried the energy of grace for their soul groups, providing them with opportunities to atone for karma, learn and practice forgiveness, to find their light through their connections with the one who carried the highest amount of light. The spiritual, emotional, and physical cost to Lightworkers has been great as they have returned to the earth plane in countless lifetimes so that their soul groups and the human family could have an opportunity to heal their soul wounds through their sacrifice and intervention. These Lightworkers held the vibration, light and promise of ascension for the world and now the moment of fulfillment has arrived.

The new Christ Consciousness is present because so many have been willing to attain Spiritual Mastery, to ascend into their divinity, shine their Light with confidence and rekindle their Source connections. The cross of the martyr has been replaced with the light of knowing and each can now find their own way. The Light is there for all to see and choose. Every choice is right and an indicator of one's level of growth and healing or whether they need more experiences with their karma.

The obligations to lead others into healing are released with the new Christ Consciousness. Participating in lessons is voluntary and honoring everyone's choices through affirming the integrity and wholeness of their path allows each one to effortlessly move into higher dimensions of experience. There is no need to suffer on behalf of others, as each one can choose spiritual wholeness and the embodiment of their divinity and mastery for themselves. The choice of karmic experience is now truly a choice that is available to all so the cross of atonement can be released to allow everyone can step into their light. Each person lights the way for others without taking on their darkness in the process. Each person can find their way as the Light shines brightly for all. This is a completion of a mission that releases everyone from the responsibility of being the light for the world so they can be a light in and of the world and in that process, light the world as it embodies its own Christ Consciousness and completes its ascension journey..

Consider these questions for your personal mastery journey:

How do you express Christ Consciousness in your life?

What can you do to be in integrity with your level of spiritual growth and express your highest vibrations?

Is there anyone in your life that you are carrying the cross of atonement for? Can you release it, and them, remember that everyone walks in and has their own light?

Who have you held the light for, in your life, and can you release yourself and them from this soul level promise?

Are you ready to release your soul group, contracts and karmic lessons with those you have held this energy for throughout many lifetimes?

How can you express your mastery in your life? Practice that every day to remind yourself that you are divine, powerful and a beacon of light for yourself and for the world.

Do you see yourself as a martyr or a master? Are there people and situations (including yourself) you can forgive so you can embrace your mastery and release your martyrdom?

Here we are at the end of this mastery journey. It has been a long and winding road, at times difficult beyond our ability to cope and at other times, more blessed than we could imagine. So what's next? Do we stop here? Is ascension the end of the road for us? Far from it. As with all aspects of our journey, each ending is the opening to a new beginning and every beginning requires an ending. So as we say good-bye to the old world and welcome a new paradigm, we start on a new journey. Each step leads to the next and while our journey never ends, we are now connected to our mastery, which takes our journey to a new and different level.

The Next Steps

So we come to the end of a journey and of course we want to know, 'what's next?' Is ascension the end of the road for us? Are we finished with the lessons and learning? Do we receive some kind of reward for our efforts that allows us to bypass every problem and challenge for the rest of our life? We want that to be the case but we know that it isn't. As we ascend into higher dimensions we will have a foot in both worlds, our third dimensional home will still be the place in which we live and work. But we will experience it through higher energetic vibrations. Every emotion exists at multiple levels of vibration and we connect with those that match our own vibration. The pain, suffering and fear of the third dimension will not completely go away but we can choose the level of these energies that we wish to experience in our life.

Each level of mastery we achieve brings its own lessons and blessings. As we have learned in these chapters, everything in our life emanates from a potential reality that we choose for ourselves from an unlimited array of possibilities. What we choose represents the only choice we can make at any point in time because it is the only choice we are aware of. When we are ready for something else the need for change propels us into choosing another path.

Everything we experience exists for the fulfillment of our life purpose of healing. We can have the most joyful, fulfilling life experiences when we are detached, aware that life is a journey of learning, healing, growth and transformation, and nothing more. Everything we give meaning to represents an attachment that holds an important life lesson for us. With this information we can use our soul group relationships in ways that help us release karmic energies, which is their ultimate purpose.

We can accomplish much when we understand life as a process of spiritual initiation and see how every situation and person plays a role in our evolution from human being to spiritual human. We do not lose our humanity with ascension; instead, we gain access to Spirit. It is through this connection that we can achieve the joy, peace, love and abundance that our heart wishes for and knows is a potential for us. When this wish is made from the ego's perspective we see life as an endless challenge; when it is made from the high heart or our connection to Spirit we know that everything we desire is waiting for us and anything that blocks it is part of our lesson in learning, healing, growth and transformation.

With mastery we are aware of the role we play in the human family and how we are all connected. Imagine a world where everyone was aware of this—it is where we are heading on our ascension journey. Every level of ascension we successfully complete, which means that every lesson we understand and bring to closure through healing, every fear we address and overcome, and every time we can extend unconditional love to ourselves and others, marks the completion of a level of ascension. We do not have wait for this to happen, it is happening now and we are all part of it.

Do not worry about whether you are doing this in the right or best way for this is your journey, your path, your ascension cycle and you are doing it in the best, right and most perfect way for you. Celebrate your successes, be grateful for your journey at this time, appreciate yourself, your life, your teachers and lessons because it is through them that ascension becomes possible.

Above all, remember to love yourself unconditionally and extend that love to everyone and to the world. Heaven on earth happens when we remember our connections and intentionally create the paradigms of peace, joy, love and abundance that are possible for the world. That is, and has always been, the purpose of our journey here, the goal of ascension and what we will know as the new earth.

Appendix

In this section you will find three exercises that you can use as part of your mastery journey. They are:

The Forgiveness Exercise
The Self Love Inventory
Releasing the Fear

The Forgiveness Exercise

Take a piece of paper and draw a line down the middle so you have two columns. On the left side of the paper, begin writing the names of every person who has ever done something to hurt you in any way, no matter how insignificant the situation was. Do not judge any situation, just write down the names as they come to you.

Now in the right column write down what they did or said to you. Again, do not judge any situation, simply write down what comes to your mind when you think of that person and how they have hurt you. Your comments do not have to be lengthy, a few words will do. If you feel they require more time and space, do a separate forgiveness exercise just for them.

This exercise may take some time to complete and it may be an emotional experience for you, so give yourself plenty of time to work on it. It may take several hours or even a few days, as you may not be able to complete it in one sitting.

Once you have completed this exercise, read through your list out loud, reading the person's name and what you are forgiving them for and then state that you are now ready to give them unconditional love. For example,

"Mom, I forgive you for always criticizing me and I now release you with unconditional love and healing."

Then, you are going to burn your list to forever release yourself and them from the karma. To do that, get a large, fireproof container and go outside, if possible. You will also need some matches, a large jar or glass of water, to put the fire out if necessary. Please be safe while doing this, do not burn your list indoors, near flammable materials or in an area where you can set plants or building materials on fire.

When you have prepared your area, take your list and tear it into small pieces as you say:

"I now release all of you and myself from any and all karmic relationships across all lifetimes and in all directions of time. I now forgive you and love you unconditionally and release you to live your life in peace."

Then put the pieces of your list in the fireproof container and light them with a match. As they burn, imagine that the smoke carries away all of the lifetimes of karma, along with all of the emotions associated with it. When the paper is completely burned and has cooled, take the ashes and bury them in your garden or sprinkle them in your yard. You can also take them to a place that you consider to be sacred and scatter or bury them there.

You are free. If you find that you think of these incidents occasionally, remind yourself that you have released them and they are gone. It will take some time before you train your mind to release all thoughts of the past, but time and practice will make that happen. You can do this exercise as often as you need to and you may need to perform it several times for some people in your life.

To keep the flow of forgiveness moving in your life, each time you feel have an emotional reaction to someone such as anger or fear, forgive them. Remember that this person is part of your healing journey and before you judge yourself or them ask what role they are playing in your soul's evolution and how you contribute to theirs. This will allow you to understand the true reasons for your connection and interaction so you can forgive them and release that connection.

A Self-Love Inventory

Before you read on, take a few minutes to think about any relationships in your life that may reflect your lack of self-love. If you are doing everything in your power to get someone to love, accept, respect and honor you and they are not cooperating, it's time to take a self-love inventory. It doesn't matter who the relationship is with or what kind of relationship it is, including those that are work related, with an intimate partner, a parent or other family member or a friendship that is not serving you. Every relationship in your life that is challenging and unfulfilling reflects an area where you do not love yourself.

For this exercise you will need a piece of paper and some quiet time alone. On the left side of the paper, write down the name of a person with whom you are currently having or have had a difficult relationship. On the right side of the paper, write down why this relationship is so difficult--ask yourself what it is about this relationship that makes you uncomfortable. For example, is this a person who criticizes you, doesn't take you seriously, doesn't respect you, won't accept you, or won't give you the consideration, attention and validation you want?

This is your list and it is an inventory of your life, so some or none of the examples here may fit your individual situation.

This list may take some time to complete, so do not rush through it. Take your time to really think about it and don't worry if you can't get it completed in a single session. You may have to take several days or more to complete your list. Or you may have to do this exercise in stages, creating different lists for family, friends, partners and others in your life.

Once you have your list of names completed you are ready for the second part of this exercise. In this part you will shift the energy of your challenging relationships so you will use the list you just completed to identify the energy you need to shift within yourself to change your connection to that person.

On a second sheet of paper and taking the names from the list that you just completed, on another sheet of paper, you are going to write some positive affirmations using the items on the right side of your paper.

To give you an idea of what your list could look like, if one of the items on your list reads:

Boyfriend	treats me disrespectfully
Boss	criticizes me
Parents	judge me for my life choices

Then your affirmations would read:

Everyone in my life treats me with respect now.

Everyone in my life speaks to me in a loving, kind way.

I am mindful of my life choices and use conscious intention to make powerful choices.

Continue writing these affirmations until you have addressed each name on your list. Remember that you are writing these in a positive way and in the present moment, as if it were happening right now. So do not write in the future, write in the present moment.

Remember that the way that people treat you reflects how you love your-self. Wherever others are criticizing, judging or treating you disrespectfully is a reflection of energy that you are sending out into the world. In order to get people to treat you differently, you need to start treating yourself differently. It's a process that must start with you and while you may not see overnight results (but it is possible) any change you seek in the energy that others use to connect with you begins with the love you have for yourself.

You will keep these lists for reference. Put the list of names and affirmations in a safe place so that you can refer to them occasionally and see what has changed with the people whose names you wrote on it. Some will change, others will leave your life.

Read the positive affirmations out loud three times a day, in the morning, afternoon and before you go to bed. Read them with conviction, putting feeling into what you are reading.

After a week, notice any changes that are occurring in your relationship life. Are people treating you any differently? Have some people left your life?

When you shift your energy and begin affirming what you want in your life, the people who cannot honor that will no longer be part of your life. And they will be replaced by those who can.

Remember to read your affirmations every day--it takes time to retrain your mind to embrace new ways of thinking and developing a foundation of self-love is essential to moving into your spiritual mastery.

Releasing the Fear

This exercise will help you to identify the fears that you are currently experiencing in your life. Any emotion, including fear, can be changed once we identify and know what we are dealing with. So to release yourself from fear you first have to identify what it is that you are afraid of.

Take a sheet of paper and at the top, write

"I am afraid of/that ..."

Then list all of the things that you are afraid of. Be completely honest with yourself. You will not be showing this list to anyone, so it doesn't matter what you write down. You want to be sure that you list as many fears as possible, include anything that can hold you back from moving forward with your own life. Even if it sounds silly, write it down anyway. You could write:

My partner won't love me
I'll be alone
I'll hate myself or others will hate me
I won't be able to find another job
I'll never have another relationship
I'll be laughed at or humiliated
I won't be able to find a place to live

This is just a sample for you to use and your list can be as long or as short as you like. If you need to, continue on the back side and use as many sheets of paper as necessary.

When you have finished with your list, read each item out loud, beginning with "I now release myself from the fear of/that ..." As you affirm that you are releasing yourself from this fear, you are shifting this energy and allowing a higher vibration to become possible for you.

Congratulate yourself on your good work. You will also be reading this list to yourself daily, along with your affirmations, so that you can program your mind to accept that none of these fears pertain to you any more.

Made in the USA
Lexington, KY
15 April 2012